Macroeconomic
Alternatives

Macroeconomic Alternatives

Martin Bronfenbrenner

Kenan Professor of Economics
Duke University

AHM Publishing Corporation
Arlington Heights, Illinois 60004

To all my teachers, colleagues, students, and acquaintances who have won macroeconomic arguments with me over the eventful half-century beginning in 1929.

Contents

Preface

This study of *Macroeconomic Alternatives* was eight years and three continents in gestation. Chapter 1 began in Japan, and revisions are ending in England. In the course of these eight years, more water and less oil flowed under our bridges than is considered in the pages which follow. The phenomena of "Nixonomics and stagflation," in particular, subjected macroeconomic analysis in America and elsewhere to a severe test, which much economic journalism claims that it has failed. (I disagree; this book will explain my disagreement.)

Another of the book's principal purposes is the reason for its title. I seek to present classical, Marxian, Keynesian, and monetarist macroeconomics in confrontation, and to permit the reader as voter to choose intelligently between and among them. (But alas, adherents of the first two faiths will, with justification, feel slighted at least in terms of space!)

A third purpose, also related to the title, has been to speak four languages more or less simultaneously: English, geometry, algebra, and econometrics. I hope to qualify the reader for further progress along any methodological line or combination of lines which appeals to him—and to tolerate the others. (Here it is the mathematical economist and econometrician who may fault my simple-minded adherence to simple-minded linear models, and the limitations of my econometrics to final results.)

To include this material, what did we perforce omit or slight? Economic and doctrinal history, for two things; the international dimension, for a third. If this volume becomes "Macro I" of a longer program, I think of "Macro II" as concerned with economic dynamics, economic development, public finance, and/or monetary theory—as it is at Duke. I accordingly point in these directions in preference to international finance or to computer simulation.

For textbook purposes, I aim at students with better-than-average preparation in elementary economics or no-worse-than-average preparation in intermediate economic theory. Background in recent world and American economic history is assumed, if not formal course work. It is also helpful that students realize in advance that "Economics is a serious subject," that

they be in the upper half of their university's I.Q. distribution, and that their choice of a macroeconomics course be inspired by the subject and/or its teacher rather than by requirements, time schedules, "any port in a storm," or by pure chance.

Returning to this manuscript, I can list my creditors in six groups:

(1) My betters past and present, whose ideas and results I have appropriated with (I hope) maximum acknowledgement and minimum distortion.

(2) My student guinea-pigs over 25 years, including both the Wellesley College sophomores who found one version of this manuscript too demanding and the Duke University doctoral candidates who found another version insufficiently challenging.

(3) My research assistants and error-detectives, including particularly Clifford Goalstone (formerly of Duke) among students, Thomas Havrilesky (Duke) and Hiroshi Ohta (Aoyama Gakuin) among colleagues, and likewise P. T. Ellsworth (formerly of Wisconsin) who permitted my first experience as a macroeconomics teacher by taking leave to Sri Lanka.

(4) My wife Teruko, our children Ken and June, and even our dog Georgie, who bore with me during larger or smaller portions of the eight years aforementioned—or who left home when the burden became too great.

(5) The succession of typists and secretaries, American, English, and Japanese, to whom I have submitted amateurish typescripts with fear and trembling. Katie Frye and Bonnie Swenson (both at Duke) endured longer than any others, but also quit for reasons unconnected with *Macroeconomic Alternatives!*

(6) The staffs of AHM Publishing Corporation in Arlington Heights, especially Harlan Davidson and Maureen Trobec, and of Phoenix Publishing Services in San Francisco, especially Douglas Pundick, who kept the manuscript moving during my travels and whose proof-reading and indexing are both much better than my own.

And in conclusion:

> Myself when young did eagerly frequent
> Doctor and saint, and heard great argument
>   About it and about, but evermore
> Came out by the same door wherein I went.

Thus Omar the Tentmaker, or rather his translator. This has not been true for me—at least, not within economics. I hope it will not prove true

for too many of my readers. Should they indeed come out by the same macroeconomic door wherein they enter, I hope their reasons for retaining their original allegiances among *Macroeconomic Alternatives* will become more rational than the conjuring with Great Names—Smith, Marx, Keynes, Friedman—or Great Epithets—radical, reactionary; practical, compassionate; liberal, conservative; socialist, capitalist—which provide slogans and thought-substitutes for too many of our voters, while my fellow economists struggle with maximum-likelihood n-stages estimates of the marginal rate of obfuscation under rational expectations!

Martin Bronfenbrenner

Brighton, Sussex, England

December, 1978

Part

I

Social Accounting
and
Macrostatic
Theories

Chapter
1

Introduction: Macroeconomics and Microeconomics

DEROGATORY INTRODUCTION

We begin with an American radical's root-and-branch attack on our entire subject:

> Microeconomics! Macroeconomics! These formidable terms greet beginning students, and a textbook filled with diagrams increases their apprehensions. However, the real difficulty is not the strangeness of a new terminology or even the mathematical rigor applied to the subject matter. More important is the fact that orthodox micro- and macro-economics fails to integrate its theoretical structure with institutional realities. The result is a pseudo-science biased in favor of the status quo, one that fails to shed much light on the problems that plague America.[1]

No one, not even a textbook writer, sets out deliberately to produce "pseudo-science biased in favor of the status quo." It goes without saying, therefore, that we reject Mermelstein's conclusion; but this is an issue for the reader to decide for himself. We suggest only that some part of the formidable strangeness of our terminology, and some part of our failure to "integrate theoretical structure with institutional realities," may be due to the artificial distinction between microeconomics and macroeconomics. The distinction has been convenient; it is, however, not cut and dried, let alone sacred. It may quite conceivably be moribund. Some of you who read this may even help to bury it, if you go on to more advanced economic work.

MICROECONOMICS! MACROECONOMICS!

The maiden name of microeconomics was "value theory." It has been concerned with the determination of individual prices, both of inputs and of outputs, and also with the determination of groups or clusters of closely related prices. Its underlying assumptions include the constancy of both the national income and product and of the prices and quantities of certain incompletely specified "other goods" produced and consumed. This is well enough for strawberries and perfumers' labor. It leaves us a little queasy when applied to steel, or houses, or unskilled labor as a whole. (Can we really ignore the national income effects, direct and indirect, or large changes in important variables like these?)

The maiden name of macroeconomics was "the theory of money and prices." An apter choice might perhaps have been "the theory of money and price *levels*." In the orthodox tradition of this ancestor of our subject, changes in real national income and product tended to be neglected as

---

[1] David Mermelstein, *Economics: Mainstream Readings and Radical Critiques* (1970) p. 66 (running quotation).

short-run or disequilibrium phenomena unworthy of notice. (There was also an unorthodox tradition, however, for which this was decidedly untrue.) Modern macroeconomics, or aggregative economics, deals with the definition and determination of certain basic economic aggregates. The precise number of these aggregates, in other words the degree of aggregation, differs from one treatment to another. Ordinarily included, however, are the levels of real income, consumption, and investment, the level of employment, and the level of general prices. An important assumption guiding the degree of aggregation is that the composition of the aggregates makes little difference and can safely be neglected. For example, all investment in plant and equipment is ordinarily lumped together without distinguishing between "Smithian" investment (which increases employment unambiguously) and "Ricardian" investment (which has important labor-saving effects).[2] For another example, public expenditure is often treated as a whole, or broken down only into public consumption, public investment, and transfer payments. It may be important, however, to know whether it is tax-financed or deficit-financed, whether it produces goods and services usable and desired by the populace at large, goods and services usable only for military purposes, or nothing whatever beyond "made work" for civil servants. For a third example, issues involving the distribution of aggregate wealth and income as between income classes, between functional shares like labor and property, between racial groups, etc., are conventionally ignored when we deal with the determination of aggregate consumption and investment. It goes without saying that this theoretical indifference to the composition of economic aggregates has come under attack from many quarters over the entire range from New Left to Old Right, and including Mr. Mermelstein.

In sum, the distinction between microeconomics and macroeconomics is both somewhat artificial and somewhat irritating. It has been called "scandalous." But it has also been extremely useful and convenient. An open question is, Where do we go from here? Some writers, one of the greatest being Karl Marx, have attempted "Roman riding" on both subjects at once. It is usual to consider Marx the economist (as distinguished from Marx the philosopher, the historian, the sociologist, the prophet, etc.) to be fundamentally a value theorist with macroeconomic accompaniment to his microeconomic themes and variations. Others consider him fundamentally a macroeconomist with an elaborate microeconomic prelude or overture. At the other extreme from Roman riders like Marx, some writers

---

[2] The "Smithian-Ricardian" dichotomy has been introduced by Paolo Sylos-Labini, who has found it quantitatively significant in econometric studies of the Italian economy.

ride one horse only and ignore the other. However, problems arise in the theory of income distribution, the theory of capital and interest, and the theories of exchange-rate variation and unilateral transfers in international trade. This is not the place to consider these problems in depth, beyond suggesting what the problems are. Microeconomic treatments sometimes seem to yield different answers from macroeconomic ones; the answers seem to be either inconsistent with or unrelated to each other. It has not been easy to bridge the gaps between them in usable (as distinct from purely formal) fashion. Part of the trouble may be that the microeconomic tradition has been more *gründlich*, i.e., based upon apparent psychological regularities of individual behavior as in the case of consumer demand theory, while the macroeconomic tradition has been more *practical*, i.e., more willing to accept empirical shortcuts without asking embarrassing questions about their philosophical or psychological bases.

But the bulk of scholarship and research aiming at welding microeconomics and macroeconomics into a coherent whole (like the welding of algebra and geometry into analytic geometry) has been neither Roman riding nor complacency. It has run along two distinct lines. The first of these lines has been statistical and econometric. It involves breaking down coarse aggregates into finer ones, in the hope of producing better short- and even long-term projections, forecasts, or predictions of the economic future. The second line of progress has been synthetic. It explores what are called the microfoundations of macroeconomic functions.[3] It hopes to justify a set of macroeconomic functions, not necessarily the conventional one, on the basis of computer simulation and the mathematical theory of aggregation, as applied to a sample of microeconomic functions.

It is too early to predict whether either of these outposts on the frontier of economic research will turn out to be anything more than dismal swamp or whether they will provide the knowledge we are lacking. Even if these two outposts are eventually abandoned, perhaps some *tertium quid* will supply the results we are waiting for. (Eminent physicists, including Einstein, have tried and failed for generations to unify the foundations of mechanics, light, and electricity.) The excuse for our foray into middle-brow methodology is to suggest that economics is not complete, dead, and ready for commitment to memory, but that fundamental work remains for future generations to undertake. You yourself have a chance to supply to economics the "unified field theory" that Einstein did not quite succeed in supplying to physics.

---

[3] An influential example (at a level more advanced than this book) has been a collection of studies edited by E. S. Phelps and entitled *Microeconomic Foundations of Employment and Inflation Theory* (1970).

STATICS AND DYNAMICS

The initial and longer part of our study deals with macroeconomic statics, or macrostatics for short. It is sometimes called macroeconomics proper, to distinguish it from economic growth or business fluctuations. In macrostatics we shall consider a capitalist economy with given population, tastes, resources, technology, and social institutions, and investigate the effects of isolated once-and-for-all, unanticipated changes taken one at a time, under the protection of *ceteris paribus*. Also, we shall usually ignore expectations of change, and we shall slice time into periods long enough for the effects of our various perturbations to work themselves out during the periods in which they occur. When we say, in effect, $y = f(x)$, we do not have to "date" x and y, nor do we have to specify that x and y refer to the same time period t. In fact, the dating notation $y_t = f(x_t)$ is pedantic in a macrostatic context.

Under the head of macrodynamics, we shall discuss some problems of growth, fluctuations, and prediction, all in an elementary way. We shall be handicapped here by the relatively underdeveloped state of these disciplines, and the greater degree of remoteness of macrodynamic theory from the institutional facts of economic development. In macrodynamics, the several restrictions mentioned above are either removed or modified. It is common, for example, for a growth theorist to treat the labor force L as a function of population growth over time, such as $L_t = L_0 e^{nt}$. (Here L_0 is the value of L at some arbitrarily selected time t_0, n is the growth rate of L per unit of time, and e is the base of natural logarithms.[4]) It is also common to treat technological progress in a similar way, by coupling an exponential multiplier e^{gt} to an aggregate production function, g being a rate of technological progress per unit of time. (Do not be concerned if much of this is Greek, or higher mathematics, at starting. There will be time to learn or review the mathematics you will need, in the process of working with it.)

Also, we no longer require in macrodynamics that the effects of any variable x_t be limited to its own future values x_{t+1}, x_{t+2}, ... This is why we need to date our variables, as in the expression $y_t = f(x_{t-1})$. In addition, relations involving rates of change, or relations involving summations and integrations are classified as dynamic. We might, for example, have $y = f(\dot{x})$, where $\dot{x}$ is the time derivative

---

[4] Formally,

$$e = \lim_{n \to \infty} \left(1 + \frac{1}{n}\right)^n$$

$$\frac{dx}{dt},$$

or

$$y_t = f(\int x \; dt).$$

The possibilities are endless. So are the temptations to play elegant mathematical games with minimal economic meaning.

A MACROECONOMIC WORLD VIEW

A typical macroeconomic view compresses an economy into a small number of economic sectors—Households, Business, Government, Saving-Investment, and sometimes also International or Rest-of-the-World. This compression means that macroeconomists have little to say about transactions *within* sectors, such as occur when a steel company sells sheet steel to an automobile company, or when a central government shares revenue with local units.

If each economic sector is an economic decision maker, what does it make decisions about? Fundamentally, about sectoral stock of assets or wealth, and about inter-sector flow of receipts and expenditures. (The distinction between a stock and a flow is important. Wealth, assets, and liabilities are all stock concepts with no time dimension. Receipts, expenditures, and income are all flow concepts with time dimensions, as when we measure income in dollars per month or year. Ordinarily a flow represents the net change in a stock per unit of time; in mathematical terms, a flow is a time derivative of a stock, and a stock is the time integral of a flow.) In macroeconomics, our attention is concentrated primarily on flows, and only secondarily on stocks.

All intersector flows are necessarily expenditures of one sector and receipts of another, in accordance with decisions made in both sectors. This is even true of payments of wages, interest, and rents, where it may not be obvious. Such *factor payments* are not only expenditures of the business (or government) sector but also receipts of the household sector. This is because households are treated as ultimate owners of human and physical capital, which they rent to business firms or to government agencies.

Since every individual intersector flow is at once an expenditure of one sector and a receipt of another, it follows that the total expenditures of all sectors taken together must equal the total receipts of all sectors taken together. This identity is called the *circular flow* of income payments; it can be represented as a flow chart or as an accounting balance. The size of the flow per time period is subject, of course, to continuous change. When such a change takes place, macroeconomists usually see the changes

in receipts and expenditures as taking place within a single accounting period. Consider, for example, a thrift campaign in which households spend less for the products of business. The fall in household expenditures is matched by the corresponding fall in business receipts. Similarly, a rise in personal income taxes is recorded as a rise in household expenditures and government receipts.

An individual sector seldom balances its receipts and its expenditures. Thus households normally receive more than they spend; the difference is called *saving*. Business, on the other hand, usually incurs higher expenditures for investment and growth than it receives from undistributed profits and additions to its reserves. This is why the business sector is almost always a net *dissaver* and a net borrower from households.

Household expenditures are divided into the two categories of *consumption* and *investment*. (With regard to investment, a household is treated like a business firm. As for saving, we have just seen that it is not an expenditure but a refraining from expenditure.) The allocation of receipts between consumption, investment, and saving is made by the household sector after the government sector has collected personal taxes, of which personal income taxes are the most important. The distinction between consumption and investment is imprecise. Investment is the purchase of a newly-produced business asset like a tractor on the family farm.[5] Purchase of a newly-built house or apartment is also called an investment, even though the property is bought with no thought of future sale or rental. But household purchase of newly-issued debt or equity securities (bonds or stocks), which business uses to finance its own purchases of business assets, is regarded as saving and not investment, for reasons we shall explain below. Purchase of *preexisting* business assets, securities, and houses are at once investments (to the purchasers) and disinvestments (to the sellers) and have no physical effects on the macroeconomy. Macroeconomists therefore tend to ignore them. Household expenditures that are neither investments nor tax payments—nor the security purchases we class as disguised saving—are lumped together as consumption.

Businesses do not consume. Business expenditures are however divided into those *current* and those on *capital* account. Goods and services purchased on current account are used up once and for all in a single productive process; their costs are called business *expenses*. They include labor and raw materials, power, fuel, light, and so on. Goods purchased on capital account are used over long periods, and are subject only to gradual

---

[5] A family farm is at once a household and a business. Pedantically speaking, the farm-as-household saves and entrusts the savings to the farm-as-business, which invests them in the tractor.

depreciation. Land, buildings, and machinery are in this class. Business expenditures for new capital goods—new goods on capital account—are called business *investments*.

When business buys new physical assets or capital goods, and finances the purchase by selling securities to households, it would be double-counting to reckon both the purchase of the capital goods and the purchase of the securities as separate investments. Macroeconomics follows the physical assets rather than the paper securities. Accordingly, business is regarded as the investing sector in this case. The household sector is regarded as a pure saver, although the individual buyers of the new business securities doubtless think of themselves as investors along with the business firm that has purchased the new physical capital.

Macroeconomists distinguish *nominal* from *real* receipts and expenditures. They also distinguish receipts and expenditures *ex ante* and *ex post*. A nominal flow is evaluated at current prices, while a real flow has been revalued (deflated) statistically in terms of a constant price level. (The statistical device used for the deflation is called an *index number*.) The *ex ante* value of an economic quantity is its value as planned or as estimated in advance. Its *ex post* value is that actually received or spent. In a world of perfect certainty and complete information, each *ex post* would equal the corresponding *ex ante* value, just as nominal and real values would be equal in a world of constant price levels. In the real world, however, *ex ante* and *ex post* values are ordinarily different. A family's consumption and saving plans *ex ante* are revised upward *ex post* after the principal breadwinner has received an unexpected promotion; they are revised downward *ex post* when the principal breadwinner loses his job or becomes ill. In the first example, *ex post* expenditures will generally exceed *ex ante* expenditures; in the second example, the inequality is reversed. In the macroeconomy, an improving state of confidence raises *ex post* receipts and expenditures over their *ex ante* values; deteriorating confidence has the opposite effect.

Macroeconomic theorists treat these distinctions as clear and unequivocal. In practice there are many gray areas. Many classifications depend on statistical conventions, which differ from time to time and place to place. Here are two examples: (1) Price index numbers are in only imperfect agreement, so that real quantities are estimated differently, depending on which index number series is used to deflate the nominal quantities; (2) The distinction between current and capital accounts in business and governmental budgets is not clear either. Optimistic firms, municipalities, and even central governments may get into difficulties by financing current expenses out of capital budgets; New York City was an example in the 1970s. On the other hand, firms have been prosecuted for tax evasion when they treated capital charges as business expenses and deducted them from

personal and corporate income. The published figures on these and similar matters are estimates, usually in accord with established accounting and statistical practices of the times and places to which the estimates refer.

A SNEAK PREVIEW

We conceive our representative reader as a serious student. He or she has been introduced to macroeconomics in an elementary course, but may have since forgotten a considerable amount of its contents. He or she agrees with Edwin Cannan that "economics is a serious subject," both in itself and for *him*, even if it is not a formal "major" or "minor" of his academic concentration. With such a reader in mind, we have planned this book along these lines:

Two chapters (2 and 3) endeavor to answer questions about the macroeconomic aggregates themselves. What do we mean precisely by such macroeconomic aggregates as employment, unemployment, and the national income? Are the volume of employment (as a proportion of full employment or the labor force) and the size of gross national product (adjusted for changes in population and the price level) satisfactory indicators of success in macroeconomic policy? Insofar as they are less than perfect, what are the principal conceptual and statistical "bugs" we should watch for?

The next group of chapters (4 through 11) considers macrostatistics. The basic question of macrostatic theory is: Does the economy tend to full employment? The classical system, beginning with Adam Smith's "invisible hand," answered this question in the affirmative (chapter 4). So do many conservatives and practical men today, for reasons which add to implicit acceptance of classical reasoning. The Marxian system (chapter 5) answers the same question in the negative, incidental to establishing certain macrodynamic "laws of motion" that imply the downfall of capitalism. The presently dominant Keynesian system (chapters 6 and 7) also answers the basic question negatively, although its policy implications are reformist rather than revolutionary. Chapter 9 takes up the "maturity and stagnation" implications some writers draw from that (and other) systems. A neoclassical counterrevolution (chapters 10 and 11) suggests that the classicals may not have been so far wrong after all. (Chapter 8 is an empirical interlude concerned with the real world forms of the principal Keynesian building blocks or "functions.")

Chapters 12 through 15 consider macrodynamics. Chapter 12 is growth theory. It does not deal with today's less developed countries (LDCs), but investigates whether the growth path of a capitalist economy is stable, or whether any departure, either upward or downward, will be cumulative. Chapters 13 and 14 deal more explicitly with fluctuations around growth

paths; it is these fluctuations which are often called business cycles. The main questions here are, of course, what are the causes for these perturbations and how they can be controlled (assuming some control is desirable). Chapter 15, finally, introduces the practical attempts to combine macrostatic and macrodynamic analysis for purposes of economic forecasting, usually for the relatively short term.

Most textbooks devote separate chapters to matters of theory and matters of policy or applications. Usually the connections between them are more tenuous and less direct than they should be. This book adopts instead (except in chapters 8 and 15) a "sandwich" approach. Organized on the basis of economic analysis, it tries to indicate in passing both the policy problems that gave rise to particular analytical structures and also the policy implications of each major item of analysis, under the assumption that it is correct.

TRUE CONFESSION

The writer has at various times been called everything from a flaming radical to a black reactionary. He considers himself more nearly a nineteenth-century than a twentieth-century liberal,[6] more nearly a neo-classical economist than a Keynesian or a Marxist in economic theory, and more nearly a monetarist than a fiscalist in macroeconomic policy. And once inflationary psychology has taken hold of an economy, he must also admit skepticism of either slackening or eliminating such psychology without the threat of substantial departure from "full employment at whatever cost"[7] or making that threat credible without accepting something closer to depression than to recession.

Some of these positions are unpopular; a few are even extreme. But any writer worthy of his salt, ink, and typewriter must somehow communicate with persons in less than one hundred percent agreement with his own views. An economics course should not be an amen session. At the very least, a writer should present, without poisoning the wells of argument, positions conflicting with his own. So it will be, we hope, in the present instance. The coming chapters will tell to what extent our hopes for fairness and communicability are justified.

---

6 The writer has attempted to spell out the several distinctions between these two positions in "Two Concepts of Economic Freedom," *Ethics* (April 1955).

7 The title of an essay by Jacob Viner (*Quarterly Journal of Economics* (August 1950), reprinted in J. Viner, *The Long View and the Short*). The opposite view, combining full employment and "reasonable" price stability, relies on wage-price guidelines or incomes policies administered within the constraints of a basically free economy.

Chapter
2

Some Economic Aggregates

MACROECONOMICS AND SOCIAL ACCOUNTING

This chapter, and the next as well, detour into macroeconomics via social accounting. The purpose of the detour is to assist in answering questions like those posed in the previous chapter: What do we mean precisely by such macroeconomic aggregates as employment, unemployment, and the national income? Are the volume of employment (as a proportion of full employment or the labor force) and the size of gross national product (adjusted for changes in population and the price level) satisfactory indicators of success in macroeconomic policy? Insofar as they are less than perfect—as they are—what are the principal conceptual and statistical "bugs" one should watch for?

Since so much macroeconomic discussion runs in terms of theoretical constructs like C (consumption), I (private investment), Y (the national income or product, which we shall find distinct through related measures), r (the rate of interest), M (the money stock) and many more,[1] we should avoid the fetishism of ascribing to such constructs independent lives of their own, apart from the people comprising the societies to which they refer. It is also important to have quantitative estimates of their values at particular times and places, if we are to judge the nature and significance of the relations between them. "Where you cannot measure, your knowledge is meager and unsatisfactory," as the physicist Lord Kelvin said in a quotation hackneyed by overuse.[2]

Unfortunately for the high hopes of economics as a science, the quantitative estimates or measurements of our theoretical constructs are only proxies or surrogates for the entities the purists have in mind. Furthermore, the estimates must be made with attention to the convenience of practicing statisticians as well as to the needs of theorists, politicians, civil servants, or businessmen. This has meant that the workaday practices of statistical estimation, the short cuts and the rules of thumb, have varied from time to time and from place to place. They have tended over time to greater complexity and plausibility as collection and computation methods have developed. In one South American country, for example, the national income was for a time estimated as ten times the national budget; such crudity is no longer practiced anywhere. In general, comparability of macroeconomic data is somewhat greater over time within one country than across geographical boundaries, despite the best efforts of the United Nations Secretariat to secure uniformity in both dimensions. It is an

---

[1] The symbol M is also used frequently for imports, when macroeconomics becomes involved in international complications.

[2] A fellow ex-student of Jacob Viner reminds me of Viner's postscript to this quotation: "And when you *can* measure, your knowledge is often *still* meager and unsatisfactory."

ethnocentric mistake to assume, with many Americans, that other countries should use the same set of macroeconomic concepts as the United States, or the same set of short cuts and rules of thumb to aid in their computations.

Neither do we know with sufficient generality the sensitivity of our statistical estimates, or our statistical tests of alternative theories, to what are apparently minor peculiarities of statistical procedure. More than conundrums, horrible examples exist to keep us not only alert but worried. An American example explored by Robert J. Gordon in the *American Economic Review* (June 1969) is the statistical "disappearance" of $45 billion of private investment made by the U.S. government during World War II and subsequently transferred to private companies. This investment in plant and equipment was originally lumped together with government expenditures, i.e., treated separately from private investment. The national income accounts were unaffected when title was transferred, even though the original expenditures would have been considered as investment had the eventual owners made them originally on their own accounts.

Many of us have sampled the problems of measuring such economic aggregates as the general price level by the use of index numbers. These numbers, as conventionally estimated, assume that if the price level has doubled for the rich, it has doubled for the poor; if it has doubled in the North, it has doubled in the South; if it has doubled in the city, it has doubled on the farm, and so on. Do we really want to assume this? Even if we do, should we use wholesale prices, retail prices, a national income deflator (which includes implicit items), or some broader index that includes items of wealth along with income? How are the various components of the index to be weighted; in particular, how should the weights appropriate to a base period be combined with those appropriate to the period for which we are computing the index? What allowance, if any, should be made for nonmonetary "fringe" elements in prices, for quality changes in individual goods, for unavailability at quoted prices, for divergence between official and free market (black market) quotations? Are prices to be measured gross or net of sales and excise taxes? At special sales or at ordinary times? At quality shoppes or at discount houses? Equally difficult problems appear in measuring all our aggregates. They are all solved in practice, in one way or another, by some crude guideline that overlooks the difficulties. However, as has been said, the solutions vary from place to place and from time to time, usually reflecting the progress of data collection methods.

EMPLOYMENT AND UNEMPLOYMENT

Much discussion and disputation in macroeconomics—especially in macroeconomic policy—is about problems of employment and unemploy-

ment. These concepts are fundamentally obvious, but the problems of measurement are extraordinarily difficult.

When an individual above minimum working age decides to seek work (other than housework in his or her own home), he or she joins the *labor force*. When an individual decides to retire, to become a full-time student or housewife (instead of working), he or she leaves the labor force, at least temporarily. Once in the labor force, an individual is considered as *employed* if he has a job, even if he is not actually working when his status is investigated. (He may be at home because of illness or accident; he may be on vacation or on strike; he may be laid off for a short period.) An employed person need not be an employee of anyone else; a self-employed accountant, doctor, lawyer, or beautician is employed. An individual who is in the labor force but not employed is counted as *unemployed*. However, an individual not in the labor force is never reckoned as unemployed. Thus a wealthy man or woman who leads *la dolce vita* may be a loafer or a parasite, but he or she is not unemployed because he or she has made no decision to seek work. Also, a worker who, after losing one job, simply remains at home for a month without actively looking for another job, is not counted as unemployed although he may consider himself unemployed and even be drawing unemployment compensation.

Unemployment is measured in terms of numbers of workers and as a percentage of the labor force. It is often subclassified as *frictional, cyclical,* and *structural*. The frictionally unemployed are unemployed only for short periods, as between jobs. Teachers are sometimes classified as frictionally unemployed during summer vacations, and professional baseball players as frictionally unemployed during the winter months. (Such frictional unemployment is sometimes classified separately as *seasonal*.) Cyclical unemployment is associated with recessions and depressions; it declines in periods of prosperity or boom. Structural unemployment is related to skills that are obsolete or regions that are declining. Many sharecroppers and other tenant farmers in the Cotton Belt became structurally unemployed when displaced by mechanical cotton pickers. When a Navy yard is closed, its ship-repair specialists are structurally unemployed, even though their skills may be in short supply at some other Navy yard a thousand miles away. Functionally illiterate high school dropouts are structurally unemployed if they are not considered worth hiring or training at the current minimum wage rates. Published unemployment statistics classify the unemployed on various bases (age, sex, marital status, education, type of job, length of unemployment) from which estimates of unemployment by type can be attempted. Nobody, however, asks an unemployed man whether he considers his unemployment frictional, cyclical, or structural.

Macroeconomic interest is centered primarily on cyclical and secondarily on structural unemployment. Because they generally ignore frictional unemployment, American macroeconomists often consider measured unem-

ployment, figures below four or even five percent of the labor force as equivalent to "full employment." Many countries with more stringent definitions (one or two percent) will be found to consider only workers dismissed from jobs (excluding those entering the labor force), or workers eligible for unemployment compensation (which requires a waiting period after a job is lost). Or they may be excluding such categories as the very young, the very old, immigrants, or married women from their computations.

If an unemployed person is willing to accept work at the clearly definite going wage rate in a job for which he is obviously qualified (but not overqualified), he is considered *involuntarily* unemployed. But if an unemployed person is holding out for "something better"—higher wages, more meaningful work, training for promotion, pay for potential as well as actual qualifications—he is considered *voluntarily* unemployed. In the absence of a single market wage rate or qualification set for a job, an unemployed worker who insists on the highest wage rate and/or the lowest qualifications within a realistic range, is considered to be *search*-unemployed. Macroeconomic concern is centered upon involuntary unemployment, including those sorts of search-unemployment which appear to be rejection of substandard or demeaning wages and working conditions. Some economists think *all* long-term unemployment is search-unemployment. (According to this controversial view, a searcher with realistic criteria for job acceptance approaches involuntary unemployment at one end of a scale or continuum, while another searcher with unrealistic criteria approaches voluntary unemployment at the other end.) Published statistics do not subdivide the unemployed along the lines mentioned in this paragraph, and some writers suspect but cannot prove that involuntary unemployment does not exist. (To what extent, they go on to inquire, should relief and unemployment compensation payments be used to subsidize workers' searches for better jobs than they would have to accept in the absence of such payments?)

The unemployment and labor force "numbers" are collected monthly on a sample basis, and without deduction of the number of unfilled vacancies from the number of the unemployed. (Unemployment, then, is reported gross and not net of unfilled vacancies.) Numerous other critics would expand the concept of unemployment further to include such categories as *disguised unemployment* (on "made work"), *underemployment* (part-time employment and/or employment not utilizing the workers' skills and other qualifications), and *subemployment* (at "poverty levels" of wages and other benefits).

MISCELLANEOUS MEASUREMENT PROBLEMS

There are other problems of measurement comparable with these in importance and vexation. For example, macroeconomists have much to

say about the rate of interest and its role in the economy. But how can we justify the distillation of a single rate of interest from the structure of observed market rates appearing monthly in, say, the *Federal Reserve Bulletin?* Macroeconomists also have much to say about the money supply and its importance, but what line should separate that body of assets called money from other groups entitled "other liquid assets" or possibly "money substitutes"? The list could go on and on, to cover practically every one of the key concepts of macroeconomic analysis.

THE FIRM: FROM INCOME STATEMENT TO GNP CONTRIBUTION

But our major concern, in this and the following chapter, is with the national income accounts proper. It is convenient to begin with the Gross National Product (GNP) and develop the other accounts from GNP by appropriate, or at least conventional, additions and subtractions. For GNP itself, we postulate an economy composed of firms (including households and nonprofit institutions) that employ labor or sell products. This definition permits us to build up GNP from the accounts of individual firms.

The two fundamental and interrelated accounts of a firm are its *balance sheet* and its *income statement.* The balance sheet is a snapshot of a firm's position at a moment of time, usually the end of a calendar or fiscal year. (Because the critical time is known in advance, it is often possible to apply "window dressing" to published balance sheets.) The balance sheets of individual firms can be and are consolidated into estimates of national wealth, broken down on the asset side by type of wealth and on the liability side by type of ownership. Such statements, however, do not concern us here. Rather, we concentrate upon the income statement, also called the profit-and-loss statement. This is a motion picture rather than a snapshot. It is a motion picture of the firm's income and expenditure flows between two predetermined dates. Although susceptible to window dressing, it involves some of the aggregates important to social accounting. It is, therefore, a useful starting point.

For the simplest form of income statement, consider a firm with constant inventories. It sells all it produces, its total cost is identical with the cost of the goods it sells, and its income is derived exclusively from its sales. An example of its income statement is given in table 2-1. Expenditures are on the left and receipts (gross income) on the right,[3] in what is known as a T-account.

---

[3] This is consistent with the balance sheet convention that puts assets on the left side of a T-account, with liabilities and net worth on the right side.

Table 2-1
Income Statement for an Individual Firm

Expenditures	Receipts
Payments to Other Firms	Income from Sales
Cost of Goods Sold	
Miscellaneous	
Payments to Inputs	
Wages and Salaries	
Property Income	
Payments to Governments	
Total: Total Expenditures	Total: Total Receipts

As a balancing item in this account, all profits (including negative profits, or losses) are included in "payments to inputs," usually in "property income." We should also note that table 2-1, although called an income statement, does not actually distinguish between payments to other firms on what is called "income account," i.e., for goods used up during a single period (raw materials, components, fuel and light), and payments on "capital account" for longer-lived buildings, machinery, and equipment. In the business world, the income statements of private firms and government enterprises (but not of governments proper) stress this particular distinction. However, this important issue of private accounting need not concern us just yet in national-income accounting.

The first step in the pilgrim's progress from income statement to GNP contribution is the *production statement* (not shown). This step is conceptually simple. It consists only of assigning to the period in which production (not necessarily sales) takes place any changes in the firm's inventories of raw materials, goods in process, and final products, from which we abstracted above. First, we ascertain the money value of each addition to (reduction from) inventory, and add (subtract) this total to the right-hand side (r.h.s.) of table 2-1. To keep our accounts in balance we divide this amount between payments to other firms, payments to governments (taxes), and payments to inputs (including *anticipated* net profit or loss), and add each component to the appropriate item on the left hand side (l.h.s.) of the same table. In the case of raw materials and purchased components, of course, the entire allocation is to purchases from other firms; in other cases, statistical allocation is required.

In practice, difficulties and ambiguities arise from this procedure when there are price changes in the various inventory items. Accountants usually assume that items purchased or produced first are also used or sold first, in accordance with the physical facts for perishable items. This leads

to what is called FIFO (first-in–first-out) accounting. This method works to increase inventory profits, reported income, and tax liabilities, when prices generally are rising; it lowers them when prices are falling. During past business fluctuations, it has tended to accentuate the variability of reported business incomes. There has been a growing tendency to recognize that inventory items must normally be replaced at current prices, and therefore to value them at replacement cost as of the last purchase. This gives us LIFO (last-in–first-out) accounting. LIFO accounting increases balance sheet fluctuations but moderates those of reported business income when price levels change. It reduces reported business income systematically under sustained price inflation, as compared with FIFO, and increases it under sustained price deflation. (U.S. Treasury practice gives firms substantial leeway in inventory-accounting methods. U.S. national income accounts include an "inventory valuation adjustment" designed to treat all firms as if they had been on a LIFO basis. The purpose of this adjustment is to reduce the influence of short-term price fluctuations.)

We return to the main thread of our argument. The remaining step to a firm's GNP contribution is called its value-added statement (table 2-2). From both sides of table 2-1 (as modified by the production statement), we subtract all "purchases from other firms." The remainder is the value added by the firm, or rather by the various inputs employed directly by the firm. The firm's value added is the sum of its final sales (net of purchases) and the additions to its inventory. The sum of values added by all firms is the value added by the entire economy, and the value added by the entire economy in any time period is precisely its GNP for that period.

To repeat, each firm's value added is its GNP contribution. This means that, in all cases of sales between firms, the contribution is assigned to the

Table 2-2
A Value-Added Statement

Expenditures (Addition Method)	Receipts (Subtraction Method)

Wages and Salaries
Interest
Rent
Depreciation of Fixed
   Capital
Profit (or Loss)
Sales and Excise Taxes
Property Taxes
	Sales
	Less Purchases from
	   other firms ————
	Final Sales
	Less decrease (plus increase)
	   in inventory

Total: Value Added =====	Total: Value Added =====

producing rather than to the *buying* firm. In the case of the government, which buys goods and services from private firms without processing them further, this means that its own contribution is limited to its payment to direct inputs, i.e., its total payroll, without confronting embarrassing questions involving excess labor and so on. (Government *enterprises*, however, such as publicly-operated post offices, telephone lines, railways, or electric utilities, are treated more like private firms.)

We note also that value added may be looked upon as either a firm's "sales minus purchases," adjusted for inventory changes, or as its payments to inputs, including profits or losses. The two totals are conceptually identical. They do not always work out to be equal under the workaday rules of the workaday bookkeeping and accounting systems of workaday firms.

DIGRESSION: VALUE-ADDED TAXATION

The twentieth century has seen an important fiscal application of the abstract value-added concept (GNP contribution). This application is the value-added sales tax or VAT. Its popularity, as compared with business income taxes and with ordinary sales taxes is due less to its intrinsic merits than to its usefulness for protectionist purposes.[4] Fiscal application of the value-added concept has brought out a number of problems, which have been resolved pragmatically without reference to macroeconomics. As a result, a firm's value-added tax base, in a jurisdiction employing this tax, usually differs from its GNP contribution.

Two difficulties have been mentioned: (1) Sales outside the taxing jurisdiction are not included in the tax base, and (2) in many accounting systems the subtraction method of computation (sales minus purchases) gives a different base than the addition method (payments to inputs). A third difficulty, alluded to above, pertains to capital-account purchases. The law may allow firms to reduce the variability of their value-added tax bases over time by spreading their deductions for capital-account purchases over the estimated lifetimes of the purchased equipment rather than concentrating each deduction in the period when the asset was purchased. (Firms occasionally ask for deductions on both bases simultaneously.) Apart from these difficulties, we sometimes find special rules governing industries where value added constitutes an unusually high proportion of total sales, where competitors within the industry differ greatly in their ratios of value added

---

[4] The tax is usually deductible for all goods *exported* from the taxing jurisdiction, including raw materials, goods in process, or finished goods, and assessed on all goods *imported*.

to total sales, or where labor organizations are concerned about possible employment effects of a tax falling on payrolls more heavily than on purchases of laborsaving machinery.

THE BIG FIVE

When the GNP contributions of all firms are added, the result is a GNP statement like table 2-3. Its l.h.s. is called the *factor payment side*. It involves a finer classification of the accounts that we have called "payments to inputs" and "payments to governments" in table 2-1. Its sum is sometimes called "charges against GNP" rather than GNP proper. The r.h.s. of table 2-3 is called the *final product side*. It includes a breakdown of firm sales, partly by the nature of the product sold (consumption goods and

Table 2-3
Gross National Product Statement

Factor Payments	Final Products

Payments to Employees
  Wages and Salaries
  Supplements
Rental Income of Persons
Net Interest
Corporate Profits[1]
  Profits Tax Liability
  Dividends
  Undistributed Profits[2]
  Inventory Valuation Adjustment
Income of Unincorporated
  Enterprises
Indirect Business Taxes[3]
Capital Consumption Allowances
Statistical Discrepancy
	Personal Consumption Expenditures
	  Durable Goods
	  Nondurable Goods
	  Services
	Gross Private Domestic Investment
	  Business Plant and Equipment
	  Residential Construction
	  Net Change in Inventory
	Net Export of Goods and Services
	Government Expenditures for Goods
	  and Services
	  National
	  Local

Total: Charges against Gross National Product	Total: Gross National Expenditures

Notes: This statement is based on U.S. practice, which changes in detail from year to year and from one publication to another. Published statements are found in the July issues of the *Survey of Current Business* and in the annual *Economic Report of the President*.

[1] Including inventory valuation adjustment.
[2] Including profits of foreign branches.
[3] Net of indirect business subsidies.

investment goods), and partly by the nature of the buyer (governments and foreigners). Its sum is sometimes called gross national *expenditure* (GNE) rather than GNP proper.

Under ideal conditions, the two sides of table 2-3 balance perfectly. Given the incompleteness of the underlying accounting documentation, and the arbitrariness of the substitutes employed, they seldom do. The two sides are ordinarily estimated separately by independent teams of accountants, economists, and statisticians. Each team combines sample data from various sources with its own estimates. A balance is forced through an account called "statistical discrepancy." This account is usually small. Because attempts to minimize taxes encourage underestimates on the factor payments side, the final products side is given priority regarding accuracy; the discrepancy account is consequently placed on the factor payments side, regardless of its sign. Perhaps the least reliable entry is the "income of unincorporated enterprises"; this account is especially important in developing countries.

In addition to GNP, the U.S. national accounts include four other major measures of national income and product, for a total of five. These are the Big Five, with which most students of elementary economics become temporarily familiar. The GNP is normally the largest of the five. We consider the others in the order in which they generally appear.

1. *Net national product* (NNP) is derived by subtracting "capital consumption allowances" (primarily for depreciation and obsolescence) from both sides of table 2-2. (If capital goods were generally like forests and old wine, which gain value over the years, we would have an addition rather than a subtraction problem, and NNP would be larger than GNP.) In the actual situation, NNP is less than GNP, but two problems arise even after accountants permit individual firms wide leeway in estimating the lifetimes of various classes of equipment and in allocating depreciation charges over time. One problem arises because of price changes and the other because of technological progress. (a) The price change problem is analogous to the LIFO-FIFO problem cited above, but it is solved differently. Many firms desire some form of "replacement depreciation" that would permit nontaxable accumulation of reserves sufficient to replace at higher prices equipment originally purchased at lower prices. Such adjustments, desirable as they may be, are not usually granted by tax authorities or recognized in national accounts. (b) Capital is treated differently from inventories in part because it is subject to technological progress. Because of progress, a firm can expect to replace depreciated equipment with improved equipment of a later vintage rather than with the original type. This newer equipment may be quite different from that which it replaces, as when wagons give way to trucks, steam engines to electric power, or

open-hearth furnaces to basic oxygen converters. A firm's gain from tax-free accumulation of reserves to replace old vintages (at old prices) by new ones (at new prices) supposedly offsets its loss from the inadequacy of reserves under inflationary conditions, so that no adjustment need be made. Quantitatively speaking, this argument is weak, but it continues to prevail because the suggested reforms seem difficult to quantify in practice.

2. *Net national income* (NNI) is derived by subtracting from NNP an account called *business taxes*. Business taxes are taken net of business *subsidies*, so that NNI will exceed NNP in an economy where business subsidies exceed business taxes. The distinction between income and product concepts is an important one that was formalized by Sir John Hicks. National *product* is evaluated, as should be clear from our preceding treatment, at market price. National *income*, however, is evaluated at "factor cost." Factor cost is defined to *include* all profits and losses, whether competitive or monopolistic, but to *exclude* business taxes and subsidies. This treatment *assumes*, but does not prove, a particular theory about the incidence of business taxes and subsidies, namely, that they are shifted forward to product prices and form wedges between prices and costs. (This is not the only area of social study where a theory is logically prior to facts, or to statistics.) As for the definition of business taxes—they include excise taxes, sales taxes, and property taxes. They do *not* include corporate income and profits taxes. The exclusion of corporate income and profits taxes is based on the theory that they are *not* shifted forward, and so do not form wedges between prices and costs.

3. *Personal income* (PI) is derived by subtracting from NNI a number of accounts that are not currently paid to individuals, and simultaneously adding a number of transfers, or payments, to individuals that are not traceable to their participation in the current production. The principal deductions are net business saving, corporate income and profits taxes, and social insurance contributions. The additions include both government and business transfers. When their sum exceeds the sum of the deductions, PI exceeds NNI. (Individual transfers between friends or relatives are treated as gifts and excluded from the accounts, unless they involve remittances to or from abroad.) Government transfers include payments for relief, unemployment insurance, social security, and pensions to public employees. They also include interest charges on the public debt, on the theory that the principal was not usually used for productive purposes, so that the interest does not represent a payment for current production. Business transfer payments consist of private pensions and insurance payments made by private organizations. The interest on consumption loans is also called a private transfer payment out of disposable personal income (see point 4 below), because it does not increase produc-

tion. One might also have argued, however, that payment of this interest (on consumption loans) was for the "service" of providing consumption goods before consumers could afford them.

4. Disposable personal income (DPI) is derived by subtracting from both sides of PI an account called "personal tax and nontax payments." Personal taxes are levied on incomes, estates, inheritances, and gifts; the federal income tax dominates the account in the U.S. The nontax payments are mainly fines and fees. If a system of negative income taxes is adopted, payments under it to poor beneficiaries may be subtracted from the positive taxes paid by those above the poverty line, or they may be treated as ordinary public transfer payments. In the former case but not the latter, it is conceptually possible for DPI to exceed PI.

If the reader attempts the exercise of relating our Big Five arithmetically, he will find that a statistical discrepancy is treated like an unrecorded business subsidy if positive, or like an unrecorded business tax if negative. The justification for this treatment is pragmatic. On the final products side, the national income statistician normally begins with GNP and works down. On the factor payments side, he begins with PI and works in both directions. Linkage is made at the transition between NNP and NNI; the statistical discrepancy is used to articulate the transition.

The foregoing paragraphs have criticized many of the short cuts and rules of thumb of conventional social accounting. Such criticism does not imply that these rules are worse than alternatives, that the writer is hiding some better set of rules, or that short cuts and rules of thumb can be dispensed with entirely. It is intended to inculcate a certain healthy skepticism about any results that may depend on the short cuts and rules of thumb, and hence about the significance of minor variations, either in the aggregates or in their rates of change.

ALTERNATIVE INCOME CONCEPTS

We have concentrated attention upon the U.S. social accounts, which have been influential internationally. Many countries, however, depart more or less widely from the U.S. model, in order to adapt to their own data sources and make what they consider improvements. In addition, income series other than the Big Five can be computed from U.S. data and are widely used although not published officially on any continuing basis. Consideration of a few variants may rid us of any belief that the official U.S. model is necessarily ideal.

Double-entry systems of national accounting are commonly used in advanced countries. Some developing countries use single-entry systems,

usually including only the final product side. Developing countries often publish only one or two of the Big Five, usually the GNP and/or the NNI. In addition to serving as a check, however imperfect, upon the accuracy of statistical computations and the consistency of statistical estimates, a double-entry system permits presentation of the accounts as a *circular flow* of income and product, proceeding from business and government to household as income payments, and then back to business and government as purchasers of products and payments of taxes. A graphical system of presenting these data has been developed by the Twentieth Century Fund; we present it as figure 2-1. It is left incomplete here. The reader may find it a profitable exercise to expand such a circular flow chart, to include omitted items like (1) international transactions, (2) government sur-

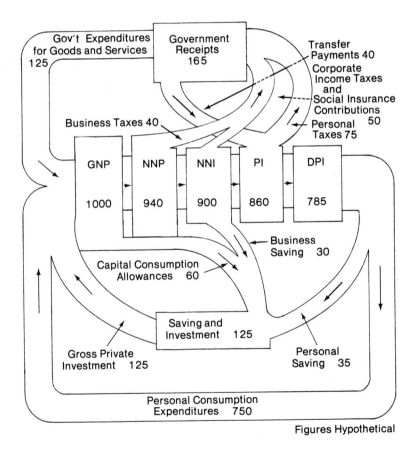

Figures Hypothetical

Figure 2-1 Twentieth Century Fund Circular Flow Chart (Plumber's Nightmare)

pluses or deficits, (3) private transfer payments, and (4) the statistical discrepancy.

The following major variations constitute a sample of social accounts used in advanced countries:

1. Rather than GNP and NNP, many countries concentrate on gross and net *domestic* product (GDP and NDP, respectively). Whereas the GNP-NNP system assigns income items to the country in which the income recipient is *living*, the GDP-NDP system assigns them to the country in which the income is *produced* directly. Consider, for example, a U.S. resident who owns Japanese securities that pay him dividends and interest. This income is included in the U.S. GNP and NNP because of the recipient's residence there. It is included in the Japanese GDP and NDP because the productivity of the capital equipment (of which the U.S. shareholder is part owner) is manifest in Japan, where the equipment is used. For a country like the U.S., whose resident individuals and firms have made extensive foreign investments, GNP is higher than GDP, and NNP is higher than NDP. For a country like Mexico, in which nonresident individuals and companies have made large investments, the reverse is the case.

2. In the USSR and many countries influenced by Soviet practice, income from services is not recognized as part of the national income or product, unless these services contribute directly to the production of material goods, as in the case of freight transportation. In this respect, Soviet practice follows the economic theories of the classical school and of Karl Marx, which limited wealth and income to material goods. To cite one anomaly of this system, production of a piano is included in the national income, but not the services of the pianist who plays it, even if the player is a professional. The USSR also uses a series called "value of output," corresponding to the sum of all firms' production statements, as considered earlier in this chapter. Critics consider such a statement to involve multiple counting. Assume, for example, that within a single period iron ore is made into steel, and the steel into a tractor. The value of the ore in this series of transactions enters into value of output three times, once in itself, once as a component of the steel, and once as a component of the tractor. Similarly, the value added to the iron ore by the steel works enters twice. The less integrated the country's economic structure, the greater the number of recorded transfers of goods between one firm and another, the larger the value of output. In the critics' view, the greater is also the problem of multiple counting, which the value-added system attempts to avoid.

3. Many countries double the number of their government accounts by separating public expenditures into public consumption and public invest-

ment. Others triple them by adding a separate category for national defense, apart from both consumption and investment. The separation of public consumption and investment is sometimes called "the Swedish budget." This system treats public and private expenditures in the same way on the final product side of the GNP statement (table 2-3), breaking both down into consumption and investment categories. It also runs counter to a common conservative belief that public expenditures are necessarily wasteful, or a form of unproductive consumption. An economic objection to the breakdown is that consumption and investment are more difficult to separate or distinguish in the public than in the private sector. A political objection under inflationary conditions is that such a breakdown makes it easy for public bodies to claim that their budgets are balanced or in surplus when only the consumption budget is in this state. They can then finance long-term projects from deficit financing, public borrowing, and monetary expansion with fewer objections than otherwise.

Within the U.S. itself, we may mention two additional aggregates, *final sales* and *discretionary income*. Final sales are defined as GNP minus that portion of investment which represents net increase in inventory. This measure attracts most attention in hard times, when the authorities need evidence that a slowdown is "only" an inventory recession. Such evidence is provided when final sales are rising more rapidly than GNP, or are rising while GNP is falling; these are common states of affairs in mild recession or in the early stages of severe ones. As for discretionary income, it is defined as DPI less some estimate of necessary or obligatory consumer expenditure. Obligatory consumption expenditure is ordinarily equated with expenditures for food, or for a more general subsistence minimum including such obligations as contract rent, insurance premiums, payments on mortgage and installment debt, etc. Consequently, discretionary income might be significantly less than DPI. Discretionary income has been found useful in estimating demand for expensive durable goods, such as automobiles, and for "consumption-type" investments of homeowners in improving their property. It is also used in estimating aggregate consumption functions in low-income countries or for low-income groups.[5]

REVIEW: NOTES ON INVESTMENT AND SAVING

Of the major categories of national income and product, "investment" gives rise to the most controversy. The man in the street thinks he is

---

[5] One form of discretionary income, the Stone-Geary system, is applied to Japanese development by Allen C. Kelley et al. *Dualistic Economic Development* (1972), pp. 46–48 and ch. 4, and by Allen C. Kelley and Jeffrey G. Williamson, *Lessons from Japanese Development* (1974), pp. 51–54 and ch. 6.

investing when he purchases real estate or securities. National income statistics only count as investment additions to the social capital—plant, equipment, residences, and inventories. A student may reasonably wonder how the two concepts are related. Consider, for example, the purchase by A of securities from B. If they are old securities, issued in some previous period, A has indeed made an investment, but it has been balanced by B's disinvestment. No net investment, therefore, has been made. (There may have been a capital gain or loss to B on the transaction, but capital gains and losses are not included in national income accounts. They represent only revaluations of existing assets and not production of new ones.)

But the securities purchased by A may not be old securities. They may be new ones, issued by C, a firm, and purchased by A through B, a broker or investment banker. In this case an investment is recorded when C spends the proceeds of the new securities for plant, equipment, or inventories. To include the securities as investment along with the investment goods would be double counting. If C does not, in fact, spend the proceeds from the new securities for investment purposes, no investment has been made from the national income viewpoint, as in the case of old securities.

Many people think of their homes as durable consumption goods, and are surprised that all residential construction is treated as investment in the national accounts, while output of automobiles, furniture, etc., enters as consumption. Most residential construction, however, is made with a view to rental income or capital gains, and not for consumption purposes by homeowners. Also, many homeowners look on their homes as investments as well as consumption goods; for some, a home is the largest investment they ever make. Consistent with their treatment of all residential construction as investment, the national accounts include in "rental income of persons" and also in "services" an estimate of the imputed rent received by homeowners from their homes. On the other hand, some people think of their jewelry, art objects, and other valuables primarily as investments. The national accounts treat these items as consumption goods when newly produced.

"Saving" is another concept with a special meaning in economics that sometimes departs from its meaning in ordinary life. For society it means reduction in the other uses of its total income, whether any individual "saver" is aware of his "saving" or not. The paradox can be illustrated by an artificially simplified case of "forced saving" or "forced frugality." Consider a primitive, fully employed, all-consumption, closed economy in which nobody saves or pays taxes. A foreigner suddenly appears with a stock of money, and makes loans that the borrowers spend for investment. Where does the offsetting saving come from, or does the investment materialize out of thin air? Actually, there has been saving. It has come from the diversion of part of the community's constant total resources away from consumption, making available the investment goods. (These

may even be the identical consumption goods, held in inventories as investments.) Nonborrowing consumers will witness price increases. These will reduce both their real income and their real consumption. As individuals they save actively neither before nor after the price increases; in each period they consume one hundred percent of their incomes. Nevertheless, saving in our sense has been forced on them behind their backs by inflation. For the society as a whole, borrowers and nonborrowers taken together, we shall see later that saving and investment turn out to be equal.

A fallacy which dies hard is the argument that the public debt should be deducted from investment and, hence, from the national income and product.[6] However, a debt is a stock and income is a flow. If the public debt should be subtracted from anything, it should be from another stock, such as national wealth, rather than from national income or any of its components. Any subtraction of debt from income would be wrong dimensionally, like subtracting velocity (distance per unit of time) from distance. Subtraction of the public debt from the national wealth would also be wrong, unless the securities representing this debt had been included in the national wealth. (In practice, securities are only included in national wealth estimates when they represent claims on assets, public or private, that are located abroad.) There seems no more reason to deduct public debt from national wealth than to deduct private debt—a suggestion seldom if ever made. And also, returning to the income account, there seems no more reason to deduct the annual or quarterly *increment* (positive or negative) in the public debt from investment and national income than to deduct the increment of private debt.

SUMMARY

We attempt several different, albeit related, things in this chapter. There is, therefore, a danger of missing the forest for the trees. The purpose of recapitulations like the one following is avoidance of this danger.

1. The introductory paragraphs relate social accounting to macroeconomic analysis.

2. Problems in measuring the price level, unemployment, and the labor force—aggregates not entering into national accounts proper—are then considered, but not solved.

3. Turning explicitly to income measurement, we build up a firm's GNP contribution from an income or payments statement, via its production

---

[6] *Interest* on the public debt, as we have noted previously, is not included in GNP, NNP, or NNI, but is included in PI and DPI.

and value-added statements.[7] This method relates private and social accounting. En route, we also note the application of the value-added statement in particular as a basis of value-added taxation.

4. Given GNP, we go on to derive the other four members of the Big Five national income series (NNP, NNI, PI, DPI), as well as final sales and discretionary income, which are less important in the American system of accounts.

5. The American system is shown to be only one possible way of setting up the social accounts. Among the alternative systems mentioned are: (a) the GDP system (which allocates income where *earned* rather than where *received*), (b) the Soviet system (based on Marxian concepts), and (c) the Swedish system (of separating public investment from public "consumption").

6. Finally, we distinguish the economist's concepts of investment and saving from the concepts of the man in the street. We argue against deducting either the public debt or its annual increment from any measure of national income, or from the national wealth (with which this book is less concerned).

---

[7] Richard Ruggles and Nancy Ruggles, *National Income Accounts and Income Analysis*, 2d ed. trace this development in considerably more detail in chapters 3–6.

Problems of Sectoring and Welfare

INTRODUCTION

This is the second chapter of a pair devoted to social accounting. Chapter 2 dealt mainly with measures of total national income and product. This chapter will look more deeply at the analytics of national income accounting by concentrating on two points: (1) how the national income is divided between sectors of the economy, and (2) to what extent, if at all, its per capita size may serve as a rough welfare index.

WHY SECTORING?

By the *sectoring* of national income accounts we mean both their division into two or more mutually exclusive sectors and the subsequent spelling out of certain intersectoral identities. There are a number of ways in which this might be done.

At one extreme, we might divide the economy into two sectors only. These might be, for example, the public and private sectors. Karl Marx, in *Das Kapital*, used a two-sector division of a purely private capitalist economy, dividing it into a Department I (producing capital goods) and a Department II (producing consumption goods). At the other extreme, we might approach microeconomics by sectoring the economy into a large table or matrix of the input and output interrelations between a large number of industries or regions.[1] A third sectoring scheme, the oldest such scheme in the history of economic thought, is the "Tableau Économique" of the eighteenth century French physiocrat François Quesnay. His division is by social classes and requires a tripartite division of the society. There is a productive sector, which includes the peasantry; a sterile class, which include artisans, industrial workers, and other elements of the nonagricultural labor force;[2] and a landowning class, which consumes or invests the surplus products of the productive peasant farmers.

We shall use none of these schemes here. Instead, we shall use a scheme developed with an eye to application of John Maynard Keynes' *General Theory of Employment Interest and Money* (1936). (Relatively little is due to Keynes himself. Following a distinction made by Axel Leijonhufvud,[3]

---

[1] Such input-output tables are used widely in many countries for both national and regional planning and forecasting, following the pioneer work of Wassily Leontief. For an introduction, see William Miernyk, *Elements of Input-Output Analysis* (1965).

[2] These people, in Quesnay's France, lived close to the margin of subsistence. In the aggregate, they could not accumulate any "surplus" by their efforts, but could only feed themselves, with nothing left over for the nobility or for the State. This may be why Quesnay regarded them as sterile.

[3] Axel Leijonhufvud, *Keynesian Economics and the Economics of Keynes* (1968).

the sectoring scheme belongs to "Keynesian economics" rather than to "the economics of Keynes.")

Before proceeding with our Keynesian sectoring scheme, we might face the question, Why sector at all? One advantage of sectoring has already been suggested by figure 2-1, which itself involves a sectoring scheme. Sectoring permits circular flows of income and expenditures between sectors to be analyzed, like the flow of the blood between the heart and the body in medical science. Another advantage of sectoring is the clarification of a number of basic identities, primarily involving saving and investment, used in theoretical analysis. A third advantage is the frequent use of sectoral totals, and relations between them, for purposes of economic forecasting.

A SECTORING SCHEME

Our initial sectoring scheme is a simplification involving only five sectors and only eleven accounts.[4] The five sectors are Production, Government, International, Households, and Saving-Investment.[5] The five accounts are presented in table 3-1. We observe that each of the eleven numbered accounts appears exactly twice, once on the l.h.s. of one sector and once on the r.h.s. of another. This means that the sum of all five sectors balances. We also note that each of the first four sectors is balanced as it stands, using as balancing items the government deficit (sector II) and personal saving (sector IV). Since the sum of all five accounts balances, and likewise the sum of the first four, it follows that sector V (Saving-Investment) must balance too. This demonstration, introduces the celebrated saving-investment identity, of which we shall hear much more.

A number of the accounts in the table may have either positive or negative signs. It is a matter of indifference whether we put these accounts on the l.h.s. or the r.h.s.; however, a positive account on the l.h.s. becomes negative on the r.h.s. and vice versa. For example, consider the government deficit account (9) on the r.h.s. of sector II, with a surplus indicated by a negative sign. It might equally well have gone on the l.h.s. entitled "Government Surplus (+) or Deficit (−)." It would remain as a balancing item.

---

[4] I am indebted to John Powelson for many details of this scheme.

[5] Use of a "production sector" rather than the more usual "business sector" permits us to dispense with the notion of "business gross product." The production sector includes nonprofit institutions such as universities; it also includes governments and households in their business capacities as employers of inputs and sellers of outputs. (Accordingly, the government sector excludes government enterprises, and the household sector excludes household business-type activities.)

Table 3-1
Simple Sectoring of National Accounts

I Production

Expenditures	Receipts
(1) Input Payments	(4) Personal Consumption Expenditures
(2) Business and Corporate Income Taxes	(5) Government Expenditures for Goods and Services
(3) Business Gross Retained Earnings	(6) Gross Private Domestic Investment
	(7) Net Exports (+) or Imports (−)
Gross National Product	Gross National Expenditures

II Government

Expenditures	Receipts
(5)	(2) ....
	(8) Personal Taxes
	(9) Government Deficit (+) or Surplus (−)
Government Expenditures	Government Receipts

III International

Expenditures	Receipts
(7)	(10) Domestic Investment in Foreign Assets and International Reserves
Balance of Trade	Balance of Trade

IV Households

Expenditures	Receipts
(4)	(1) ....
(8)	
(11) Personal Saving	
Household Expenditure	Household Income

V Saving-Investment

Expenditures	Receipts
(6)	(3) ....
(9)	(11) ....
(10)	
Investment	Saving

35

The information on table 3-1 can also be presented on an intersectoral payments table (sometimes called a payments *matrix*) like table 3-2. This table helps visualize the abstraction of treating saving-investment as a separate sector, whose receipts are saving and whose expenditures are investment.

Digression: As outlined here, tables 3-1 and 3-2 ignore transfer payments. If they had been included no column or row would have been added to GNP. For public transfer payments, sectors II and IV of table 3-1 are involved. In sector II (Government), a "transfer payments" account may be added on the l.h.s., and the deficit account (9) correspondingly increased on the r.h.s. In sector IV (Households) the new "transfer payments" account might enter as an additional receipt on the r.h.s., while the personal saving account (11) would be increased correspondingly on the l.h.s. as a balancing item. For business transfer payments, sectors I and IV are involved. On the l.h.s. of sector I (Business) we might enter a new "business transfer payments" account, and reduce correspondingly the "gross retained earnings" balancing item (3) on the same side. In sector IV, the adjustments are as in the case of public transfers, except for the nomenclature of the new account. Balance in all sectors is retained, including balance in sector V (Saving-Investment), where the rise in the personal savings account (11) is balanced partly by the decline in the business gross retained earnings account (3) on the same side, and the remainder by the increase in the government deficit account (9) on the l.h.s.

A NATIONAL ECONOMIC BUDGET

The term "nation's economic budget" was formerly applied in the U.S. to a somewhat different sectoring scheme devised by Grover Ensley, whose sectoral totals add to GNP. The title was later dropped as implying too large a role for centralized planning. The series, however, continues to be published.

It was no mean feat to devise a sectoring scheme, including transfer payments, that adds to GNP, which excludes transfer payments. This, however, has been accomplished as per table 3-3. If we ignore any statistical discrepancy, the table has four sectors: Households, Business, Government, and International. Intersectoral receipts and expenditures are computed for each sector; the balancing items are also indicated. As the pattern is presented in table 3-3, positive balances are elements of saving, and negative balances are elements of investment. The saving-investment identity is not shown as a separate balanced sector, but by the zero sum of the "Balance"

Table 3-2
Simplified Matrix of Intersectoral Income Flows

Paying Sector \ Receiving Sector	I Production	II Government	III International	IV Households	V Saving-Investment	Total
I Production		(2) Business and Corporate Income Taxes		(1) Input Payments	(3) Business Gross Retained Earnings	Gross National Product
II Government	(5) Government Expenditures for Goods and Services					Government Expenditures
III International	(7) Net Exports					Balance of Trade
IV Households	(4) Personal Consumption Expenditures	(8) Personal Taxes			(11) Personal Saving	Household Expenditures
V Saving-Investment	(6) Gross Private Domestic Investment	(9) Government Deficit	(10) Domestic Investment in Foreign Assets and International Reserves			Investment
Total	Gross National Expenditures	Government Receipts	Balance of Trade	Household Income	Saving	

Table 3-3
A National Economic Budget

Sector	Receipts	Expenditures	Balance
Households	Disposable Personal Income	Personal Consumption Expenditures	Personal Saving (+)
Business	Gross Retained Earnings	Gross Private Domestic Investment	Excess of Investment (−)
Government	Taxes less Transfers	Expenditures less Transfers	Surplus (+) or Deficit (−)
International	International Transfers	Net Exports	Excess of Transfers (+) or Exports (−)
Total	Gross National Product	Gross National Expenditure	0

column for the four sectors shown. (This result we have stated without proof.)[6]

Among the numerous uses of table 3-3 to short-term forecasting, we point out one. If the saving ratio (personal saving divided by disposable income) rises, and particularly if S rises while DPI falls, one might expect an economic slowdown, or at least the moderation of any previous overheating. If the saving ratio rises, and particularly if S falls while DPI rises, one might expect high prosperity, or at least the moderation of any previous recession.

SAVING-INVESTMENT IDENTITIES

The algebraic background of the saving-investment identities in our tables is quite simple. In the circular flow of income, one firm's spending

---

[6] The proof is too involved for our present purposes. The reader may attempt it on his own; one main trick is that transfers have been deducted from *both* government receipts *and* government expenditures.

(whether for consumption or investment) is another firm's income. Aggregating, total income equals total expenditure. This is the theme on which we are elaborating variations. Let us denote income by Y, consumption expenditure by C, and investment expenditure by I. We can then draw up a "source" equation (identity) for aggregate income, neglecting for the present both the government and the international economy:

$$Y = C + I \tag{3.1}$$

In this same truncated economy, income can be used only for consumption or nonconsumption. Nonconsumption is defined as saving and denoted by S. We can then draw up a "use" equation (identity) for aggregate income:

$$Y = C + S \tag{3.2}$$

It follows at once that I = S, which is the saving-investment identity in its simplest form. This identity is not claimed to hold for any single individual or firm. It means rather than any act of saving or dissaving by A is somehow matched by his own, or someone else's, voluntary or involuntary investment or disinvestment. Suppose consumers suddenly become more thrifty and decide to save more. What would the balancing investment be? In the short run, it would be an unplanned and involuntary accumulation of inventories of finished products, primarily by retailers. Similarly, suppose all consumers decide the world is about to end and suddenly go on a spending spree. This time the balancing *disinvestment* would be an unplanned and involuntary reduction or decumulation of inventories of finished products, starting with retailers and extending "up the line." In both cases, the formal identity between actual or ex post I and S holds.

Let us now include in our economy a set of governments, central and local. It spends in total—as injections into the circular flow of income—an amount G for goods and services. It receives in total—as *leakages* from the circular flow—an amount T in taxes and allied receipts like fines and fees. (T is usually taken net of public transfer payments, as per the expression T = Tx − Tr.) At the same time we may include the rest of the world, as reflected in the international sector. The rest of the world spends X for our economy's exports, and supplies M in imports. G and X are additional sources (injections) of income. M is a use (leakage) of income, but is treated as a deduction in the source equation, since consumption of imported goods (or investment in imported capital items) is not a direct addition to the economy's income. With these additions, the source, use, and balance equations for income become:

$$\text{Sources:} \quad Y = C + I + G + (X - M) \tag{3.3}$$

$$\text{Uses:} \quad Y = C + S + T \tag{3.4}$$

$$\text{Balance:} \quad (I - S) + (G - T) + (X - M) = 0 \tag{3.5}$$

The balance equation (3.5) tells us that the equality between private I and private S no longer holds precisely, unless $(G - T) + (X - M) = 0$. Private I exceeds private S if $(G - T) + (X - M) > 0$. The U.S. has tended historically to satisfy the requirements of this last alternative, running budget deficits and trade surpluses.

Going a small step further, we can divide exports into commercial exports, which we continue to call X, and transfer (aid) exports A. In the same way, we continue to call commercial imports M and transfer (aid) imports B. (For a net provider of foreign aid, $A > B$; for a net recipient, $A < B$.) Exports of aid goods add to domestic income like other exports, and income is spent on aid goods like other imports. The equation group (3.3–3.5) expands to:

$$\text{Sources:} \quad Y = C + I + G + (X - M) + (A - B) \tag{3.6}$$

$$\text{Uses:} \quad Y = C + S + T \tag{3.4}$$

$$\text{Balance:} \quad (I - S) + (G - T) + (X - M) + (A - B) = 0 \tag{3.7}$$

The expanded balance equation (3.7) tells us that I = S only as a first approximation, when $(G - T) + (X - M) + (A - B) = 0$. $I > S$ if $(G - T) + (X - M) + (A - B) < 0$; $I < S$ if $(G - T) + (X - M) + (A - B) > 0$. Many developing countries would like to accelerate growth by a higher level of private investment than is permitted by private saving at their current level of poverty, so that $(I > S)$. They would also like to undertake a greater level of public spending (on investment projects for the most part) than can be financed in taxes under the same poverty-stricken conditions, so that $(G > T)$. At the same time, developing countries would like to increase their international reserves by active, or at least balanced, international trade, so that $(X \geq M)$. Finally, they would like to avoid the political entanglements sometimes entailed by dependence on aid receipts, so that $(A \geq B)$. Equation (3.7) shows that these four aims, however laudable, are mutually incompatible. At least one of the quartet must be abandoned. This result has nothing to do with issues of capitalism vs. socialism, planning vs. the market, inflation vs. price stability, or "advanced-country economics" vs. some allegedly different developing-country variety. It is simply a matter of algebra.

DIGRESSION: ALTERNATIVE SAVING-INVESTMENT FORMULATIONS

We may, however, be dealing with time periods so short that income received in period 1 from expenditure in period 1 is only spent in period 2. If so, we have a "Robertson" lag and an essentially dynamic saving-investment equation. In the simplest case of a purely private closed economy:[7]

$$\text{Sources:} \quad Y_2 = C_2 + I_2 \tag{3.8}$$

$$\text{Uses:} \quad Y_1 = C_2 + S_2 \tag{3.9}$$

$$\text{Balance:} \quad Y_2 - Y_1 = I_2 - S_2 \tag{3.10}$$

Another alternative formulation writes the use equation on an anticipations basis. That is to say, it separates anticipated income Y_a into anticipated consumption and saving C_a and S_a. If we assume further that anticipated consumption plans are carried out in the aggregate, so that $C_a = C$ even though Y_a differs from Y, but that saving plans may not be carried out, we have in a private closed economy:

$$\text{Sources:} \quad Y = C + I \tag{3.1}$$

$$\text{Uses:} \quad Y_a = C + S_a \tag{3.11}$$

$$\text{Balance:} \quad Y - Y_a = I - S_a \tag{3.12}$$

Let us consider the economic meanings of equations (3.10) and (3.12). Equation (3.10) says that investment exceeds saving in the short run when income is rising, and vice versa; its development is associated with the work of Sir Dennis Robertson. Equation (3.12) says that actual investment

---

[7] Another possible lag pattern (a "Lundberg" lag) for short periods would have income earned in period 1 received only in period 2, while spending in period 1 consists of income received in period 1 from previous earnings (say, in period 0). This pattern gives us:

$$\text{Sources:} \quad Y_2 = C_1 + I_1$$
$$\text{Uses:} \quad Y_1 = C_1 + S_1$$
$$\text{Balance:} \quad Y_2 - Y_1 = I_1 - S_1$$

with the same implications as (3.10) except for details of timing.

exceeds anticipated (planned) saving if actual income exceeds anticipated income, and vice versa; its development is associated with the work of the Stockholm School of Scandinavian economists.

These alternatives to the saving-investment identity are entirely correct under their own assumptions. They do not seem as useful empirically as their Keynesian counterparts stemming from I = S. There seems little point in working with periods so short (and so inconvenient statistically) as to make the Robertsonian equation (3.10) relevant, despite the appeal of being more "dynamic." Also, anticipations data are still inadequate for any extensive use of the Stockholm equation (3.12) except in theoretical manipulations.

WELFARE IMPLICATIONS

From sectoring problems we pass to the relation between income and welfare. It has become fashionable to attack the measurement of welfare by means of (total or per capita) national income and product aggregates. This is true whether we think of welfare in general, or of economic welfare as a somehow-separable component of general welfare. This fashion is a reaction to the "growthmanship" of the 1950s and early 1960s, which subordinated other goals, including resource conservation and pollution avoidance, to maximizing measured GNP, and especially to maximizing measured growth in measured GNP. On the other hand, the reaction may go too far. We need not, for example, support those ascetic extremists of the ecological school, who insist on zero growth or *falling* GNP as a necessary condition for "safeguarding the environment" and other good things.

A high statistical correlation seems to exist between, for example, national income or GNP per capita and most of our other quantitative measures of economic and social welfare. Despite its various arbitrarinesses and allied deficiencies, per capita income may be a reasonable welfare proxy or surrogate after all. For example, consider John Ruskin's "There is no Wealth but Life!" This can be interpreted as associating welfare with high life expectancy, which is, in fact, a common demographic welfare index. On this basis, high-income countries with adequate diets and modern sanitary-medical facilities rank above low-income countries, despite the consequences of air, water, and other pollutions, and despite the propensity of the affluent to "dig their graves with their teeth."[8] A similar result

---

[8] The U.S. lies "below the curve" relating per capita income to life expectancy. We need not speculate whether this is due to longer exposure to pollution, obesity, and the sedentary way of life, to the comparative paucity and costliness of medical facilities for low-income people, or to other factors altogether.

obtains when records for single countries are examined over time, or when welfare criteria other than life expectancy are employed. In short, per capita income is a reasonable proxy for a large group of alternative welfare measures, even though the correlation (when measurable) is by no means perfect.

Among the Big Five national income and product aggregates of the U.S. system, real per capita NNI seems at first glance most useful or "least worst" as a welfare indicator for the long period, and real per capita PI or DPI for the short period. Measures net of depreciation, like NNI, are "cleaner" than gross measures like GNP for this particular purpose; one may accuse the gross measure of double counting. In practice, unfortunately, the depreciation deduction is among the most arbitrary and least reliable features of the statistical series. As between NNI and NNP, NNI is preferable because NNP, based on market prices, gives higher weights to items like liquor and tobacco, which (as luxuries, or as threats to health) are taxed heavily, and lower weights to items like public-housing rents, which (as necessities) are subsidized. As between NNI and PI or DPI, the welfare of natural persons (as distinguished from corporate entities) can be increased in the short run by transfer payments that increase PI and DPI but not NNI. Decreases in personal taxes, or negative taxes, which increase only DPI, have the same effect. It is clear, however, that such real transfers and tax remissions cannot increase without bound. It may therefore be unwise to use as long-term welfare measures series like per capita PI and DPI, which are subject to such manipulations.

Rather than welfare, GNP seems most closely related to employment, precisely because it is gross. Employment is furnished equally by replacement of old facilities and production of new ones. As for NNP, it comes conceptually closest to the theorist's Y, which usually involves measurement in market prices, but which ignores the complications of depreciation. Finally, DPI is most closely related to personal consumption and saving.

STATISTICAL ENTOMOLOGY

Numerous statistical "bugs" or anomalies, most of them apparently unavoidable, operate against the use of economic aggregates as more than first approximations to welfare measures. Some of these "bugs" are obvious. Others have been mentioned already in passing.

1. None of these aggregates takes account of resource depletion, environmental pollution, the "human-capital" costs of overwork, or (on the positive side) the intangibles summarized under the heading of "the good life."

2. All these aggregates include items that might equally well be deducted from income as costs of life in an advanced or urban economy. One example is the variety of clothing required in temperate climates, or the vagaries of fashion. Another is the costly array of services (transportation, sanitation, police and fire protection, etc.) required for contemporary urban and suburban life but not for Thoreau's *Walden* or hippie communes. A third example is the output of specialized military goods and services involved in modern military technology.

3. All these aggregates exclude household services as unmeasurable.[9] This explains the old saws about the national income rising when people take in each others' washing, or falling when a man marries his cook or housekeeper. It also explains some systematic understatement of the incomes of developing countries, relative to the income of advanced ones. A wide range of activities (baking, spinning, weaving, residential repair and construction) is usually carried on domestically in developing countries and through the market in advanced ones. In the first case but not the second, the aggregates usually miss them entirely.

4. Nearly all components of nearly all aggregates include statistical estimates. In addition, some components are *imputations* of the values of nontransactions. Two important examples are the rents that might have been received by homeowners from their residential properties, and the farm value of product consumed by farm families in their own homes.[10]

5. The entire purchased output of consumption goods is included in the aggregates,[11] but only increments (positive or negative) to the capital stock are considered investment. The distinction between consumption and investment goods is not always clear. (Coal, wood, gas, or oil for home heating is a consumption good. Its entire value is included in the aggregates, with no deductions anywhere else. Coal, wood, gas or oil for heating an office or factory is an intermediate product; its value is deducted from the value added by the office or factory where it is used.) Military goods are normally treated as consumption goods, with their full values included in the aggregates. Some believe they should be excluded, or even deducted (see number 2 above). A less extreme view would treat military goods as capital items, with only the increments included in the aggregates.

---

[9] Some women's liberation organizations insist that if household services were paid for (and included in the national income) women's self-esteem and self-respect would rise substantially.

[10] Part of the gap between measured urban and rural incomes would be closed if, instead of farm prices, the higher urban retail prices were used in estimating the value of farm-consumed produce.

[11] Even in the case of consumer durable goods like automobiles, furniture, and appliances, their entire value is counted in the period of their sale to consumers. Some writers propose that it be spread over their average estimated lifetimes instead.

6. All government activities are included. The economic contribution of governments proper (as distinguished from government enterprises like the Post Office) is their payrolls. Two problems arise: (a) the evaluation is subject to no market test; (b) government services to business are double-counted, if they are also reflected in business value added. As for government enterprises, depreciation on their capital is not deducted in the U.S. system. (Their capital is treated as though it were permanent.) This means that all the aggregates except GNP increase when a light plant or bus system is shifted from private to public ownership.

7. All the aggregates exclude criminal activities, whose definition varies with time and place. Thus, the aggregates rise when a previously criminal activity like abortion, gambling, or prostitution is legalized. They fall when production of tobacco products or alcoholic liquors is restricted or prohibited. (Assume two adjoining acres planted with opium poppies. Whiteacre's crop is used for legitimate medical purposes. Blackacre's crop is grown illegally for "junkies" at home or abroad.[12] Whiteacre's poppy crop (but not Blackacre's) is included in the national income and product.)

MEASURES OF ECONOMIC WELFARE

A measure of economic welfare (MEW), derived by Nordhaus and Tobin, aims to adjust the conventional series for many of the "bugs" mentioned in the last paragraph.[13] Briefly, the Nordhaus-Tobin MEW is NNP *plus* estimates of the value of a number of nonmarket activities such as leisure and household capital services and *minus* similar estimates of the value of a number of public and private "regrettables," "disamenities," and intermediate products—services to business (as in number 6-b above). Detail is summarized in table 3-4. For 1929, Nordhaus and Tobin estimate MEW for the U.S. as $543.6 billion in 1958 prices, as against GNP of $203.6 billion. The corresponding estimates for 1965 are $1241.1 billion (MEW) and $617.8 billion (GNP). Comparing these two years, the MEW/GNP ratio fell from 2.67 to 2.01; further adjustment for population changes would supply a further fall in the ratio on a per capita basis. Such estimates support the frequent criticisms of post-1945 American society, to

---

[12] If the *production* had been legal Blackacre's poppies would have been included at the farm value, regardless of any illegality of subsequent processing or disposal under domestic or foreign law.

[13] William Nordhaus and James Tobin, "Is Growth Obsolete?" in National Bureau of Economic Research, *Economic Growth* (1972). For an elementary summary, see Kenneth Stewart, "National Income Accounting and Economic Welfare: Concepts of GNP and MEW," Federal Reserve Bank of St. Louis *Review* (April 1974). A similar study for Japan, directed by Miyohei Shinohara, is Economic Council Japan, *Measuring NNW of Japan* (1973). (NNW stands for Net National Welfare.)

Table 3-4

GNP and MEW, 1929 and 1965
(in billions of dollars, at 1958 prices)

	1929	1965
GNP	203.6	617.8
Less: Capital consumption	−20.0	−54.7
NNP	183.6	563.1
Less: Output reclassified as "regrettables" or "intermediaries"		
Government	−6.7	−63.2
Private	−10.3	−30.9
Plus: Imputations for items excluded from national income and product		
Leisure	339.5	626.9
Nonmarket activity	87.5	295.4
Services of private and public capital	29.7	78.9
Less: Disamenities	−12.5	−34.6
Additional capital consumption	−19.3	−92.7
Minimum net investment to sustain		
MEW	543.6	1241.1

Source: Stewart, *op. cit.*, p. 21, based on Nordhaus and Tobin, *op. cit.*, p. 55.

the effect that GNP advances have been absorbed largely—some claim completely—in regrettables, disamenities, and "people pollution."

SUMMARY AND TRANSITION

The initial third of this chapter is about simple sectoring schemes in social accounting. It centers around schemes for clarifying the saving-investment identity. The middle third derives this identity algebraically in the simple case of a purely private closed economy, and then modifies it to include government, international trade, and international aid. The final third of the chapter attempts to justify the use of the national income aggregates and their rates of change as proxies for welfare measures, on the theory of frequently high correlation between the series concerned. The chapter closes with a list of several of the "bugs" in published national income statistics and a brief mention of modifications designed to measure economic welfare.

We now have an introductory acquaintance with the principal microeconomic aggregates—their meanings, their interrelations, and their approximations in published statistical series. The next series of chapters will take up rival views concerning the *determination* of these aggregates and the implications of these rival views for economic policy, including the viability of capitalism.

Chapter 4

Classical Macroeconomics

THE KEY ISSUE

The most important issue of macrostatic theory is whether or not a market economy tends toward a position of full employment equilibrium. We will adopt as our definition of full employment the balance between unfilled vacancies and involuntarily unemployed workers in all occupations at prevailing wage rates. With unemployment so defined, a classical thesis answers this question in the affirmative; the later (neo-classical) recasting of classical microeconomics left classical macroeconomics essentially unchanged. In this chapter we shall find out why the classical (and neo-classical) writers believed the market always tended to full employment as an equilibrium position. The alternative claim, of course, is that the maintenance of full employment requires public intervention in the form of fiscal and/or monetary policy, or possibly even the supplementing or replacement of the market economy by some form of centralized planning.[1] We should not lose sight of this issue in any maze of technical manipulations.

THE CLASSICAL THESIS

This classical thesis reduces unemployment to a disequilibrium. Its existence means that certain prevailing real wage rates are "too high," not in any ethical sense but in the economic sense that supply exceeds demand for labor at those rates. This conclusion follows from simple supply-and-demand analysis of unemployment in particular trades or occupations. The classical thesis generalizes this conclusion to the entire economy. Writing in the depth of the Great Depression, Edwin Cannan asserted the essence of the classical position: "General unemployment is in reality to be explained almost in the same way as particular unemployment . . . General unemployment appears when asking too much is a general phenomenon."[2]

Classical macroeconomics, and oral traditions based upon it, dominated Western economic thought over roughly the four generations (125 years) prior to the Great Depression of the 1930s. Its conclusions, if not the details of its analysis, are accepted today by many practical men—particularly the conclusion that unemployment means that real wages are too high.

---

[1] Centralized planning may be *imperative* or *indicative*. In imperative planning (the Stalinist or Maoist model), individual industries and plants are ordered to fulfill quantitative physical targets. In the less extreme indicative type of planning (the French or the Japanese model), direct commands are replaced by economic inducements. A frequent economic inducement is the demonstration that some target which seems overly ambitious to an individual industry or firm is really profitable in view of the targets or related industries or firms in the economy.

[2] "The Demand for Labour," *Economic Journal* (September 1932).

Among economists, its analysis survives on the supply side in particular, as we shall see in chapter 11. It is an error to dismiss classical macroeconomics as obsolete, outworn, or completely discredited.

The classical thesis may be stated more formally: For any nominal money supply M* and any positive price level p, there is a positive equilibrium real wage rate w_e such that, at w_e, employment N_e is equal to full employment N_f.[3] Borrowing from symbolic logic the signs $\forall$ (for any), $\exists$ (there exists), and : (such that), we may write the classical thesis as:

$$\forall(M^* \, p), \, \exists(w_e) : (N_e = N_f) \qquad (4.1)$$

This thesis is sometimes caricatured as claiming that unemployment cannot exist. This is nonsense. It means only that net unemployment (as well as net labor shortage or negative net unemployment) is a disequilibrium phenomenon. A corollary of (4.1) may be written: The existence of unemployment implies that the real wage is above its equilibrium value. Also, the existence of labor shortage implies that the real wage is below its equilibrium level. If the arrow symbol $\rightarrow$ means "implies that," we have:

$$\text{For unemployment: } (N^s > N^d) \rightarrow (w > w_e)$$

$$(4.2)$$

$$\text{For labor shortage: } (N^d > N^s) \rightarrow (w < w_e)$$

PREVIEW OF ALTERNATIVES

Nowhere has the classical thesis been accepted unanimously. Much of the objection has limped along on the "moron's crutch": "It's true in theory, but not in practice." However, formal *antitheses* were never absent. Both the Marxian antithesis (chapter 5) and the Keynesian antithesis (chapters 6–7) may be stated: No combination of nominal money supply, positive price level, and positive real wage can be counted on to assure full employment without external intervention.[4] Full employment, except as a fortuitous and temporary special case usually involving a war economy, requires for Marxists a socialist state. For Keynesians, state intervention

---

[3] A few pointers on notation: The asterisk * means "nominal" or "in money terms"; the subscript e means "the equilibrium value of"; the subscript f means "the full-employment value of."

[4] The original (1936) version of the Keynesian system ran in terms of the nominal or money wage w* (=wp) rather than the real wage w. To express this conclusion, we may substitute w* for w in equation (4.3). Subsequent developments of Keynesian economics, responding to increased sensitivity of workers and unions to price level movements, have greatly modified this feature.

(usually falling short of socialism) is required to secure the appropriate values of aggregate expenditures, the money supply, and perhaps also the level of prices, consistent with full employment. In symbols, if $\sim$ means negation, or "it is not true that," the antithesis may be stated:

$$\sim[V(M^*,p), \exists(w_e) : (N_e = N_f)] \qquad (4.3)$$

or in words: It is not true that the equilibrium wage rate involves full employment, regardless of the money stock and the price level.

A counterrevolution against Keynesian economics—a counterrevolution that some critics write off as "anemic"—has produced a synthesis of classical and Keynesian positions, which we shall take up in chapters 10–11. The resulting system leads to full employment equilibrium values. In symbols, this synthesis maintains that:

$$V(M^*), \exists(p_e,w_e) : (N_e = N_f) \qquad (4.4)$$

or "Regardless of the nominal money supply, there is an equilibrium level of prices and an equilibrium level of real wages such that full employment will be achieved." Also, the expression equivalent to (4.2) in this system is:

For unemployment: $(N^s > N^d) \rightarrow (w > w_e)$ and/or $(p > p_e)$

$$(4.5)$$

For labor shortage: $(N^d > N^s) \rightarrow (w < w_e)$ and/or $(p < p_e)$

A MODERNIZED CLASSICAL SYSTEM

The economics of the classical economists—Adam Smith, David Ricardo, the Mills, their contemporaries, and their immediate successors—was technically underdeveloped by modern standards.[5] The argument leading to the classical thesis (4.1) and its corollary (4.2) is clearer when presented in modern dress.

The classical macrostatic system can be decomposed into five parts. Four of these fit together into a four-quadrant diagram (figure 4-1). The fifth part, dealing with saving, investment, and the rate of interest,[6] is drawn separately (figure 4-2).

---

[5] In intellectual power, originality, and cogency, however, the classical economists seem to have been superior to their successors of our day. They should not be downgraded or patronized.

[6] The modern distinction between the rate of interest and the rate of profit was not commonly drawn by the classical economists, who used the term "rate of profit" in both senses.

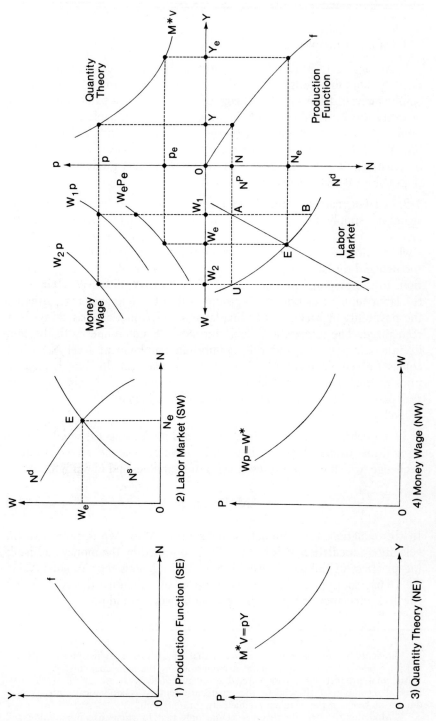

Figure 4-1 Classical Macrostatic Theory

51

The four-quadrant diagram is composed of:

1. An *aggregate production function* relating real output Y to employment N. One may consider capital as expressible either in terms of indirect employment of labor—a labor theory of value—or as a separate input whose quantity is considered constant. In either case, the principle of diminishing returns is presumed throughout the relevant range of the production function $Y = f(N)$. This means that f' or dY/dN is positive, and f'' or d^2Y/dN^2 is negative. On the diagram, this means that the production function slopes upward and is concave downward.

2. A *labor market*, reduced to an aggregate demand function N^d and an aggregate supply function N^s for homogeneous labor, in terms of the real wage rate w. The various classical and neo-classical writers presented a wide variety of wage theories. We select a *marginal productivity* theory of the demand for labor, according to which N^d is related, to a first approximation, to the marginal productivity of labor f' or dY/dN.[7] We assume that the labor supply function N^s slopes upward in the relevant range, although the possibility of backward-bending labor supply functions has always been recognized. The intersection of N^d and N^s at E determines both the equilibrium real wage w_e and the equilibrium employment level N_e, which equals full employment N_f. This strand of classical thinking is logically prior to the remainder of the system, since w_e and N_e determine the entire real part of the system. (That is, real output is determined in the labor market.)

3. A *quantity theory of money*. Here again, the classical school was no monolithic whole. Many writers did, however, assume an equation of exchange, which can be expressed with our variables and in our notation as:

$$M^*V = p\,Y \qquad\qquad (4.6)$$

In this equation, the nominal money supply M^* or Mp is given, and the velocity of circulation V is technically determined by the money and banking practices of the day. With M^* and V fixed, so is their product M^*V. By (4.6), so is p Y. In this strict form, the quantity theory therefore involves a rectangular-hyperbolic relation between Y and p.[8]

---

[7] Students of microeconomics will recall that equation of marginal productivity and the wage rate is a condition for profit maximization by the individual employer.

Marginal productivity theory entered economic analysis as an aspect of the *neo*-classical revolution at the end of the nineteenth century. The classical writers proper did not make use of the marginal productivity concept at all.

[8] "Modernized" quantity theories require only that functions like $p = p(M^*)$ and $Y^* = Y(M^*)$ exist, that they be positively sloping, and that they do not fluctuate drastically over time or with changes in public policy. They do not require any par-

4. The *money wage rate* w^* or wp. An equilibrium money wage w^* or $w_e p_e$ is determined by w_e and p_e, and a w_e^* function is drawn through their intersection point as a second rectangular hyperbola. This procedure makes the determination of the money wage a consequence of the determination of its components w and p.

These aspects of classical macroeconomic theory are presented in order on the left panel of figure 4-1. They are then combined on the right panel. The labor market (SW quadrant) is the most fundamental. It determines the real wage w_e and the employment level N_e, at which the demand and supply of labor are equal (full employment). Equilibrium employment N_e then determines equilibrium real income Y_e via the production function (SE quadrant). Real income in turn determines the equilibrium price level p_e via the quantity theory of money (NE quadrant). Finally, the intersection of w_e and p_e determine the equilibrium money wage w_e^* (NW quadrant).

A below-equilibrium real wage like w_1 (still on figure 4-1) leads to a labor shortage AB. An above-equilibrium real wage like w_2 leads to unemployment UV. Both W_1 and W_2 lead to an income level Y, which is less than Y_e, and to a price level p, which is higher than w_e.[9] The money wage w_2^* ($=w_2 p$) is higher than w_e^*, because both $w_2 > w_e$ and $p > p_e$. The money wage w_1^* may be higher or lower than w_e^*, because $p > p_e$ while $w_1 < w_e$.

A helpful way to test and improve one's mastery of an involved system like this one is to trace through the various consequences of unanticipated once-and-for-all changes, using the apparatus of figure 4-1. Six examples are provided in table 4-1 on page 54.

SAVING, INVESTMENT, AND INTEREST

Once the equilibrium income level Y_e is determined in the classical macroeconomics, a real rate of interest r—differing from the observed nominal rate, r^*, to a first approximation, by subtracting the estimated inflation rate of general prices or adding the estimated deflation rate—regulates its division between consumption and saving. The supply of real saving from a given real income Y_e was usually thought of as a positively sloped function of the rate of interest. Such a function is denoted by S in

---

ticular functional relationship between the price level p and the real income level Y. They also permit the velocity of circulation V to be one of the unknowns of a larger system.

[9] The values of w_1 and w_2 were selected so as to yield a single pair of (Y,P) values. This procedure is arbitrary, but simplifies figure 4-1. Incidentally, the "labor shortage" AB at w_1 may be either greater than, less than, or equal to, the "unemployment" UV at w_2.

Table 4-1

Nature of Change	Direction of Change in					Is Full Employment Maintainable?
	N_e	Y_e	w_e	p_e	w_e^*	
Population Increase	Rise	Rise	Fall	Fall	Fall	Yes
Technical Progress[1]	Rise	Rise	Rise	Fall	?	Yes
Increase in Nominal Money Supply	Constant	Constant	Constant	Rise	Rise	Yes
Increase in Demand for Cash Balances	Constant	Constant	Constant	Fall	Fall	Yes
Accumulation of Capital[2]	Rise	Rise	Rise	Fall	?	Yes
Increase in Degree of Monopoly[3]	Fall	Fall	Fall	Rise	?	Yes

Notes: [1] The results in this line assume "normal" technical progress, such that the marginal product of labor (as well as the total and average product) increases.

[2] The results in this line assume that the marginal product of labor increases with the accumulation of capital, i.e., that labor and capital are net complements rather than net substitutes in production.

[3] The results in this line assume that demand for labor by a monopolist is determined by *marginal revenue product* rather than the value of marginal product, and that marginal revenue product is the smaller of the two. (See any standard text covering the microeconomics of imperfect competition.)

figure 4-2. The rate of interest also regulates the demand for saving (still from the given Y_e). This demand comes largely from potential investors. It is drawn downward sloping in figure 4-2, and labelled I. At any given income level, the interest rate has two functions: (1) to equate investment and saving (productivity and thrift), and (2) to allocate income between present consumption and provision for future growth and change. (In post-classical macroeconomic systems, as we shall soon see, the interest rate plays a role in income determination, and is no longer logically posterior to a determined income level.) In conformity with the remainder of our notation, the equilibrium rate of interest is indicated by r_e on figure 4-2, while the equilibrium rate of real saving and investment is indicated by S_e.

MACRODYNAMIC DIGRESSION

From the arguments which led to these diagrams and figures, the classical economists also worked out a set of macrodynamic "laws of motion"

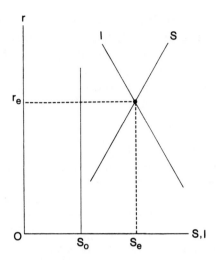

Figure 4-2   Classical Saving and Investment Theory (Y = Y$_e$ throughout)

for the capitalist economy. For suppose that the equilibrium saving and investment rate S$_e$ at interest rate r$_e$ (figure 4-2) is, as was ordinarily the case, more than the amount S$_o$ that is sufficient to replace the period's depreciation of fixed capital instruments and the period's inroads on inventories. We then have capital accumulation of S$_o$S$_e$ per period. This capital accumulation, together with population increase, are the paramount factors in classical macrodynamics or growth theory. (Much less stress was placed on technical progress than is found in contemporary growth theory.)

As capital accumulates, the production function rises. Labor demand N^d also rises, since the classical writers and their successors assumed capital and labor to be primarily *complements* rather than *substitutes* in production. As a result, the real national income Y$_e$ and employment N$_e$ both rise. The real wage rate w$_e$ also rises at least temporarily, but some part of the rise is cancelled in the long run by population growth (attributed to higher real wages) and a rise in the labor supply N^s. (For the classical school *proper* (prior to 1850) the Malthusian theory of population led to the conclusion that w$_e$ would remain constant. That is, the increase in the supply of labor would offset the increased demand for labor, thus reestablishing the old wage. The "magnificent dynamics" of the classical school embodied this conclusion. This was the "iron law of wages," the most dismal aspect of the "dismal science.")

Because of the increase in the capital stock and the presumed operation of diminishing returns to capital, the investment function (demand-for-saving function) I shifts inward (towards the origin). The equilibrium real

saving and investment quantum S_e therefore falls over time, and so does the equilibrium real rate of interest or profit r_e. These processes continue until S_e suffices for no more than capital replacement, S_o having simultaneously increased with the capital stock. Another factor ending the development process is the fall in the interest rate,[10] which discourages saving. Some classical economists believed the interest rate would eventually fall to zero, but others spoke merely of "the tendency of profits of a minimum."

The process we have just traced leads to the famous classical "stationary state," toward which economic growth supposedly tends. When it is reached, growth comes to a halt. The capital stock stops rising, and in its train the demand for labor and the size of the population do likewise. Both the real wage and the real interest rate remain constant, the wage rate at the subsistence level and the interest rate at (or near) zero. This gloomy outcome is to be postponed as long as possible by technical progress, by increased frugality at low interest rates, and by cheap food imports to raise the labor supply function.

Who gains by classical economic growth? Not the representative industrial or agricultural worker, if w_e is nearly constant. Not the representative capitalist or farmer, if the trend of r_e is downward. Society gains, in some organismic sense, from the larger labor force and capital stock resulting from the growth process. The individual supplier of labor and/or capital, however, is no better off. The predominant gainer is the *landlord*. The stock of land is presumed fixed. The demand for land rises as the economy grows and as the supply of both labor and capital increase. (Both labor and capital are, in the large, complementary with land in the process of production.) The result is a rising income share accruing to the landed class.

After about 1850, the orthodox economists' faith in Malthus's principle of population was increasingly eroded and replaced by faith in technological change counteracting the force of diminishing returns to both capital and labor. Anticipations of the stationary state faded away and were replaced by a substantial measure of complacency. This complacency, however, was justified by an appeal to the historical facts of the advanced countries rather than by any formal restructuring of the "magnificent dynamics" of the earlier generation of economists.[11]

---

[10] The saving function S shifts to the right as growth proceeds and income rises. This delays the fall in S_e but accelerates the fall in r_e.

[11] The outstanding exception to this generalization is Joseph Schumpeter's *Theory of Economic Development* (1912).

THE DEPRESSION CASE

Having completed an exposition of the classical macroeconomic model, we can pass to criticism, concentrating upon the static aspects. According to the conventional critique the classical theory was somehow proved wrong by the Great Depression, and then superseded by something called the Keynesian Revolution. This is hardly rigorous; how can a theory be proved wrong (within its own assumptions) by events (which often violate these assumptions)? It is also incorrect.

We turn back to equation (4.1) to examine both what it claims and what it does not claim. It does indeed imply that even at the low money supply and price levels of 1931–1933, a positive real wage existed at which full employment could have been restored, had M* and p remained constant at these levels. It does not indicate how long the restoration process might have taken. More important, it does not claim that, at the *falling* levels of M* and p, which marked that disastrous period of capitalist economic history, the equilibrium adjustments would have been fast enough to restore full employment, or even to keep unemployment from rising. It "blames" for unemployment not only real (and money) wages that were "too high" for the existing values of M* and p, but also certain public policies that permitted M* and p to fall as far and as fast as they did. It also implies support for policies that might have eased and accelerated the adjustment process by *reversing* the post-1929 declines in M* and p.[12]

THREE THEORETICAL FLAWS

There are, however, at least three important theoretical flaws in the classical macrostatic picture—in addition to the extreme aggregation that pervades macroeconomics and irritates its critics. These flaws are (1) the dichotomy between the real and monetary aspects of the model, (2) the absence of an aggregate demand function for output, particularly any pattern showing the influence of wage rates and employment upon aggregate demand, and (3) inadequate attention to the problem of wage rigidity. We consider each of these defects in turn.

---

[12] This statement is itself controversial. It disagrees with the "Austrian" interpretation of neo-classical macroeconomics as blaming depression on the failure of the price level to fall *pari passu* with technical progress, and denying the possibility of healthy recovery until such apparent deflation had taken place. The best source of this view is Friedrich von Hayek, *Prices and Production* (1931).

THE CLASSICAL DICHOTOMY[13]

On figures 4-1 and 4-2, everything "real" (Y_e, N_e, w_e, S_e, I_e, r_e) is determined without reference to the top half (NE and NW quadrants) of figure 4-1. On the other hand, the levels of prices and money wages are determined entirely on those two quadrants, in the sense that changes in M^* and V always affect p and w^*, but affect nothing else in the system.

What is wrong with this depiction of money as a "veil" over real quantities? Nothing whatever, if the velocity of circulation V is determined entirely by technical conditions or "ways of doing business," and is unaffected by prices and interest rates. But insofar as choice is also involved—how much money individuals and firms hold in their portfolios, in preference to real assets or securities expressing claims to real assets—this choice is left unexplained.[14] Suppose, for example, a general shortage induced by the exhaustion of important domestic productive resources or the cutting off of foreign ones. After the resulting rise in general prices—which has required no rise in the supply of money—individuals and firms feel constrained to hold larger nominal cash balances. If the money supply does not rise, this entails a fall in the velocity of circulation V. It also means that individuals and firms reduce their holdings of other assets, such as physical capital including inventories. If they hold less physical capital their demand for labor also falls, so that cash balances become an indirect substitute for labor. With less employment of both capital and labor, output also falls. The fall of output and employment sets off in its turn a decline in prices, reversing part of the previous rise. This whole process illustrates a two-way relationship between the money and real aspects of the economy that is overlooked in the classical model. This model, to repeat, treats as given or exogenous the velocity $V \left(= \dfrac{pY}{M^*} \right)$ and its reciprocal $\left(\dfrac{M^*}{pY} \right)$, the proportion of income held in cash. These quantities should be considered unknown or endogenous in the macrostatic system.

SAY'S LAW AND SAY'S IDENTITY

The classical macroeconomic system includes demand and supply functions of homogeneous labor. It also includes a production function, which

---

[13] This section attempts to simplify an argument of Don Patinkin, *Money, Interest and Prices* (1956), ch. 8.

[14] It may also be inaccurate to regard M^* as given, when the monetary authorities operate to adjust the money supply to what they perceive as changes in the demand for money.

substitutes for an aggregate supply function of the homogenized output constituting the national product. But where is the demand side of the output market?

With few exceptions, the classical economists accepted, in one or another form, a principle ascribed to Adam Smith's French disciple Jean Baptiste Say called Say's Law of Markets. Say's Law maintains that in the aggregate, supply creates its own demand, so that aggregate supply and demand functions are identical, and no aggregate demand function is required of a system containing an aggregate supply function (or a production function). The argument behind Say's Law either assumes a barter economy with money absent or assigns a mere accounting role to money. The producer of good A, so runs the argument, either wishes to consume A himself or exchange it directly or indirectly for goods B,C, ... The same is true, *mutatis mutandis*, for the producers of B,C, ... Therefore, while A,B,C, . . . may be produced in the wrong proportions, there can be no excess supply of all goods taken together. Rather, an excess supply of A was itself evidence of—indeed, it constituted—an excess demand for one or more of the other goods in the economy. The problems arising from such imbalances were entirely microeconomic problems of relative prices, soluble on free markets by the operation of supply and demand. Critics occasionally pointed out that if the (A,B,C, . . .) economy included one or more goods not currently being produced for the market—land, money, antiques—or even goods whose maximum currently producible increment was insignificant compared to the stock accumulated in the past—gold, precious stones, houses—a shift in demand to nonproducible goods might produce a surplus of the currently producible ones. Such criticism, however, had little impact outside the economic underworld of dissidents, heretics, and cranks.

It was never made clear what Say's Law implied about the general price level. Two possible interpretations have been christened by Oskar Lange "Say's Law" and "Say's Identity." They may be written, in our symbols:

$$\text{Say's } \textit{Law} \quad \exists(p_e) > 0 : (Y^s = Y^d) \tag{4.7}$$

(There exists some positive equilibrium price level P_e, at which aggregate supply Y^s equals aggregate demand Y^d.)

$$\text{Say's } \textit{Identity} \quad V(p), (Y^s = Y^d) \tag{4.8}$$

(At any price level whatever, aggregate supply equals aggregate demand.)

It is clear that the classical economists and their successors accepted (4.7). Indeed, most still do—including the present writer. It is not clear to what extent, if at all, they also accepted the more extreme (4.8) and the

related (4.1), or whether statements implying acceptance of Say's Identity were merely slips of the pen.[15]

WAGE RIGIDITY

The relation between wage rigidity and full employment is illustrated in figure 4-3. In the relevant range of this figure, the labor supply function S_n is flat; labor supply is perfectly elastic with respect to the real wage. The equilibrium wage rate is w_e, with employment at N_e; there is nothing new here. However, N_f workers are willing to accept jobs at W_e ($N_f > N_e$); involuntary unemployment at equilibrium equals N_eN_f, a positive quantity. Both classical and neo-classical economists saw this problem, when they saw it at all, as a short-run aberration unworthy of much attention. One should simply wait for the supply function N^s to return to a less patholog-ical pattern, like $N^{s'}$. After it did so, the equilibrium real wage would fall to w'_e, equilibrium employment would rise to N'_e, and involuntary un-employment would be eliminated.

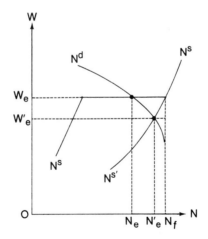

Figure 4-3   The Wage Rigidity Problem

---

[15] If we interpret classical macroeconomics as accepting only Say's Law, there is an ambiguity in figure 4-1. There, an equilibrium price level is determined, but there is no evidence that this p_e is also the p_e of (4.7). If we interpret classical macroeconomics as accepting Say's Identity as well, the question arises, what difference does the price level make? Furthermore, why should the society hold one quantity of money rather than another? And how can we take account of shifts in demand as between goods and money? Acceptance of (4.8) consigns us to a special-case world, with the velocity of circulation indeed fixed behind the backs of the economic actors. In such a world, the strict quantity theory of money can indeed take over the aggregate-demand-curve role of determining the general price level, as it does in figure 4-1.

We may distinguish three subcases of wage rigidity. In case (1), the wage rate w_e denotes some physical or psychological subsistence minimum. In case (2), w_e is a conventional, or possibly a collectively bargained, wage rate significantly higher than any subsistence minimum. In case (3) w_e is a previous rate that workers expect will shortly be restored. The analysis of these subcases is different.

In case (1), the interval N_eN_f represents not only involuntary unemployment but a "redundant" labor supply. This redundance is usually traceable to overpopulation. Economic policy is a matter of waiting for elimination of the surplus population, or for a rise in N^d resulting from accumulation and growth. Neither policy requires starvation to kill off the surplus population, as was alleged by opponents of classical economic "pig philosophy."[16] To avoid starvation, classical economic policy relied upon emigration, delayed marriage, spacing of children—by continence rather than contraception or abortion—as well as infant mortality, to chisel away at population redundancy. To quote the Irish bard Thomas Moore on Thomas Malthus, whom we have mentioned as the classical spokesman in demographic matters:[17]

Come, Malthus, and in Ciceronian prose
Show how a rutting population grows,
Till all the produce of the earth is spent
And brats expire from lack of aliment.

In the more usual cases of wage rigidity, N_eN_f represents no demographic redundancy. In these cases, classical economic policy is to wait for unemployment to wear down workers' resistence to cuts in their real wages or moderate their expectations—as well as for economic growth to raise the demand for labor. A student critic in this writer's class has called this policy "waiting for Godot." This observation would have been inappropriate for Victorian Britain, where a number of factors made the wage earner's position precarious and lessened his power to resist wage reductions:

1. The level of workers' real wages and incomes. This is at least as important as any "juicy" institutional factor. In the early nineteenth century, these wages and incomes were seldom high enough to provide any cushion

---

[16] Neither did classical economic policy preclude this cold-hearted outcome. See Cecil Woodham-Smith, *The Great Hunger* (1962) for an account of the attitudes of British economists toward the victims of Irish potato famines in the 1840s.

[17] This is "long run" Malthus, the youthful author of the *Essay on Population* (1798). In later life, he became "short run" Malthus, devoted major attention to problems of depression and unemployment, rejected Say's Law, and was recognized by Keynes among his own precursors! (The appendix to this chapter outlines Malthus's short-run analysis.)

of saving or security for loans, either of which might have supported strikes against wage cuts or searches for better jobs.

2. The status of trade unions. During the period in which classical thinking developed, these organizations were illegal conspiracies in restraint of trade.

3. The systems of relief and of unemployment insurance. The British system, following the "New Poor Law" (1834), required relief recipients to enter workhouses, suffer the indignities of separation between family members, and toil under conditions deliberately made less desirable than regular employment. There was no such thing as unemployment insurance until the twentieth century. (Regarding the "poorhouse" aspect of nineteenth-century working-class life, Charles Dickens's *Oliver Twist* is a social document.)

4. Imprisonment for debt. The unemployed nineteenth-century worker could seldom tide himself over a period of unemployment by borrowing. Even if he could obtain a loan without adequate security, he faced the prospect of indefinite imprisonment for debt if unable to repay it. (Dickens's *Little Dorrit* had a good deal to say about imprisonment for debt.)

5. The criminal justice system. It was likewise difficult for the nineteenth-century unemployed worker to subsist by the variety of minor crimes known collectively today as "hustling." Penalties for petty theft, in particular, were severe and included capital punishment. Convictions were also easier, because legal aid was not available to the indigent defendant, and trial for petty crimes was before a single judge with no jury.

6. Vagrancy laws. Persons "with no visible means of support" could be jailed at hard labor for "vagrancy" without benefit of jury trials if their actions impressed the local constabulary as suspicious, or if they were reported as potential criminals to local justices of the peace.

7. Suffrage restrictions. Why did the British (and American) electorates of the early and middle nineteenth century tolerate the arrangements sketched above? In Britain, the working classes were largely disfranchised until the 1860s. In most American states, manhood suffrage came a generation earlier, but racial and religious prejudices operated against "wild Irish" immigrants and free blacks, who bore between them a disproportionate share of unemployment.

One cannot infer that the entire range of circumstances listed above was necessary to reduce wage rigidity to its dimensions of 1850. These arrange-

ments may have included a good deal of economic overkill. It is, however, incumbent on those advocating the summary restoration of downward real-wage flexibility to ask themselves whether they are prepared to recommend reinstatement of any or all of the antilabor institution of mid-Victorian Britain, and if not, how they propose to get "from here to there."

SUMMARY

This chapter begins by asserting that the key problem of macrostatics is whether or not the economy tends toward a position of full-employment equilibrium. It states the classical thesis (that it does), the Marxian and Keynesian antitheses (that it does not), and a contemporary synthesis closer to the classical position. Because the classical thesis, and oral traditions based on it, remain strong in the business community and in conservative circles, and also because much contemporary thought makes use of it, the chapter denies that classical macroeconomics has been killed off, and claims that it was more than a historical curiosum.

In classical economic thinking, unemployment results exclusively from wage rates being above their equilibrium values. Similarly, labor shortages imply that wage rates are below their equilibrium values. The chapter includes a demonstration deriving these results in "modern dress"; the "modern dress" features a four-quadrant diagram. We then go on to explore certain macrodynamic implications of the classical system, including the iron law of wages, the tendency of profits to a minimum, and the stationary state. After approximately 1850, these results require modification; but the classicals themselves never reconstructed their theory to take economic and institutional changes into sufficient account.

After completion of this expository material, attention shifts to the criticisms of the classical system (some of which we shall see followed up by Keynesian economics in particular). Three criticisms are (1) unrealistic dichotomy between real and monetary aspects of the system, (2) neglect of aggregate demand, as related especially to the labor market, and (3) neglect of problems emanating from the downward rigidity of wage rates. This criticism is not an indictment of the original Classical School (1800–1850), whose institutional assumptions fit their period of history. Rather, it concentrates on their successors (of 1850–1930), who failed to adapt the classical system adequately to developments after 1850. Regarding the Great Depression itself, we further suggest that (along with favoring wage reductions) classical writers might have opposed letting the money supply fall, and might never have advocated the unconstrained deflation associated with the economic orthodoxy of that time.

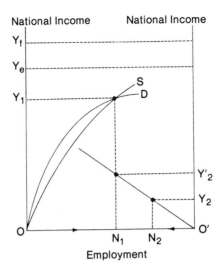

Figure 4A-1 Malthusian Macroeconomics

Appendix 4a

MALTHUSIAN MACROECONOMICS

Many dissenters and heretics—in addition to Marx, Keynes, and their disciples—have rejected part or all of the classical macroeconomics. For an early example, let us consider Malthus, a contemporary of Say and Ricardo. As a young man, Malthus concerned himself with long-run economic problems and was the principal codifier of the demographic doctrine that bears his name. A generation later, his interest shifted to the short-run problems of the depression that followed the Napoleonic Wars. He became a conservative underconsumptionist who justified the British aristocracy by its necessary role in maintaining employment by the "unproductive consumption" of personal services. Obviously, Malthus did not accept Say's Identity.

We owe to Robert Eagly a formal summary of Malthus's position.[1] Let OO' (figure 4A-1, horizontal axis) be the labor supply, which we have called N_f in other diagrams, and let the vertical axis Y of the same figure be labor income only. Employment is divided between two sectors, productive (read

---

[1] Robert V. Eagly, *The Structure of Classical Economic Theory* (1974), ch. 5 (II). Our figure 4A-1 is adapted from a diagram included in a preliminary version of Eagly's study but omitted from the final one.

rightward from 0) and unproductive (read leftward from 0'). "Pseudo" demand and supply of goods or income in the productive sector are represented by D and S in terms of employment and not of price; this is why we call them pseudo D and S. The slope of S represents marginal cost per worker. It is not exclusively a wage rate; the curvature of S arises from diminishing returns. All we need say about D is that it includes demand from both sectors of the economy, slopes upward, and intersects S from above. The point of intersection determines an equilibrium position, which we assume to be unique. At equilibrium ON_1 workers are employed in the productive sector, producing Y_1. At the same time, the landed aristocracy and others in the nonproductive sector employ or patronize $N_2 0'$ workers as domestics, doctors, lawyers, teachers, etc., at an average compensation given by the slope of the ray through 0'. An amount Y_2 of what we would call income—but classical economists would not—is generated from their services. Vertical addition of Y_1 and Y_2 gives equilibrium (labor) income Y_e. At Y_e, $N_1 N_2$ workers remain unemployed.

The Malthusian remedy for this unemployment is for the unproductive consumers of the second sector to hire the $N_1 N_2$ unemployed workers in unproductive uses. They would generate an additional $Y_2 Y_2'$ of income and raise total labor income to its full-employment level Y_f. Malthus seems to assume that these unproductive consumers have the wherewithal to increase employment to this extent, without reducing their purchases from the productive sector. Like the classical economists, he also assumed that the price level did not affect real variables such as employment; unlike them, he assigned no role in his system to changes in either real or money wage rates. Perhaps he may be interpreted as considering the real wage to be given at the subsistence level.

Contemporary writers in the tradition of the later Malthus put the government in the role of the Malthusian unproductive consumer, and see public agencies, civil and military, rather than the red-coated fox-hunting squirearchy of Malthus's England, as the "employers of last resort."

Chapter

5

Marxian Macroeconomics

ECONOMICS IN THE MARXIAN SYSTEM

Karl Marx was a philosopher first and a social scientist second, but the social science of economics came to play a crucial role in Marxian philosophy. It is no accident that Marx's unfinished masterpiece, *Das Kapital*, was a treatise on economic theory.

Marx felt that society was capable of generating a surplus over basic human needs and that the size of this surplus grew with time and technological progress. In his own day (mid-ninteeenth-century) Marx believed this potential surplus to be so large that reasonable men could, aided by modern technology, produce all they could reasonably desire to consume and abolish the economic problem of scarcity altogether. In practice, however, the social surplus had always been expropriated by one or another exploiting class (slave owners, feudal lords) which owned some strategic means of production (slave labor, agricultural land). The rest of society had remained in economic misery and psychological alienation. This alienation, Marx was convinced, lay at the root of such social pathologies as crime, violence, and vice, which conventional thinkers blamed on the poor themselves or on human nature in general.

Marx went on to apply to concrete historical process a dialectic of thesis, anthesis, and synthesis that his teacher Hegel had applied primarily to abstract ideas and to processes of human understanding. Whereas Hegel had thought of human development as a synthesis of the abstract ideas of Freedom and Order (neither of which could be understood without reference to the other), Marx saw history as a succession of struggles between possessing economic classes (thesis, in a scheme called "dialectical materialism"), and oppressed economic classes (their antitheses).

Dialectical materialism—standing Hegalian idealism on its head and applying it to material problems of the real world and of actual people—led Marx to two conclusions about capitalism: (1) Capitalism was not uniquely harmonious with unchanging human nature. Instead, it too was a system of conflict (contradiction) between a capitalist or bourgeois class (thesis), which owned the basic means of production (primarily capital goods), and a working class or proletarian class (antithesis). This conflict was no different from previous conflicts between slave owners and slaves or between feudal lords and serfs. (2) Capitalism would not be permanent. It would be replaced in the coming class struggle by socialism. Socialism would be a classless society in which (because the social surplus was now so large) the whole process of conflict and alienation might end (after a period of proletarian dictatorship) in a better and more harmonious state of society, which Marx called communism.

This vision brought Marx into conflict with classical economics, which saw free-market capitalism as "the obvious and simple system of natural

liberty," even if it led to an uninspiring stationary state dominated by un-inspiring landlords and inhabited by workers doomed to subsistence wages. Small wonder that, for all Marx's respect for Ricardo in particular, he be-came a bitter critic of classical economics, or that his initial large-scale economic work was a *Critique of Political Economy* (1859). For Marx the social philosopher, the function of economics was to demonstrate and illustrate, for the capitalist regime, the persistence of class struggle, the impossibility of class harmony, and the inevitability of social revolution. History had done this for the slave and feudal systems of the past; eco-nomics was to do it for the capitalist system of his own day. En route to this philosophical goal, it was necessary for Marx to overturn the classical economics, which pointed instead to a quietist stationary state.

Marx never became a *sehr geehrter Herr Professor Doktor Geheimrat* in the nineteenth-century German tradition. He had aspired to this dignity as a young Ph.D. in philosophy. His political heterodoxy, combined with his ethnic background,[1] precluded this career, but Marx remained (among other things) a *sehr geehrter Herr Professor Doktor Geheimrat* in spirit. One aspect of this spirit was Marx's refusal to be satisfied with merely criticizing the systems of the great Hegel in philosophy and the great Ricardo in economics. Marx had to map his criticism with a complete sys-tem of his own. The result was *Das Kapital*.

Das Kapital was never finished. Volume I was published during Marx's lifetime. Volumes II and III were published after Marx's death, from manuscript notes edited by Marx's friend and collaborator Friedrich Engels.[2] We attempt here to reconstruct a macroeconomic system out of fragments from all three volumes, and to guess where the whole might have led. This task is worthwhile because of the influence *Das Kapital* has exercised both on supporters and opponents of Marxian socialism. It is comparable to conjuring up the missing movements of Schubert's Un-finished Symphony, solving Dickens's *Mystery of Edwin Drood*, or carrying forward Coleridge's *Kubla Khan* from the point where anonymous visitors interrupted the flow of his inspiration. There have been many previous reconstructions of the Marxian system; this writer's greatest debt is to Paul Sweezy's *Theory of Capitalist Development* (1942).

We shall interpret the Marxian economic model as a macroeconomic one for a closed, private, competitive economy, producing a homogenous national product.[3] Only one input is used, namely, homogeneous labor,

---

[1] Marx was of Jewish descent, although his father had been converted to Luther-anism. He did not consider himself Jewish.

[2] A projected volume IV dealt with the history of economic thought. It was pub-lished (in three volumes) under the title *Theories of Surplus Value*, edited by Karl Kautsky after Engels's death.

[3] This interpretation is itself questionable. There is no lack of strictly microeconomic

which may be used (in the amounts socially necessary) either directly or indirectly. Indirect application of labor involves the use of previously produced income in capital goods form.

The aggregate value produced can be symbolized as W, measured in hours of homogeneous labor time. This feature gives us a labor theory of value, on which Marx insisted more strenuously than any classical economist. W is further divisible into three parts, each measured in the same units of labor time: constant capital C, variable capital V, and surplus value S. Raw materials and depreciation, reduced to labor hours, are the components of C, which we interpret as a *flow* of services rather than a *stock* of instruments.[4]

V is related to direct labor, primarily manual. Although measured in labor hours, it is not equal to the number of hours actually worked, but to the (smaller) number required to produce the output purchased with the workers' wages. If A works 40 hours a week for a wage that will repurchase the product of only 25 hours of labor, his weekly stint represents 25 (not 40) hours of Marxian V. The remaining 15 hours of his time the worker A contributes to the surplus value S. Property incomes are paid out of surplus value; administrative salaries and other overheads also come out of S. In Marx's view, they go primarily to members of the property-owning bourgeois class. In any event, the skeletal algebra is:

$$W = C + V + S \tag{5.1}$$

The exploited manualist A described above puts in 40 hours of labor per week for wages that buy only 25 hours of product. We can express his wage rate w in labor hours per hour, or as a pure number. It is the ratio of variable capital V to value added V + S. In the case of our hypothetical A, this wage rate is 25/40 or .625. Under equilibrium conditions, the wage rate is equal for all workers, and less than unity:

$$w = \frac{V}{V + S} \quad \text{or} \quad \frac{1}{w} = 1 + \frac{S}{V} \tag{5.2}$$

If the wage rate w is equal for all workers, so must be the ratio S/V. To this ratio Marx assigns the symbol S'. It is called the *rate of surplus value*

---

analysis in *Das Kapital*. Many Marxist writers insist that the system can only be understood if its microeconomic features—the multiplicity of investment and consumption goods—are taken into explicit account. In the appendix to this chapter, we shall follow Marx's practice of subdividing the economy into Departments I and II, producing, respectively, a homogeneous investment good and a homogeneous consumption good.

[4] Much of Marx's analysis uses a time period equal to the average turnover period of the social capital stock, so that the flow and stock are equal numerically. It is therefore difficult to be sure which concept Marx had in mind.

and, sometimes, the *rate of exploitation*. In our hypothetical example, S' is 15/25 or .60. (Marxist estimates of its value in contemporary America run in excess of unity.) Algebraically, we can express S' in terms of the wage rate w:

$$S' = \frac{1}{w} - 1 \quad \text{or} \quad S' = \frac{1 - w}{w} \tag{5.3}$$

Marx takes pains to distinguish the rate of surplus value S' from the rate of profit P'. P' is, to a first approximation, S/(V + C) over a period in which the capital stock turns over precisely once. Division of a numerator and denominator by V transforms the last expression to:

$$P' = \frac{S'}{1 + \dfrac{C}{V}} = \frac{S'}{1 + k} \tag{5.4}$$

The C/V term in this denominator will be important for later analysis. Marx calls it the *organic composition of capital*, and it is conventionally symbolized by k. The more capital-intensive production becomes, the greater the value of capital per worker or per man-hour, the larger is k.

If the capital stock turns over in 1/d periods rather than in one period, the capital flow C + V is equal to d times the capital stock K. Computing the rate of profit on K, therefore:

$$P' = \frac{S}{\dfrac{C + V}{d}} = \frac{S'd}{1 + k}$$

The equations (5.1–5.4) constitute the skeleton of a labor theory of value. They do not, however, constitute a complete equilibrium system. The four equations are associated with seven unknowns (W,C,V,S,w,S',P'); we take d and K as exogenously given. If the Marxian system is not to be discarded for circular reasoning, additional constraints must be placed upon the variables.

Marx apparently considers as determined by prevailing institutions, or by prevailing techniques of production, many relations that conventional economists consider as varying with relative prices. In this respect, much contemporary structural economics and management science (including input-output analysis and linear programming) has agreed with the

Marxian view of the world. We shall examine a number of these structural relations. Some of these are basically definitional while others purport to describe behavior.

The first of these structural relations we have already noted. It is the organic composition of capital k. Marx usually viewed k as independent of wage or profit rates; it should, therefore, be regarded as technically given, and not as unknown in the Marxian system:

$$\frac{C}{V} = k \qquad (5.5)$$

We next recall the relation between the given stock K of social capital and the unknown C and V flows of constant and variable capital:

$$\frac{C + V}{d} = K \quad \text{or} \quad Kd = C + V \qquad (5.6)$$

with the capitalization rate d also taken as given. This coefficient is also, as we have seen, the reciprocal of the turnover period of capital.

Nothing in the Marxian system requires full employment of labor. On the contrary, Marx and the Marxists see both gross and net unemployment as normal. The economic function of this net unemployment, for Marx, is to hold wage rates close to a subsistence level. Unemployment plays for Marx the role Malthusian population theory played for the classical school, in enforcing an "iron law of wages." If we denote by V_o, and take as given, the economy's maximum supply of variable capital at any time, we can define an unemployment percentage U as:

$$U = 1 - \frac{V}{V_o} \quad \text{or} \quad U = \frac{V_o - V}{V_o} \qquad (5.7)$$

which falls to zero when $V = V_o$ in the special case of full employment.

At some risk of violence to Marx's own text, we can introduce a generalized function in our Marxian model:

$$U_t = U(S'_{t-1}) \quad \text{so that} \quad S_t' = U^{-1}(U_{t+1})^5 \qquad (5.8)$$

---

[5] If the function $U = U(S')$ is monotone (steadily) increasing, there exists a monotone inverse function $S' = U^{-1}(U)$ that is also increasing.

with the derivative dU/dS' positive. Equation (5.8) attempts to summarize the maldistribution-overproduction-underconsumption aspect of Marx's thought. It relates *present* unemployment to *past* rates of surplus value or exploitation, and the *present* rate of exploitation to the *prospective* unemployment rate. The literary-economic argument corresponding to (5.8) is that less output can be bought back at higher exploitation rates than at lower ones, and, therefore, less labor will be employed to produce the smaller output.

This completes our exposition of the simplest short-run Marxian system. It is not strictly static; the dynamic element involves the lag in equation (5.8). Our version is a general equilibrium one, comprising the eight equations numbered (5.1–5.8). There are also eight unknowns—the seven listed above, plus one more (U). The terms k, d, K, and V_o are all given.

Digression: Equality or balance between the number of equations and the number of unknowns of an economic system or model is a *prima facie* condition for the logical consistency of that system or model, and logical consistency is the special virtue of general-equilibrium economics. It is, however, no more than *prima facie* evidence, since equations may be inconsistent with each other or dependent upon each other. The balance we have shown here is neither a necessary nor a sufficient condition for the existence of a solution to the system, let alone a unique solution or an economically meaningful one.[6] A dangerous trap, which we hope to avoid at all times, is an equation system that can be partitioned into two or more subsystems with separate sets of variables. Although such a system appears to be in balance, one or more of the subsystems may be *circular* (with fewer equations than unknowns) and one or more subsystems may be *inconsistent* or *overdetermined* (with more equations than unknowns). We claim only that balance of equations and unknowns is *prima facie* evidence of logical consistency. (Similarly, an excess number of unknowns is only *prima facie* evidence of circular reasoning, and an excess number of unknowns is only *prima facie* evidence of inconsistency.)

---

[6] To make the argument less abstract, consider an elementary supply-demand model. Its two equations are the supply and demand curves of any elementary text; its two unknowns are price and quantity; there is normally a unique solution. If the supply function is ruled out—as in some versions of utility theories—the system is normally circular. If a fixed price or quantity is additionally imposed, as in a regime of direct controls, the system is normally overdetermined. Special problems arise, of course, if supply and demand functions do not cross (for positive prices and quantities) or if they cross more than once.

LAWS OF MOTION OF CAPITALISM

Marxian macrodynamics argues that, rather than progressing indefinitely or approaching any stationary state, the capitalist economy will follow a trend leading to increasingly severe stagnation in the long run.[7] This economic stagnation will furnish, either directly or indirectly, the major spark for the socialist revolution. It may set off the revolution directly if the misery of the workers, especially the underemployed and unemployed workers, becomes unbearable. It may set off the revolution indirectly, if capitalist countries resort to imperialism and war to extricate themselves from stagnation, and arm their workers to do the fighting.[8]

To begin the exposition of Marxian long-run macrodynamics, we return to (5.4), which defines the rate of profit P':

$$P' = \frac{S'}{1 + k}$$

whose time derivative dP'/dt is:

$$\frac{dP'}{dt} = \frac{1}{(1 + k)^2}\left[(1 + k)\frac{dS'}{dt} - S'\frac{dk}{dt}\right] = \frac{1}{1 + k}\left(\frac{dS'}{dt} - P'\frac{dk}{dt}\right) \quad (5.9)$$

Equation (5.9) is a key to the Marxian macrodynamic system, including "Marx's Law" of the falling rate of profit. Our first question is, can the profit rate be expected to trend downward over time; in calculus terms, is dP'/dt negative? The organic composition of capital k rises over time, Marx argues (dk/dt is positive). It rises because capital normally is accumulated faster than population and employment grow. It also rises because part of the capital accumulation takes the form of research and development. This results in technical progress, and technical progress tends to be laborsaving. Unless the exploitation rate S' rises sufficiently—unless dS'/dt exceeds

---

[7] *Das Kapital* also includes (in volume II) an entirely different growth theory, composed of arithmetical examples suggesting the self-contained expansion of capitalism in a manner anticipating post-Keynesian developments. However, the apocalyptic strain has been more influential among Marxists and is more consistent with Marx's political position.

[8] Nikolai Lenin, *Imperialism, the Highest Stage of Capitalism* (1916) developed these ideas more fully a generation after Marx's death than Marx himself did in his lifetime.

P' dk/dt in (5.9)—the profit rate P' will fall as time passes and as k rises. [This is "Marx's Law" of the falling rate of profit; it is not propounded in Marx as any more certain than our (5.9) makes it out to be.] If the law holds, P' will fall eventually to a level at which further net investment is not worth the risk involved. This analysis is good English classical economics.

But when P' has fallen to the point where further net investment vanishes, Marx's Herr Geldbeutel (Mr. Moneybags) reacts in a manner quite unlike his English classical counterpart. Rather than increasing consumption when investment peters out, Geldbeutel will attempt to hoard and not to spend his entire receipts of surplus value. He may even attempt liquidation of investments he had made previously. The result of this failure of expenditure and this attempted hoarding is an upward trend of unemployment. Such a trend is called by Marxist writers a *liquidity* (or liquidation) *crisis* or depression, with the profit rate having fallen below some minimum level P'_{min} required for full expenditure of the economy's surplus value. In his polemics against opponents, Marx uses the falling rate of profit particularly against people we would call today liberal reformists. (If reformists propose to salvage or humanize capitalism by raising wages or improving working conditions, will they not make the profit rate fall faster, and hasten the liquidation crisis?)

The argument of Marx's law of the falling rate of profit has supposed that the exploitation rate S' does not rise to the point where dS'/dt exceeds P' dk/dt in (5.9). Marx is by no means dogmatic in denying that S' may rise to this extent, particularly as a consequence of the concentration of capital and the trend toward monopoly that he supposed would wipe out (proletarianize) the small capitalist and bourgeois middle classes. But can a rising exploitation rate save capitalism in the long run, even if it should overcome the falling rate of profit? No, say Marx and the Marxists. If capitalist monopolies and cartels raise the rate of surplus value sufficiently, they can, of course, maintain or even increase the rate of profit on whatever is sold. But how much can be sold, or rather, how much can be bought? In our Marxian model, equation (5.8) says that, as the exploitation rate S' rises, the unemployment rate U will also rise, albeit with a time lag. If we identify stagnation with secularly rising rates of unemployment, stagnation is not avoided.[9] The particular sort of depression or crisis haunting the economy in this case, however, is not a liquidation crisis as before; Marxists call it a *realization* crisis. In a realization crisis, the amount of out-

---

[9] Anatol Murad has suggested that if population growth is sufficiently slow, stagnation may be marked by labor *shortages* rather than by unemployment. The important characteristic of a crisis, in such a view, would appear to be falling *employment* rather than rising *unemployment*.

put on which a high rate of profit can continue to be realized becomes increasingly inadequate to keep the labor force employed. The spectre of a realization (overproduction, underconsumption) crisis is used by Marx and the Marxists in polemics against apostles of "self-government in business," cartels, trade associations, "orderly marketing," and "rationalization" as saviors of capitalism. Their constant question is, Where will purchasing power come from?

Das Kapital leaves it unclear whether the liquidation or the realization crisis should be considered the major vehicle of capitalist stagnation. The majority view among Marxian economists assigns primacy to the liquidation crisis, and therefore to the falling rate of profit. The majority view among Marxian noneconomists assigns it to the realization crisis, and therefore to the capitalist tendency to overproduction. A third possibility involves a dilemma or contradiction. If there exists some unemployment rate U_{max}, above which increasing misery will bring on the socialist revolution, the dilemma argument runs that there will eventually be no profit rate of P'_{min} or above consistent with an unemployment rate of U_{max} or below, i.e., high enough to avoid a liquidation crisis and low enough to avoid a realization crisis. Marx himself would presumably have been willing to take his revolution in any or all of these three ways.

The three stagnation patterns just described can be illustrated diagrammatically. On figure 5-1, the horizontal axis measures time, and therefore indirectly k, the organic composition of capital. The vertical axis measures the profit rate P'. Let us combine equations (5.4) and (5.8):

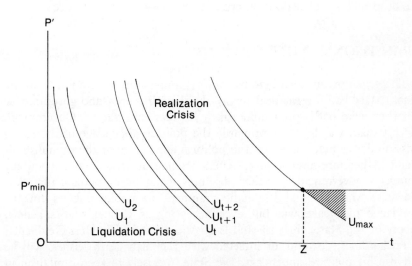

Figure 5-1   Long-Term Marxian Macrodynamics

$$P' = \frac{S'}{1 + k} = \frac{U^{-1}(U_{t+1})}{1 + k}$$

implying that to any value of S' there corresponds a single unemployment rate U. Also, the unemployment rate U_2 corresponding to S'_2 at any time is higher than the unemployment rate U_1 corresponding to S'_1 at the same period of time, if S'_2 exceeds S'_1. As time passes and the organic composition k rises, the profit rate P' falls for any preassigned level of S' (and of U), by the argument of (5.9). This explains the downward slope of the several U functions on the diagram. Eventually, for any U, P' falls below P'_{min}, which is drawn horizontal (trendless). After P' crosses P'_{min}, the economy is in a liquidation crisis, and hoarding tendencies set in. Employment cannot be maintained, and unemployment rises as time passes. (This is a strict falling-profit-rate interpretation of Marx.)

Alternatively, P' can be maintained above P'_{min} by raising the rate of surplus value, but each time S' is raised, the unemployment rate rises as well, by (5.8). (This is a strict overproduction-underconsumption interpretation of Marx, particularly if we postulate no falling tendency in the profit rate P'.)

For the dilemma interpretation, finally, let U_{max} be the highest tolerative unemployment rate, if one is to avoid revolution. Denote by Z (Zusammenbruch, or collapse) the time at which U_{max} and P'_{min} intersect on figure 5-1. After time Z there is no profit rate that can avoid both liquidation and realization crises at an unemployment rate at or below U_{max}. The only choice for the capitalist system is between the devil of liquidation crisis, the deep blue sea of realization crisis, or conceivably both at once.

TRANSITIONAL NOTE

The economy outlined here has neither a monetary system nor a government. Marx had a great deal to say about both money and governments, but they were both epiphenomenal in his economic theory. Government, in particular, was to Marx primarily the political appendage of the ruling class; under capitalism, it was the political appendage of the capitalists. It seemed, therefore, useless to anticipate significant social reform from any bourgeois government, whether absolute monarchy or parliamentary democracy. Marx applied the same argument to public policies for the avoidance of breakdown, but even accepting as Gospel Marx's general theory of the State, this last step is questionable. Unless Herr Geldbeutel is extraordinarily stupid, or infected with Freudian death wishes, will he not use his political appendage, the State, precisely to keep capitalism in being, reasonably prosperous as well as reasonably capitalistic? May there not be certain specialized tasks he might assign the State to perform more

effectively than he or his business associates can perform them in the private economy? Among possible devices to be assigned the capitalist political appendage by the capitalist class may be the manipulation of public expenditure, taxation, and the monetary system. In the following chapters we shall consider what these manipulations may be and how they may operate, independently of the degree of capitalist control of the State power.

SUMMARY

This is a difficult chapter to summarize. Much of the material is more nearly relevant to the study of socialist economics or comparative economic systems than to macroeconomic theory. Perhaps the main reason for introducing the Marxian system is to demonstrate that it is a tightly reasoned and high-level analysis of the capitalist economy, rather than the emotional, not to say irrational, diatribe non-Marxists consider it. The Marxian short-run (macrostatic) system involves chronic unemployment. The long-run (macrodynamic) system investigates so-called "contradictions of capitalism" that lead to disaster. Three possible routes, culminating in collapse, are indicated: (1) through the falling rate of profit, (2) through overproduction or underconsumption, and. (3) through a sort of dilemma between the other two. The last section raises the question of whether public action (even under a capitalist-dominated government) might not stave off the debacle indefinitely, by assuring profit for the capitalists and/or purchasing power for the masses, over and above what is supplied by the private economy. With this question in view, we begin in the next chapter to dissect the Keynesian system.

Appendix 5a

A TWO-SECTOR MARXIAN MODEL

As we said in footnote 3, Karl Marx was never so exclusively macroeconomic as we have presented him. He worked with two sectors that he called departments: Department I produces a homogeneous investment good and Department II produces a homogeneous consumption good. The relations between these two departments were an essential part of Marx's thinking.[1]

---

[1] A number of later writers extended the Marxian system to three and to n departments, at the cost of substantial mathematical complexity. See, for example, Michio Morishima, *Marx's Economics* (1973).

Sectoring involves a number of microstatic complications that we have avoided thus far. Not only must we solve for more unknowns, but the two departments must be articulated together in a single system. Beginning as before with the *labor theory of value*, we have a pair of equations corresponding to (5.1). (Subscripts refer to departments):

$$W_1 = C_1 + V_1 + S_1 \tag{A5.1}$$

$$W_2 = C_2 + V_2 + S_2 \tag{A5.2}$$

Values measured in units of labor time are not necessarily proportional to prices, even to the long-run competitive equilibrium prices that Marx calls *prices of production*. His argument can be put in terms of ratios p_i of prices to values. This relation is such that the sum of labor-time surplus values equals the sum of money profits in the system:[2]

$$S_1 + S_2 = p_1 S_1 + p_2 S_2 \tag{A5.3}$$

The wage rate w is uniform between the two departments as an equilibrium condition. Corresponding to (5.2) we again require two equations:

$$w = \frac{V_1}{V_1 + S_1} = \frac{V_2}{V_2 + S_2} \quad \text{or} \tag{A5.4}$$

$$\frac{1}{w} = 1 + \frac{S_1}{V_1} = 1 + \frac{S_2}{V_2} \tag{A5.5}$$

If the wage rate is uniform between departments, so is the rate of surplus value S/V or S'. Equation (5.3) continues to hold but we give it another number:

$$S' = \frac{1}{w} - 1 \quad \text{or}$$

$$S' = \frac{1-w}{w} \tag{A5.6}$$

---

[2] Marx is ambiguous on this point, also indicating that the sum of the labor values $(W_1 + W_2)$ should equal the sum of money values $(p_1 W_1 + p_2 W_2)$. We do not in general obtain the same p_i values in both cases.

Our most difficult problem arises in terms of the rate of profit P′. It should also be uniform between departments as an equilibrium condition. But if we write, instead of (5.4):

$$P' = \frac{S_1}{C_1 + V_1} = \frac{S_2}{C_2 + V_2} \quad \text{or}$$

$$P' = \frac{S'}{1 + k_1} = \frac{S'}{1 + k_2}$$

we come face to face with what the great Austrian critic of Marx, Eugen von Böhm-Bawerk, called "the great contradiction" in the Marxian system.[3] For though we can see why the S′ terms in the numerators must be equal, there is no reason why the C/V (or k) terms, the organic compositions of capital, should be equal. Is there any way out of this dilemma? Böhm-Bawerk was sure that there was not.

Marxists insist that there is a way out, but disagree as to its nature. One escape hatch involves the price-value ratios p_i of (A5.3); one of these p_i is generally above unity and the other below unity. If neither is unity, we may replace (5.4) by (A5.7-8) directly below, leaving to the next paragraph the explanation of the complications.

$$P' = \frac{[p_1 S_1 + (p_1 - p_2)V_1]d}{p_1 C_1 + p_2 V_1} = \frac{[p_1 S' + (p_1 - p_2)]d}{p_2 + p_1 k_1} \quad \text{(A5.7)}$$

$$P' = \frac{[p_2 S_2 + (p_2 - p_1)C_2]d}{p_1 C_2 + p_2 V_2} = \frac{[p_2 S' + (p_2 - p_1)k_2]d}{p_2 + p_1 k_2} \quad \text{(A5.8)}$$

The expansions in (A5.7-8) as compared with (5.4) arise from necessary shifts (1) from labor-hours to money, and (2) from flows to stocks:

1. Shifts from labor-hours to money: (a) In the numerators, each term in S_i is multiplied by the appropriate p_i. (b) In addition, each numerator includes a remainder term $(p_i - p_1)C_i + (p_i - p_2)V_i$, allotted to S_i as allowance for the monetary evaluations of C_i as $p_1 C_i$ and of V_i as $p_2 V_i$. (C_i is adjusted by p_1 because constant capital consists of investment goods; V_i is adjusted by p_2 because the variable capital represented by a worker's

---

[3] Böhm-Bawerk, *Karl Marx and the Close of His System* (1949; original German edition, 1896), ch. 3.

labor consists of consumer goods bought with his wages.) In Department I, $i = 1$, $p_i = p_1$, and so the term in C_1 vanishes in the numerator of (A5.7). In Department II, $i = 2$, $p_i = p_2$ and the term in V_2 vanishes in the numerator of (A5.8).

2. Shifts from flows to stocks. It is customary to relate profit to the stock of capital rather than the flow of its services. For a (given) capital stock K we apply (5.6) and write:

$$\frac{C_1 + C_2 + V_1 + V_2}{d} = K$$

where the term in d represents a rate of capitalization. We treat this capitalization rate as uniform, both between departments and for constant and variable capital. We also treat d as a technological given at any point in time. If we use $(C_i + V_i)/d$ in the denominators of (A5.7–8) instead of simply $(C_i + V_i)$, the changes involve dividing each denominator (multiplying each numerator) by d.

We now have eight equations (A5.1–8) as the skeleton of a labor theory of value, as against thirteen unknowns (W_1, W_2, C_1, C_2, V_1, V_2, S_1, S_2, p_1, p_2, w, S', P'). To balance the system, a number of additional constraints may be placed upon the variables.

One of these constraints is supplied by equating aggregate *supply* and *demand* in the two departments. The resulting equation is simpler in value than in money terms. In Department I (investment goods), aggregate supply W_1 is $(C_1 + V_1 + S_1)$. Aggregate demand for its ouput is divisible into (1) replacement demand $C_1 + C_2$, the flow of constant capital, and (2) expansion demand, which consists of some (unknown) proportion that we call g (a "growth coefficient") of the flow of surplus value $S_1 + S_2$. (Workers' investment is neglected as near zero.) The equation of supply and demand for Department I is, therefore:

$$C_1 + V_1 + S_1 = C_1 + C_2 + g(S_1 + S_2) \quad \text{or}$$

$$V_1 + (1 - g)S_1 = C_2 + gS_2$$

(A5.9)

In Department II (consumption goods) aggregate supply is W_2 or $(C_2 + V_2 + S_2)$. Aggregate demand for the output of Department II is again divisible into (1) the variable capital $V_1 + V_2$, required to maintain and expand the labor force, and (2) the remaining surplus value $(1 - g)$ $(S_1 + S_2)$, consumed by capitalists, by unproductive workers, or by addi-

tional workers hired by capitalists to expand the future social output. Equating these expressions, we again derive (A5.9), rather than any independent expression:

$$C_2 + V_2 + S_2 = V_1 + V_2 + (1 - g)(S_1 + S_2) \quad \text{or}$$

$$C_2 + gS_2 = V_1 + (1 - g)S_1$$

Five *structural relations and identities* also assist in balancing the system. The first two are the organic compositions of capital $k_i (= C_i/V_i)$. The third equation is (5.6), expanded and renumbered. The fourth equation is an equilibrium proportion or capital-consumption ratio, which we call h, between W_1 and W_2. The fifth and last equation is an expanded version of (5.7), the definition of an unemployment rate:

$$k_1 = \frac{C_1}{V_1}, \quad k_2 = \frac{C_2}{V_2} \qquad \text{(A5.10–11)}$$

$$\frac{(C_1 + C_2) + (V_1 + V_2)}{d} = K \qquad \text{(A5.12)}$$

$$h = \frac{W_1}{W_2} = \frac{V_1(1 + k_1 + S')}{V_2(1 + k_2 + S')} \qquad \text{(A5.13)}$$

$$U = 1 - \frac{V_1 + V_2}{V_0} = \frac{V_0 - (V_1 + V_2)}{V_0} \qquad \text{(A5.14)}$$

In the two-sector model, we introduce two *generalized functions*. The first, relating unemployment to the rate of surplus value with a lag, is (5.8) with a new number. The second defines the growth coefficient g of (A5.9) as a function of three variables, (W_2, h, P'), with all derivatives nonnegative. This final equation also takes liberties with Marx's original text. In the numerous arithmetical examples in *Das Kapital*, Marx treats as a constant (usually ½) the term we call g. Subsequent critics, particularly Rosa Luxemburg, have claimed that Marx's fixing of g at ½ involved him in contradictions.[4] These contradictions can be avoided by making g—the

---

[4] Luxemburg's question was, Where is the purchasing power to come from to purchase the large increases in W_1 and W_2 that are to result from economic growth, or, in Marx's terms "expanded reproduction" with half the surplus value invested in constant capital? [Rosa Luxemburg, *The Accumulation of Capital* (1913, English translation, 1951).]

percentage of surplus value reinvested in constant capital—an unknown. Our argument is that the higher total consumption W_2, the required capital-consumption ratio h, and the going profit rate P', the higher the proportion of total surplus value that will be invested in the output of Department I.

$$U_t = U(S'_{t-1}) \quad \text{or}$$

$$S'_t = U^{-1}(U_{t+1})$$

$$\text{(A5.15)}$$

$$g = g(W_2,h,P') \qquad \text{(A5.16)}$$

This scheme of sixteen equations corresponds to sixteen unknowns, the thirteen listed above plus three more (g,h,U) added in later equations. Exogenous or technologically given variables are (k_1,k_2,d,K,V_0).

The macrodynamic aspects of the Marxian system follow from the macrostatics of this system in the same way as they follow from the simplified one-sector system.

Chapter
6

The Simplest
Keynesian Models

ESTABLISHMENT ECONOMICS

A simplified *classical* macroeconomic system, with complacent growth replacing the stationary state, may be the macroeconomics of the "silent majority." A simplified *Marxian* system is the official macroeconomic analysis of *capitalism* in the socialist East. Similarly, a simplified *Keynesian* macroeconomic system captured at least the temporary allegiance of the Anglo-American "liberal establishment" at mid-twentieth-century. Indeed, if any system can still claim the special status of orthodoxy in Western Europe and North America, it is probably this one. This chapter and the following three will consider Keynesian macroeconomics, emphasizing its theoretical, structural and policy implications, as well as its empirical supports.

We have mentioned the alleged differences, emphasized most fully by Leijonhufvud, between "Keynesian economics"—which we shall treat in detail—and "the economics of Keynes"—which we shall do little more than mention. John Maynard Keynes (Lord Keynes) was concerned naturally with "depression economics" during the 1930s.[1] His generalization of macroeconomics was from a classical system tending toward full-employment equilibrium to a vaguely outlined system, possibly tending toward stagnation, in which full-employment equilibrium was only a special case. This was "the economics of Keynes"—a series of tracts for the times, centering about one major masterpiece, the *General Theory* of 1936. The refinement and formalization of this system, plus extension to the postwar worlds of economic exhilaration, price inflation, and growthmanship, were left to disciples in Britain, America, and elsewhere. The result has been Keynesian economics. Its development began well before Keynes's death;[2] its divergences from Keynes's personal oral tradition were accelerated by the Master's passing in 1946. Since World War II, it has been Keynesian economics, rather than the economics of Keynes himself, which has influenced liberal establishment policy. It is, therefore, Keynesian economics which we emphasize here; almost none of the technical apparatus, in particular, can be found in the *General Theory*.

We shall develop the Keynesian system in a series of increasingly complex models of a closed economy with a stable price level—none of them de-

---

[1] Keynes's 1940 pamphlet, *How to Pay for the War*, was influential in extending the economics of Keynes to exhilaration conditions. Like most wartime writing, however, it assumed an early postwar relapse into renewed depression.

[2] This writer reads Keynes's last published essay, "The Balance of Payments of the United States" (*Economic Journal*, June 1946), with its reference to "modern stuff gone silly and sour," as a protest against what Keynesians were making of Keynes. If so, it was ineffective; an additional dozen years would be required to verify Keynes's last forecasts (of U.S. balance of payments difficulties and the transformation of "dollar shortage" to "dollar glut").

vised by Keynes himself. (For the benefit primarily of readers with training in international economics, an appendix will shed the single country, closed economy straitjacket.) Our particular sequence of models will number five:

1. Model I considers income and expenditures in a purely private economy in which all investment is exogenous and unaffected by interest rates.[3]

2. Model II, also included in this chapter, adds a government that engages in aggregative fiscal policy, as regards both its expenditures and its tax receipts.

3. Models III–V are postponed until chapter 7. Model III introduces the rate of interest as a determinant of both public and private investment.

4. Model IV adds a fixed money stock and demand functions for it. (From this point on, we use the so-called "Hicksian cross" or "Islamic" technique of IS and LM functions.) At the same time, the arsenal of public policy is expanded to include monetary manipulation, as we consider the rival claims of "monetarists" and "fiscalists" for dominance in macro-economic policy.

5. Model V makes the money supply itself a function of the income level, the rate of interest, the size of the fiscal deficit or surplus, and the autonomous decisions of the monetary authorities.

Except as otherwise indicated, all the variables of all these models will be expressed in "real" terms. This means that nominal values are "deflated" for changes in price levels, so that all "dollars" have constant purchasing power. This procedure implies that the price level makes no difference to the real variables, although its actual or anticipated rate of change may influence them. Keynes himself preferred to express his aggregates in "wage units," deflating by the wage rate rather than the price level. His wage unit corresponds to Marx's hour of socially necessary homogeneous labor. The conventional method of deflation by the price level is more convenient statistically; Keynes's usage impounds technical progress in the wage unit.

KEYNESIAN MODEL I: THE STATE OF NATURE

Keynesian Model I is a review of material covered in elementary courses.[4] Its notation may be new. It may be helpful, if you recall the notation of

---

[3] Appendix A to this chapter extends to two countries the analysis of Model I.

[4] Elementary courses that place more than half their stress on macroeconomics and special advanced or honor sections of other courses, usually include aspects of Models II–IV as well.

some earlier presentation, to translate arguments and derivations back and forth between that notation and this one.

In Model I, we are in the state of nature, with no government sector; or if there is a government, it spends no money and levies no taxes. In this anarchist utopia, real income and expenditure are composed of real private consumption and investment only. In terms of our source equation for income (chapter 3) $Y = C + I$ only. All monetary magnitudes are expressed as the units of constant purchasing power.

Aggregate planned, real consumption C depends upon anticipated real income Y alone. The relation between consumption and income is simplified as a first approximation to a linear consumption function $C = C_o + cY$.[5] In this consumption function C_o is the vertical-axis intercept, i.e., the value of C when Y is zero; c is the slope of the consumption function, i.e., the change in C when Y increases by one unit. (See figure 6-1.) With rare exceptions both the intercept C_o and the slope c are positive. The slope, known in economics as the *marginal propensity to consume* or m.p.c., cannot exceed unity if Model I is to have a stable solution. (A demonstration of this point must wait until later in the chapter.) The m.p.c. should be distinguished from the *consumption ratio* or average propensity to consume (a.p.c.) C/Y or $c + (C_o/Y)$. The a.p.c. is seen graphically as the slope of a ray or radius vector from the origin to the relevant point on the consumption function. More than geometry links the m.p.c. and the a.p.c.; they both relate to consumption behavior. But we should recognize that they contain distinct pieces of information. For example, it does not follow that because "the poor" have a higher a.p.c. than "the rich" they must have a higher m.p.c. as well, or that total consumption will increase with egalitarian redistribution of income and decrease with antiegalitarian redistribution.[6]

---

[5] Functions of this form fit the data extremely well over short periods (annual data covering approximately a decade) but the goodness of fit is statistically misleading insofar as C forms a large part of Y. The implications of this form of consumption function for long-term extrapolation are unfortunately disconfirmed. This disconfirmation is one of the principal problems to be discussed in chapter 8.

[6] The student can persuade himself of these points by hypothetical arithmetical examples like the following:

Assume a total income of 200, divided equally between two groups, called simply Group 1 and Group 2, whose respective consumption functions are:

Group 1: $C_1 = .90 \, Y_1$ (a.p.c. = .90, m.p.c. = .90)
Group 2: $C_2 = 25 + .75 \, Y_2$ (a.p.c. = 1.00, m.p.c. = .75)

When one unit of income is shifted from Group 2 (higher a.p.c.) to Group 1 (lower a.p.c.), total consumption *rises* by 0.15, the amount by which $(m.p.c.)_2$ exceeds $(m.p.c.)_1$.

Investment is taken in the non–Wall Street sense of net addition to the social physical capital stock of plant, equipment, residential housing, and inventories. In this initial model, planned investment real I is equal in any period to some constant I_o. This constant may fluctuate widely from period to period according to what Keynes called the "animal spirits" of individual and corporate investors. These fluctuations Keynes believes to be the main causes of observed economic instability.

Another symbol we shall use is A, which represents all "autonomous" expenditures independent of Y. In this model, $A = C_o + I_o$. Autonomous expenditure, including both C_o and I_o, is often referred to as "high-powered," because of its capacity to generate a "multiplier." (The meaning and measurement of this multiplier is discussed below.)

Whatever income is not spent for consumption is saved (by definition). Saving that is not intended for investment may be intended for lending or for hoarding, usually in monetary form, but money is not mentioned in Model I. Similarly, any excess of investment over saving is intended to be financed by borrowing or dishoarding, but Model I includes no stock of assets from which such dishoarding can occur. Much of macroeconomics, and not only the Keynesian variety, is concerned with the problems raised when plans to lend, borrow, hoard, or dishoard, reasonable enough for individuals, cannot be fulfilled in the community at large because of lack of "finance."

The world of Model I, summarized verbally above, can be compressed further into a set of four equations:

$$Y = C + I \qquad (6.1)$$

$$C = C_o + cY \qquad (6.2)$$

$$I = I_o \qquad (6.3)$$

$$A = C_o + I_o \qquad (6.4)$$

Only the consumption function (6.2) is a true behavioral equation purporting to describe variations in economic behavior. (6.1) and (6.4) are definitional identities, while (6.3) is a behavioral constant.

The four-equation system (6.1–6.4) can be solved algebraically for each of its four unknowns (Y,C,I,A) in terms of its statistical constants (C_o,I_o,c). The most useful solution for our present purposes is the solution for Y:[7]

---

[7] A simple solution substitutes (6.2) and (6.3) directly into (6.1):

$$Y = C + I = (C_o + cY) + I_o = (C_o + I_o) + cY$$

$$Y = \frac{A}{1-c} = \frac{C_o + I_o}{1-c} \qquad (6.5)$$

The same solution is obtainable diagramatically as the equilibrium value Y_e on a "Keynesian cross" (figure 6-1). The horizontal axis of this diagram is Y, real aggregate income. The vertical axis is used for any of the several components (sources and uses) of income, such as C or I; it may also be used for Y itself. A 45-degree line expresses the circular-flow (equilibrium) condition of equality between income and expenditure, i.e., between income and the sum of its components. The same equality is expressed by the *intersection* of the 45-degree line with the vertical sum (C + I) and the C and I functions. This vertical sum is called the aggregate *expenditure* function; it should not be confused with the aggregate *demand* function involving the price level, which we shall encounter later on.

The intersection of the aggregate expenditure function and the 45-degree line gives the equilibrium income level Y_e, *provided* that this value lies

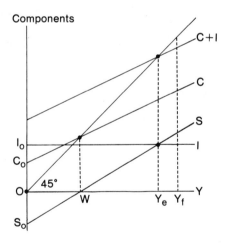

Figure 6-1   Keynesian Cross

Then, using (6.4):

$$Y = A + cY$$

from which:

$$Y - cY = (1-c)\,Y = A$$

so that (6.5) follows at once.

within the productive capacity Y_f of the economy at full employment. More generally, the equilibrium income is the *smaller* of the two values Y_e and Y_f. A solution like $Y_e < Y_f$, such as that on the diagram, involves equilibrium at less than full employment.

We should also consider the private saving function S in relation to investment I. The saving function, which includes both personal and corporate saving, is equal to $Y - C$ by the use equation of income. In this Keynesian model, using the consumption function (6.2):

$$S = Y - (C_0 + cY)$$

$$= -C_0 + (1 - c)Y$$

$$= S_0 + sY$$

where s [$= 1 - c$] is the marginal propensity to save (m.p.s.), S/Y is the saving ratio or average propensity to save (a.p.s.), and $S_0 = -C_0$. By equation (6.1), investment I [$= I_0$] also equals $Y - C$. On figure 6-1, the S function and the horizontal line I therefore cross at the point corresponding to the equilibrium income Y_e. The saving function also crosses the horizontal axis at point W, directly below the intersection of the consumption function and the 45-degree line. The point W is called the Wolf Point, in honor not of any economist or statistician named Wolf but rather "the wolf at the door."

But we argued in chapter 3 that, ignoring fiscal surpluses, fiscal deficits, and the balance of trade, $I = S$ identically at all times. Here this equality reappears as an equilibrium condition. Is there not an inconsistency? Not really; the apparent contradiction is purely verbal. In chapter 3, we were discussing actual, realized, statistical, or *ex post* values of S and I. Here we consider planned, intended, or *ex ante* values; the S function, the I function (and also the C function) represent the plans. Undesired and unplanned inventory accumulations and decumulations, in particular, do not enter the *ex ante* I function, although they enter into the recorded *ex post* values of I. This definitional shift changes the saving-investment equality from the identity of chapter 3 to an equilibrium condition in formal Keynesian models.

Digression: Several pathological cases complicate the above analysis, at least in theory. For example, had the slope c of the consumption function (6.2)—the m.p.c.—exceeded unity, a unit rise in Y would have increased both consumption and total expenditure by more than one unit. In figure 6-2 (panels a and b) both C and $(C + I)$ cut the 45-degree line from

below. The result is instability. For consider the case of $Y > Y_e$. Expenditure exceeds income in this disequilibrium case where income was already "too high," and pulls income further from its equilibrium value of Y_e. Similarly for an initial $Y < Y_e$. These cases explain why we consider $c < 1$ as a *stability condition* for the model (6.1–6.4) and its solution (6.5).[8] But the status of $c < 1$ as a stability condition does not imply anything about the real world. (Keynes himself referred to $0 < c < 1$ as a "fundamental psychological law," of aggregate consumption, but proclamation of a law does not insure enforcement.) A third pathological case (figure 6-2, panel c) combines a negative C_o with a normal m.p.c. Here Y_e is stable, but at an impossible and meaningless negative value. None of these three cases has yet been observed over significant periods; all are regarded as theoretical curiosa.

MULTIPLIERS

Equation (6.5) expresses the equilibrium solution of the simplest Keynesian model of equations (6.1–6.4). Utilizing the saving function S, the solution (6.5) may be written:

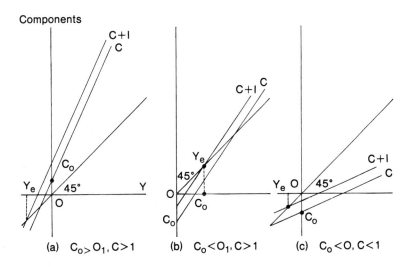

Figure 6-2   Consumption Function Pathology

8 The "boundary value" of c is unity. The boundary value $c = 1$ rules out any solution whatever if $A \neq 0$, and produces a "neutral equilibrium" if $A = 0$. (In a neutral equilibrium case, $C + I$ is identical with the 45-degree line throughout its length, and any Y value whatever is an equilibrium solution.)

$$Y = \frac{A}{1-c} = \frac{A}{s}$$

We can differentiate (6.5) with respect either to autonomous expenditure A as a whole, or to the investment or consumption component of A.[9] The result is called the general or standard *multiplier*; we denote it by μ. It indicates the increase (decrease) in Y to be expected under stable equilibrium conditions from a unit increase (decrease) in any element of autonomous expenditure. Algebraically, it is the reciprocal of the m.p.s., and exceeds unity whenever the m.p.s. is a positive proper fraction.[10] Because the value of μ exceeds unity, we speak of autonomous expenditures as being *high-powered*, in the sense of giving rise to income increases greater than themselves. The statement of our result is:

$$\frac{\partial Y}{\partial A} = \mu = \frac{1}{1-c} = \frac{1}{s} \tag{6.6}$$

Digression: Equation (6.6) is not a universal multiplier formula, although students have memorized it as one. (In Appendix A of this chapter, (6.6) is modified for a two-country case with trade between the countries.) For example, we can also compute a *rotation* multiplier for a change in the m.p.c., or c. Defining the result as μ_c, we obtain from (6.5):

$$\frac{\partial Y}{\partial c} = \mu_c = \frac{A}{(1-c)^2} = \mu Y \tag{6.7}$$

The geometry of figure 6-3 may help visualize the algebra of (6.6–6.7). In the standard or shift multiplier computation, $(C + I)$ becomes $(C + I)'$

---

[9] Students innocent of the differential calculus can follow the derivation of (6.6) by replacing A in (6.5) by $A' = A + 1$ and comparing the new value Y' with the previous value Y. A derivation proceeds as follows:

$$Y' = \frac{A'}{1-c} = \frac{A+1}{1-c} = \frac{A}{1-c} + \frac{1}{1-c} = Y + \frac{1}{1-c} = Y + \frac{A'-A}{1-c}$$

It follows immediately that:

$$\frac{Y'-Y}{A'-A} = \frac{1}{1-c}$$

which is the multiplier formula in algebraic dress.

[10] Values of c inconsistent with stability yield infinite or negative values of the multiplier. Also, negative values of s, arising from consumption functions sloping in the "wrong" direction, yield fractional values of the multiplier.

by the addition of one unit $(=\alpha\beta)$ of autonomous consumption expenditure C_o or autonomous investment expenditure I_o. The equilibrium income level then rises by $\mu(=\alpha\gamma)$ units, from Y_e to Y'_e. The standard multiplier is then μ or (on the diagram) $\alpha\gamma/\alpha\beta$. But if the income change from Y_e to Y'_e results from a rotation of the aggregate expenditure function $(C + I)$ to $(C + I)''$ through the angle ϕ, the corresponding rotation multiplier μ_c is $Y\mu$, by (6.7). On the diagram, the product of μ and Y is a shaded area, labelled μ_c. A handicap to its acceptance is the variability of its value with the time period over which Y is measured.

Digression: Many multiplier puzzles or conundrums were explored in the early Keynesian literature. Some of these retain their interest. For example: (1) Is the multiplier a velocity of circulation of money, in modern dress? (2) Does the multiplier exercise its effect immediately and without time lag? (3) If there is a time lag, by what process of period analysis does the multiplier take effect? (4) If the process of (3) requires a number of discrete periods, what is the length of each such period, in terms of ordinary calendar time? These questions are considered in order.

1. The standard multiplier is never a velocity of circulation, even though published numerical estimates of μ and V may be equal in a particular economy. The two are dimensionally different. The multiplier is a pure number, without a time dimension. The velocity, on the other hand, has a time dimension; it is the number of times money turns over per period; it is twelve times as large for a year as for a month.

2. When the aggregate expenditure function shifts from C + I to

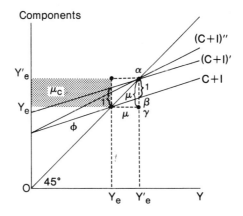

Figure 6-3   Shift and Rotation Multipliers

$(C + I)'$ or $(C + I)''$, the shift in the *equilibrium* income Y_e is indeed immediate and without time lag, as Keynes maintained. But the adjustment of the *actual* income Y from its initial value—which we assume equal to Y_e—to the new equilibrium value Y_e' requires an extended period. The process of adjustment is often presented as an exercise in period analysis. Thus, suppose a unit rise in autonomous expenditure A, which is maintained at the higher value throughout the adjustment period. In the first period, the unit rise in C + I raises Y by one unit, and no more. In the second period, an additional rise in Y is given by the m.p.c., or c, which represents the incremental expenditure from the first period's income increase. In the third period, there is a further rise of c^2 from the second period's income increase; in the nth period, the incremental income increase is c^{n-1}, all with a constant c. The total effect, spread over n periods forms (under stable conditions) a geometric series, whose sum is precisely the multiplier μ:[11]

$$1 + c + c^2 + \cdots + c^{n-1} = \frac{1}{1 - c} = \mu \qquad (6.8)$$

3. In no case does a single, nonmaintained rise in A, however high-powered A may be, generate directly any permanent increase in Y.[12] Error on this point has been pervasive. For example, the first Roosevelt administration in the U.S. (1933–1937), hoped to induce recovery by "pump-priming"—a burst of increased public spending in 1933–1935 that was largely discontinued in 1936–1937. The historical record suggests that the discontinuance of "pump-priming" actually helped bring on the "secondary depression" of 1937–1939.

---

[11] Denote by Σ the sum of the series in (6.8):

$$1 + c + c^2 + \cdots + c^{n-1} = \Sigma \qquad (6.8a)$$

so that

$$c + c^2 + c^3 + \cdots + c^n = c\Sigma \qquad (6.8b)$$

Subtracting (6.8b) from (6.8a), we have:

$$1 - c^n = \Sigma(1 - c), \text{ so that } \Sigma = \frac{1 - c^n}{1 - c}$$

In the limit, as n increases without bound, the value of Σ is $\frac{1}{1 - c}$ for a fractional c, which is the stability condition for (6.5).

[12] There may be indirect or secondary effects, operating through investment by a mechanism known as the *accelerator*. (This mechanism, in its simplest form, relates I to the time change of income, or dY/dt.) Consideration of the accelerator will be delayed until chapter 8.

4. The multiplier time period appears to be the sum of two parts. The first part is a Robertson lag between the receipt and the expenditure of income. The second part (in a monetary economy) is the reciprocal of the *marginal* velocity of circulation of money. This marginal velocity differs from the measured or *average* velocity when the average is sensitive to changes in the nominal money supply.[13] If a rise in the nominal money supply generated expectations of accelerated inflation, people would hurry to spend their money, V would rise, and the multiplier time period would be affected more rapidly than the increase in (average) V would indicate.

EXPANSION AND CONTRACTION GAPS

Keynesian multiplier analysis was applied widely to the "inflationary gaps" of World War II and its aftermath. The same analysis has been extended retrospectively to the "deflationary gaps" of the 1930s, but the expressions "inflationary" and "deflationary" are sometimes misleading, especially here since money has not entered the picture. Furthermore, an inflationary gap may exist without measured inflation, in a regime of price controls and rationing. A deflationary gap may also exist without measured deflation—or even with measured inflation—in a regime of administered prices and wages. We prefer the expressions "expansion gap" and "contraction gap," without explicit reference to price-level changes.

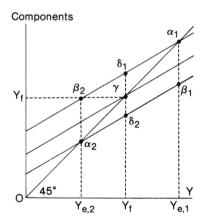

Figure 6-4   Expansion and Contraction Gaps

---

[13] If V is the average velocity of circulation and M* is the nominal money supply, the marginal velocity of circulation is:

$$\frac{d(M^*V)}{dM^*} = V + M^* \frac{dV}{dM^*}$$

A (moneyless!) expansion gap exists when Y_e exceeds capacity output Y_f (as, for example, in figure 6-4). The size of this gap, however, is not $Y_f Y_{e,1}$ in this diagram, but $Y_f Y_{e,1}/\mu$, not $\alpha_1 \beta_1$ but $\gamma \delta_1$, which (by figure 6-3 and its supporting argument) can be shown equal to $\alpha_1 \beta_1/\mu$. What is the rationale of this definition of the gap? Simply that a maintained reduction of A or of C + I by $\gamma \delta_1$—and not by $\alpha_1 \beta_1$—will reduce $Y_{e,1}$ to capacity output Y_f. A reduction of A or of C + I by the full $\alpha_1 \beta_1$ would constitute over-kill. Similarly, a contraction gap exists when $Y_{e,2}$ falls short of Y_f (on figure 6-4), as in depression or recession conditions. But again, its size is not $Y_{e,2} Y_f$ as one might first suppose, but $Y_{e,2} Y_f/\mu$; not $\beta_2 \alpha_2$ but which equals $\beta_2 \alpha_2/\mu$. The rationale is the same as in the case of the expansion gap in the opposite direction.

Digression: Let us drop temporarily the assumptions of a constant Y_f and p. Let us suppose instead that real Y_f can increase with anticipated nonactual Y*. This may occur if people's willingness to work increases. Such a motivational change may result from a phenomenon economists call "money illusion,"[14] or by such related reasons as greater ease in avoiding or settling industrial disputes. If Y_f increases with anticipated Y, the policy implications of gap analysis become complex. Turning to figure 6-5, which has as its axes actual and anticipated income—we suppose an initial expansion gap of $\alpha_1 \beta_1/\mu$. This gap can be eliminated by reduction of C + I to (C + I)', perhaps by some sort of thrift campaign, but at the cost of reducing the national income by YY'. This amount appears small, but in the real-world situation of a slow-growing country, it may comprise the bulk of that economy's real growth. On the other hand, income can be raised by YY'' by an increase of C + I to (C + I)''. This expansion, how-ever, would increase the expansion gap to $\alpha_2 \beta_2/\mu$ and probably accelerate the inflation. This type of dilemma is faced constantly or intermittently, not only by developing countries, but by developed countries desirous of increasing their measured growth rates.

Suppose that nothing is done about the expansion (or contraction) gap. The result may be looked upon as a hidden tax (or subsidy) on the receipt of income in money rather than real terms, or on the holding of wealth in money terms. In the expansion case, it is probable that the price level will rise, from "too much money chasing too few goods," and that the rise will be faster, the larger the gap as a percentage of Y_f.

---

[14] In an economy affected by money illusion, "a dollar is a dollar," regardless of its purchasing power. People react in the same way to changes in nominal and changes in real income and wealth, ignoring any accompanying changes in the price level. In the illustration in the text, they may be induced to "work harder," or to settle industrial disputes more readily, by prospects of higher money incomes all round, which cannot in the aggregate be fulfilled in real terms.

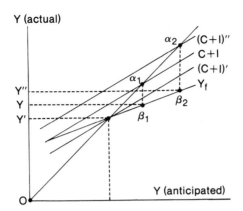

Figure 6-5   Dilemma of Gap Policy

This inflation is a hidden tax on individuals and firms whose incomes or assets are fixed in terms of money, and a hidden subsidy on individuals and firms with negative money assets (net money debts). It is less likely that the price level will fall in the contraction case of "too many goods chasing too little money." (The temptation is strong to reduce the output of goods and the employment of labor instead of reducing prices.) But insofar as the price level falls in the contraction case, the resulting deflation is a hidden subsidy to individuals and firms whose incomes or assets are fixed in terms of money, and a hidden tax on individuals and firms with net money debts.

The hidden tax and subsidy rates are normally higher for *unanticipated* than *anticipated* inflations and deflations. Many individuals attempt to avoid the hidden taxes of inflation by purchasing goods—ranging from real estate and common stocks to jewelry and *objets d'art*—called *inflation hedges*. The prices of these goods tend to rise more quickly than the general price indexes in periods of inflation, and fall more quickly in periods of deflation. Inflation is a hidden subsidy to those producing and holding inflation hedges, and deflation a hidden tax upon them.

In addition, the fact and prospect of significant price-level changes in either direction, anticipated or not, imposes a utility loss on individuals by imposing additional elements of avoidable risk and uncertainty upon them. Individuals must shift from what would otherwise be preferred patterns of expenditure and asset holding to what would otherwise be inferior ones as insurance against the risks of both inflation and deflation, or as self-insurance against the uninsurable uncertainties of fluctuating price levels. (This argument applies only to the risk-averse majority of the economic population. Utility gains and real benefits for the risk-preferring majority may result from fluctuating price levels.)

PARADOXES OF SAVING AND SPENDING

Suppose there is a successful thrift campaign in a situation with no expansion gap. This campaign raises the saving function *permanently* by an amount dS_o [$= -dC_o$], and therefore lowers the expenditure function by dC_o. (We assume no change in the investment function.) This fall in autonomous expenditures lowers equilibrium income, which falls by more than dS_o. Allowing for the operation of the multiplier, equilibrium income will fall by μdS_o. This phenomenon is called the *paradox of saving*—increased thrift lowers the income level. The increment dS_o of saving in this paradoxical case is also called *abortive*. For equilibrium S must remain equal to the unchanged I_o. The income fall is just sufficient for saving (with the increased saving ratio) to equal I_o. The attempt to increase saving has not resulted in increased voluntary investment;[15] that is why it is called abortive.

There can also be a paradox of *spending*. In the presence of an expansion gap, suppose a successful consumption-spending (antithrift) campaign, again with no change in the investment function. Or suppose a successful investment-spending campaign, with no change in the propensity to save. All that happens in either case is the raising of the expansion gap. It increased by dC_o in the first illustration and by dI_o in the second. There is no increase in *real* income or expenditure, which remains at the predetermined level Y_f. Y_e indeed rises (by way of the multiplier) by μdC_o or μdI_o as the case may be. However, this can only increase the expansion gap, since full employment already prevails; the maximum attainable equilibrium income can increase no further. To rephrase our conclusion, equilibrium income is not necessarily Y_e; it is the *lower* of Y_e and Y_f. As for the paradox of spending, the practical result is that an increased desire (propensity) to spend *ex ante* fails to increase real expenditure *ex post* when $Y_e \geq Y_f$.

Victims of inflation taxes react to these taxes, by reducing their real consumption. The reduction of consumption is called *forced saving*. Forced saving by consumers is an important explanation of the effectiveness of inflationary finance in diverting a country's resources from consumption to government, and possibly also increasing the country's capital stock and eventual measured growth rate. At the same time, from the victims' point of view, a paradox is involved. Inflation has forced them to reduce their real saving, and sometimes also their saving ratios (S/Y). It seems anomalous to talk of forced saving in cases where their own real saving has actually fallen, in view of our definition of saving as nonconsumption.

---

[15] During the period of income fall (from Y_e to $Y'_e = \mu dS_o$) there was a temporary increase in involuntary inventory investment, which kept *ex post* I and S equal throughout the adjustment process.

KEYNESIAN MODEL II: FISCAL POLICY

We have touched on public policy in connection with Keynesian Model I, notably in our discussions of expansion and contraction gaps and the paradoxes of thrift and spending. Since Model I has no provisions for government we have implicitly assumed that these policies represented the "general will" or collective choice of the community. It is apparent, however, that Model I is very limited in scope. It is the task of Model II to introduce the government explicitly. Along with the government, Model II introduces one important sort of public policy, namely fiscal policy. The cost of these refinements is a model more complex than Model I but also more useful.

Our fiscal policy variables are: (1) government expenditure G for goods and services, (2) government transfer expenditures Tr, (3) government taxes and allied receipts Tx, and (4) government receipts net of transfers $T(= Tx - Tr)$.

This model is still elementary. The new government sector includes the entire range of national, regional, and local governments. One tax is treated like another; one overall income tax can represent the entire elaborate public receipt and public transfer system in microcosm. Also, government spending G for goods and services is treated as an autonomous constant G_o, which becomes an element in autonomous expenditures A. We now have $A = C_o + I_o + G_o$.

A new behavioral equation is added, in the form of a tax function. This function represents government receipts (net of transfers) as a linear function of the national income, $T = T_o + tY$. The slope t of the tax function is the marginal propensity to tax (m.p.t.). It is assumed nonnegative and less than unity.[16] The intercept T_o is probably negative. In the transition from Model I to Model II, our initial behavioral equation, the consumption function (6.2), is changed in form. Consumption now depends upon *disposable* personal income, defined as Y-T, rather than upon Y alone. This change is reasonable, particularly where taxes are deducted at the source.

Model II can be expressed as a set of six equations in the six unknowns Y,C,I,G,T,A. These equations are:

$$Y = C + I + G \tag{6.9}$$

$$C = C_o + c(Y - T) \tag{6.10}$$

---

[16] This coefficient can be zero in a system where all revenue is raised by poll taxes and where no transfer payments are made.

$$T = Tx - Tr = T_o + tY \tag{6.11}$$

$$I = I_o \tag{6.12}$$

$$G = G_o \tag{6.13}$$

$$A = C_o + I_o + G_o \tag{6.14}$$

of which only (6.10) and (6.11), are strictly behavioral. The other four equations are behavioral constants, definitional identities, and equilibrium conditions.

Model II can be solved for Y by easy stages.[17] The equilibrium solution is:

$$Y = \frac{A - cT_o}{1 - c + ct} = \frac{A - cT_o}{1 - c(1 - t)} \tag{6.15}$$

whose stability condition is $c(1 - t) < 1$. (When t is a positive fraction, this permits c, the m.p.c., to exceed unity.)

A family of four multipliers (6.16–6.19) can be derived from (6.15):[18]

$$\mu = \frac{\partial Y}{\partial A} = \frac{1}{1 - c + ct} \tag{6.16}$$

$$\mu_c = \frac{\partial Y}{\partial c} = \frac{Y - T}{1 - c + ct} = \mu(Y - T) \tag{6.17}$$

$$\mu_{T_o} = \frac{\partial Y}{\partial T_o} = \frac{-c}{1 - c + ct} = -c\mu \tag{6.18}$$

---

[17] One solution begins by substituting (6.11) in (6.10):

$$C = C_o + c(Y - T_o - tY) = C_o - cT_o + (c - ct)Y \tag{6.10a}$$

Then we substitute (6.10a), (6.12), and (6.13) in (6.9) simultaneously:

$$Y = C_o + I_o + G_o - cT_o + (c - ct)Y$$

$$Y(1 - c + ct) = C_o + I_o + G_o - cT_o$$

Using the definitional identity (6.14):

$$Y(1 - c + ct) = A - cT_o$$

from which (6.15) follows at once.

[18] Of these multipliers, (6.16) and (6.18) can be derived by the student innocent of the differential calculus, using the method of footnote 9, shown earlier in this chapter. The other multipliers, (6.17) and (6.19) are more difficult to compute.

$$\mu_t = \frac{\partial Y}{\partial t} = \frac{-cY}{1 - c + ct} = \mu_{T_0} Y = -c\mu Y \qquad (6.19)$$

The standard multiplier μ can now be used to estimate the effects of changes in G_0 as well as in C_0 and I_0. The m.p.c. rotation multiplier is μ_c as before. The values of both these multipliers, however, are numerically smaller than in Model I because of an additional tax *leakage* from Y, represented by the t term (unless this term is zero) and combined with the savings leakages or $1 - c$ of Model I. Also, the numerator of μ_c changes from national income Y to disposable income $Y - T$.

The two new multipliers (6.18–6.19) refer to a shift and a rotation, respectively, in the tax function (6.11). They are taken with respect to the coefficients T_0 and t. They permit us to estimate the effects of different sorts of tax changes upon the national income. We denote them by μ_{T_0} and μ_t respectively.[19]

At this point we might consider the common sense of the difference between (6.16) and (6.18). Why should the multiplier effect of public expenditures on income be higher than the multiplier effect of public transfer payments (negative taxes)? Why should it more than overbalance the (negative) multiplier effect of taxes, or of taxes less transfer payments? And why should an increase in expenditures balanced by an increase in taxes have any nonzero multiplier effect at all? In terms of our symbols, why do we have:

$$\frac{\partial Y}{\partial G} = \frac{\partial Y}{\partial A} > \frac{\partial Y}{\partial Tr} = -\frac{\partial Y}{\partial T_0}$$

and

$$\frac{\partial Y}{\partial G} + \frac{\partial Y}{\partial T_0} > 0$$

The economic justification of the algebra is that when G rises by one unit, that unit is itself a unit of expenditure and, therefore, an addition to

---

[19] We can also combine the last two multipliers into a single multiplier μ_T for a simultaneous change in both tax parameters T_0 and t, such as results from general fiscal reform. We then have:

$$\mu_T dT = \mu_{T_0} dT_0 + \mu_t dt = \mu_{T_0} (dT_0 + Ydt)$$

In numerical application of this formula, the Y value used should not be the pre-reform value Y_e but $(Y_e + \mu_{T_0} dT_0)$.

Y. On the other hand, the increase in T does not itself reduce Y, since T does not enter into Y as defined in (6.9).[20] We can proceed further along this line and suggest a balanced-budget multiplier μ_b of unity, by means of period analysis. Since G is included in autonomous expenditures A, the multiplier applicable to dG is the standard μ. This multiplier can be expressed in Model 2 (taking account of the expenditure "leakage" through taxation), as the series:

$$1 + c(1 - t) + [c(1 - t)]^2 + \cdots + [c(1 - t)]^{n-1}$$

The multiplier generated by a tax change dT_0 is the same series, but lacks the initial value of unity. If $dG = dT_0$, with the multipliers working in opposite directions, the difference between the two series is precisely unity, regardless of the value of t, the m.p.t., and c, the m.p.c.

On the other hand, letting B represent the size of the government budget, we may write:

$$\mu_b \, dB = \mu dG + \mu_{T_0} \, dT_0 \tag{6.20}$$

with t given. Choosing units such that $dB = dG = dT_0 = 1$, and substituting multiplier values from (6.16) and (6.18), we derive:

$$\mu_b = \frac{1 - c}{1 - c + ct} = (1 - c)\mu$$

which does depend on t and c. It is unitary when $t = 0$, but otherwise fractional. Which estimate of μ_b is correct for a positive m.p.t.—the unitary estimate of the last paragraph or the fractional estimate of the present paragraph? We seem to have an inconsistency on our hands, if not a contradiction.

The resolution of this inconsistency depends upon the *income level* at which the taxation increment dT is to balance the expenditure increment dG. (The relation between total G and total T, paradoxically, has nothing to do with the balanced budget multiplier.) In (6.20) there is a balance *ex ante*, at the income level prevailing *before* the budgetary change. After the change has worked itself out, dT will exceed dG for a budgetary in-

---

[20] If our income variable had been disposable income Y − T instead of Y, and our tax function had been $T = T_0 + t(Y + T)$, some of our results would have been different. The reader is invited to explore this byway on his own.

crease, and vice versa for a budgetary decrease. To obtain the unitary value of μ_b, the budget balance is taken ex post. At the original income level, dG will exceed dT for a budgetary increase, and vice versa for a budgetary decrease. (Appendix B of this chapter is devoted to the mathematics underlying this statement.)

In closing expansion and contraction gaps, it is important to remember that μ_b is seldom zero. Suppose an expansion gap is accompanied by inflation. In addition, suppose it is thought expedient to increase G still further, perhaps for national defense. We now ask: By how much must the tax function be shifted upward—by how much must T_o increase—if the expansion gap is not to increase and the inflation accelerate? The answer is not simply the increment dG. Instead, it is given by solving the following equation for dT_o, which makes use of the multiplier (6.18) and whose right hand side is the *product* of the standard multiplier and the initial increment of the gap:[21]

$$\mu dG + \mu_{T_o} \, dT_o = \mu (dG - c \, dT_o) = 0 \qquad (6.21)$$

The same analysis is applicable if G is cut back in the presence of a contraction gap, or if dT_o is given with dG to be determined.

A technical feature of (6.21) is that neither the budget as such nor the balanced-budget multiplier μ_b need enter the analysis, although they of course could.[22] More important economically is the implication that, for an expansion gap to be frozen (with a fractional m.p.c.), any expenditure increase must not only be *matched* but actually *exceeded* by an accompanying tax increase. This uncomfortable result was christened the *principle of overfinance* by Kenneth Boulding in *Reconstruction of Economics* (1949). Being uncomfortable to the representative legislator, it is "impractical." (However impractical, it is unfortunately true.)

FISCAL FLEXIBILITY

We have seen that the standard multiplier (6.16) of Model II is smaller than its counterpart (6.6) of Model I, as a consequence of a positive tax

---

[21] If the desired change in the expansion gap is nonzero—call it dZ—the r.h.s. of (6.21) will be μdZ. (The reader can work out variations on (6.21) when the m.p.t. t is to be changed instead of, or in addition to, the shift parameter T_o.)

[22] Taking μ_b as unity and dB = dG, implying $dT_o = 0$, we would have,

$$dB = dZ$$

so that dZ cannot be zero if dB is nonzero.

leakage indicated by the m.p.t. This difference may be advantageous or disadvantageous to the policymaker or adviser, depending on circumstances. If the prior situation is a desirable one—with full employment, high growth, price-level stability—and some disturbance dA sets in, such as a change of investors' "animal spirits," the policymaker prefers a low multiplier so that the equilibrium level of income is not greatly altered. He then praises the *built-in flexibility* of a fiscal system with a high m.p.t. On the other hand, if he confronts a situation of high unemployment and/or rapid inflation, and if the disturbance dA is in the right direction, the policymaker wants his multiplier high, and complains of *fiscal drag* when a low multiplier slows down the desired change.

Built-in flexibility involves only the damping effect of an *existing* tax function and its parameters upon the multiplier μ and the income change dY. A broader form of fiscal flexibility, called *formula flexibility*, permits the authorities, in addition, to modify within limits certain tax-function parameters—our T_0 and t—automatically and without legislative approval, in response to specified signals from the side of unemployment or price movements.[23] In the U.S., formula-flexibility proposals have failed thus far to overcome Congress' jealousy of its fiscal prerogatives.

Digression: *The Effectiveness of Built-In Flexibility* Musgrave and Miller defined as a measure of the *effectiveness* of built-in flexibility the percentage by which the multiplier declines when (6.16) is substituted for (6.6) with a given set of tax parameters.[24] The measure goes to zero when the tax function makes no difference and to unity when the multiplier (6.16) goes to zero. The analysis involves two new concepts: (1) the *average propensity to tax* (a.p.t.)—(T/Y) or t + (T_0/Y), which we shall call τ—and (2) a *tax elasticity* E, or (dT/dY)(Y/T).

We define the Musgrave-Miller effectiveness coefficient a as:

$$a = \frac{\mu_0 - \mu}{\mu_0} = \frac{\dfrac{1}{1-c} - \dfrac{1}{1-c+ct}}{\dfrac{1}{1-c}} = \frac{ct}{1-c+ct}$$

In these expressions, the new term μ_0 is the standard multiplier (6.6) as in Model I, with t = 0 and no fiscal flexibility. A tax elasticity E can be developed:

[23] Formula-flexibility proposals vary with regard to responses to unemployment inflation, i.e., to contraction gaps accompanied by price increases.

[24] Richard A. Musgrave and Merton C. Miller, "Built-In Flexibility," *American Economic Review* (March 1948).

$$E = \frac{dT}{dY}\frac{Y}{T} = \frac{t}{\tau}$$

so that $\qquad\qquad t = E\tau \quad$ and accordingly

$$a = \frac{cE\tau}{1 - c + cE\tau} \qquad\qquad (6.22)$$

which varies directly, not only with the tax elasticity E and the tax ratio τ, but also with the m.p.c. For the U.S., the value of a has been estimated as close to .5 and the value of τ as approximately .3. This implies that, with c estimated at .8 and μ_o at 5, the American fiscal system provides a tax elasticity E of 1.2 and reduces the multiplier μ to 2.5. When the operation of the multiplier is moving the system away from Y_t, either downward to recession or upward to inflationary boom, we praise the system because its built-in flexibility is so large, and we may wish a were larger. But at the same time, when the system is moving *toward* Y_t under its own power in recovery, we may complain of *fiscal drag* as slowing its recovery, and wish a were smaller.

DIGRESSION: MORGENTHAU'S DREAM

We mentioned previously the discrediting of the New Deal pump-priming efforts of 1933–1935 by the secondary depression of 1937–1939. An ideological successor to the theory of pump-priming was a theory of a permanent budget deficit that would nevertheless be self-liquidating. This theory is associated with the name of the New Deal Secretary of the Treasury, Henry Morgenthau, Jr., who had previously been a fiscal conservative. Ignoring complications traceable to time lags and to interest payments on the public debt, Morgenthau hoped that additional public spending might increase the national income and generate an increase in tax receipts sufficient to pay off the accompanying deficit, with no change in tax function (6.11). Translated into algebra, the theory was that:

$$t(\mu dG) = dT = dG$$

or, choosing units such that $dT = dG = 1$:

$$\mu t = 1$$

The last equation smacks of perpetual motion. It is a little too good to be true. In fact, it can be shown to require a value of c inconsistent with economic growth, or alternatively, a value of t that reduces it to a tautology. For, when we substitute the value of μ from (6.16):

$$
\begin{array}{c|c}
\multicolumn{2}{c}{t = 1 - c + ct} \\
\hline
c(1 - t) = 1 - t & t(1 - c) = 1 - c \\
c = 1 & t = 1
\end{array}
\qquad (6.23)
$$

The left-side development of (6.23) involves division by $1 - t$ and assumes $t \neq 1$. It results in $c = 1$ and $\mu = 1/t$. With $t > 0$, this assumes stationary conditions. All increments of income (after taxes) are spent for consumption, and net saving and investment are both zero. The right-side development of (6.23) involves division by $1 - c$ and assumes $c \neq 1$. It results in $t = 1$ and $\mu = 1$. (The first result makes the budget deficit illusory.) More realistic parameter values ($c = .80$, $t = 0.25$, whence $\mu = 2.5$) yield $\mu t = 0.625$. This means that a one-dollar expenditure increment eventually generates 62.5 cents of the revenue increment required for its financing, without allowance for interest.

We can extend a similar analysis to a tax cut, which may mean a reduction in T_o and/or a reduction in t. If a *reduction* in either parameter will finance itself through multiplier effects, an *increase* will also raise no additional revenue, as per the doctrine of diminishing returns from taxation.[25] We shall examine both the "shift" case (involving dT_o) and the "rotation" case (involving dt).

1. The shift case requires that, if T_o rises by 1 unit:

$$
t\mu_{T_o} = -dT_o \quad \text{or} \quad 1 + t\mu_{T_o} = 0
$$

Applying the multiplier formula (6.18) reduces this to:

$$
1 - \frac{ct}{1 - c + ct} = \frac{1 - c}{1 - c + ct} = 0
\qquad (6.24)
$$

which requires an m.p.c. of unity or an (m.p.s. + m.p.t.) of zero.

---

[25] The diminishing returns doctrine goes further, claiming that an *increase* in either parameter of the tax function will *decrease* total receipts. [Compare Martin Bronfenbrenner, "Diminishing Returns from Federal Taxation?" *National Tax Journal* (December 1970).]

2. The rotation case requires that:

$$\frac{d}{dt}\,(tY) = Y + t\frac{dY}{dt} = Y + t\mu_t = 0$$

The appropriate multiplier formula is now (6.19). Its application yields:

$$Y\left(1 - \frac{ct}{1 - c + ct}\right) = 0$$

with implications the same as those of (6.24).

THE BURDEN OF A PUBLIC DEBT

A standard conservative reproach against Keynesian economics has been the equanimity with which it regards both budget deficits and public debts. All Keynesians recognize that such deficits must be financed, that their financing by the printing press (however indirect) will be inflationary at or above full employment, and that inflation is a hidden tax. But if deficits are financed instead by the sale of public securities, do their carrying charges (interest plus provision for repayment) constitute some sort of burden on the future? There is considerable argument over this issue. (The conventional "burden on future generations" assertion is sometimes carried to the point of deducting public—but not private—debt from national wealth as estimated statistically.[26]) In the remainder of this section, we discuss a number of forms of the debt-burden argument, including denials that any such burden can exist when the debt is held domestically—when "we owe it to ourselves."

When a private household, a private firm, or a local government agency contracts a debt, it imposes a future burden upon itself, its successors, or its constituency. A superficial argument treats the general public treasury as a bigger if not better individual, firm, or village bank account. The gen-

---

[26] Some such deduction would be legitimate if domestically held public securities were regarded as elements of national wealth, but they are not.

We did not discuss national wealth accounting in chapters 2–3. National wealth accounts are, however, macroeconomic aggregations of the *balance sheets* of households and firms. Like private balance sheets, national wealth accounts use a double-entry system. The asset side (l.h.s.) lists and evaluates the physical assets involved; the liability side (r.h.s.) indicates the ownership of these assets. It is as erroneous to subtract an r.h.s. item (public debt) from an l.h.s. item (public assets) as to subtract the value of bond and mortgage debt from the value of privately held land, buildings, and equipment.

eral public as general-government taxpayers are then like family members, corporate stockholders, or local taxpayers. When their households, firms, or villages get "in the red," they and their successors must "make good" the deficits by some form of belt tightening. Therefore, they feel an interest in seeing their households, firms, or villages stay "out of the red" and pursue "sound finance." This microeconomic outlook, however, ignores altogether the macroeconomic effects of public spending and taxation. Or, alternatively, it treats all multipliers as zero, as though full employment and full capacity were always maintained by other forces. The argument may be traced to the classical macroeconomics of our chapter 4, where equilibrium involves full employment, although the classical economists themselves—notably Ricardo—took a more sophisticated view (see below).

We take leave of the conventional wisdom of the business community. As its antithesis, we consider next the conventional wisdom of the liberal intellectuals. Keynesian economics, as interpreted in the "functional finance" of A. P. Lerner,[27] assures us categorically that the public debt—at least its domestically held portion—cannot be a burden on future generations, and that its size is a matter of secondary concern. Deficit financing, it is claimed, gives control over real resources to the government, at only a minimal "transactions cost" to taxpayers. If these real resources would otherwise be unemployed (as in the presence of a contraction gap) there is no burden on anyone at any time. If deficit financing shifts resources from alternative (private) use, command over them has been surrendered directly or indirectly by the public-security buyers of the present generation. Their surrender is the consequence of their having purchased public securities instead of other resources. As for the future, the only problem is a distributional one when the debt is serviced. There is redistribution from the taxpayers' to the bondholders' heirs, insofar as these classes do not overlap. Problems may, of course, arise, as with any other redistributions. There are administrative (transactions) costs. Society's willingness to supply labor (and other productive inputs) may be effected (either way), and so may the social income, if "bondholders" and "taxpayers" react asymmetrically to changes in their disposable incomes. But such effects are secondary; they involve no significant burden on a generation as a whole, which lumps bondholders and taxpayers together. The conclusion remains, that a country's national debt can only be a burden to the country's inhabitants if its holders are foreigners.

We have ascribed to David Ricardo a more sophisticated burden theory than the "conventional" one given above. Ricardo can indeed be inter-

---

[27] Abba P. Lerner, *Economics of Control* (1944), ch. 24, or *Economics of Employment* (1951), ch. 8.

preted as accepting Say's Identity and as denying that public expenditure can increase employment. But if failure of expenditure to increase employment does not constitute a burden in itself, whence does the burden arise? Ricardo's argument against public debts had as its basis what is now called the *crowding out* of more productive private investment. With equilibrium income constant at Y_e (figures 4-1 and 4-2), and with the saving function S given (and interest-inelastic), the financing of an increased public debt raises the "investment" demand schedule I. It also raises the equilibrium real rate of interest r_e, not shown on this diagram. It is the rise in the interest rate that displaces private expenditures, primarily private investment expenditures. It is this displacement which constitutes crowding out. Crowding out, in turn, lowers the country's growth rate and with it the income levels of future generations. Herein lies its burden—in terms of alternatives foregone, rather than in "real" or "pain" costs. The transfer of resources from private investment to public expenditure lowers growth because, in standard classical doctrine, private investment is generally used productively, while public expenditure goes largely for the "unproductive consumption" of warfare and courtly luxury. (Modern critics add, much of it goes for relief payments and similar transfers to nonworkers.) The Ricardian position depends centrally upon this fact situation, which he assumed without much discussion. Were public expenditure, either for directly productive purposes or for the "social infrastructure" of development, more productive in the long run than the private investment it displaces, a modern Ricardian might come out on the other side of the "burden" debate.

Buchanan has developed a quite different "sophisticated classical" theory of debt burden in the mid-twentieth century.[28] Buchanan turns the Keynesian argument against itself. To him, a completely voluntary action by a rational man—such as the transfer of purchasing power to a government by purchase of bonds or other securities—cannot constitute a burden. Neither can the compulsory redemption of interest-bearing public securities, which deprives him of interest income, constitute a benefit. On this basis, let us reconsider the "we owe it to ourselves" argument of the functional financiers.

Suppose two generations, generation 1 (when a given debt increment is incurred through deficit financing) and generation 2 (when this increment is serviced, as to both principal and interest, from tax receipts). Let us also compare the *wealth* rather than the income positions of "taxpayers" and "bondholders," including in wealth the capitalized benefits of public services and deducting from wealth the capitalized burdens of (discounted)

---

[28] James Buchanan, *Public Principles of Public Debt* (1958).

future taxes. The benefits of debt-financed public services are assured to accrue primarily to generation 1, and also to fall as the gentle rain from heaven upon domestic taxpayers and bondholders impartially. In generation 1, therefore, we find a net benefit (negative burden) for taxpayers. They obtain more public services than they have paid for; their wealth positions therefore improve. There is at the same time no burden on bondholders— and here is Buchanan's departure from functional finance—because they have bought public securities *voluntarily*, and their wealth positions have not deteriorated as a result of this transaction. In generation 2, there is a burden on taxpayers. They must now pay for "expired" public services; their wealth positions are affected adversely by anticipated future taxes for debt service, even if the debt instruments take the form of "consols" or perpetual annuities. But there is no offsetting benefit to bondholders. When debt is redeemed, they must involuntarily exchange their securities as they come due, for noninterest-bearing cash. (If the surrender had been voluntary, it would have been made previously on the open market, without waiting for the redemption date.) If the debt takes the form of consols, bondholders neither gain nor lose at the margin. In neither case do the bondholders benefit. Taking each generation as a whole, by adding the wealth positions of taxpayers and bondholders, there is a net benefit to generation 1 and a net burden to generation 2.[29] Within Buchanan's framework, however, his conclusions may be upset if the benefits of public expenditure are divided sufficiently favorably to generation 2 to offset the intergenerational division of actual and accrued taxes.

SUMMARY

This chapter is the first of a pair devoted to exposition of the Keynesian macroeconomic system, which has the best claim to orthodoxy in the capitalist world of the mid-twentieth century. The chapter takes up the two simpler models of a series of five, leaving the other three (which include interest and money) for chapter 7.

The first half of this chapter reviews the macroeconomic materials included in introductory economics textbooks. Keynesian Model I is limited to a purely private closed economy in a "state of nature" with all

---

[29] Buchanan goes on to show that the division of the burden is not affected by the *residence* of the bondholders—i.e., his result is the same for an externally held debt as for an internally held one. He also shows that his results are not affected by the *ex post* advisability of the deficit-financed projects, i.e., by the relation between the value of the public services and the value of the securities issued to finance them. (The total benefits to each generation are raised or lowered by these considerations, but not the intergeneration differential.)

investment autonomous. The mechanics of this model, centering in the multiplier, are presented with and without recourse to the differential calculus. Among the policy applications attempted at this stage are the effects on consumption of income redistribution among economic groups with different consumption propensities, the paradoxes of spending and saving (including forced saving), and the analysis of expansion and contraction gaps. On the technical side, we pay more attention to the distinction between *ex ante* and *ex post* relations (between saving and investment), to problems of stability, and to "rotation multipliers" than do most introductory treatments. Also, a number of multiplier "conundrums" are considered, and one of them is applied to the case of pump-priming.

Keynesian Model II introduces the government and one aspect of public policy. This is fiscal policy, dealing with aggregate expenditures and taxes (both net of public transfer payments). The mechanics of the model and its train of multipliers are again explored on two levels. The policy applications include the balanced-budget multiplier in two forms, the principle of overfinance in gap analysis, built-in and formula flexibility, and "Morgenthau's dream" of continuous deficits continuously liquidating themselves by multiplier effects. The final section compares four rival views on the issue of whether or not the "burden" of a public debt can be shifted to future generations—the "sound finance" view that there *is* a shiftable burden, the "functional finance" view that there is none (unless the debt is held by foreigners), and two compromise suggestions, by Ricardo and Buchanan respectively.

Appendix 6a

MODEL I IN AN INTERNATIONAL SYSTEM

We can introduce international economics into our Keynesian Model I in an elementary way.[1] Let the international economic system consist of two countries, 1 and 2. Let Country 1 be "our country," and let it be *active*; that is to say, let all changes and disturbances originate there. Country 2, "the rest of the world," is then passive, responding to changes in Country 1.

---

[1] This treatment is based on Jaroslav Vanek, "Appendix E—The Foreign Trade Multiplier," in Charles P. Kindleberger, *International Economics*, 3rd ed. (1963). Vanek and Kindleberger, however, limit C and I to expenditure on domestic goods.

Each country has a linear import function ($M = M_o + mY$)[2] with m the marginal propensity to import (m.p.i.) and (M/Y) $= m + (M_o/Y)$ the average propensity to import (a.p.i.). These import functions imply that each country's imports depend only upon its own income and that the relative prices of imports and other goods are unimportant. (Such assumptions depart from the microeconomic theory of international trade.)

With real exports denoted by X, we have $X_1 = M_2$ and vice versa. Applying Keynesian Model 1 and the two import functions to the two countries' source equations for income, we have:

$$Y_1 = C_1 + I_1 + X_1 - M_1 = C_1 + I_1 + M_2 - M_1$$

$$Y_1 = C_{o1} + I_{o1} + M_{o2} - M_{o1} + c_1Y_1 + m_2Y_2 - m_1Y_1$$

and

$$Y_2 = C_{o2} + I_{o2} + M_{o1} - M_{o2} + c_2Y_2 + m_1Y_1 - m_2Y_2$$

We may write autonomous expenditure A in each country as:

$$A_1 = C_{o1} + I_{o1} + M_{o2} - M_{o1}$$

and

$$A_2 = C_{o2} + I_{o2} + M_{o1} - M_{o2}$$

so that:

$$Y_1 = A_1 + c_1Y_1 + m_2Y_2 - m_1Y_1$$

---

[2] Income Y includes net exports ($X - M$) so that it is more accurate to write:

$$M = M_o + m(Y + M)$$

whence

$$M = \frac{M_o}{1 - m} + \frac{m}{1 - m} Y.$$

We ignore this refinement here.

and

$$Y_2 = A_2 + c_2 Y_2 + m_1 Y_1 - m_2 Y_2$$

letting $1 - c = s$ in each country we obtain:

$$(s_1 + m_1) Y_1 - m_2 Y_2 = A_1$$

$$-m_1 Y_1 + (s_2 + m_2) Y_2 = A_2 \qquad \text{(6A.1)}$$

We are primarily interested in consistent solutions for Y_1 and Y_2. Equations (6A.1) can be solved determinantally for these variables. (They can of course be solved by other methods as well.):

$$Y_1 = \frac{\begin{vmatrix} A_1 & -m_2 \\ A_2 & s_2 + m_2 \end{vmatrix}}{\begin{vmatrix} s_1 + m_1 & -m_2 \\ -m_1 & s_2 + m_2 \end{vmatrix}} = \frac{(s_2 + m_2) A_1 + m_2 A_2}{s_1 s_2 + m_1 s_2 + m_2 s_1} = \frac{\left(1 + \dfrac{m_2}{s_2}\right) A_1 + \dfrac{m_2}{s_2} A_2}{s_1 + m_1 + m_2 \dfrac{s_1}{s_2}}$$

and likewise

$$Y_2 = \frac{\left(1 + \dfrac{m_1}{s_1}\right) A_2 + \dfrac{m_1}{s_1} A_1}{s_2 + m_2 + m_1 \dfrac{s_2}{s_1}} \qquad \text{(6A.2)}$$

From equations (6A.1–2) we can compute both own-country multipliers $\partial Y_i / \partial A_i$ or μ_{ii} and cross-country multipliers $\partial Y_i / \partial A_j$ or μ_{ij}.

$$\mu_{11} = \frac{1 + \dfrac{m_2}{s_2}}{s_1 + m_1 + m_2 \dfrac{s_1}{s_2}} \qquad\qquad \mu_{22} = \frac{1 + \dfrac{m_1}{s_1}}{s_2 + m_2 + m_1 \dfrac{s_2}{s_1}}$$

$$\qquad \text{(6A.3)}$$

$$\mu_{12} = \frac{\dfrac{m_2}{s_2}}{s_1 + m_1 + m_2 \dfrac{s_1}{s_2}} \qquad\qquad \mu_{21} = \frac{\dfrac{m_1}{s_1}}{s_2 + m_2 + m_1 \dfrac{s_2}{s_1}}$$

Equations (6A.3) treat dA_1 and dA_2 as mutually independent. This is a special case, since M_{o2} is a component of A_1 and vice versa. To generalize

somewhat, we recall that Country 1 is the "active" country, where initial changes in autonomous spending occur to which the "passive" country reacts. Suppose first that Country 1's exports are competitive with Country 2's production, and that the rise in A_1 is a rise in the physical quantity of these exports. Then, when A_1 rises by one unit, some proportion λ of the increase will be at Country 2's expense—a fall in A_2 by λ units, λ being usually a negative fraction. (Similarly, a unit fall in A_1 would then result in an λ-unit rise in A_2.) If Country 1's exports are complementary with Country 2's production, as in raw-material cases, λ would be positive if a rise in A_1 represents a rise in physical quantity, but negative if it represents a rise in relative price. (We therefore have four cases. To which of them does the oil crisis of the 1970's correspond, with OPEC in the "active" role of Country 1?) In general:

$$dA_2 = \lambda dA_1 \qquad (6A.4)$$

with no similar expression applying to A_1 in the active country, and with λ taking either sign. Only (μ_{11}, μ_{21}) of the multipliers of (6A.3) remain relevant:

$$\mu_{11} = \frac{1 + (1 - \lambda)\dfrac{m_2}{s_2}}{s_1 + m_1 + m_2 \dfrac{s_1}{s_2}} \qquad \mu_{21} = \frac{(1 + \lambda)\dfrac{m_1}{s_1} + \lambda}{s_2 + m_2 + m_1 \dfrac{s_2}{s_1}} \qquad (6A.5)$$

Two important special cases of (6A.5) arise when the international coefficient λ approaches zero and -1. As λ approaches zero, we return to our earlier solutions of (6A.2–3). At another extreme, where λ approaches -1, as by direct economic aggression on the part of Country 1, (6A.4–5) simplify to:

$$Y_1 = \frac{A_1 + \dfrac{m_2}{s_2}A_{o2}}{s_1 + m_1 + m_2 \dfrac{s_1}{s_2}} \qquad Y_2 = \frac{\left(1 + \dfrac{m_1}{s_1}\right)A_{o2} - A_1}{s_2 + m_2 + m_1 \dfrac{s_2}{s_1}}$$

$$\mu_{11} = \frac{1}{s_1 + m_1 + m_2 \dfrac{s_1}{s_2}} \qquad \mu_{21} = \frac{-1}{P_2 + m_2 + m_1 \dfrac{g_2}{s_1}}$$

The qualitative economic implications of this analysis should not be lost in the algebra: (1) In member countries of an international system, m.p.i.

as well as m.p.s. (or m.p.c.) are involved in multipliers: (2) Shifts in X_o and M_o generate multipliers like other components of A. The multipliers of X_o and M_o are equal numerically, but opposite in sign. (3) It is therefore legitimate to compute trade-balance multipliers for changes in $X_o - M_o$, but not for changes in $X - M$; (4) All these multipliers depend on both countries' propensities to save and to import. It is erroneous to ignore the rest of the world in estimating even domestic multipliers for countries in an open economy. (Furthermore, the rest of the world should be considered as a set of consumers and savers, not merely as importers and exporters.) (5) When $s_1 \neq s_2$ and $m_1 \neq m_2$, world income $Y_1 + Y_2$ is not independent of its international distribution. With involuntary unemployment in both countries, world income is raised by transfers from the country with the higher *leakage coefficient* $(s + m)$ to the country with the lower leakage coefficient, and lowered by a transfer in the opposite direction.

Appendix 6b

THE *EX POST* BALANCED BUDGET MULTIPLIER

In this appendix we derive a value for the ex *post* balanced budget multiplier μ_b. This multiplier has been defined as the effect upon the national income of an equal change in both taxes (net of transfers), T, and public expenditures (for goods and services), G. We shall employ our standard tax equation $T = T_o + tY$, as estimated from the (unknown) value of the national income Y *after* the budgetary change has worked itself out.[1] The conventional wisdom of practical men regards this multiplier as zero, and some economists have calculated "deficit multipliers" based on the size of the budgetary deficit or surplus. The actual value of μ_b in this case, however, is unity.

These conditions can be expressed as a differential equation:

$$dG = dT = dT_o + (Y\, dt + t\, dY)$$

from which we shall use the expression for Y dt:

$$Y\, dt = dG - dT_o - t\, dY \qquad (6B.1)$$

---

[1] The proof is adapted from R. G. D. Allen, *Macroeconomic Theory* (1967), p. 147.

Because nonfiscal variables are held constant, we may use a simplified function:

$$Y = Y(G, T) = Y(G, T_o, t)$$

from which we have

$$dY = \frac{\partial Y}{\partial G} dG + \frac{\partial Y}{\partial T_o} dT_o + \frac{\partial Y}{\partial t} dt = \mu dG + \mu_{T_o} dT_o + \mu_t dt$$

Substituting multiplier values from (6.16, 6.18, and 6.19), we obtain:

$$dY = \mu[dG - (cdT_o + cY\ dt)] = \frac{dG - c(dT_o + Ydt)}{1 - c + ct} \qquad \text{(6B.2)}$$

We next substitute for Y dt its value from (6B.1), and multiply through by $1 - c + ct$:

$$(1 - c + ct)dY = dG - c(dT_o + dG - dT_o - t\ dY)$$

The terms in c dT_o cancel on the right, and there is a term in ct dY on each side. What remains is only:

$$(1 - c)dY = (1 - c)dG$$

whence, if $c \neq 1$:

$$dY = dG = dT$$

which is the condition for a unitary value of the balanced budget multiplier μ_b.

Chapter 7

Further Keynesian Models

PROSPECTUS

The full title of Lord Keynes's masterpiece is *The General Theory of Employment Interest and Money.* Our introduction to Keynes in the last chapter has had virtually nothing to say about either interest or money. The present chapter will fill this lacuna.

Figure 7-1 presents the Keynesian system as an oversimplified scheme of one-way causation, rather than one of mutual interaction or general equilibrium.[1] Capitalized terms are the principal *causative factors* (prime movers) of the system. Omitted from chapter 6, they will be explained in later sections of the present chapter. Italicized terms are the principal *effects* of the system; we have already encountered them. Arrows indicate directions of causation; parentheses indicate mechanisms of causation.

The lacuna in our exposition of the Keynesian system—the roles of interest and money—will be filled by stages. Model III, specifically, will introduce interest and derive an IS locus of values of national income and interest rates, such that planned (*ex ante*) saving equals planned (*ex ante*) investment. Models IV–V will introduce (real) money, first (Model IV) in fixed supply, and then (Model V) in variable supply. Models IV–V will derive an LM locus of national income and interest rates, such that the demand for real money balances equals the real stock of money. An IS-LM confrontation was worked out originally by Sir John Hicks,[2] is sometimes called the "Hicksian cross"; we shall also refer to it as the "Islamic diagram."

The introduction of monetary variables (Models IV–V) raises an important question for macroeconomic policy. Is money important in the Keynesian prescription? Or is fiscal policy all that matters, as per Model II? Policy recommendations—Keynesian, post-Keynesian, or anti-Keynesian—

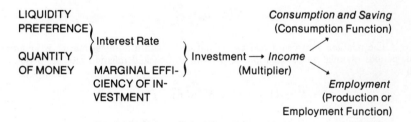

Figure 7-1 Diagrammatic Summary of the Keynesian System

---

[1] For a more elaborate diagram, see Dudley Dillard, *Economics of J. M. Keynes* (1948), p. 49, fig. 3.

[2] John R. Hicks, "Mr. Keynes and the Classics: A Suggested Interpretation," *Econometrica* (April 1937), reprinted in M. Gerald Mueller, *Readings in Macroeconomics,* no. 10.

that stress the monetary side are often lumped together under the head of "monetarism." "Fiscalism," by contrast, is a label that lumps together proponents of the opposite policy line. As a statistical matter if nothing more, the proportion of self-styled Keynesians is substantially higher in the fiscalist than in the monetarist ranks, while the proportion of self-styled anti-Keynesians is higher among the monetarists.

KEYNESIAN MODEL III: VARIABLE INVESTMENT

Our previous treatment of investment as entirely exogenous is un-satisfactory, since (if not *the* most volatile element) investment is *among* the most volatile elements in income.[3] This can be seen by comparing national income accounts for periods of prosperity and recession—the in-vestment total varies more widely than consumption. Yet in our first two Keynesian models, private investment was the plaything of entrepreneurial "animal spirits," while public expenditure varied only by reason of explicit policy decisions. How far can such characterizations take us?

We now relax the exogeneity assumption to the limited extent of acknowledging both real private investment and real public expenditure to be dependent upon a real rate of interest r.[4] Even this relaxation leaves the private investment function $I(r)$ highly volatile. In addition to pure animal spirits (a random variable), I may shift with Y itself,[5] with the rate

---

[3] One common measure of the volatility of a function is its coefficient of variation over a given time period. If the standard deviation of a variable x is denoted by σ_x and its arithmetic mean by M_x, its coefficient of variation is the quotient:

$$(\text{c.v.})_x = \frac{\sigma_x}{M_x}$$

[4] The relations between a real rate of interest r and a nominal rate r* is important in periods of inflation or deflation. If $\dot{p}$ is the anticipated inflation rate per period, we have:

$$1 + r^* = (1 + r)(1 + \dot{p}) \quad \text{whence} \quad r^* = r + \dot{p} + r\dot{p}$$

[5] Sensitivity of I to Y, as in an investment function of the form:

$$I = I_o + iY \qquad (i > 0)$$

gives us *induced* investment. In Models I–II, consideration of induced investment would raise multiplier values to what have been called *supermultipliers* or *expansion coefficients*, with:

$$\frac{1}{1 - c - i} \quad \text{replacing} \quad \frac{1}{1 - c}$$

in multiplier formulas.

of change in income dY/dt, with the rate of technical progress of the economy somehow estimated, with the "monetary environment" and its stability and/or with the relation between the real social capital stock K and the desired stock $\hat{K}$.[6] James Tobin stresses a ratio, which he denotes by q, between the *value* of total assets (estimated from the total value of bonds and equities on security markets) and the estimated *reproduction cost* of these assets. A high value of q—above, say, 1.10 or 1.15—encourages investment, while a value below 1.00 discourages investment. (Can you see why?) We ignore for the present such elements of volatility, sometimes called shift variables, even though their effects often appear to swamp those of the interest rate itself in econometric models, such as we will take up in chapter 8.

We shall lump I and G together in a single investment function with $d(I + G)/dr < 0$. In linear form; we assume:

$$I + G = I_o + G_o - ir \qquad (I > 0) \tag{7.1}$$

where i represents the slope of the investment function.

Economists call functions like (7.1) *marginal efficiency* functions as well as investment functions. The marginal efficiency of any investment (m.e.i.) is the *highest* interest rate r at which this investment is considered worthwhile. For a worthwhile (profitable) investment, the present value of the stream of anticipated returns resulting from that investment (with allowance for uncertainty and discounted at the interest rate under consideration) exceeds the cost of the investment, including the present values of whatever future expense stream the present investment may require. Any investment profitable at rate r is also profitable at any lower rate of interest. On a diagram like figure 7-2, the marginal efficiency function cannot slope upward because it gives a *ranking* of profitable investment projects; however, it may be vertical if the coefficient i of (7.1) is zero.

There is much unresolved dispute about the shapes of marginal efficiency (m.e.i.) or investment functions, both as related to aggregates like our I + G and to particular investment types, such as plant and equipment investment, inventory accumulation, and residential construction. The linear form (7.1) is a simplified special case. Under American conditions it is generally agreed that private residential construction, bond-financed public construction, and public utility investment[7] are relatively interest-

---

[6] Sensitivity of I to (dY/dt) is called the *acceleration principle*, and sensitivity to $(K - \hat{K})$ is called the *stock-adjustment principle*. These are two important, and to some extent rival, elements in empirical investment functions.

[7] Public utility companies may not count as costs, for rate-making purposes, principal and interest on "imprudent" investments. This doctrine is sometimes extended to

elastic. Externally financed business investment[8] seems to occupy an inter-mediate position. Internally financed business investment appears dom-inated by comptrollers' notions of "permanent" interest rates[9] and is relatively unaffected by short-term changes in market rates. It seems a reasonable generalization that large firms are less dependent than small ones upon external financing. Consequently policies of "tight money" and "credit squeeze" impede investment plans of large firms less than those of small and particularly of growing firms.

The curvatures as well as the slopes of m.e.i. functions are both uncertain and important for policy decisions. While, to repeat, we use in this chapter linear m.e.i. functions like figure 7-2a, this choice is for convenience only. A linear function has an infinite radius of curvature. Downward-sloping m.e.i. functions with high radii of curvature would justify policymakers in giving only secondary attention to the interest-rate effects of their decisions, because variations in r lead to uniform and predictable variations in I + G.

---

cover "imprudently high" interest cost on investments financed in periods of high interest rates.

[8] "External financing" may take the form of borrowing from banks, issuance of debt securities (bonds), or sale of equities (stock). "Internal financing" involves the ex-penditure of the firm's undistributed profits, its reserve for depreciation, contingencies, etc.

[9] **Digression:** The "permanent" values of economic variables play important roles in much post-Keynesian thinking. For an interest rate r, the corresponding permanent rate r^p is presumed to change only slowly between periods $t-1$ and t. One common assumption uses the equation:

$$r_t^p - r_{t-1}^p = \beta(r_t - r_{t-1}^p)$$

where β is a positive fraction $(0 < \beta < 1)$.

To express r^p in terms of observed values exclusively, we write:

$$r_{t-1}^p = \beta r_{t-1} + (1-\beta)r_{t-2}^p$$

whence:

$$r_t^p = \beta[r_t + (1-\beta)r_{t-1}] + (1-\beta)^2 r_{t-2}^p$$

Repeating over n periods, the infinite series yields, by mathematical induction:

$$r_t^p = \beta[r_t + (1-\beta)r_{t-1} + (1-\beta)^2 r_{t-2} + \cdots + (1-\beta)^n r_{t-n}] + (1-\beta)^{n+1} r_{t-n-1}^p$$

Since β is a fractional parameter, the last term can be dropped as near zero, giving us an estimate of r_t^p in terms of observed values, $r_t, r_{t-1}, r_{t-2}, \cdots, r_{t-n}$. (We leave for chapter 8 the problem of the estimation of the parameter β.)

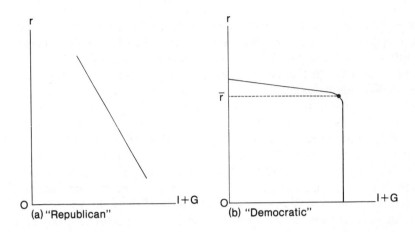

Figure 7-2 "Republican" and "Democratic" Marginal Efficiency Functions

Some such view is associated with economic conservatism; in the United States, with the Republican party. A rival position can be translated into figure 7-2b, and is associated with the liberal wing of the American Democratic party. In this view, the real (usually also the nominal) interest rate should always be kept low, mainly to avoid "unjust enrichment" of "finance capital" but also because interest rate increases are "too hot to handle."[10] Below some critical value r̄, the m.e.i. is vertical; changes in r have little or no effect upon I + G, so why permit them at all? At the critical value r̄, which is both unknown and variable, increases in r choke off I + G in dangerously large amounts. This m.e.i. function has a low radius of curvature, and suggests for policy that r not be allowed to rise. (Keynes himself favored policies that would permit r to fall to near-zero, and hoped for "the euthanasia of the rentier.")

Digression: In the *General Theory* Keynes wrote in terms of the marginal efficiency of *capital* (m.e.c.) rather than of m.e.i. (At the same time, he stressed a distinction between marginal efficiency and the conventional notion of marginal *productivity*; marginal efficiency is estimated over long periods, and includes the allowances for futurity and uncertainty that managers make in estimating the present values of cost and return streams.) There has subsequently arisen much discussion about the precise relationship between m.e.i. and m.e.c. One easy solution is to imagine that Keynes meant by m.e.c. what his followers were to call m.e.i. (When capital and

[10] There are an infinite number of market interest rates and regulated interest rates at any moment of time. Another policy problem arises, if r is to be used as a parameter, from the imperfect correlation between the various market rates. Compare Warren L. Smith, *Macroeconomics* (1970), pp. 280–294.

investment are considered net of depreciation and obsolescence, a change in I is also, except for its dimension, a change in K.) A more complex solution includes in m.e.i. dynamic considerations regarding the *speed of adjustment* of K to changes in r; m.e.c. does not consider speeds of adjustment. We adopt (as in figure 7-3) a compromise solution that identifies m.e.i. with m.e.c. are identical only in a special case, namely, when the actual capital stock K at the beginning of our period is precisely equal to the desired stock $\hat{K}$ at the ruling permanent interest rate. If we have at starting a capital shortage $(K < \hat{K})$, m.e.i. exceeds m.e.c., particularly at low interest rates, by a factor related to making up the arrears, slowly at high rates and quickly at low ones. Conversely, if the economy has excess capacity at starting $(K > \hat{K})$, m.e.i. falls short of m.e.c. by a factor related to "depreciating off" excess capacity quickly at high rates or slowly at low ones. In both cases of $K \neq \hat{K}$, m.e.i. appears more interest-elastic than m.e.c. As a matter of positive economics, m.e.i. is the more important of the two notions, when one deals with short-run problems.

We are ready for the formalities of Model III proper. It will not yield a solution for the equilibrium income Y_e, but only an equilibrium *function* or locus of (Y,r) combinations such that $[I + G = S + T]$ ex ante as well as ex post. From such a function or locus, we can determine Y_e only if the equilibrium interest rate r_e is known, and vice versa. We cannot determine both unknown equilibrium values at once. Our "function or locus of (Y,r) combinations" is usually called the IS function, with all variables real, from its $I = S$ ex ante property under conditions of budgetary balance. Another name is the CE (commodity equilibrium) function, since at each point we have ex ante equilibrium of total income and expenditure. (In an international economy we should have for each country, $[I + G + X = S + T + M]$.)

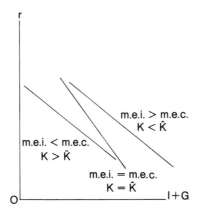

Figure 7-3 Marginal Efficiency Functions, m.e.i. and m.e.c.

In algebraic terms with linear functions, Model III differs from Model II only by including an interest rate term in the determination of I and G.

$$Y = C + I + G \tag{7.2}$$

$$C = C_0 + c(Y - T) \qquad (0 < c < 1) \quad (7.3)$$

$$T = T_0 + tY \qquad (0 < t < 1) \quad (7.4)$$

$$I = I_0 - i_1 r \qquad (i_1 > 0) \quad (7.5)$$

$$G = G_0 - i_2 r \qquad (i_2 > 0) \quad (7.6)$$

$$I + G = I_0 + G_0 - (i_1 + i_2)r = I_0 + G_0 - ir \qquad (i > 0) \quad (7.7)$$

$$A = C_0 + I_0 + G_0 {}^{11} \tag{7.8}$$

Substituting as in Model II, we can solve for Y as a function of r or for r as a function of Y. Both solutions represent the same IS function, which is linear and slopes downward. Either solution can be used as a formula for the IS function; the use of Y as dependent variable is the more common:

$$Y = \frac{A - cT_0}{1 - c + ct} - \frac{i}{1 - c + ct}\, r \tag{7.9a}$$

$$r = \frac{A - cT_0}{i} - \frac{1 - c + ct}{i}\, Y \tag{7.9b}$$

---

[11] The solution process is essentially review. We begin as before, substituting the tax function into the consumption function [here (7.4) into (7.3)]:

$$C = C_0 + c(Y - T_0 - tY) = C_0 - cT_0 + (c - ct)Y$$

then adding (7.7) and substituting in (7.2):

$$Y = C_0 - cT_0 + (c - ct)Y + I_0 + G_0 - ir$$

collecting terms, and using (7.8):

$$(1 - c + ct)Y = C_0 + I_0 + G_0 - cT_0 - ir = A - cT_0 - ir$$

from which (7.9a) follows at once. Alternatively, we may shift the term in ir to the l.h.s. and the term in Y to the r.h.s.:

$$ir = A - cT_0 - (1 - c + ct)Y$$

which gives (7.9b).

and

$$\frac{\partial r}{\partial Y} = -\frac{1 - c + ct}{i} < 0 \quad (\text{where } 1 - c + ct > 0 \text{ for stability}).$$

Our old multipliers can be computed from Model III and equation (7.9a). The familiar autonomous expenditure multipliers of chapter 6, involving the consumption function, tax function, and autonomous expenditures, are the same as in Model II. Two new multipliers are a shift multiplier with respect to the interest rate r and a rotation multiplier with respect to the slope i of the investment or m.e.i. function. We may call these multipliers μ_r and μ_i respectively:

$$\mu_r = \frac{\partial Y}{\partial r} = -\frac{i}{1 - c + ct} = -i\mu \quad \text{and} \quad \mu_i = \frac{\partial Y}{\partial i} = -\frac{r}{1 - c + ct} = -r\mu$$

It will be noticed that the denominators of these multipliers must be positive if they are to operate in the expected direction. It is for this reason that we expect the IS function to slope downward. If $(1 - c + ct)$ were negative, these multipliers would be "pathological." It is this result to which the stability condition alerts us. But including induced investment, either with or without the additional effect of the interest rate upon the consumption-investment decision, might rationalize in extreme cases an upward-sloping IS function. We should then rewrite (7.3) and (7.7) as:

$$C = C_o + c_1(Y - T) - c_2 r \tag{7.3a}$$

$$I + G = I_o + G_o - ir + jY \tag{7.7a}$$

and leave the remainder of the proof (together with explorations of possible policy significance) for the reader.

Digression: There are seven unknowns in Model III—Y, C, I, G, T, A, and r. To these, there correspond only six independent equations. The system (7.2–7.8) appears at first glance to provide a solution, since it includes seven equations. However, (7.7) is the sum of (7.5) and (7.6), so that only two of the equations (7.5–7.7), inclusive, are independent of each other, and Model III is an open one. The statement that Model III is not closed is equivalent to the statement that equations (7.9a–b) cannot be solved for Y and r in terms of the constants of the model, but can only be solved for Y in terms of r and vice versa.

A geometric solution like figure 7-4 illustrates quite readily the effects of shifts in our various functions. This diagram is a four-quadrant one, of the type already encountered in chapter 4. If we reserve the NE quadrant on this diagram for the IS function itself, with horizontal axis Y and vertical axis r, we can allot the other quadrants consecutively. Proceeding in the clockwise direction, we have:

1. SE, horizontal axis Y and vertical axis $S + T$. A saving-plus-tax function, which equals $Y - C$ by the source equation for income (chapter 3). Its algebraic formulation is:

$$S + T = Y - C = Y - [C_o + c(Y - T_o - tY)] =$$
$$- (C_o - cT_o) + (1 - c + ct)Y$$

which is linear. Its upward slope is necessitated by our stability condition, that is,

$$\frac{\partial(S + T)}{\partial Y} = (1 - c + ct) > 0$$

2. SW, horizontal axis $I + G$ and vertical axis $S + T$. The ex-post saving-investment identity, indicated as a 45-degree ray through the origin.

3. NW, horizontal axis $I + G$ and vertical axis r. The marginal efficiency function in the form (7.7):

$$I + G = I_o + G_o - ir \qquad \left(\frac{\partial r}{\partial(I + G)} = -\frac{1}{i} < 0\right)$$

While the IS function is readily derivable by either algebraic or geometric manipulations, these manipulations may conceal its economic meaning. To help understand the economics, the reader should verify on his own the reasons for and directions of the shift in IS that would result from each of the changes considered in table 7-1 on page 127.

QUANTALUMCUMQUE CONCERNING MONEY

The indeterminacy of Model III is the price we pay for introducing the interest rate while failing to introduce the other market it most directly concerns—the money market. As it turns out, all we need to "reclose" the economy and render our system of equations determinate is the explicit introduction of money. We have been inching in this direction already.

126

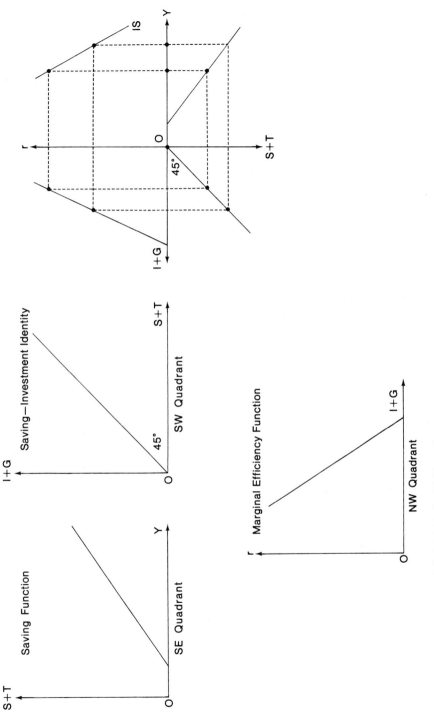

Figure 7-4 Keynesian Model III: the IS Function

Table 7-1
Model III: Shifts in the IS Function

Change	Quadrant Primarily Affected	Shifts in IS Function (Y, given r)	(r, given Y)
Increased "business confidence"	NW	rise	rise
Increased public expenditures for goods and services	NW	rise	rise
Increased public transfer payments	SE	rise	rise
Increased world demand for domestic exports*	NW	rise	rise
Increased domestic demand for imports*	SE	fall	fall
Increased protection for home industry*	SE	rise	rise
Increased thriftiness	SE	fall	fall
Increased taxation	SE	fall	fall

* For purposes of this exercise, the S + T axis should be labelled S + T + M and the I + G axis, I + G + X.

For example, any *ex ante* excess of saving over investment may represent an increased demand for money (increased *ex ante* hoarding), and any *ex ante* excess of investment over saving may represent a decreased demand for money or increased *ex ante* dishoarding.[12] As for the supply of money, we begin by considering it fixed in real terms or as varying proportionately with the price level in nominal terms. (The real money supply is made variable in Model V.)

Introduction of money into macroeconomic analysis does not require a complete course on monetary theory, or on banking and finance. At the same time, borrowing from these disciplines is unavoidable, as are evasions of their unsolved problems. In macroeconomics, we shall suppose that we know unequivocally what money is, and also that the "moneyness" or liquidity of all monetary forms is the same.

A commodity has a high *liquidity* if its holder feels a near-perfect probability of receiving a real price for it at least equal to its present real price

---

[12] From this point on, we usually speak of investment in the broad sense of I + G + X or I + G + (X − M), and of saving in the broad sense of S + T or S + T + M. We shall also use M as a symbol for the real money stock; the context should clarify whether M means "money" or "imports" in any particular discussion.

at the moment he desires to dispose of it. In identifying certain goods as money, we are supposing the existence of one or more commodities that have high liquidity, and whose utility to consumers and productivity to business firms depends primarily upon this liquidity attribute. Additionally, we suppose that no monetary commodity bears significant nominal interest, although its real rate of return is positive in deflation and negative in inflation.[13] We admit, of course, the existence of money-substitutes or near-moneys, mainly interest-bearing liquid assets such as short-term public securities, deposits in savings banks, savings and loan shares, etc. At the same time, we assume a "break in the chain of substitutes" for any monetary commodity; this break leaves no doubt as to which assets are monetary and which are not. We also assume these money substitutes or near-moneys to be complementary in demand with other interest-bearing assets as against money. In other words, when a change in the interest rate changes the relative attractiveness of money and interest-bearing capital assets generally, these "interest-bearing capital assets" include money-substitutes or near-moneys.

Digression: In most communities, the distinction between money and other commodities is by no means clear. In the U.S., for example, the conventional definition of money includes only currency held by the public outside banks, plus demand deposits other than interbank ones. Many economists, notably Milton Friedman, have advocated inclusion of savings deposits in commercial banks (which are often treated in practice like demand deposits) but not in other institutions. Still broader definitions, including other sorts of liquid assets, have been employed in statistical studies by other economists. These are also attempts at complex definitional forms, which add a number of components, weighted by econometrically-estimated "degrees of moneyness."

We have said that the demand for investment goods as a function of the rate of interest is often called a marginal efficiency function. Similarly, the Keynesian term for the demand for money is called a *liquidity*, or *liquidity preference*, function. The liquidity preference function represents not only active and conscious demand for money as a consumption or investment good, but also a large passive and inert residual after demands for other resources are met. Functionally speaking, liquidity preference is usually related both to the national income Y and the interest rate r, as a first approximation. The higher the income level Y, the more the amount of

---

[13] If money bears interest at a real rate ρ—which may be negative under certain "stamped money" schemes—the terms of our models require respecification as $r - \rho$.

money demanded. Money, in other words, is what microeconomists call a normal rather than an inferior good. (This result is entirely plausible.) On the other hand, the higher the interest rate, the higher is the cost of holding money—meaning the alternative or opportunity cost in terms of interest income foregone. Accordingly, the amount of money demanded is expected to move inversely to the rate of interest. Using the symbol L to represent a liquidity function we write:

$$M = L(Y,r) \qquad \left(\frac{\partial L}{\partial Y} > 0,\ \frac{\partial L}{\partial r} \leq 0\right) \qquad (7.10)$$

Many writers specify the liquidity function (7.10) more precisely. They consider (7.10) a *separable* function, meaning that it is decomposable into one function of Y alone and another function of r alone, with interaction terms neglected. This interpretation is particularly convenient for the graphical analysis of our models, since our geometry will assume strict separability. We, therefore, adopt the following liquidity function:

$$M = L_1(Y) + L_2(r) \qquad \left(\frac{dL_1}{dY} > 0,\ \frac{dL_2}{dr} \leq 0\right) \qquad (7.11)$$

The function L_1 represents the demand for money balances for transaction purposes. Keynes separated the demand for ordinary transactions from the demand for extraordinary (large or unanticipated) transactions, such as loan repayments, illnesses, accidents, unusual bargains. Only the first sort of demand he called *transactions* demand proper. For the second sort of demand he used the term *precautionary* demand. (Our L_1 abandons his distinction.) The function L_2 represents what Keynes called the speculative motive for holding money balances; it is sometimes called *liquidity preference proper*. M_1 is a statistical estimate of the amount of money held by individuals and firms for transactions (and precautionary) motives related primarily to the level of income; M_2 is a statistical estimate of the amount held by individuals and firms for speculative motives related primarily to the interest rate. (No coin, bill, or bank deposit bears any label allocating it to M_1 or to M_2.)

It seems paradoxical to reckon the holding of money as speculative. The term "speculation" is usually reserved for holdings of questionable oil stock and water-logged real estate. To Keynes, however, the holding of monetary assets had speculative aspects; one might hold money believing that interest rates would rise or that the price level would fall. This perfectly rational behavior can act as a hedge against capital losses incurred by

buying other assets too soon. It is also clear that Keynes thought of trans-action and precautionary demands for money as dependent primarily on income, and speculative demand as dependent primarily on interest rates. How seriously he would have taken the extreme separability assumption of (7.11) is uncertain.[14]

More controversial is another Keynesian specification, this time applying to the speculative demand function L_2 of (7.11). According to this specifi-cation, at a low but positive value of r—possibly about two percent—individuals and firms will hold unlimited quantities of money in the speculative belief that the interest rate must soon rise, and in the judgment that the subjective value of liquidity is more than two cents on the dollar. At two percent, therefore, any monetary expansion will be absorbed entirely in speculative balances rather than in increasing the level of economic activity. This is the doctrine of *absolute liquidity preference* or of the *liquidity trap*. It is similar to, but independent of, the Marxian concepts of "minimum rate of profit" and "liquidation crisis" that we met in chapter 5. As far as Keynes was concerned, a liquidity trap constituted a possible pit-fall of capitalism. It is unclear whether he felt that Britain was actually in such a trap even in the deep depression of the early 1930s.

KEYNESIAN MODEL IV: FIXED MONEY STOCK

Formally, Model IV is a supplement added to Model III. We sum-marize this "supplementary" aspect by including the IS function (7.9a) together with the strictly monetary equations (7.11-7.14) which follow:

$$M = L_1(Y) + L_2(r) \tag{7.11}$$

$$L_1(Y) = m_1Y \qquad (m_1 > 0) \tag{7.12}$$

$$L_2(r) = M_{20} - m_2r \qquad (r > r_0) \qquad (m_2 > 0) \tag{7.13a}$$

$$r = r_0 \tag{7.13b}$$

$$M_0 = M - M_{20} \tag{7.14}$$

$$Y = \frac{A - cT_0}{1 - c + ct} - \frac{i}{1 - c + ct}r \tag{7.9a}$$

---

[14] Standard inventory theory indicates that the volume of investment in inventories is related to the interest rate as an element in the cost of holding them. Any cash balance can be looked upon as a special type of inventory. A number of economists have therefore related the transactions demand for money to the interest rate; an influential example has been W. J. Baumol, "The Transactions Demand for Cash: An Inventory Theoretic Approach," *Quarterly Journal of Economics* (May 1952).

Constancy of the real quantity of money[15] and the separability of the liquidity function are both embodied in (7.11). Equation (7.12) combines the transaction and precautionary demands for money; m_1 is a structurally-determined positive constant, related inversely to the velocity of circulation V. The two branches of (7.13) correspond to a downward-sloping linear function (7.13a) with intercept M_{20} and slope $(-m_2)$ for interest rates above r_0, and a liquidity trap denoted by (7.13b) for $r = r_0$. Equation (7.14) introduces the term $M_0[=M - M_{20}]$ as a notational simplification. Equation (7.9a) was derived above in Model III.

No single solution of equations (7.11–7.14) is possible because (7.13) has two distinct and alternative branches. [In mathematical terms, (7.13) is not an algebraic function.] There are two separate solutions. The major solution is for (7.11, 7.12, 7.13a, and 7.14). The minor solution consists of (7.13b) alone, and is simply $r = r_0$. (The economic relation between the two solutions is the liquidity trap at r_0.) The major solution is not a single equilibrium value Y but a locus of (Y,r) values such that the demand and supply of money are in equilibrium *ex ante*, as with the IS function (7.9). Substituting (7.12) and (7.13a) into (7.11), we have:

$$M = m_1 Y + (M_{20} - m_2 r)$$

or, using (7.14):

$$M_0 = m_1 Y - m_2 r$$

which can be solved for Y in terms of r or vice versa:

$$Y = \frac{M_0}{m_1} + \frac{m_2}{m_1} r \qquad (r > r_0) \qquad \textbf{(7.15a)}$$

$$r = \frac{m_1}{m_2} Y - \frac{M_0}{m_2} \qquad (r > r_0) \qquad \textbf{(7.15b)}$$

The combination of (7.15a) for interest rates above r_0 and (7.13b) for $r = r_0$ is usually called the LM function, with L signifying liquidity and

---

[15] Constancy of M may result from either (1) a constant nominal quantity of money M* with a stable price level or (2) the operation of a strict quantity theory of money, by which changes in M* and p are proportional and the quotient (M*/p) or M, does not vary.

M money. Some writers call the same combination an ME (monetary equilibrium) function. The liquidity trap, if it exists, precludes $r < r_0$.

The interaction of LM and IS functions restores to our sequence of models the closure interrupted in Model III. Model III comprised seven unknowns with only six independent equations. Model IV has added three new monetary unknowns $[M_0; M_1 = L_1(Y); M_2 = L_2(r)]$, M itself being given. It has also added four new independent equations [(7.11), (7.12), (7.13a or 7.13b), and (7.14)]. The entire Model IV, therefore, is in balance with ten equations and ten unknowns.

We can derive the LM function and illustrate Model IV by means of another four-quadrant diagram, figure 7-5. We again reserve the NE quadrant for the LM function itself with horizontal axis Y and vertical axis r. (The IS function is superimposed from figure 7-4.) As before, we allocate the other three quadrants consecutively, proceeding clockwise:

1. SE, horizontal axis $\hat{Y}$, vertical axis M_1. The transaction and precautionary demand for money, equation (7.12).

2. SW, horizontal axis M_2, vertical axis M_1. Equation (7.11), with the constancy of M expressed by a 45-degree line.

3. NW, horizontal axis M_2, vertical axis r. The speculative demand for money, represented by the two forms of equation (7.13), including a liquidity trap at r_0.

The LM function is derived readily on figure 7-5. It has three branches and is therefore not an algebraic function.

1. A vertical branch at $Y = Y$ occurs at an interest rate high enough to eliminate the speculative demand $(M_{2_0} - m_2 r = 0)$. In this vertical branch, expenditure changes (shifts in IS) affect only r but not Y. This portion is sometimes misleadingly called the *classical range* because constancy of the real income level corresponds to the classical macroeconomics of chapter 4. (But does $\hat{Y}$ entail full employment?)

2. A horizontal branch at $r = r_0$ expresses, as we have said, the liquidity trap. This portion is sometimes called the *Keynesian range* because, in this range, shifts in IS affect only Y. This result also corresponds to extreme fiscalism, as distinguished from monetarism, as we shall see below.

3. A diagonal or intermediate branch between (1) and (2) is sometimes called the *intermediate range*. In this portion, changes in either IS or LM affect both Y and r. This intermediate range leaves the way open for both fiscal and monetary policy actions.

As with earlier models, the geometric manipulations involved in figure 7-5 may conceal the economic meaning. To help understand the economics

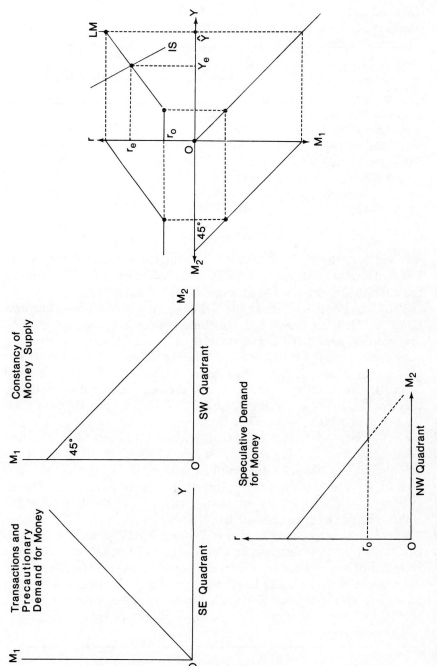

Figure 7-5 Keynesian Model IV: the LM Function

Table 7-2
Model IV: Shifts in LM Functions

Change	Quadrant Principally Affected	Shifts in LM	
		(Y, given r)	(r, given Y)
Increased "business confidence"	NW	rise	fall
Stock market crash	NW	fall	rise
Fall in general price level	SW	rise	fall
Spread of credit cards	SE	rise	fall
Abolition of check payment system	SE	fall	rise

involved here the reader may verify for himself the nature of the shift in LM that would result from each change considered in table 7-2, assuming the intermediate range of LM in which (7.15a–b) hold:

The IS-LM diagram forming the NE quadrant of figure 7-5 is sometimes called a "Hicksian cross" and sometimes an "Islamic diagram."[16] This diagram illustrates much Keynesian analysis, as we shall see. (At the same time, there is doubt of its fidelity to "the economics of Keynes.") At first glance (figure 7-6), it may seem inconsistent with the Keynesian cross of Model I, since nothing seems to prevent the two analyses from leading to different equilibrium income levels. In figure 7-6, the Hicksian cross (upper panel) gives us Y_e, while the Keynesian cross (lower panel) gives us Y_e' as our solution. The inconsistency is a chimera since the Keynesian-cross analysis takes the interest rate as given. If its value is a disequilibrium one like r_0 as distinguished from r_e, the Keynesian cross may be misleading until the expenditure function is shifted from the line labeled $(C + I)_{r_0}$ — which assumes an interest rate r_0 — to the line $(C + I)_r$, which is based on the equilibrium rate r_e.

The IS-LM intersection of figures 7-5 and 7-6 ($Y = Y_e$, $r = r_e$) is an equilibrium point. It may also be a full-employment point, but it need not be. The full employment income level Y_f (not shown) may lie either to the left or right of Y_e. It would be strange to find it lying to the right of $\hat{Y}$ in figure 7-5. This is because $\hat{Y}$ is reached with no money whatever held for speculative purposes; if any unemployment should persist at this income

---

[16] The eight quadrants of figures 7-4 and 7-5 are also called the "magnificent seven." Not "magnificent eight," because the NE quadrants of the two figures have the same axes and are combined into one.

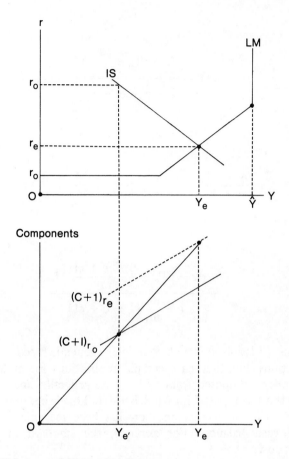

Figure 7-6   Hicksian and Keynesian Crosses

level with all money spent for transactions, the wage rate must be a dis-equilibrium one, or the labor supply function must be horizontal as in the wage-rigidity case of chapter 4.

Equilibrium values of Y and r are easily derived, if we know which of the three branches of LM is relevant. We usually use the intermediate one. In this case, we can solve for Y in terms of the parameters of Models III and IV, eliminating r by equating the IS and LM solutions for r in (7.9b) and (7.15b). In the same way, equating the IS and LM values for Y in (7.9a) and (7.15a), we can solve for r in terms of the same parameters. Thus:

$$\frac{A - cT_o}{i} - \frac{(1 - c + ct)}{i}Y = \frac{m_1}{m_2}Y - \frac{M_o}{m_2}$$

leads to:

$$Y = \frac{A - cT_o + \dfrac{i}{m_2} M_o}{1 - c + ct + i\dfrac{m_1}{m_2}} \tag{7.16a}$$

while

$$\frac{A - cT_o}{1 - c + ct} - \frac{ir}{1 - c + ct} = \frac{M_o}{m_1} + \frac{m_2}{m_1} r$$

gives us:

$$r = \frac{A - cT_o - \dfrac{1 - c + ct}{m_1} M_o}{i + \dfrac{m_2}{m_1} (1 - c + ct)} \tag{7.16b}$$

Equations (7.16a–b) are not completely general, based as they are on linear functions, but they have certain implications for multiplier values. The multipliers computed from (7.16a) are generally smaller in absolute value than those computed for Models I–III. This is because an additional leakage from the circular income flow has been recognized—leakage into speculative cash balances. For example, the standard multiplier μ or $(\partial Y/\partial A)$ is now:

$$\mu = \frac{\partial Y}{\partial A} = \frac{1}{1 - c + ct + i\dfrac{m_1}{m_2}} \tag{7.17}$$

which is smaller than $1/(1 - c)$ (Model I) or $1/(1 - c + ct)$ (Models II–III), unless i is zero, m_1 is zero, and/or m_2 is infinite. These exceptions imply, respectively, that r influences neither I nor G, that no money is held for transactions purposes, and that no money is held in speculative balances.

In addition, a monetary multiplier enters the analysis for the first time.[17]

---

[17] This monetary multiplier should not be confused with a better-known "money multiplier," which relates the changes in the total money stock to changes in the monetary base.

Defining it as μ_{M_o}, it is the effect on real income of changes in the money supply. Its value is:

$$\mu_{M_o} = \frac{\partial Y}{\partial M_o} = \frac{\dfrac{i}{m_2}}{1 - c + ct + i\dfrac{m_1}{m_2}} = \frac{i}{m_2}\mu \qquad (7.18)$$

which is positive unless i is zero or m_2 is infinite, cases considered above. In other words, money has a definite role in the Keynesian system.

MONETARISM AND FISCALISM

The monetarist-fiscalist controversy concerns the relative efficacy of these two types of policy. In the following paragraphs, we shall examine the controversy in a "contraction gap" context of increasing income from Y_e to Y_f. By an "expansionary" ("contractionary") shift in either IS or LM we shall mean a shift to the right (left) of whichever function we are talking about, on diagrams like figures 7-5 and 7-6, with a higher Y for any r. By fiscal policy or fiscalism we shall mean concentration of policy upon shifts in IS;[18] by monetary policy or monetarism we shall mean concentration upon shifts in LM.

In the usual case (the intermediate range of LM), either fiscal or monetary policy can be effective, or the two can be combined in any of an infinite number of combinations. The quantitative aspects of choosing the policy mix are called "fine tuning" the economy, usually in a derogatory tone. The effects of monetarist and fiscalist expansion differ principally in that monetarist expansion tends to lower the interest rate (encouraging investment and growth) whereas fiscalist expansion tends to raise the interest rate and concentrate expansion upon interest-inelastic consumption[19] and government expenditures. This difference in composition is no small matter.

In four extreme cases only one type of policy will be effective— fiscal or monetary, as the case may be. These cases are associated with horizontal or vertical IS or LM functions, and are summarized in figure 7-7. We should not be surprised to find ardent fiscalists assuming one or both

---

[18] Fiscalists often include, as elements of fiscalism, whatever shifts in LM may be necessary to keep r from rising (in an underemployment situation). Holding r at its previous level will eliminate the multiplier-attenuating effects of the i term in equations like (7.9a) and (7.16a).

[19] Interest-elastic consumption is confined largely to items purchased on the installment plan and other forms of consumer credit. Other consumption is relatively interest-inelastic.

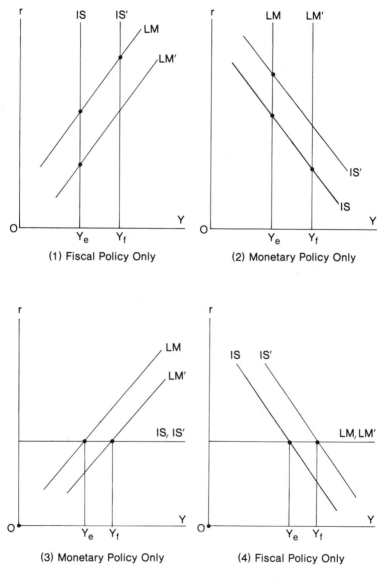

Figure 7-7　Monetary vs. Fiscal Policy

"fiscal policy only" cases, numbered (1) and (4) below and on the diagram, while ardent monetarists assume one or both "monetary policy only" cases (2) and (3).

1. *Vertical IS*. Here shifts of LM affect only r, so that only fiscal policy works upon Y, as in the shift from IS to IS'. This case is associated with

an absolute ceiling on the amount of profitable investment at any positive interest rate; such a ceiling is assumed by the "stagnation thesis" of much Keynesian thinking (see chapter 9).

2. *Vertical LM* (the so-called classical range). Here shifts in IS, arising from fiscal policy changes, affect only r and not Y. Furthermore, the composition of income shifts away from private investment and toward the government sector. Only monetary policy can affect Y, as in the shift from LM to LM'. Increases in G "crowd out" equivalent amounts of I.

3. *Horizontal IS.* Here a "horizontal shift" in IS has no meaning, and again only monetary policy is effective upon Y. This case corresponds to a classical interest theory, according to which the equilibrium rate of interest, determined by nonmonetary considerations such as "productivity and thrift," is perfectly income-elastic.

4. *Horizontal LM* (the so-called liquidity trap). Here a "horizontal shift" in LM has no meaning, and only fiscal policy is effective. The action of monetary policy in this case has been called "pushing on a string."

Digression: The ultimate choice between monetary and fiscal policy might be influenced by their impact on investment and growth. Two other considerations that influence this policy choice include personal income distribution and the balance of payments.

1. Distributional egalitarians hate high interest rates. Rightly or wrongly, they identify debtors with "the poor" and creditors with "the rich." They accordingly favor easy monetary policy to raise the income level, and tight fiscal policy to close expansion gaps. In the U.S., such thinking has been associated with populism and agrarianism. Creditor interests, including bankers and bondholders, tend to take the opposite tack in each case.

2. Suppose our country confronts a balance of payments problem with the rest of the world, in the sense that its international reserves are running low.[20] (We ignore the possibility of solving its problems through currency revaluation, protectionism, exchange controls, or similar measures.) At income level Y_e (on figure 7-8), it estimates that the interest rate r_b—which may be either above or below r_e—is the lowest rate that can attract enough foreign capital and retain enough domestic capital to keep its balance of payments in equilibrium with $Y = Y_e$. As Y rises above Y_e, the balance of trade deteriorates because of increased imports. To offset

---

[20] This is the ordinary meaning of "balance of payments difficulties." However, a number of countries (the U.S. in 1930–50, West Germany and Switzerland much of the time since 1960) have been embarrassed by the accumulation of undesired international reserves.

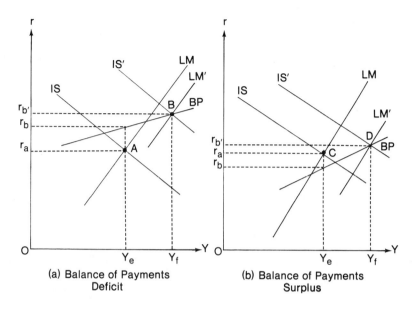

Figure 7-8   The Balance of Payment Function

increased imports, the interest rate consistent with balance of payments equilibrium must rise above r_b, to attract more capital. The upward-sloping function BP of figure 7-8 is a locus of (Y,r) points estimated to keep the country in balance of payments equilibrium. Points below BP on the diagram are eventually excluded on international economic grounds, since they involve balance of payments deficits. If income is to rise from Y_e to Y_f, the monetary-fiscal policy mix should be chosen to keep the interest rate at or above r_b. If the country has an undesired payments deficit (outflow of international reserves) as in figure 7-8a, its policy mix should include measures aimed at raising interest rates, attracting foreign capital, and restoring payments equilibrium. In the case drawn on the diagram, a combination of an easy monetary policy with an expansive fiscal policy moves the economy from A to B; an optimum combination of Y_f and payments equilibrium is reached at B. Such consistency, however, cannot always be counted upon; tight money must sometimes be combined with a loose budget to raise the interest rate sufficiently. If the country has an undesired payments surplus (accumulation of international reserves) as in figure 7-8b, its policy mix should include measures aimed at lowering interest rates, inducing capital outflow, and (again) restoring payments equilibrium. Once again, in the case drawn on the diagram, a combination of easy money with an expansive fiscal policy moves the economy from C to an optimal position at D. But again, such consistency cannot always be

relied on. In the real world, this time, budgetary tightness may have to be combined with easy money to keep the interest rate down.

QUANTALUMCUMQUE CONCERNING MONEY (PART II)

Now that we have finished our discussion of Model IV, Model V is looming over the horizon. Model V introduces variability in the money supply. As an overture to Model V, this section discusses the determination of the nominal quantity of money. With regard to this determination, there are two extreme positions, between which most economists compromise. At one extreme is the claim that, by manipulating what is sometimes called the *monetary base* or *high-powered money*, the monetary authorities have complete control over the entire money supply, when they choose to exercise it. At the other extreme is the view that the authorities' decisions can be counteracted by other public agencies, by domestic commercial banks, in international money markets ("Eurodollars"), and by the non-banking public, or are so hemmed in by legislation,[21] that the authorities are, if not entirely helpless, in no position for "fine tuning" operations.

The following treatment of the determination of the money supply is based upon the work of Cagan.[22] In this notation, the money supply M

---

[21] By "monetary authorities" are meant in most countries the Ministry of Finance and/or the Central Bank—in the U.S., the Treasury Department and the Federal Reserve System.

The legislative restrictions on their actions may be either anti-inflationary or anti-deflationary in intent. A requirement of convertibility of the national currency into gold is anti-inflationary. Imposition of upper limits on the authority's holding of gold or foreign exchange is anti-deflationary; so is the requirement that the authority support prices of public securities at predetermined levels.

[22] Phillip Cagan, *Determinants and Effects of Changes in the Stock of Money, 1875–1960*, ch. 1 (3).

The derivation of equation (7.19) proceeds as follows:

$$\text{Since } M = C + D \qquad 1 = \frac{C}{M} + \frac{D}{M} \quad \text{and} \quad \frac{D}{M} = 1 - \frac{C}{M}$$

The derivation of M/B is then:

$$\frac{M}{B} = \frac{C + D}{C + R} = \frac{\dfrac{C + D}{M}}{\dfrac{C + R}{M}} = \frac{1}{\dfrac{C}{M} + \dfrac{R}{D} \cdot \dfrac{D}{M}} = \frac{1}{\dfrac{C}{M} + \dfrac{R}{D}\left(1 - \dfrac{C}{M}\right)}$$

from which (7.19) follows at once.

If we differentiate (7.19) with respect to the three variables B, (R/D), and (C/M), the first of the three partial derivatives is positive and the other two are negative.

is composed of currency C and bank deposits D held by the public, while the monetary base B is composed of currency plus bank reserves R. In symbols, M = C + D while B = C + R. From these definitions, Cagan derives the relation:

$$M = \frac{B}{\frac{C}{M} + \frac{R}{D}\left(1 - \frac{C}{M}\right)} \qquad (7.19)$$

which makes M an increasing function of B and a decreasing function of both the banks' reserve ratio (R/D) and the currency ratio (C/M) that divides money holding between currency and bank deposits.

We concern ourselves with formulas like (7.19) because each independent variable (B,R/D,C/M) is controlled within limits by a different element in society. The monetary authorities control the monetary base B within limits set by the general government. The commercial banks control the reserve ratio (R/D), above a legal limit itself made flexible in practice by banks' borrowing privileges from the central bank. The general public controls the currency ratio (C/M), however unconsciously, by shifting its money supplies between currency and bank deposits. It follows that control over the money supply is distributed between three groups—four, if we include the nonmonetary sector of the general government, or five, if we include "the rest of the world." It is accordingly difficult to allocate the credit when monetary policy seems to be going well, or the blame when it seems to be going badly.

In keeping with the technique of analysis thus far adopted, we limit ourselves to a linear supply function of M alone. Using M^s to distinguish the money supply from the money demand M^d:

$$M^s = M^s_o + n_1 Y + n_2 r + g(G - T) \qquad (n_1 > 0), (n_2 > 0), (g > 0)$$
$$(7.20)$$

which embodies in the constant term M^s_o the decision of the monetary authorities and also the money supply of the preceding period. Equation (7.20) also implies that banks will expand their loans, and the deposits resulting from such loans, more readily the larger is national income, and the greater the rate of interest earned by loan expansion. It also says that, at any time, a certain fraction g of the public deficit is financed directly or

indirectly by central bank monetary expansion.[23] If there is a net surplus in the public sector, of course, this implies monetary contraction.

KEYNESIAN MODEL V: VARIABLE MONEY STOCK

Model V does not require much explanation, being little more than a rerun of Model IV. It substitutes the variable money supply of (7.20) for the constant money supply of (7.11). It also modifies or drops certain specialized assumptions relating to the liquidity function. These are (1) strict separability of the monetary demand L_1 and the speculative demand L_2, and (2) the liquidity trap. Instead of equations (7.12–7.13) we write a single equation expressing the demand for money as:

$$M^d = M_o^d + m_1 Y - m_2 r \tag{7.21}$$

and redefine M_o in (7.14) as:

$$M_o = M_o^s - M_o^d \tag{7.22}$$

These minor modifications give us, as Model V, a five-equation linear system. It includes (7.9a) from Models III–IV in simplified form ($G = G_o$, $T = T_o$, as per note 23).

$$M^s = M_o^s + n_1 Y + n_2 r + g(G - T) \tag{7.20}$$

$$M^d = M_o^d + m_1 Y - m_2 r \tag{7.21}$$

$$M_o = M_o^s - M_o^d \tag{7.22}$$

$$M^d = M^s \tag{7.23}$$

$$Y = \frac{A - cT}{1 - c} - \frac{ir}{1 - c} \tag{7.9a}$$

---

[23] Karl Brunner has proposed in correspondence that M^s be related to the weighted sum or integral of $[g(G - T)]$ over time rather than to the public deficit $(G - T)$ of its own period. This is correct, but we think of M_t^s as equalling $M_{t-1}^s + (dM^s/dt)$. With M_{t-1}^s embodying the integral and included in M_o^s, it does not seem unreasonable to relate the coefficient g to the current deficit alone.

We treat G and T in (7.20) as constants to simplify the algebra ($G = G_o$, $T = T_o$). As a result t, the marginal propensity to tax, goes to zero, and ($i = i_1$; $i_2 = 0$) in (7.5–6). The appendix to this chapter removes these simplifications.

For the Hicksian LM function, the first four equations (7.20–7.23) yield simple algebraic solutions for both Y and r:[24]

$$Y = \frac{M_o + g(G - T)}{m_1 - n_1} + \frac{m_2 + n_2}{m_1 - n_1} r \qquad (7.24a)$$

$$r = \frac{m_1 - n_1}{m_2 + n_2} Y - \frac{M_o + g(G - T)}{m_2 + n_2} \qquad (7.24b)$$

Simultaneous solution of equations (7.9b) and (7.24b) gives us Y_e, while simultaneous solution of equations (7.9a) and (7.24a) gives us r_e. These values satisfy both the IS and the LM conditions. That is to say, they provide both equality of planned saving and investment and equality of the planned demand and supply of money. The results appear formidable, but are derived without difficulty from simple equations:[25]

---

[24] A simple derivation begins by subtracting (7.21) from (7.20). By (7.23), the l.h.s. of the difference is zero, and the constant term on the r.h.s. is M_o by (7.22). This leaves:

$$0 = M_o + (n_1 - m_1)Y + (m_2 + n_2)r + g(G - T)$$

Moving the term in Y to the l.h.s., this becomes:

$$(m_1 - n_1)Y = M_o + (m_2 + n_2)r + g(G - T)$$

from which (7.24a) follows at once. Or, leaving only the term in r on the r.h.s., an alternative development gives:

$$(m_1 - n_1)Y - [M_o + g(G - T)] = (m_2 + n_2)r$$

which yields (7.24b).

[25] To derive (7.25a), we equate (7.9b) and (7.24b):

$$\frac{A - cT}{i} - \frac{1 - c}{i} Y = \frac{m_1 - n_1}{m_2 + n_2} Y - \frac{M_o + g(G - T)}{m_2 + n_2}$$

multiply by $i(m_2 + n_2)$, and collect terms in Y on the r.h.s.:

$$(m_2 + n_2)(A - cT) + i[M_o + g(G - T)] = [(m_2 + n_2)(1 - c) + i(m_1 - n_1)]Y$$

The initial solution for Y is:

$$Y = \frac{(m_2 + n_2)(A - cT) + i[M_o + g(G - T)]}{(m_2 + n_2)(1 - c) + i(m_1 - n_1)}$$

$$Y = \frac{A - cT + \dfrac{i[M_o + g(G - T)]}{m_2 + n_2}}{1 - c + \dfrac{i(m_1 - n_1)}{m_2 + n_2}} \qquad (7.25a)$$

$$r = \frac{A - ct - \dfrac{1 - c}{m_1 - n_1}[M_o + g(G - T)]}{i + \dfrac{m_2 + n_2}{m_1 - n_1}(1 - c)} \qquad (7.25b)$$

Of the multiplicity of multipliers that can be derived from (7.25a), the most important are the standard multiplier μ for autonomous expenditure generally, a new and special multiplier μ_G for public spending specifically, and the monetary multiplier μ_{M_o}. Their values are cumbersome compared to the earlier ones we have encountered:

$$\mu = \frac{\partial Y}{\partial A} = \frac{1}{1 - c + \dfrac{i(m_1 - n_1)}{m_2 + n_2}} \qquad (7.26)$$

$$\mu_G = \frac{\partial Y}{\partial G} = \left(1 + \frac{gi}{m_2 + n_2}\right)\mu \qquad (7.27)$$

$$\mu_{M_o} = \frac{\partial Y}{\partial M_o} = \frac{i}{m_2 + n_2}\mu \qquad (7.28)$$

but division of numerator and denominator by $(m_2 + n_2)$ gives (7.25a).

To derive (7.25b), we equate (7.9a) and (7.24a)

$$\frac{A - cT}{1 - c} - \frac{ir}{1 - c} = \frac{M_o + g(G - T)}{m_1 - n_1} + \frac{m_2 + n_2}{m_1 - n_1}r$$

multiply by $(m_1 - n_1)(1 - c)$, and collect terms in r on the r.h.s.:

$$(m_1 - n_1)(A - cT) - (1 - c)[M_o + g(G - T)] =$$
$$[(1 - c)(m_2 + n_2) + i(m_1 - n_1)]r$$

The initial solution for r is:

$$r = \frac{(m_1 - n_1)(A - cT) - (1 - c)[M_o + g(G - T)]}{i(m_1 - n_1) + (1 - c)(m_2 + n_2)}$$

but division of numerator and denominator by $(m_1 - n_1)$ gives (7.25b).

These multipliers are somewhat larger than the corresponding multipliers of Model IV. This is because they include a "negative leakage" or "injection" in the positive response of the money supply to the "needs of trade" as manifest in changes of Y. In addition, the multiplier for G becomes larger than the multipliers for other autonomous expenditure elements like C_o and I_o because of the monetary response to changes in the public deficit. The multipliers for taxation also have larger (negative) values for the same reason; for example:

$$\mu_T = -\left(c + \frac{gi}{m_2 + n_2}\right)\mu \qquad (7.29)$$

In geometric terms (figure 7-9) we leave the domain of four-quadrant diagrams, and enter a domain where LM functions need no longer slope upward. On the left-hand panel of figure 7-9, several demand and supply functions for money are labelled L_i and M_i respectively, and expressed as functions of r alone. However, the subscript i (i = 1,2,3,) is an index of the income level Y_i on the right hand panel, with $Y_2 = Y_e$. The sign of the slope of the locus determined by the (L_i, M_i) intersections on the left panel is also the slope of the LM function on the right panel. Referring back to the algebra of equation (7.24a), the normal upward slope of LM implies $m_1 > n_1$; in words, this implies that the demand for money is more

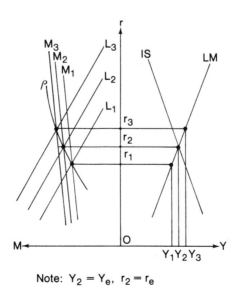

Note: $Y_2 = Y_e$, $r_2 = r_e$

Figure 7-9   LM Derivation—Variable Money Supply

sensitive to income changes than is the supply. The diagram shows this standard case, with the L_i more widely spaced than the M_i; the opposite case is by no means impossible.

STABILITY CONSIDERATIONS

In our discussion of the Islamic diagram, we have been assuming that a downward-sloping IS function and an upward-sloping LM function ensure static stability.[26] We have also been assuming that one of IS or LM, but not both simultaneously, could become horizontal or vertical without disturbing stability. Now we find in Model V the suggestion that LM might slope negatively. It is time, therefore, for a fuller discussion of macrostatic stability.

In considering the stability of Models IV–V, we assume:

1. In a disequilibrium situation, the adjustment of the interest rate r tends to be more rapid than that of the income level Y.

2. For any income level Y, I > S for r values below the IS function, and I < S for r values above the IS function.

3. For any income level Y, L > M (excess demand for money) at r values below the LM function, and L < M (excess supply of money) at r values above the LM function.

4. Disequilibria with I > S and L ≤ M lead to increased expenditure and income, as do disequilibria with L < M and I ≥ S. Disequilibria with I < S and L ≥ M lead to decreased expenditure and income, as do disequilibria with L > M and I ≤ S.

With this background, we take up two "unorthodox" cases generated by Model V, in which LM slopes downward.[27] In the first case (figure 7-10a) the absolute value of the slope of LM is the lower, so that the interest-elasticity of IS is higher absolutely then that of LM. In the second case, (figure 7-10b) the absolute value of the slope of LM is the higher, so its

---

[26] Students recalling the "cobweb theorem" of microeconomics will recognize the additional assumption that adjustments of IS and LM occur at the same speed. As we shall see in our macrodynamic section (chapter 14) Sir John Hicks founds a "monetary cycle" on the opposite assumption that LM adjustments are faster than IS ones. [Hicks, *The Trade Cycle* (1949).]

[27] Readers may find it helpful to repeat this analysis, combining an upward-sloping LM function with the unorthodox upward-sloping IS functions considered briefly in connection with our Model III.

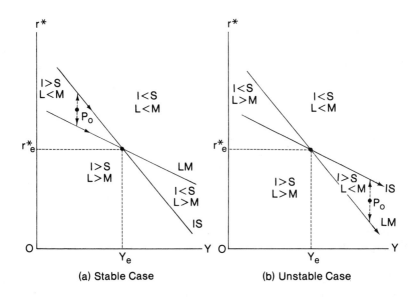

Figure 7-10   Stability Analysis—Islamic Diagram

interest elasticity is lower. The diagram area is divided into four quadrants, according as $I \gtrless S$ and $L \gtrless M$.

We begin with an arbitrary disequilibrium point P_0 on figure 7-10. We suppose an initial interest adjustment, but in which direction and how far? According to the classical "productivity and thrift" approach to interest theory (chapter 4), the initial adjustment is to IS, where productivity (investment) and thrift (saving) are in balance. A Keynesian liquidity-preference approach to interest theory suggests rather an initial adjustment to LM, where liquidity preference and the money supply are in balance. Under either interest-theory assumption, our first case (figure 7-10a) is consistent with macroeconomic stability. If the initial movement of r is a classical one to IS, it leaves $L < M$ when $Y < Y_e$, and vice versa. If the initial movement of r is a Keynesian one to LM, it leaves $I > S$ when $Y < Y_e$, and vice versa. In each instance, the subsequent movement of the income level is toward Y_e, as indicated by the arrows on the diagram.

In the same way, and under either interest-theory assumption, our second case (figure 7-10b) is one of macroeconomic instability. Again we begin with an arbitrary disequilibrium point P_0. If the initial movement of r is to IS (productivity and thrift), it leaves $L > M$ if $Y < Y_e$ and vice versa. If the initial movement is to LM (liquidity preference), it leaves $I < S$ if $Y < Y_e$ and vice versa. In each instance, the subsequent movement of Y is away from Y_e, as indicated by the arrows on the diagram.

We can therefore conclude that the Hicksian cross or Islamic diagram

illustrates a stable situation if IS slopes downward and lies above LM for $Y < Y_e$ and below LM for $Y > Y_e$. The orthodox result (negatively-sloping IS, positively-sloping LM) satisfies this condition. An ultra-unorthodox one (positively-sloping IS, negatively-sloping LM) would not. In an unstable macroeconomy, of course, the case for substantial and detailed public intervention or planning is stronger than in a stable one.

DIGRESSION: LOANABLE-FUNDS INTEREST THEORY

Rivaling Keynesian liquidity preference for primacy in monetary interest theory is a *loanable-funds* analysis developed independently by Knut Wicksell in Sweden, Sir Dennis Robertson in the U.K., and H. J. Davenport in the U.S. This section attempts to fit loanable-funds theorizing into the framework of macroeconomic stability analysis in an Islamic diagram or Hicksian cross framework.

Loanable-funds interest theory may be interpreted in this framework as implying that the net supply of new securities or bonds, denoted by B and identical with the net demand for loanable funds, is roughly proportional to $(I - S)$. It is zero when $I = S$, meaning that the net supply of securities does not change, and negative when $S > I$, meaning that new issues are less than retirements. The theory may also be interpreted as implying that the net supply F of loanable funds, identified with the net demand for new securities, is roughly proportional to $(M - L)$ (excess supply of money). It is zero when $L = M$, meaning that the supply of loanable funds is constant, and negative when $M > L$, meaning that demand has shifted from securities to money. At flow equilibrium $(Y = Y_e, r = r_e)$ with $I = S$ and $L = M$, the demand and supply of loanable funds are also equal to each other (at zero).[28]

Let BF (in figure 7-11) be the locus of points such that $B = F$. It passes through the point (Y_e, r_e). It is drawn falling as income rises, a special case which implies that, starting at any income level on BF,

---

[28] We can obtain the same result from Walras's Law. Walras's Law (a generalization of Say's Identity) says that the demand for goods and services *plus* the demand for new securities *plus* the demand for additions to the money supply is identically equal to the sum of the corresponding supply terms. At points on LM, the demand and supply of the monetary increment are in balance. It follows that the demand and supply of securities are in balance where IS and LM intersect, i.e., that BF passes through this intersection.

But holders of *stocks* are not inert. What if holders of preexisting stocks of cash or securities wish to reduce their holdings at going rates of return? Does flow equilibrium suffice for stock equilibrium, or for the full equilibrium of stocks and flows taken together? Apparently not. Our approach should be interpreted as treating an excess stock supply of old securities as a positive component of both the flow supply of new ones and the flow demand for the monetary increment. Also, market equilibrium is *stock-flow* equilibrium (stocks and flows combined).

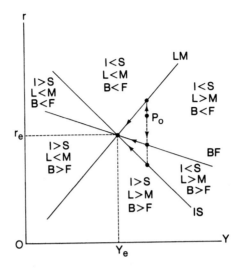

Figure 7-11   Loanable Funds Interest Theory

$(\partial S/\partial Y) > (\partial L/\partial Y)$, producing a relative scarcity of bonds and raising their prices. (A rise in the bond price is a fall in the interest rate.) Furthermore, at any income level Y, $B > F$ at rates of interest below the BF function, and vice versa. It should therefore be clear that BF lies between IS and LM. It should also be clear from figure 7-11 that if, starting from disequilibrium at P_o, the initial adjustment of r is to BF rather than to IS or LM, our "stability conclusions" are not disturbed by introduction of loanable-funds interest theory into consideration.

ANOTHER DIGRESSION: THE STEIN TABLE

The so-called Stein table represents an application of the Islamic diagram (with IS sloping downward and LM upward).[29] The purpose of Stein's analysis is to determine from historical data the dominant causes of observed simultaneous variations in Y, in r, and also in V, the velocity of monetary circulation. Possible candidates for this honor, in Stein's scheme, are three in number:

1. Real factors, under which head are classified shifts in the total expenditure and saving functions as reflected in IS;

---

[29] Jerome L. Stein, "A Method of Identifying Disturbances which Produce Changes in Money National Income," *Journal of Political Economy* (February 1960). (Stein applied his analysis to Y*; we apply it to Y.)

Table 7-3

Causation of Changes in (Y, r, V)

			Direction of Change in		
Dominant Cause			Y	r	V
1. Real Factors	(Shift in IS)		+	+	+
2. Money Supply	(Shift in LM)		+	−	−
3. Money Demand					
(Change in V)			+	−	+

2. Shifts in the money stock or the money supply function, reflected in LM;

3. Shifts in the demand for monetary assets (changes in velocity of circulation). These are likewise reflected in LM; increased demand for money implies both increased LM and lowered V.

Considering only cases of increased Y, table 7-3 illustrates Stein's results.

A fourth conceivable sign combination or row in table 7-3 would be $(+, +, -)$. To produce such a combination, several causes presumably have acted with nearly equal force. A shift in demand from money and securities to real goods, for example, may have dominated the change in interest rates, while a rising money supply has prevented any rise in measured velocity of circulation.

An increase or rightward shift in IS is a sufficient cause for the combination in line 1 of table 7-3. It will itself produce these results in the absence of changes in LM, as when demand shifts only from securities to goods. Similarly, a decrease in the demand for money (in favor of securities only, if IS does not change) will by itself produce the effects indicated in line 3. Line 2, however, is on a different logical footing. An increased money supply is a *necessary* condition for the combination $(+, -, -)$, meaning that it is difficult to imagine any alternative way for this combination to come about. Increased money supply is not, however, a *sufficient* cause of a declining velocity of circulation.[30]

---

[30] Under certain circumstances one expects $[\partial V / \partial M < 0]$; these have been elevated at times into a general theory, notably by the Radcliffe Committee in the U.K. One such circumstance is the possible deep-depression liquidity trap, where increases in M

THE LIQUIDITY TRAP: AN ALTERNATIVE EXPLANATION

We can also use the apparatus of Models IV–V to examine an alternative explanation of the controversial liquidity trap. We have mentioned Leijonhufvud's concern, now shared by many others, that the Keynesian system as outlined here may be little more than a travesty of Keynes himself. The liquidity trap is a case in point. Leijonhufvud interprets this trap, or rather the apparent historical evidence of its importance, as largely a statistical artifact. The apparent trap results, in this view, from the monetary authorities (central bankers) allowing the money supply to fall when the ostensible needs of trade decline, rather than permitting the interest rate to do so.

We illustrate this argument by the Islamic diagram (our Model IV), although Leijonhufvud doubts the validity of this construction in representing "the economics of Keynes." On figure 7-12, however, the M_2 and LM curves are drawn as algebraic functions, without the liquidity-trap horizontal segments of figure 7-5 and 7-6. Introduce into figure 7-12 a contractionary disturbance in the real or IS sector—a downward shift of the consumption or the m.e.i. function, causing the IS function to shift from IS to IS'. Instead of keeping M constant and permitting the interest rate to fall from r to r', Keynes accuses the bankers (in this interpretation) of contriving or permitting a fall to M'. The fall in the money supply shifts the LM function from LM to LM'. More important, holding the interest rate at r causes the income level to fall from Y, not only to Y' but to Y'', with a consequent worsening of employment problems as well. It is the artificial constancy of r as represented by the horizontal segment AB on figure 7-12 that constitutes a pseudo-liquidity trap; it should not be confused with a real one.

Keynes himself, faced with the policy problems set off by a fall in IS, would not content himself by holding M passively constant. He would advocate some activist combination of (1) reversing the fall in IS by fiscal policy, and (2) expanding the money supply beyond M by monetary policy. Our discussion is intended to indicate some of the primarily economic issues involved in the choice among fiscal and monetary elements in the policy mix.

---

are absorbed in hoards of M_2 with near-zero velocity. Another such circumstance is "tight money" at the height of an inflation, where use of money substitutes can offset at least temporarily the effects of falling dM by increased V. In the general case, the effect of M on V depends upon the effect of dM upon the distribution of M between high-velocity M_1 and low-velocity M_2. If the monetary increment is so distributed as to raise the overall (M_1/M_2) ratio, V will presumably rise; if its distribution lowers this ratio (or is accompanied by other circumstances lowering it), V will fall as in table 7-3.

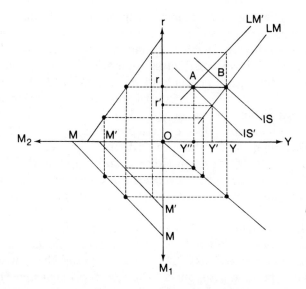

Figure 7-12   Alternative Interpretation of Liquidity Trap

SUMMARY

This chapter touches on a number of subjects not indicated by its title. Its principal purpose is the extension of the Keynesian analysis of chapter 6 to include interest and money, measured in real terms. Both formal models and policy applications are introduced.

Interest comes first in Model III as a crucial variable purporting to explain variations in both private investment I and public expenditures G. We develop an investment or marginal efficiency function in linear form, thereby taking sides (for simplicity's sake) in a policy controversy about the actual shape of such a function (if it exists). Using the investment function, we next derive a locus IS of all values of income Y and the interest rate r at which planned investment (plus public expenditure) equals planned saving (plus taxes net of transfers). This function takes the place of equilibrium solutions for either Y or r; each of these variables can only be determined if the other is given; also, IS presents them as related inversely to each other.

The resulting failure of determinacy is repaired by the introduction of a fixed money supply in Model IV. The demand for money, or liquidity preference, is separated into two aspects: transactions demand, dependent primarily upon income, and speculative demand or liquidity preference proper, dependent primarily on the interest rate and possibly involving a liquidity trap or absolute liquidity preference at some minimal interest

rate r_0. The locus of income-interest combinations at which the sum of these demands equals the fixed money supply is drawn as a nonalgebraic LM function with three branches or ranges. The intersection IS and LM functions (the Hicksian cross) gives equilibrium values of both Y and r, which do not correspond generally to full employment but leave contraction or expansion gaps. For the contraction gap (recession or depression) case, we see that the gap can, in general, be closed by fiscal policy operating on IS, by monetary policy operating on LM, or by any of an infinite number of combinations of the two. Extreme cases (vertical or horizontal IS or LM), however, leave no choice open. We close the discussion of Model IV on a policy note, by considering a few factors not reflected in the function slopes of IS or LM, which might influence the choice of a policy mix.

The only new element in Model V is the variability of the money supply, depending not only upon decisions of the ostensible monetary authority but also of commercial banks, the government, and the nonbank public. Algebraically, the money supply is treated as dependent upon the income level, the interest rate, and the fiscal deficit. Even with proportionality or linearity assumptions throughout, the algebra of this model becomes "hairy." The principal new qualitative conclusion is that multipliers, which have become steadily smaller in absolute value from Models I through IV when successive leakages are introduced, become larger when money-supply effects (injections) are also considered.

Our next topic is the stability of the solution of IS-LM models (Models IV–V). We show that the LM function may slope downward without threatening the stability of the model; the IS function may also slope upward, but at least one of the two functions must have the expected slope. We then show, for several rival interest theories, a key determinant of stability: on conventional diagrams, IS must lie above LM at income levels below equilibrium, and below LM at income levels above equilibrium. (We assume that a unique intersection point exists between IS and LM in all cases.)

The final topics return to policy applications of the Hicksian cross. These are (1) the Stein table for assessing causation in historical cases of income change, and (2) an alternative explanation for the liquidity trap in terms of bankers' refusal to let interest rates fall.

We close with a warning. Throughout our discussion of IS and LM curves we have identified IS with the real economy and LM with the monetary economy. It has been convenient to treat this dichotomy as absolute and to treat the IS and LM curves as completely independent constructs. Such treatment can be misleading; the real and monetary sectors cannot be so readily isolated. For example, if there should suddenly be a change in thriftiness conditions affecting the IS curve, liquidity

preference might *as a consequence* be altered simultaneously, affecting the LM curve, if "thriftiness" meant "demand for larger cash balances." Or suppose an economy in equilibrium to be suddenly disturbed by an increase in the money supply. Until this money is absorbed, there will be an excess supply of money that will be counterbalanced by an excess demand for goods and/or bonds. The excess demand for goods will shift the IS curve outward, until all excess demands are eliminated. These examples should alert us to the pitfalls of naive manipulation of the Islamic apparatus, particularly of ignoring the interdependence of IS and LM functions. These functions are independent in practice only in the highly special case where changes in IS (or LM) are absorbed or reflected entirely by the bond market without affecting LM (or IS).

Appendix 7a

EXPANDED MODEL V

THE EXPANSION

We have used as a money-supply equation for Model V:

$$M^s = M^s_o + n_1 Y + n_2 r + g(G - T) \qquad (7.20)$$

with G and T exogenous constraints. If, as suggested in note 23, we readmit their dependence on Y and r respectively, as by:

$$G = G_o - i_2 r \quad \text{and} \quad T = T_o + tY$$

and reexamine Model V, the solutions for Y and r become, after considerable algebra:

$$Y = \frac{A - cT_o + \dfrac{i[M_o + g(G_o - T_o)]}{m_2 + n_2 - gi_2}}{1 - c + ct + \dfrac{i(m_1 - n_1 + gt)}{m_2 + n_2 - gi_2}} \qquad (7A.1a)$$

$$r = \frac{A - cT_o - \dfrac{(1 - c + ct)[M_o + g(G_o - T_o)]}{m_1 - n_1 + gt}}{i + \dfrac{(1 - c + ct)(m_2 + n_2 - gi_2)}{m_1 - n_1 + gt}} \qquad (7A.1b)$$

These expressions reduce to (7.24a–b) when g and t are zero, so that G and T equal G_o and T_o, respectively.

Equations (7A.1a–b), cumbersome in themselves, generate interesting multipliers. The standard multiplier is, from (7A.1a):

$$\mu = \frac{\partial Y}{\partial A} = \frac{1}{1 - c + ct + \dfrac{i(m_1 - n_1 + gt)}{m_2 + n_2 - gi_2}} \tag{7A.2}$$

which, while still larger than the corresponding expression for Model IV [equation (7.17)], is smaller than that for Model V [equation (7.26)] unless $i_2 > t$, which is extremely unlikely. The multipliers for public expenditures, taxes, and the money supply are, respectively:

$$\frac{\partial Y}{\partial G_o} = \left(1 + \frac{gi}{m_2 + n_2 - gi_2}\right) \mu \tag{7A.3}$$

$$\frac{\partial Y}{\partial T_o} = -\left(c + \frac{gi}{m_2 + n_2 - gi_2}\right) \mu \tag{7A.4}$$

$$\frac{\partial Y}{\partial M_o} = \left(\frac{i}{m_2 + n_2 - gi_2}\right) \mu \tag{7A.5}$$

all of which are larger in absolute value than those indicated by (7.27–7.29) unless μ in (7A.2) is significantly less than its value in (7.26).

Chapter

8

A Taste of
Macroeconometrics

QUESTIONS TO BE CONSIDERED

Our Keynesian models are composed of equations in large numbers. The majority of these equations are definitional identities (tautologies) or equilibrium conditions. Only a minority, which make the models tick, claim to describe actual human behavoir. These "behavioral" equations include consumption functions, import functions, tax functions, investment functions, liquidity functions, and money-supply functions.

We assume that all these functions exist and can be isolated statistically. We also represent them in linear form, because linear equations are easiest to handle algebraically. (If any dependent variable Y is a linear function of n independent variables $X_1, X_2, \ldots, X_n$, we have in our notation:

$$Y = Y_o + y_1X_1 + y_2X_2 + \cdots + y_nX_n \tag{8.1}$$

with the signs of Y_o and of the y_i terms determined by stability conditions, by simple economic reasoning, or by casual empiricism.)

This is not good enough for practical application. The responsible financial journalist, social critic, civil servant, or intelligent voter has reason to wonder:

1. Whether such entities as consumption, investment, and liquidity functions exist outside the economist's imagination, and whether they do not fluctuate too erratically to be useful.

2. Whether such functions, if they exist, can be represented by linear functions, or whether other functional forms, while more complex, fit the data significantly better.

3. Whether our theory has selected the most significant set of independent variables for these functions, or whether it has swept equally significant or more significant ones under the rug.[1]

4. Whether our static assumption that Y at time t is influenced only by $(X_1, X_2, \ldots, X_n)$ of the same time period is as true or as helpful as a dynamic formulation allowing for leads and lags, such that, for example, Y_t may be influenced by $X_{i,t-1}, X_{i,t-2}, \ldots$, as well as or instead of by $X_{i,t}$.

5. Whether our constant terms, such as Y_o in (8.1), are really constants, or whether they depend in some systematic way upon other variables, either

---

[1] Readers of leftist persuasion may have already smelled one or more rats in our aggregation of workers' and capitalists' consumption into a single C term, and our ignoring income distribution throughout—both *personal* distribution between rich and poor and *functional* distribution between labor and property.

included in or omitted from our theory. (In economics, to some extent, "everything depends upon everything else.") The omitted variables may not even be "economic" by the usual classification; they may be social, political, or indeed natural-scientific. (Consider the effect of earthquakes, epidemics, floods, droughts, or simple "bad weather" upon real income in agricultural regions.)

6. Whether we have proxies or surrogates for unobservable variables, and whether these really correspond to what we intend to measure. (Where interest rates or total imports are controlled, for example, how can any theory that uses their free-market values be applied?)

At least one leading macroeconomics text places its major stress upon econometric measurement of Keynesian-type functions,[2] and assumes that students have obtained substantial background in statistical techniques. Some other texts either avoid empirical functions altogether, or accept a particular set of quantitative results without raising embarrassing questions. In this chapter we compromise by discussing problems and controversies that have arisen in fitting to actual data a sample of three Keynesian functions:

1. The aggregate consumption function.

2. The investment function for plant and equipment, which is quantitatively the most important investment function.[3]

3. The liquidity function.

In addition, we shall touch upon a broader issue raised originally by Friedman and Meiselman;[4] namely, Does the Keynesian system as a whole fit the data as well as the old-fashioned quantity theory of chapter 4? Another way of phrasing this question is, Is the Keynesian multiplier μ more or less stable than the velocity of circulation V? (Monetarists believe V the more stable of the two.)

---

[2] Michael K. Evans, *Macroeconomic Activity* (1969).
[3] The other principal elements in private investment activity are inventory investment and investment in residential housing. No overall investment function has yet been found that fits the sum of all three components in any satisfactory manner.
[4] Milton Friedman and David Meiselman, "The Relative Stability of the Velocity of Circulation and the Investment Multiplier," in Commission on Money and Credit, *Stabilization Policies* (1963). A prime source on the subsequent "F-M controversy" is the September 1965 issue of the *American Economic Review*.

CONSUMPTION FUNCTIONS

THE PROBLEMS

Since personal consumption expenditure comprises over ninety percent of disposable personal income, it should occasion no surprise that the early consumption functions fitted to annual data for 1929–41 fitted almost perfectly.[5] In linear form they were also well-behaved, with C_o terms positive and c terms positive fractions. The goodness of fit, however, means little. Any variable is correlated perfectly with itself, and almost perfectly with ninety percent of itself.

Trouble arose with these early consumption functions, less from statisticians' worries about tautology than from economists' concern with the economic implications of the results. For example:

1. Short-run and long-run data were inconsistent with each other. If a short-run function for 1929–41 is extrapolated forward mechanically, it forecasts a steadily *falling* consumption ratio or a.p.c. $(C/Y) = c + (C_o/Y)$, as Y *rises*. By the same token, backward extrapolation implies that past generations' a.p.c. was higher than that for 1929–1941; indeed, it implied that our ancestors were net dissavers. On the other hand, long-run statistical studies by Simon Kuznets indicate that a.p.c. has, in fact, been reasonably constant in the U.S. since the Civil War, rather than moving inversely with Y.

2. In addition, the 1929–1941 functions grossly underestimated consumption for the postwar period after 1946, not only for the 1946–1948 years of pent-up demand, but quite permanently. (This error was, as we shall see in chapter 15, a major cause of the notorious 1944–45 "postwar forecasts" of employment returning to deep-depression levels approximating ten percent of the civilian labor force.) During the period after 1950, the long-run a.p.c. has continued fairly steady, and there has been a rise in the m.p.c., or c, as computed from short-run consumption functions. Long-run and short-run consumption functions are compared on figure 8-1.

3. In addition to aggregate data, we also have "cross-section" consumption functions by family income classes. These functions indicate that (except for the lowest family income classes) the m.p.c. as well as the a.p.c. falls as income rises. These effects, particularly the variable m.p.c., are not reflected in the macroeconomic consumption function.

---

[5] Consumption functions using *quarterly* data, however, fit best with an allowance for a one-quarter lag between receipt of income and some part of its expenditure.

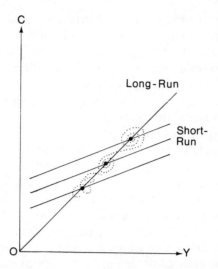

Figure 8-1   Long-run and Short-run Consumption Functions

4. When we standardize by income classes, blacks save more than whites, property-owners save more than workers, farmers save more than urban folk, and small business and professional men save most of all. Should not whatever factors cause these differences also have some effect on the aggregate consumption function?

5. We recall from chapter 4 on the classical macroeconomics and particularly from the dependence of both real saving and real investment upon the real rate of interest, with the national income at its (full-employment) equilibrium level. If saving is dependent on interest, so too must be consumption. Furthermore, contemporary studies of demand for durable consumption goods of the sort often called "consumers' capital" (automobiles, furniture, electrical appliances, etc.) show strong interest-rate effects.

RELATIVE-INCOME HYPOTHESES

Relative-income hypotheses of the consumption function are directed at solving problems (1-2) of the last paragraph. They treat the *short*-run "Keynesian" consumption functions of figure 8-1 as fundamental, and treat the *long*-run "post-Keynesian" consumption function as a resultant of the shifts from one short-run function to another.

Three simple explanations of the apparent upward drift of the consumption function over time are (1) growth of the national wealth, both total and per capita, (2) increased expenditure and improved technology in advertising and salesmanship for expenditure items (with which advertising

and salesmanship for saving have not kept up),[6] and (3) increased social security and other welfare state activities, plus private pensions. The standard self-justification of "Madison Avenue" is the second element of this trio, although it sounds strange in inflationary times. As for the apparent rise in the m.p.c., it can be ascribed plausibly to some combination of the second and third—advertising, salesmanship, and pensions in the private sector, welfare-statism in the public sector.

We owe to James Duesenberry a more refined relative-income hypothesis, which stresses phenomena called "interdependence" and "demonstration" effects.[7] Duesenberry argues from the undoubted fact that individual tastes in consumption expand with income to include additional goods and more expensive varieties—for example, from radio sets to black-and-white television sets to color television sets—via emulation of those wealthier than ourselves, who can afford them first and show their advantages to others. Duesenberry also believes, with Veblen and his followers, that expansion of our tastes is accelerated by desires to distinguish ourselves in the public eye from those worse off than ourselves, who cannot afford novelties and improvements.

The combination of these "interdependence" and "demonstration" effects can be illustrated at the individual level by supposing that a consumer's income first rises, then falls back to its original level. Duesenberry argues that his consumption follows one consumption function on the way up, but a higher consumption function on the way down, because he has acquired a higher living standard in the interim. Although he returns to his initial income level he will not return to his initial consumption level. His final a.p.c. will normally be higher than his original one, and his saving ratio will normally have fallen.

On the macroeconomic level, suppose $\hat{Y}$ to be the economy's highest previous level of real disposable income—ignoring taxes and tax function. Ignoring Duesenberry's insights, we can modify our consumption function to:

$$C = C_o + c_1 Y + c_2 \hat{Y}$$

witih (C_o, c_1, c_2) all positive and both c terms less than unity. Changing our dependent variable to the consumption ratio to avoid statistical tautology, we get:

$$\frac{C}{Y} = c_1 + \frac{C_o}{Y} + c_2 \frac{(\hat{Y})}{Y} \qquad (8.2)$$

---

[6] Compare Julian Simon, "The Effect of Advertising upon the Propensity to Consume," Chapter 8 of Simon, *Issues in the Economics of Advertising* (1970).

[7] Duesenberry, James S. *Income, Savings and the Theory of Consumer Behavior* (1952) chapters 2–4, 7.

with the last term representing the relative-income effect. (Alternative forms of (8.2) have included $\hat{C}$ (highest previous consumption) rather than $\hat{Y}$.) The implications of (8.2) can be worked out in two dimensions on a diagram like figure 8-2.

Let us begin at Y_1, with previous maximum income $\hat{Y}_1$. Consumption follows the function C_1, assuming aggregate income to rise, until the crucial level $\hat{Y}_1$ is reached. Then m.p.c. rises on a two-dimensional figure, and we follow some approximation of the long-run consumption function, until some higher level $\hat{Y}_2$ is reached. Now suppose a recession or depression, from some external cause. Consumption will decrease as income falls, but it will follow the consumption function C_2 rather than C_1, since the relevant $\hat{Y}$ value has changed from $\hat{Y}_1$ to $\hat{Y}_2$. (The arrows on the diagram make the path easier to follow.) We know that the upward shift exists, but the detail of figure 8-2, particularly the corner at $\hat{Y}_1$, is difficult to identify in practice. If it exists, it cannot be distinguished readily from any other random oscillation of observed (Y,C) values around any statistical consumption function.[8]

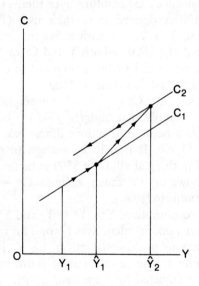

Figure 8-2   Relative-Income Hypothesis

---

[8] The omnipresence of these oscillations makes it erroneous to estimate m.p.c. by simply comparing dC with dY in successive observations of C and Y. This method gives us dC/dY values that fluctuate widely, sometimes becoming negative or exceeding unity. This erroneous method is used by many people; the results are used, equally erroneously, as arguments against Keynesian theory.

PERMANENT-INCOME HYPOTHESIS

Friedman's *Theory of the Consumption Function* (1957) takes a different tack. To Friedman, the long-run consumption function is the fundamental one, and is determined by long-run (wealth) considerations. As a proxy for wealth or assets, he uses "permanent" income. Short-run consumption functions, on the other hand, are statistical artifacts explainable by deviations of measured from permanent income. If we divide both Y and C into permanent components (Y^p, C^p) and transient components (Y^t, C^t) Friedman argues that we should expect for the long-run consumption function:

$$C = \alpha Y^p \quad (\alpha \cong .88) \tag{8.3}$$

while there is little or no correlation between Y^t and either C^p or C^t.

How have these concepts been made operational? To begin with, Friedman adjusts both measured Y and measured C by spreading the values of durable consumption goods expenditure over their estimated lifetimes to approximate the utilities derived from their use. (For example, a new $4,000 automobile, sold in Year 1 with a five-year estimated life and no scrap value, is entered at $4,000 in both Y and C for Year 1 in the official series discussed in chapter 2. Friedman proposes to enter $800 in each of the five years of the automobile's estimated life.)

On the consumption side, C^p is planned consumption, C^t is unplanned, and $C = C^p + C^t$. A family that budgets $500 for health care in a given year and spends $2,000 because of serious illness has, on this account, C^p of $500 and C^t of $1,500. If it is lucky enough to encounter no health problems and spend nothing at all, C^p is $500 as before, while C^t is $-$500. In the aggregate, however, Friedman assumes $C^p = C$, so that $C^t = 0$. (The C figure is the adjusted one.)

As in the case of consumption, $Y = Y^p + Y^t$ and Y^t is negative when Y is less than Y^p. When a poor student lives beyond his means in anticipation of a lucrative business or professional career, his Y^t is negative. It is also assumed that at time t, the representative individual's concept of his permanent income is adjusted by a constant positive percentage β of the amount by which his actual income Y_t diverges from his previously estimated permanent income Y^p_{t-1}. We have, therefore:

$$Y^p_t - Y^p_{t-1} = \beta(Y_t - Y^p_{t-1}) \quad \text{or} \quad Y^p_t = \beta Y_t + (1 - \beta)Y^p_{t-1} \tag{8.4}$$

and similarly:

$$Y_{t-1}^p = \beta Y_{t-1} + (1 - \beta) Y_{t-2}^p$$

$$Y_{t-2}^p = \beta Y_{t-2} + (1 - \beta) Y_{t-3}^p$$

and so on. Combining all these results into a series by mathematical induction (adding successive terms to equation (8.4)) we get:

$$Y_t^p = \beta Y_t + \beta(1 - \beta) Y_{t-1} + \beta(1 - \beta)^2 Y_{t-2} + \cdots + (1 - \beta)^{n+1} Y_{t-n-1}^p$$

but since β is a fraction, the last term can eventually be dropped as near zero—Friedman often uses 17 as his value for n. The remainder involves only observed values of Y on the r.h.s.:

$$Y_t^p = \beta Y_t + \beta(1 - \beta) Y_{t-1} + \beta(1 - \beta)^2 Y_{t-2} + \cdots +$$

$$\beta(1 - \beta)^n Y_{t-n} = \beta \sum_{i=0}^{n} (1 - \beta)^i Y_{t-i}$$

We must still estimate α and β. To do so, we return to equation (8.3). Changing the time subscript, this equation implies:

$$C_{t-1} = \alpha Y_{t-1}^p \quad \text{or} \quad Y_{t-1}^p = \frac{C_{t-1}}{\alpha}$$

which can be substituted into equation (8.4):

$$Y_t^p = \beta Y_t + \frac{1 - \beta}{\alpha} C_{t-1}$$

and the whole r.h.s. substituted back into (8.3):

$$C_t = \alpha \left(\beta Y_t + \frac{1 - \beta}{\alpha} C_{t-1} \right) = \alpha\beta Y_t + (1 - \beta) C_{t-1} \tag{8.5}$$

Equation (8.5) can be fitted by ordinary least squares, and both α and β can be estimated from its parameters. (Friedman obtains approximately 0.88 for α.) Furthermore, if a constant term C_0 is added to (8.5), it usually proves statistically insignificant—very close to zero.

Digression: Friedman makes, as we have seen, the extreme assumption that consumption is based *entirely* on permanent (anticipated) income (which may be a proxy for the wealth data that are not available) and *not at all* on transient income. This extreme assumption can be modified by adding a term in Y_t^t or $(Y_t - Y_t^p)$ to (8.5). Other modifications of Friedman's procedures involve estimating permanent income by looking forward in time rather than backward as Friedman does.

Even in modified form, the permanent-income hypothesis explains why a poor student consumes at a higher level and contracts debts (makes negative savings) more readily than a poor workman with the same income. The permanent-income hypothesis also explains why black men save more than whites at any income level, i.e., why the consumption function for blacks appears lower on a per-capita or per-family basis than that for whites. (The existence of race prejudice makes the average permanent income of blacks at any current income level lower than the average permanent income of whites receiving the same income.)

Friedman also applies equation (8.3) to the family income distribution at a given time. His explanation of the low saving ratios of "the poor" is that observations of a group of poor families include a large number of families for whom Y^p exceeds Y (and Y^t is negative), and only a small number for whom the opposite is true. It follows that the representative poor family bases its consumption habits upon an income *higher* than the income it currently receives. The same analysis holds, with appropriate reversals, for the high saving ratios of "the rich." If the low observed saving ratios of poor families reflect primarily the influence of negative transitory incomes and the high observed saving ratios of rich families reflect primarily the influence of positive transitory incomes, it may well be that neither a permanent nor a transitory personal income redistribution in either direction will have any significant permanent effect upon total consumption. Such, indeed, is Friedman's unorthodox view; he does not, however, deny that a higher degree of equality might shift the *pattern* of consumption away from both inferior and luxury goods to what might be called normal consumption goods.[9]

Values of α, the propensity to consume, may, however, vary as between

---

[9] **Digression:** Duesenberry offers different explanations for certain of these phenomena. He suggests that families' saving ratios depend principally upon their positions in the income distribution of their communities and not upon their absolute incomes. A family in the top decile of its income distribution will have a higher saving ratio than a family in the second decile, and so on; furthermore, neither saving ratio will change greatly with economic growth. As for the black-white disparity in the U.S., prejudice and segregation result in a black family ranking higher in the black community than a white family with the same income in the white community.

social classes and by income sources. Friedman believes that it moves inversely with the interest rate, because high rates encourage saving and discourage the installment purchases of durable goods. The propensity to consume also varies inversely with the importance of income from physical capital in permanent income, so that a "capitalist" saves more than a "proletarian" with the same income. Farmers and independent businessmen have unusually high saving propensities, because their access to credit is limited relative to their desires for growth and protection of their enterprises, and because they may be paying off debts contracted while acquiring their fixed assets and stock in trade. If one wishes to increase consumption by income redistribution, then, one should tax independent entrepreneurs (however poor) and subsidize wage and salary earners (however rich).

Relating the short-run functions to the long-run functions offers no problems for the permanent-income hypothesis. Where short-run functions lie NW of the long-run one (in figure 8-1) conditions of recession or depression prevail; Y^p exceeds Y in the aggregate, and consumption accordingly exceeds αY. Where short-run functions lie SE of the long-run one, conditions of boom or prosperity prevail; Y exceeds Y^p in the aggregate, and consumption accordingly falls short of αY.

DIGRESSION: QUASI-DYNAMIC HYPOTHESES

In this section we shall examine the *wealth-adjustment hypothesis*, the *life-cycle hypothesis*, and the *disequilibrium hypothesis*.

The wealth-adjustment hypothesis focuses upon the saving function. It begins with an identity: net saving S_t during period t is a change in wealth W. In symbols, $S_t \equiv W_t - W_{t-1}$. If now $\hat{W}_t$ is an individual's or a society's desired stock of wealth, to which adjustment is only partial, we may write:

$$W_t - W_{t-1} = S_t = \beta(W_t - \hat{W}_{t-1}) \qquad (8.6)$$

where β is yet another adjustment coefficient, treated as a constant positive fraction.

Is desired wealth not infinite? Not if present consumption must be sacrificed for its accumulation through saving and investment. (The fable of King Midas is in point.) Rather than being infinite, $\hat{W}_t$ is assumed equal to γY_t, with the constant γ assumed positive and greater than unity. Substituting this value of $\hat{W}_t$ in (8.6) gives:

$$S_t = \beta\gamma Y_t - \beta W_{t-1} \quad \text{or} \quad \frac{S_t}{Y_t} = \beta\gamma - \beta\frac{W_{t-1}}{Y_t} \qquad (8.7)$$

From this equation, S declines as W rises (with a constant Y) in accord with our earlier explanation for an upward drift of the consumption function. The m.p.s. (dS_t/dY_t) is $\beta\gamma$, which implies an m.p.c. of $(1 - \beta\gamma)$. The saving ratio also declines as wealth rises relative to income. (This implication differs from that of the permanent income hypothesis and does not seem to be verified for the long-run consumption function.)

The m.p.s. changes over time with both β and γ. Pensions and social insurance schemes may be expected to cause γ and m.p.s. to fall and m.p.c. to rise. As for the interest rate r, which does not enter directly into (8.7), a rise imposes capital losses (lowering W). It also lowers the price of future income in terms of present consumption. Both these indirect effects of rising r are expected to raise the coefficient γ, causing m.p.s. to rise and m.p.c. to fall. The opposite is naturally true for a fall in r.

The *life-cycle hypothesis* of consumption and saving is an extension of the permanent-income hypothesis. Whereas Friedman, for example, assumed $C = \alpha Y^p$ as per (8.3), with α exogenous, the life-cycle hypothesis treats α as variable with age, family size, and wealth, as well as anchoring it in microeconomic considerations. While the hypothesis has several variants, the simple form (8.8) below is due primarily to Ando and Modigliani.[10]

This form of the hypothesis assumes (in its first approximation) that each consumer seeks to allocate his income and other consumable resources between consumption and saving so that his anticipated consumption level remains approximately constant for the remainder of his estimated life—with no concern for his heirs. In symbols: Let (C,Y,Y^p) be as in (8.3); let the representative consumer have L years of estimated life remaining, of which N are anticipated to be working years; and finally, let W be the value of his *non–income-earning* assets or wealth, unreflected in Y. We then have:

$$C = \frac{Y + NY^p + W}{L} \qquad (8.8)$$

By (8.8), a consumer's basic m.p.c. or $(\partial C/\partial Y^p)$ should vary directly with N and inversely with L. His basic a.p.c. or (C/Y^p) also varies directly with both Y and W. Ando and Modigliani show that these presumptions are confirmed by statistical data.

The unconventional and disturbing *disequilibrium hypothesis* of Stephen Marglin maintains that: "households tend to spend whatever they can lay

---

[10] Albert K. Ando and Franco Modigliani, "The 'Life-Cycle' Hypothesis of Saving," *American Economic Review* (March 1963).

their hands on. Households do not save . . . except inadvertently—when their incomes are rising faster than they can adjust their spending."[11]

It follows that equilibrium saving must be done almost entirely by non-households, i.e., by corporations, and saving is the main thing "bosses do." "A simple algebraic formulation of this hypothesis," Marglin states "is a linear equation relating the rate of change of consumption $\dot{C}$ to saving— which can be thought of as a reflection of [adjustment] yet to take place— and to the rate of change of current income $\dot{Y}$:"

$$\dot{C} = \Theta(Y - C) + \delta\dot{Y}$$

where the parameter Θ measures the speed of adjustment of saving to an equilibrium value in which all income would be spent and the parameter δ is a short-run m.p.c. But a more general formulation, allowing for the possibility of some portion of equilibrium income being saved, is the one Marglin actually fits:

$$\dot{C} = \Theta(kY - C) + \delta\dot{Y} \tag{8.9}$$

in which k, the long-run m.p.c., would be close to unity if this hypothesis were correct.

Using quarterly data (which yield $\Theta/4$ rather than Θ itself), substituting differences for rates of change, and averaging where necessary, Marglin fits (8.9) in the form:

$$C - C_{-1} = \frac{k\Theta}{4} \frac{(Y + Y_{-1})}{2} - \frac{\Theta}{4} \frac{(C + C_{-1})}{2} - \delta(Y - Y_{-1})$$

$$C = A_1 C_{-1} + A_2 \frac{(Y + Y_{-1})}{2} + A_3 (Y - Y_{-1}) \tag{8.10}$$

and estimates the three A_i statistically. From the three A_i he goes on to estimate (Θ, k, δ) for the U.S. (1953–68) as 0.898, 0.976, and 0.533 respectively. The first two of these results Marglin considers as confirming the disequilibrium hypothesis of saving, while the third is less meaningful.[12]

---

[11] Stephen Marglin, "What Do Bosses Do?" Part II, *Review of Radical Political Economics* (Spring 1975).

[12] It works out algebraically that:

$$A_1 = \frac{1 - \Theta/8}{1 + \Theta/8} \qquad A_2 = \frac{k\Theta/4}{1 + \Theta/8} \qquad A_3 = \frac{\delta}{1 + \Theta/8}$$

INVESTMENT FUNCTIONS

CONTRAST WITH CONSUMPTION FUNCTIONS

Consumption-function estimators enjoyed short-lived euphoria when simple linear functions fitted annual data so well over 10–12-year short runs prior to World War II. Investment-function estimators could never be so complacent. At least four major difficulties became apparent very early:

1. Private investment has three principal components—business plant and equipment investment, inventory investment, and residential housing. Functions fitting one component reasonably well, founder on the others. No aggregate function for I as a whole appears to be usable outside the classroom, although Tobin's "Magic q" (chapter 7) may be promising. Our discussion here will run in terms of the largest and most important component, plant and equipment.

2. Since I = S ex post, there are *identification problems* as between functions explaining the two. The nature of these problems can be clarified by reference to microeconomic supply and demand analysis. Suppose we have a series of demand functions D_i and supply functions S_i shifting over time, whose intersections we observe as a set of points P_i (figure 8-3). Identification problems are these: Under what circumstances does a function fitted statistically to the observations P_i represent a supply function or a demand function? Under what circumstances is it a hybrid of the two? In the hybrid case, under what circumstances can we distill from the hybrid (and from other information) unbiased statistical estimates of the parameters of the supply function, the demand function, or both? In macroeconomics, investment and saving functions present similar problems to the budding or blooming econometrician.

3. The relevant cost of additional capital to a firm considering investment is not always the interest rate. It may be its marginal capital cost, which includes a risk premium. In addition, the more a representative firm ex-

---

so that:

$$\Theta = \frac{8(1 - A_1)}{1 + A_1} \qquad k = \frac{A_2}{1 - A_1} \qquad \delta = \frac{2A_2}{1 + A_1}$$

Incidentally, Marglin reports an extremely good fit to (8.10), with $R^2 = 0.99984$ for a fifteen-year period of nearly 60 observations.

On this entire topic, compare Dale Jorgenson, "Econometric Studies of Investment Behavior," *Journal of Economic Literature*, as criticized by Lawrence Klein and Robert Eisner, *Journal of Economic Literature* (March 1974).

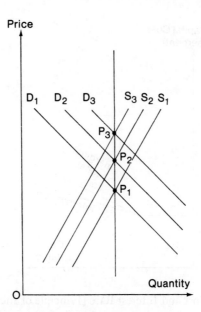

Figure 8-3   Identification Problem Illustration

pands its borrowing (on a given equity) the higher will be the interest rate it must pay, not only on its new but on its old investment.[13] This result is explained not only by imperfections of competition but from the "principle of increasing risk" associated with either reducing a firm's equity or piling an increasing debt upon that equity. Diagrammatically, the relationship is as drawn in figure 8-4 even under pure and perfect competition, when allowance is taken of reactions on the interest cost of old debt.

4. As Keynes and the financial press both tell us, there seems to be a margin of "confidence," "market psychology," "animal spirits," or simply free will (as opposed to determinacy) involved in the fluctuations of investment activity, even in the aggregate. This margin is reflected in deviations (errors) in investment functions, which may not lower materially the computed correlation coefficients of these functions, but may make the functions nonetheless suspect. (Large residual errors can be associated with high correlation coefficients because of the high variability of investment itself.)[14]

---

[13] By a "rise in the interest rate on old investment" we mean a fall in the market value of the debt or equity securities representing the old investment. This fall imposes capital losses upon present holders.

[14] **Statistical Digression:** Let $y_2 = f(x)$. If r is a correlation coefficient between x and y, then r^2 measures the closeness of fit of $f(x)$. (The coefficient r^2 is often called a

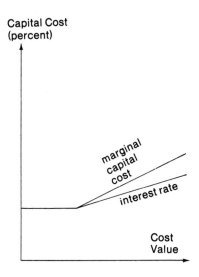

Figure 8-4   Capital Cost and Interest Rate (Principle of Increasing Risk)

THE DESIRED CAPITAL STOCK

A simple explanation for investment in period t is as a partial or complete adjustment of the real capital stock K_{t-1} at the beginning of the interval to its desired value $\hat{K}_t$. A schema of this kind is called a *capital-stock adjustment* model; such models are numerous.

A capital-stock adjustment process in period t can be divided into two subprocesses. The first subprocess is a change in the desired capital stock itself, symbolized by $(\hat{K}_t - \hat{K}_{t-1})$. The second subprocess is an adjustment of the actual capital stock to the desired stock of period t − 1, an adjustment which takes time to complete. This process is symbolized by $\beta(\hat{K}_{t-1} - K_{t-1})$, the adjustment coefficient β being as usual positive and no larger than unity. In addition, we assume $[\hat{K}_t = \gamma^Y{}_t]$ and $[\hat{K}_{t-1} = \gamma^Y{}_{t-1}]$; the coefficient γ is a *desired capital-output ratio* whose aggregate value is assumed constant in the short run. (Estimates of its value are often between 2.5 and 3.5).

---

coefficient of determination.) Let σ^2 be the variance of the dependent variable y about its own mean, and S^2 the variance of y about the function $f(x)$, i.e., the variance of the estimate $f(x)$. Then we have, by definition of r^2:

$$r^2 = \frac{\sigma^2 - S^2}{\sigma^2} = 1 - \frac{S^2}{\sigma^2}$$

If σ^2 is sufficiently high, r and r^2 can both approach unity while S^2 remains high.

Combining these insights, we may replace the I_o term of our elementary investment functions by the expression:

$$I_{o,t} = \alpha(\hat{K}_t - \hat{K}_{t-1}) + \beta(\hat{K}_{t-1} - K_{t-1})$$

where $\alpha(0 \geq \alpha \geq -1)$ is yet another adjustment coefficient, this time an adjustment of *actual* investment to the change in *desired* capital stock. Moreover, since $[\hat{K}_t = \gamma Y_t]$ and $[\hat{K}_{t-1} = \gamma Y_{t-1}]$:

$$I_{o,t} = \alpha\gamma(Y_t - Y_{t-1}) + \beta\gamma Y_{t-1} - \beta K_{t-1}$$

or, denoting $(Y_t - Y_{t-1})$ by dY/dt:

$$I_{o,t} = \alpha\gamma \frac{dY}{dt} + \beta\gamma Y_{t-1} - \beta K_{t-1} \tag{8.11}$$

The first term on the right of (8.11) represents the *accelerator* or the *acceleration principle* (or simply "the relation"), which relates net investment to the rate of change in income or sales. This notion antedates Keynes; it was introduced nearly simultaneously by Albert Aftalion in France and J. M. Clark in the U.S. shortly before World War I. The second term of (8.11) represents *induced investment*, such as has appeared in the footnotes of chapter 7. The third term represents the damping effect of existing capital stock, which becomes particularly obvious if it includes excess capacity $(K_{t-1} > \hat{K}_{t-1} = \gamma Y_{t-1})$.

ACCELERATORS, SIMPLE AND FLEXIBLE

A simple or naive accelerator model is a special case of (8.11). It ignores the last two terms by considering the coefficient β as near zero. It also assumes investment to be interest-inelastic. (Interest inelasticity implies that the i term of $I = I_o - ir$ is also near zero.) Equation (8.11) reduces, therefore, to

$$I = k \frac{dY}{dt} \tag{8.12}$$

where the coefficient k equals $\alpha\gamma$ in (8.11). We shall see this equation in many forms in our studies of both growth and fluctuation theory in later chapters.

However convenient analytically and expositorily, the simple accelerator (8.12) has one critical disadvantage. It fits the data badly, even with a constant term added. Apparently k is not a constant in the absence of the other variables of (8.11). At least, k falls below its "normal" value in the presence both of excess capacity and near-full employment. The overhang of excess capacity needs no special explanation. The problem at or near full or over-full employment is the scarcity of resources (both labor and materials) for carrying out ambitious investment programs.

To improve this poor statistical fit (shown largely by research of Jan Tinbergen), economists have turned to "flexible accelerators." A *flexible accelerator* allows for the process of capital stock adjustment taking more than one time period, so that (8.12) expands to:

$$I_t = k_0 + k_1 \left(\frac{dY}{dt}\right)_t + k_2 \left(\frac{dY}{dt}\right)_{t-1} + \cdots + k_n \left(\frac{dY}{dt}\right)_{t-(n-1)}$$

Among American economists, Robert Eisner has been the principal proponent of this approach. In one of a series of empirical studies,[15] Eisner combined the flexible accelerator with business profits in what he calls a "basic accelerator and profits model," and included also the influence of capital-stock factors. Let S represent sales, P profits, F total fixed capital, D depreciation, and N fixed assets net of depreciation. Eisner's model may then be written:

$$\left(\frac{I}{F}\right)_t = k_0 + k_1 \left(\frac{S_t - S_{t-1}}{S_t}\right) + k_2 \left(\frac{S_{t-1} - S_{t-2}}{S_t}\right) + \cdots + k_4 \left(\frac{S_{t-3} - S_{t-4}}{S_t}\right)$$
$$+ k_5 \frac{P_t}{F_t} + k_6 \frac{P_{t-1}}{F_t} + \cdots + k_8 \frac{P_{t-3}}{F_t} + k_9 \frac{D_t}{F_t} + k_{10} \frac{N_t}{F_t}$$

It has been applied both at the microeconomic level (to individual firms) and at the macroeconomic level (to broad industrial groups).

Eisner's sales-change coefficients (k_1 through k_4) were uniformly positive and frequently summed to about 0.5, whereas the profit coefficients (k_5 through k_8) were statistically insignificant and varied in sign, summing to approximately zero. Eisner also reported the rapidity of depreciation and

---

[15] Robert Eisner, "A Distributed Lag Investment Function," *Econometrica* (January 1960). See also Robert Eisner and Robert H. Strotz, "Determinants of Business Investment," in Commission on Money and Credit, *Impacts on Monetary Policy* (1963), pp. 173–178.

obsolescence as an important factor, with the k_9 coefficient significantly positive but the k_{10} coefficient sometimes negative.

CAPITAL COST CONSIDERATIONS

One might wonder while reading our discussion of capital cost under increasing risk and inspecting figure 8-4, how such notions could be made operational either for the firm or the economy. The answer is, unfortunately, that they are not yet operational as they stand. At the same time, proxies or surrogates have been substituted, to the satisfaction of some critics.

A frequent approach has been to include in investment functions variables representing the liquidity position or the cash flow of borrowers.[16] The more favorable a borrower's liquidity position, the less the differential between his capital cost and the pure rate of interest. A variant of basically the same approach has been to include in the investment function an index of common-stock prices, or the rate of return on high-grade corporate bonds. A high stock price index, or a low bond yield, can be interpreted in the same way as a favorable liquidity position; the issuer of equities, or of bonds, need not pay a large premium over the rate of interest r. (It is unusual to include numerous financial variables in a single investment function, because financial variables are highly intercorrelated. To include several intercorrelated dependent variables in a single equation biases the statistical results and gives rise to *multicollinearity* problems.)[17]

An alternative approach is associated with the name of Dale Jorgenson,[18] who devised and used a compound variable, which he called c and which includes the interest rate, to represent the cost of capital. Jorgenson's c is computed from the interest rate r by the elaborate formula:

$$c = q \left(\frac{1 - uv}{1 - u} d + \frac{1 - uw}{1 - u} r \right) \qquad (8.13)$$

---

[16] A company's cash flow is the sum of its undistributed earnings (usually net of corporate taxation), its dividend payments, and the net addition to its reserves.

[17] **Statistical Digression:**   Assume a point in the (x,y) plane, around which all observations of y (the dependent variable) are clustered tightly. This means that y is at or near its mean value, and is independent of x, while x is equally independent of y. If, however, one fits a regression line y = f(x), including the superfluous variable x, random variation may produce a line with any slope whatever. Similarly, the line x = g(y) might have any slope whatever. Detecting and adjusting for meaningless fits (resulting from inclusion of superfluous variables) is called a multicollinearity problem. Geometrically, a multicollinearity problem results from fitting an n-dimensional surface to a set of points in (n − m) − dimensional space.

[18] Dale Jorgenson, "Capital Theory and Investment Behavior," *American Economic Review* (May 1963). This essay also includes the rationale of equation (8.13).

where q and d are respectively a price index of capital goods and the rate of depreciation. The additional parameters (u,v,w) introduce tax considerations; they are, respectively, the total tax rate on corporate income (including the personal income tax on the dividend receiver), the proportion of depreciation deductible for corporate income tax purposes, and the proportion of interest payments similarly deductible.

THREE REPRESENTATIVE FUNCTIONS: HICKMAN, JORGENSON, EVANS

Investment function studies have flourished like ragweed, which itself outflourishes the green bay tree. G. R. Post's encyclopedic bibliographical contribution to the Eisner-Strotz survey (footnote 15) includes 55 "interview, questionnaire, and case studies"; 155 empirical, quantitative studies "not involving parameter estimation"; 70 empirical, quantitative studies "involving econometric estimation"—and ends in 1963. For illustrative purposes we consider—in addition to the Eisner essay—three estimates by Bert Hickman, Dale Jorgenson, and Michael Evans.[19]

Hickman's investment function is basically an induced-investment model. Fitted to annual U.S. data for 1949–1960, it yields an extraordinarily high multiple-correlation coefficient (.989). In addition to his macroeconomic equation reproduced here, Hickman fits similar but separate functions, sometimes with additional variables, to such branches as manufacturing, railroads, agriculture, etc. He excludes the interest rate altogether, and includes (substitutes?) a time trend, of which we will hear more later. The function, primarily in logarithmic form, is

$$\log I_t = .0833 + .1235 \log Y_t + .1157 \log Y_{t-1}$$
$$- .2594 \log K_{t-1} - .0016 \, t.$$

Hickman interprets the negative sign of the last term as implying some degree of stagnation in the American economy, both from relatively-falling investment and from the multiplier it generates. An alternative explanation seems more plausible (with the aid of hindsight), in view of later events. This alternative view is that Hickman's "time trend" represents the effect

---

[19] Bert G. Hickman, *Investment Demand and U.S. Economic Growth* (1965): Jorgenson, *op. cit.*; also his contribution to James Duesenberry et al., *Quarterly Econometric Model of the U.S.* (1965); Michael K. Evans, "A Study of Industry Investment Decisions," *Review of Economics and Statistics* (May 1967); also *Macroeconomic Activity, op. cit.*, ch. 5.

of rising interest rates in the eleven-year period covered by his data. (The interest rate variable, however, fits less well statistically than the time trend during the eleven "Hickman" years.)

Jorgenson's investment function is mathematically more complex than any other we consider. It also professes the closest reliance upon the profit-maximizing methodology of microeconomic analysis, because of its stress on capital cost. Its most general form is:

$$I_t = \mu(\Theta)(\hat{K}_t - \hat{K}_{t-1}) + \delta K_{t-1}$$

fitted to quarterly data. (This form was expanded in studies subsequent to 1963.) Some of Jorgenson's symbols are unfamiliar. $\mu(\Theta)$ is a power series in the lag operator Θ. (Detailed explanation is too complex for treatment here; Jorgenson's application gives him lag patterns that rise sharply for two or three quarters, then fall off more gradually.) The coefficient δ is a depreciation rate. The desired capital stock $\hat{K}$ is defined not as αY but as

$$\alpha \left(\frac{pY}{c} \right)$$

where p is a price index of output and c the cost of capital as per equation (8.13), which involves the rate of interest. As for the coefficient α, it is unity on the average and in the long run, but is sometimes adjusted to smoothe the K series. If we denote by dK_{t-i} the term $(\hat{K}_{t-i} - \hat{K}_{t-(i+1)})$, a representative sample of Jorgenson's results is:

1. For durable manufacturing industries:

$$I_t = 0.00099 \ d\hat{K}_{t-3} + -.00079 \ d\hat{K}_{t-4} + 0.00054 \ d\hat{K}_{t-5} +$$
$$1.242 \ (I_{t-1} - \delta K_{t-4}) - 0.394 \ (I_{t-2} - \delta K_{t-5}) + 0.0256 \ K_{t-3}$$

2. For nondurable manufacturing industries:

$$I_t = 0.00058 \ dK_{t-6} + 1.220(I_{t-1} - dK_{t-4}) -$$
$$0.420(I_{t-2} - dK_{t-5}) + 0.0184 \ K_{t-3}$$

The separation of the function into two parts was made because durable goods industries appear to behave in a significantly different manner from other manufacturing industries. The signs for existing capital stock (lagged three quarters) appear "wrong" at first glance, but presumably reflect de-

preciation and obsolescence. The terms $(I_{t-1} - dK_{t-(i+3)})$ allow for the incomplete or exaggerated capital-stock adjustments of prior quarters; the lumpiness of investment may account for the irregularity of the signs.

Evans' investment function stresses the combination of two principal components of both the m.e.i. function and the marginal capital cost function. The two m.e.i. components are the volume of output and the size of the existing capital stock. The two marginal capital cost components are the interest rate (or more precisely, the corporate bond yield), and the corporate cash flow. A special capacity-utilization ratio and a stock-price index are also included. Another special feature is the use of two-quarter average values of most independent variables; this device tends to smooth the fluctuations of these variables. The function is fitted to quarterly data for the manufacturing sector only; the multiple-correlation coefficient is 0.935. All parameters have the expected signs. The equation itself is:

$$I_{pm,t} = -11.48 + 5.28\, C_{p,t-1} + 0.0453\, \frac{X_{m,t-5} + X_{m,t-6}}{2}$$

$$+ 0.1888\, \frac{L_{m,t-5} + L_{m,t-6}}{2} - 1.539\, \frac{r_{L,t-5} + r_{L,t-6}}{2}$$

$$+ 0.0783\, \frac{SP_{m,t-1} + SP_{m,t-2}}{2} - 0.0309\, \frac{K_{m,t-5} + K_{m,t-6}}{2}$$

This equation also includes a number of unfamiliar symbols. Their meanings are:

I_{pm} Gross private domestic investment, manufacturing sector ($billion, 1958 prices)
C_p Capital utilization ratio
X_m Gross physical output, manufacturing sector
L_m Corporate cash flow, manufacturing sector
r_L Yield, high grade corporate bonds, all sectors
SP_m Stock price index, manufacturing sector
K_m Capital stock value, manufacturing sector

LIQUIDITY FUNCTIONS

FIVE SPECIAL PROBLEMS

In addition to the standard problems of existence and stability, five special issues have developed in relation to the fitting of empirical liquidity, or monetary demand, functions:

1. Is there an appropriate counterpart for our theoretical M*, which represents the nominal money supply? Is there an unambiguous dividing line between money on the one hand and money-substitutes (other liquid assets) on the other?

2. Does the demand for the real money stock M, as defined, depend primarily upon some variant of real national wealth W (another stock), upon some variant of the national income or product Y (a flow), or possibly both?

3. In addition to W or Y or both, does the demand for M depend significantly upon the rate of interest? If so, what is the interest-elasticity of the demand for M? Furthermore, what observable interest rate or rates should be used to represent the theorist's conventional symbol r? Should nominal values be used, or should they be adjusted for actual or anticipated inflation rates; if so, how?

4. What is the evidence for the existence of the Keynesian liquidity trap (*absolute* liquidity preference, with infinite interest-elasticity of demand for M), which we assumed in certain models of chapter 7?

5. If both the demand for money and the supply of money depend upon Y and upon r, how are we to distinguish liquidity functions from money supply functions, or from hybrids of the two? (This is another identification problem of the sort encountered earlier in this chapter with regard to investment functions.)

Before the importance of these issues was realized, liquidity theory (like consumption theory) enjoyed a period of euphoria, exemplified in a well-known article by Tobin.[20] Tobin attempted to isolate the speculative demand for money, the so-called liquidity preference proper. His monetary variable was a conventional one—cash and demand deposits held by the public, in nominal terms—taken net of a certain proportion of the national income. [This deducted proportion, equal to the lowest historically-recorded (M/Y) ratio (1929), was taken to represent the "requirements" of the transactions demand for money.] Tobin also used a long-term nominal rate of interest. Over a generation of generally-falling interest rates ending in 1946, a two-dimensional diagram in M and r alone displayed the Keynesian liquidity trap in all its glory. Extension beyond 1946, however, to a period of rising nominal rates, showed the liquidity function following a

---

[20] James Tobin, "Liquidity Preference and Monetary Policy," *Review of Economics and Statistics* (May 1947), reprinted in Arthur Smithies and J. Keith Butters, eds., *Readings in Fiscal Policy* (1955).

path widely divergent from (less interest-elastic than) the path developed by Tobin for earlier years.

ALTERNATIVE MONETARY DEFINITIONS

The conventional or narrow definition of money, frequently indicated by M_1, includes "outside" currency in circulation plus demand deposits in commercial banks. Broader definitions include one or more other liquid assets—savings deposits, government securities, overdraft privileges, savings and loan shares, etc. Two analytical arguments for their inclusion are that their holders usually think of them as secondary monetary reserves, and that in a rise in liquidity preference—a shift in demand to money balance from "bonds" or securities—the demand for these liquid assets tends to rise like the demand for M_1, rather than falling like the demand for securities in general. (And vice versa, in case of a fall in liquidity preference.) An analytical argument on the other side is that all these near-moneys bear interest whereas M_1 does not, so that inclusion of near-moneys in the money supply muddies our estimate of the interest-elasticity of the liquidity function.[21]

A compromise solution has been the use of a concept called M_2, advocated by Milton Friedman and his associates.[22] M_2 is defined as M_1 plus savings deposits in commercial banks (but not in other institutions). A continuous series for M_2 dates back (in the U.S.) further than the series for M_1. In addition, Friedman finds functions using M_2 generally more stable and better fitting (less volatile) than similar functions using M_1. Later writers carry the Friedman expansion further, devising M_3, M_4, . . . M_n series which include additional categories of liquid assets or "money substitutes."

Another suggestion is to use an artificial composite unit of money, which treats a dollar of near-money as something less than a dollar of M_1. For

---

[21] **Digression:** The same argument is valid against inclusion of demand deposits in M where they bear interest, as they did in the U.S. prior to 1933, and currently do in many foreign countries. (It is common for the depositor to choose between receipt of interest and the right to draw checks on his account.)

[22] Milton Friedman and Anna J. Schwartz, *Monetary History of the U.S.* (1963). (This use of M_1 and M_2 is not to be confused with that in chapter 7, where they referred to money held for transactions and speculative motives respectively.)

The observed correlation between M_1 and M_2 is sometimes quite low. Friedman believes irregularities are caused by legislation forbidding payment of interest on demand deposits and setting ceilings on rates payable on savings deposits. In the absence of such legislation he believes the correlation would be much higher. See Milton Friedman, *An Economist's Protest* (1972), p. 60f.

example, V. K. Chetty proposes a pair of related composites M_a and M_a', such that:[23]

$$M_a = [M^{.954} + 1.020\ T^{.975} + .880\ MS^{.959} + .616\ SL^{.981}]^{1.026}$$

$$M_a' = (M + T) + .880\ MS + .615\ SL$$

where M is our M_1, T is time deposits in commercial banks, MS is savings deposits in mutual savings banks, and SL is saving and loan shares. Chetty's $(M + T)$ is therefore Friedman's M_2.

THE INDEPENDENT VARIABLES

A wide variety of liquidity functions have been fitted, varying in the choices and specifications of the independent variables to be included, the periods covered, and the algebraic forms of the functions fitted. Two useful summaries of this work have been made in a monograph by David Laidler and an essay by Ronald Teigen.[24] Results derived from the Teigen study are presented below in table 8-1. All writers use American data. Several choose the ratio (M/Y) or (M/Transactions) rather than M itself as dependent variable, and thereby bind the income or transactions elasticity at unity; these cases are denoted by asterisks in the table. Most writers used a short-term interest rate. Use of a long rate, as in the cases denoted by L in the table, generally increased the interest-elasticity. The first Bronfenbrenner-Mayer fit is not comparable with the others. It aimed at the speculative demand exclusively; other researchers have abandoned the attempt to subdivide monetary demand in the early Keynesian manner.

Omitted from table 8-1 is a Friedman study of 1959, which relates the demand for nominal money (including time deposits) to nominal perma-

---

[23] V. Karuppan Chetty, "On Measuring the Nearness of Near-Moneys," *American Economic Review* (June 1969). The details of Chetty's econometrics are beyond the scope of this discussion.

[24] David Laidler, *The Demand for Money: Theories and Evidence* (1969), ch. 8; Ronald F. Teigen, "The Demand for and Supply of Money," in Warren L. Smith and Ronald F. Teigen, *Readings in Money, National Income, and Stabilization Policy* (rev. ed., 1970). Our table 8-1 is based on Teigen's table 1 (p. 84). Both Laidler and Teigen include full references of the studies included in the table. A later study is John T. Boorman, "The Evidence on the Demand for Money," chapter 22 of Thomas M. Havrilesky and John T. Boorman, *Current Issues in Monetary Theory and Policy* (1976). On money supply functions, compare also Robert H. Rasche, "Review of Empirical Studies of the Money Supply Mechanism," Federal Reserve Bank of St. Louis *Review* (July 1972).

Table 8-1
Principal Elasticities of Demand for Money

Author and Period	Interest Elasticity	Income Elasticity	Wealth Elasticity	Permanent Income Elasticity	Transactions Elasticity
Latané 1954 (1919–52)*	−.70 (L)	1.0	—	—	—
Latané 1960 (1909–58)*	−.85	1.0	—	—	—
Stedry 1959 (1919–58)*	−.21	—	—	—	1.0
Bronfenbrenner and Mayer 1960 (1919–56)	−1.12	—	3.93	—	—
Ibid.	−.22	—	−0.19	—	—
Meltzer 1963 (1900–58)	−.78 (L)	—	1.01	—	—
Teigen 1964 (1953–64)	−.10	1.1	—	—	—
Chow 1966 (1894–1958)	−.75 (L)	—	—	1.05	—

nent income and to a "permanent" price level estimated by Friedman along the same lines as permanent income.[25] Friedman estimates the permanent-income elasticity of the liquidity function at 1.8, making money clearly a luxury good by the ordinary microeconomic definition of the term. The fit is close enough to induce Friedman to doubt the existence of any non-zero interest rate elasticity. A zero elasticity means that the LM curve of Keynesian models is vertical, and supports monetarist as against fiscalist policy conclusions. In later work, Friedman modifies this view to the extent of accepting interest-elasticity estimates of $-.15$, in the low range of the estimates presented in table 8-1.

IDENTIFICATION PROBLEMS

All these estimates have generally assumed, at least implicitly, the world of our Keynesian Model IV, in which the money supply is determined autonomously by the monetary authorities. Introducing the complications of Model V—taking account of money supply *functions*—introduces the identification problem of distinguishing a liquidity function from a money supply function, if both depend on the levels of income and interest. The isolation of single functions is a matter for an econometrics text or treatise; it boils down to using (for liquidity-function purposes) not the actual values of M but our estimates of these values as they would have been under "normal" relations between the money supply and the *monetary base* (sometimes called high-powered money). The results of three such studies, also summarized by Teigen, are reproduced as table 8-2. These studies distinguish between demands for currency, for demand deposits, and for time deposits. They also use two separate interest rates, r (the nominal rate on three-month Treasury bills) and r_t (the nominal rate of time deposits). As usual, certain of the differences between the computed interest-elasticities can be traced to differences in specification. The first author (de Leeuw) uses a private-security rate rather than a Treasury bill rate in measuring interest-elasticity of demand for currency and demand deposits; the other two authors (Goldfeld and Teigen) use a long-term bond rate in measuring the interest-elasticity of demand for time deposits; the third author (Teigen) ignores the currency component of the money supply.

---

[25] Milton Friedman, "The Demand for Money: Some Theoretical and Empirical Results," *Journal of Political Economy* (August 1959). Compare also Friedman, "Interest Rates and the Demand for Money," *Journal of Law and Economics* (October 1966). Both papers are reprinted in Friedman, *The Optimum Quantity of Money and Other Essays* (1969).

Table 8-2
Interest Elasticities of Demand for and Supply of Money

Author and Period	Elasticity of Demand for Currency		Elasticity of Demand for Demand Deposits		Elasticity of Demand for Time Deposits		Elasticity of Supply of Money	
	r	r_t	r	r_t	r	r_t	r	r_t
de Leeuw 1965 (1948–62)	−.36	−.14	−.35	−.17	−.37	.68	.22	−.35
Goldfeld 1966 (1950–1962)	−.07	−.14	−.11	−.18	−1.62	.37	.25	−.08
Teigen 1969 (1953–64)	—	—	−.10	−.43	−2.82	3.76	.14	−.10

THE LIQUIDITY TRAP

The range and scatter of these econometric estimates—all relating to a single country in a time interval of two generations or less—inspire no great faith in econometrics as the magic key to bringing all economists of all schools into unanimity. One point of near unanimous agreement, however, should not be overlooked. There is no evidence for the existence of an ultra-Keynesian or ultra-fiscalist liquidity trap—an infinite interest elasticity of demand of money—even over periods that include the Great Depression. If anything, the interest-elasticities are relatively low; to this extent a monetarist view of economic life is strengthened.

THE FRIEDMAN-MEISELMAN CONTROVERSY

THE FRIEDMAN-MEISELMAN THESIS

The Friedman-Meiselman study cited above (footnote 4) raised the overall econometric question, Does a simple Keynesian system perform better than a simple classical system, namely, the quantity theory of money? Dividing nominal Y into autonomous expenditure A and induced expenditure B, Friedman and Meiselman, (hereafter F-M), claim that the quantity of money M is a more efficient estimator of induced expenditure B than is autonomous expenditure A. The use of B rather than Y as dependent variable may seem unusual; its purpose is elimination of the bias resulting from estimating Y from some portion of itself, such as A. In addition F-M claim that dM, the change in nominal M, is generally more efficient than dA, the change in nominal autonomous expenditures, in estimating dB, the change in induced expenditure. A third related claim is that, when both nominal M and nominal A are used in a multiple regression to estimate nominal B (or, in the difference-equation case, when both nominal dA and nominal dM are used to estimate nominal dB), the coefficients of M or dM are always statistically significant, while those for A or dA may not be.

All these results cumulate in the statistical suggestions that the classical velocity of circulation V may be more stable over time than is the Keynesian multiplier μ, so that A and dA are redundant variables in estimating B or dB. The economic implication, going a step further, makes the entire Keynesian "revolution," if not a backward step, a false alarm in the history of macroeconomic analysis.

THE REBUTTALS

Rebuttals to F-M were not long in appearing. Two replies, one by Ando and Modigliani, the other by Mayer and de Prano, appear (with rejoinders

by F-M) in the September 1965 issue of the *American Economic Review*. The multifarious points raised in the Keynesian rebuttal by the generally-Keynesian critics may be summarized under two heads: (1) the specifications of the A and M variables, and (2) the direction of the causation between M and Y (or between M and B).

1. The critics contend that F-M's results are not statistically robust. That is to say, they are qualitatively sensitive to minor changes in the definition (specification) of their A and M variables; different specifications will often make the Keynesian variable A perform better than the quantity-theory variable M. In particular, F-M's specification of A [and therefore of B, which equals $(Y - A)$], are "wrong" in Keynesian terms. This point may be clarified, using the models and symbols of our chapters 6–7. For one thing, the Keynesian system is interpreted in a completely nonmonetary fashion. Our A was defined as $(C_o + I_o + G_o)$ for a closed economy, or as $(C_o + I_o + G_o + X_o - M_o)$ for an open economy with international trade;[26] this usage takes account of an autonomous component of consumption, of the influence of interest rates on private and public investment, and also of the influence of income upon the volume of imports. Expansions, allowing for tax functions, might have been $[C_o + I_o + (G_o - cT_o)]$ for the closed economy, and $[C_o + I_o + (G_o - cT_o) + (X_o - M_o)]$ for the open one. F-M use instead $[I + (G - T) + (X - M)]$. Their simplification treats all investment, all government spending for goods and services, all taxes, and all imports as exogenous; on the other hand, it treats all consumption as induced, and assumes a balanced-budget multiplier of zero.

2. A perennial policy issue in monetary economics has been whether monetary authorities (including as an authority the metallic-standard "rules of the game") should have full control over the size of the money stock, or whether the banks and the public should be permitted to influence M as well, by varying the reserve and currency ratios (R/D) and (C/M) of chapter 7. The first view, concentrating authority and responsibility in Treasuries, Central Banks, or full metallic standards, is associated with the *currency school*. The second view, whose proponents prefer an "elastic currency" expanding and contracting in response to the "needs of trade," is associated with the *banking school*. Whatever the normative pros and cons of the rival positions,[27] the banking school has won out in practice in leading industrial countries. As a result, M has tended to vary in the same

---

[26] As in other contexts involving international trade, the symbols M and M_o refer here to imports (and their autonomous component) rather than to the money supply.

[27] A history of monetary economics from a viewpoint strongly opposed to the banking-school position is L. W. Mints, *A History of Banking Theory* (1945).

direction as Y; the direct relationship is embodied in the money-supply function of our Keynesian Model V (chapter 7). It is the contention of F-M's critics that the correlation between M and B represents predominantly causation from Y to M through this money-supply function, so that the relation would vanish in a regime of monetary rules that reduce such a function to a vertical line. F-M, on the other hand, have interpreted the direction of causation as primarily from M to Y to B, and propose a regime of monetary rules as a stabilization device.[28] The conflict between these two interpretations is still another unresolved identification problem.

SUMMARY

The four main bodies of this chapter are surveys or digests of econometric studies. They attempt to avoid any higher level of statistical proficiency than most macroeconomists can claim.

In connection with *consumption functions*, which fit deceptively well in the short-run, there are incongruities between long-run and short-run functions; reliance on the short-run functions contributed to the unduly pessimistic "postwar forecasts" of 1944–47 in the U.S. We also presented several hypotheses that propose to account for the incongruities themselves. These hypotheses include a *relative-income* hypothesis, a *permanent-income* hypothesis, a *wealth-adjustment* hypothesis, a *life-cycle* hypothesis, and a *disequilibrium* hypothesis. (The last three of these involve macrodynamic as well as macrostatic analyses.) None of the five, unfortunately, will exclude entirely any of the others.

In connection with *investment functions*, statistical fits have been less encouraging from the outset. Apparently no single function explains all three principal private-investment components (plant and equipment, inventories, residential housing); in this chapter, we limit ourselves to the first of these components. Even here, there is disagreement as to the principal explanatory factors (other than the rate of interest), and likewise to the importance of the rate of interest itself. As investment-function hypotheses we have considered *capital-stock adjustment* and *acceleration*. (An acceleration model is one that attributes explanatory force to rates of income *change* over time, (dY/dt), rather than to income itself.) We have also considered three concrete studies of the American scene, by Hickman, Jorgenson, and Evans, respectively. These indicate the range and divergence of hypotheses applied; we have not attempted to choose between them.

In connection with *liquidity functions* (demand functions for money),

---

[28] Friedman's views are presented in his A *Program for Monetary Stability* (1959) and his *Inflation: Causes and Consequences* (1963), reprinted in his *Dollars and Deficits* (1968), ch. 1.

there remain divergent views as to the specification of the money stock; the usefulness of distinguishing transactions from speculative demand functions for money; the relative explanatory importance of measured income, permanent income, and wealth (which in practice capitalizes property income at a permanent interest rate, but ignores labor income); the comparative relevance of short-term and long-term interest rates for estimating the interest-elasticity of demand for money; and the method of distinguishing the liquidity function from the money-supply function in practice. While none of these issues have been resolved definitively, there is considerable agreement that the Keynesian liquidity trap (infinite interest-elasticity of demand for money) is not found in historical data. Indeed, there is a minority view that the interest-elasticity of demand for money is close to zero, i.e., that the LM curve of simple Keynesian models is nearly vertical, and that the scope for fiscal policy is small as compared to that of monetary policy.

In connection with *the F-M controversy* of the mid-sixties, the F-M thesis is that a simplified Keynesian system, interpreted in a purely fiscalist manner with no monetary sector, is outperformed in estimating induced expenditure under U.S. conditions by a simplified classical system exemplified by the quantity theory of money. This implies that the Keynesian multipliers are less stable (more volatile) than the velocity of monetary circulation. To these conclusions, F-M's critics reply that the results are sensitive to minor changes in the specifications of the rival determinants, autonomous expenditures A and the money stock M; that F-M actually misinterpret Keynes and misspecify the A variable; and that F-M's results are subject to interpretation as causation from A to Y to M, rather than as causation from M to Y to induced expenditures B.

In all four of these macroeconometric samplings, there remains plenty of work to be done. None of the conclusions is cut and dried; none of the controversies is resolved; there is little danger of the reader's thinking otherwise. The real dangers are the lazy man's proposition that nothing is knowable, that research is a waste of time, that voters and legislators might as well follow Goldwater's Law ("In your heart, you know I'm right"), or alternatively, that any clever fellow can "prove" or "disprove" anything whatever by the statistical legerdemain of regression plus correlation. To such skeptical doubts we can answer, not too forcibly, that one should not jump to nihilistic conclusions on the basis of a single generation of inconclusive research. It is more true than this chapter shows, that even among the existing inconclusive models there are clearly better and clearly worse ones, clearly promising and clearly unpromising ones. We have tried to sample from the better specimens and let the others go down the drain. One cannot "prove anything by statistics" to a sophisticated audience; one purpose of a chapter like this one is to increase the sophistication of intelligent laymen, as regards defense against questionable statistics.

Chapter 9

Economic Stagnation?

STAGNATION AND KEYNESIAN ECONOMICS

A recurrent policy interlude in our theoretical and statistical exposition of the Keynesian macroeconomic system (chapters 6–8) has concerned monetarism, fiscalism, and the disagreement between their respective advocates. We now deal separately with another recurrent policy issue, "economic stagnation," alias the "mature economy thesis." This thesis has been propounded most positively, and related most closely to the Keynesian system, by Alvin H. Hansen, often called "the American Keynes." It was purported at least intermittently by Keynes himself.[1] It does not however, follow logically from the Keynesian system; one can be a Keynesian without being a stagnationist, just as one can be a stagnationist without being a Keynesian.

Visceral hostility to the "un-American" stagnation thesis—a supposed corollary to the Keynesian doctrine of equilibrium at less than full employment—engendered an emotional repugnance to Keynes and all he stood for. It also created a widespread confusion between the Keynesian and Marxian systems. (Marxian macrodynamics, as we have seen in chapter 5, involves stagnationist projections of the capitalist future.) On a personal basis, hostility to stagnationism probably cost Hansen the first chairmanship of the Council of Economic Advisers in 1946, a post for which he had been recommended widely by fellow-economists.

In this chapter, we consider Keynesian stagnationism in its Hansen version, and also compare it with two non-Keynesian forms of stagnationism. One of these is neo-Marxist, developed from the left-wing Marxist position that we have seen already; the other is a more conservative version made famous by Joseph Schumpeter.

DIGRESSION ON LOGIC

Many intelligent laymen consider stagnationism a dead issue. To some, the case has been proved by the increased importance of the public sector, particularly the military subsector, in the American economy. To a larger number, the case has been disproved by the absence of any marked long-term upward trend in American unemployment as a percentage of the labor force. Is either of these positions valid, and if so, which one?

---

[1] The standard statement of Hansen's position is "Economic Progress and Declining Population Growth," *American Economic Review* (March 1939), his presidential address to the American Economic Association, reprinted in Gottfried von Haberler, ed., *Readings in Business Cycle Theory* (1944), ch. 18. An earlier stagnationist statement by Keynes, along similar lines, is "Some Economic Consequences of a Declining Population," *Eugenics Review* (April 1937).

Suppose we are considering, as an exercise in pure logic, the proposition "A implies B," often written $(A \Rightarrow B)$, on the basis of observations "not-A" and "not-B," often written $(\sim A, \sim B)$. What can we infer from these observations about the truth-value of the proposition itself? Quite obviously, nothing whatever. But let us substitute for the bloodless neutrality of "A implies B" the stagnationist thesis that a predominantly private economy with a public sector no more important than during the Harding-Coolidge "normalcy of the 1920s"—A—implies one or another form of "economic stagnation"—B. We observe that the comparative importance of government has nearly tripled since 1929; the (G/Y) ratio (Using GNP as our approximation to Y) rose from 8.2 percent in 1929 to 22.6 percent in 1970, and hence we have $(\sim A)$. We also observe that the American economy has not stagnated over the period since 1929 as a whole, whatever may have happened during the Great Depression of the 1930s, or during shorter intervals like 1958–60, 1969–71, or 1974–76; hence we also have $(\sim B)$. From this evidence the typical conservative jumps to the conclusion that the stagnation thesis has been disproved, that the issue is closed, and that stagnationism is a matter of only antiquarian interest. From this same evidence the typical radical jumps to the opposite conclusion, arguing that the shift from A in 1929 to $(\sim A)$ after 1939 is explained by the need to avoid stagnation, and also that we would have stagnated without the shift. I do not know which cynic first said that the axioms of geometry owed their acceptance to their general adaptability to people's vested interests (including their vested interests in ideas). The same is true of the principles of logic.

TWO STAGNATION CONCEPTS

It is important to distinguish between two concepts of secular stagnation.[2] The two stagnation types may appear together, or either may prevail without the other.

The first stagnation concept implies a decreasing growth rate of an economy (total or per capita or both) at an approximately constant level of employment. The decrease may represent diminishing returns to capital accumulation, as in the approach to the classical stationary state of our chapter 4. It may also be ascribed, when it occurs, to the deterioration of the environment in general and the exhaustion of specific resources (oil fields, forests, fertile soil) as anticipated by many ecologists and environ-

---

[2] Compare Benjamin Higgins, "Concepts and Criteria of Secular Stagnation," in Lloyd A. Metzler and Evsey D. Domar, eds. *Income, Employment, and Public Policy* (1948), Part I, ch. 4.

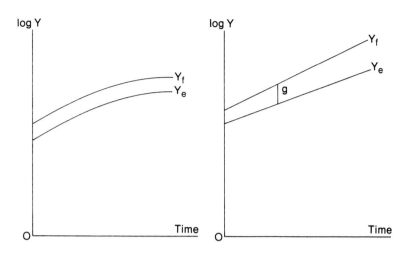

Figure 9-1   Two Concepts of Secular Stagnation

mentalists. It may be due to a decline in population or the labor force, to an increase in psychological alienation (as reflected in declining productivity growth), or to any of a myriad of other causes. It is illustrated on the left panel of figure 9-1, where the horizontal axis is time and the vertical axis is log Y, so that the slope of a straight line is the growth rate ($dY/dt/Y$). The two lines Y_f (representing full-employment conditions) and Y_e (representing equilibrium employment conditions) are drawn upward sloping but concave downward, meaning that equilibrium employment income is a constant proportion of full employment income, so that there is no long-term tendency for the equilibrium employment rate to fall. This is the stagnation concept commonly used in the theory of economic growth and development.

For our present purposes, a second concept is more relevant. It is illustrated by the right panel of figure 9-1. The setting is the same as in the left panel discussed above. Here, however, Y_f may have any concavity whatever; it is drawn as a straight line with zero concavity, implying that the growth rate of full-employment income is assumed constant, as in the "trend growth rates" used by Arthur Okun in estimating the Y_f line for the Council of Economic Advisers under the rubric "Potential GNP."[3] Y_e may also have any concavity whatever. The important point for stagna-

---

[3] "The trend growth rate, fitted to 1947–60 quarterly data, was 3.9 percent, but . . . this was not uniform throughout the period. For the post-Korean period, the estimated trend growth in potential was about 3½ percent, while for the 1947–53 period, it was near 4½ percent." Arthur M. Okun, "Potential GNP: Its Measurement and Significance," in Okun, *The Political Economy of Prosperity* (1970), p. 137.

tionism is not only that Y_e and Y_f not be parallel, but that the gap g between the two curves tends to increase over time. This means that, over time, the equilibrium rate of employment tends to fall, and the equilibrium rate of unemployment tends to rise.

THE HANSEN "FRONTIERS"

Like many Keynesians of the 1930s, Alvin Hansen accepted the stagnation thesis in its *second* form above. Like economists of all persuasions in the late 1930s, Hansen was impressed not only with the persistence of the Great Depression but with the relapse into secondary depression in 1937–1939, before recovery from the primary depression of 1929–1933 was at all complete.[4] At the same time, Hansen wondered why the Depression had come when it did, rather than one or more generations earlier or later. This explanation he believed could be found for the U.S. in the dynamics of population growth.

Hansen concentrated his attention upon the volume of investment outlets for the amount of saving forthcoming at full-employment levels of income. During the nineteenth century these "offsets to saving" had been unusually high because of the presence and importance of four "frontiers," which were, however, tending to decline in importance during the twentieth century, both for the U.S. and for the capitalist world as a whole. These frontiers were:

1. **Geographic,** the layman's meaning of "frontier"—the opening of the U.S. and Canadian West, as well as areas like Australia, South Africa, and Argentina.

2. **Natural resources,** largely geological-mineralogical—the exploitation of forests and mines and soil fertility, not only in frontier areas but well back of them, like (in the U.S.) the Pennsylvania-Ohio oil fields of the mid-nineteenth century and their Oklahoma-Texas-California successors of the twentieth. Also the Mesabi iron range, out of which two World Wars were largely fought.

3. **Demographic**—the growth of population, which provided a steadier demand (with fewer postponable elements of expenditure) than mere increases in living standards.

---

[4] In the U.S., employment had risen from 3.2 to 24.9 percent of the civilian labor force between 1929 and 1933. It had then fallen only to 14.3 percent (1937) before rising to 19.0 and 17.2 percent in the two following years. (These estimates are from *Economic Report of the President* (January 1972), table B-22, p. 220.)

4. **Technological**—the introduction of innovations of both consumption and investment goods, based successively on such major developments as the steam engine, the railroad, the internal-combustion engine, and the electric motor.

From the viewpoint of an American in the 1930s, the first frontier had disappeared domestically a generation previously, and the second was declining. (Since Hansen wrote, the oil shock and energy crisis have emphasized this decline more sharply than did any evidence available in the 1930s). The third (demographic) frontier seemed to Hansen the crucial one in its timing, and hence the title of his study. The absolute increase in population in the U.S. during the decade 1920–1930 had been lower than the absolute increase during the decade 1910–1920. It was the first time in U.S. history that the *increment* (dN/dt) had fallen, although the *growth rate* $(dN/dt)/N$ had been declining quite steadily for over a century. Demographers were currently predicting that the downward trend of (dN/dt) would extend into the indefinite future, because birth rates were falling. Barring drastic reversal of U.S. immigration policy, (dN/dt) was expected to fall to near-zero—a near-stationary population—during the last quarter of the twentieth century. As for the fourth, or technological, frontier, Hansen considered it unreasonable to expect this frontier to carry by itself the full load of off-sets to full-employment saving that it had shared previously with the other three. Hansen went even further at times in the direction of science fiction. He suggested that the capital-intensity of future innovations might decline, as the investment per horsepower was less for gasoline or electric motors than it had been for steam engines. He also had occasional doubts about the future of technological innovation as such, and did not foresee coming revolutions in air transport, television, computers, plastics, synthetics, nuclear power, solar energy, etc.

Although a stagnationist, Hansen was not a pessimist, and neither were his Keynesian followers. To supplement the closing frontiers just discussed, and particularly to compensate for the falling population increment, Hansen proposed and foresaw a fifth frontier, which might be called a *public service* frontier. This frontier was to consist of massive expansion of public works and public services—housing, highways, hospitals, schools, research facilities—without increases in tax rates.[5] It contained no important military

---

[5] Hansen did not consider seriously cutting tax rates instead, while leaving expenditures more nearly constant. In later work, he praised John K. Galbraith's *Affluent Society* (1958) with its call to remedy the "poverty which afflicts us in public services" at the expense of "affluence in private goods." (Hansen, *Economic Issues of the 1960's* (1960), p. 82.) It may be fair to read into Hansen's earlier papers an anticipation of Galbraith's position.

or even para-military components. Hansen commented ruefully to this writer a generation later, in 1970, that the U.S. military budget alone had become a higher percentage of GNP than he had ever imagined for this proposed expansion of civilian spending.

The expansion of World War II was accompanied by stagnationist "postwar forecasts" of a bigger and worse depression after its close. When no such depression developed, and when a twelve-year "baby boom" restored a demographic frontier, it became fashionable to laugh at Hansen's latter-day "dismal science." But when the birth rate fell again after 1957, and the unemployment rate took an upward trend, stagnationism enjoyed a mild revival culminating in the Kennedy-Johnson "Great Society" proposals. These programs were themselves shelved by the Vietnam War and its inflationary consequences. After the oil shock of 1973, stagnationism revived, but based upon resource exhaustion, the perils of pollution, and the alleged beauty of small-scale, slow-growth technologies—the *alternative* stagnation concept illustrated by the left-hand panel of figure 9-1.

MARXIAN CRITICISM: STEINDL

In discussing Marxian stagnationism (chapter 5), we mentioned the unimportance of fiscal and monetary policy in the Marxian scheme. (There was in this scheme no way out short of revolution.) Stagnation in the Keynesian version, however, carries its own reformist solution in a new, or public service, frontier. Marxist counterattack on such reformism has come on three fronts.

1. To raise Y_e to Y_f by monetary or fiscal expansion—i.e., by increasing aggregate demand—tends to raise the price level, as Keynes admitted and as we shall see in chapters 10–11. The Marxists were quick to stress this fact, particularly with relation to the monetary side. (Monetary expansion, some Marxist writers claim, creates "fictitious values" if the monetary increment is valued above its cost of production, as in the case of paper currency or deposit money.) Price-level inflation, especially when accompanied by the creation of fictitious values, lowers real wages. It allegedly follows that any recovery it accomplishes is achieved at the expense of the working class, because it raises the rate of exploitation, the Marxian S'. The higher the rate of exploitation, as we have seen in chapter 5, the greater the danger of "realization crises" (underconsumption), unless private demand is supplemented by "outside" public demand. What remains is not pure capitalism, but (in a phrase later made famous by Schumpeter) "capitalism is an oxygen tent."

2. It is no accident for Marxists that fiscal expansion has taken primarily military rather than civilian forms. (Neither do they blame this twist on

Soviet, Chinese, or Cuban "expansionism.") It was also no accident, in their view, that recovery from the Great Depression waited for World War II. (Neither do they think the delay can be explained by the requirements of "learning" Keynesian economics, nor have we "learned" from the 1930s to avoid repetition of their experience.) Any society is dominated, Marxists maintain, by its technical "mode of production" plus its economic institutions and the particular economic classes that control its means of production. A capitalist government, then, must be in the last analysis the agent of the capitalist class, which controls its physical capital. True, it is not in the capitalists' interest to let the economy stagnate into a situation of revolutionary breakdown, but neither is it in their interest to maintain tight labor markets in which rising wages impinge on profits. The capitalists' interest is best served by an intermediate situation, moderate prosperity without boom, employment reasonably high but less than full. Moreover, if government is to promote employment on a large scale, it should concentrate its efforts in ways that provide capitalists a *quid pro quo* of profitable and guaranteed markets, rather than in ways that involve competition with capitalist industry (such as low-cost housing), or in ways that reduce the labor supply (such as schools or welfare payments). The obvious and simple way out is spending on government order, which is primarily military on a "cost-plus" basis. Everything else is, to a Marxist, little more than cosmetic. Paul Baran and Paul Sweezy sum up U.S. developments since 1945 from a Marxist viewpoint:[6]

> It is of course in the area of defense purchases that most of the expansion has taken place—from about 1 per cent of GNP to more than 10 per cent, accounting for about two thirds of the total expansion of government spending relative to GNP since the 1920's. This massive absorption of surplus in military preparations has been the key fact of postwar American economic history. Some six or seven million workers, more than 9 percent of the labor force, are now dependent for jobs on the arms budget. If military spending were reduced once again to pre-Second World War proportions, the nation's economy would return to a state of profound depression, characterized by unemployment rates of 15 per cent and up, such as prevailed during the 1930's.

3. Aimed directly at the frontier theory is a methodological argument by Josef Steindl,[7] that an economic system should be logically self-contained, so that one should not be content to explain tendencies so important as

---

[6] Paul A. Baran and Paul M. Sweezy, *Monopoly Capital* (1966), p. 152. For later statements, see Sweezy "Capitalism, for Worse," *Monthly Review* (February 1974) and "Keynesian Chickens Come Home to Roost," *ibid.* (April 1974).

[7] Josef Steindl, *Maturity and Stagnation in American Capitalism* (1952), Ch. 12.

stagnation by extraneous forces like frontiers or sunspots without a fuller examination of the economy itself, its internal structure as well as its macro-economic aggregates. Attempting such an analysis, Steindl has himself devised a neo-Marxist stagnation theory that we shall now examine.

Why are there, in a mature capitalist economy, insufficient outlets in the private sector for the saving generated at a full employment level of income? Such an economy, Steindl maintains, must be viewed as a dual structure. One sector is dominated by monopolies and oligopolies, while the other remains basically competitive; the boundaries between the sectors are constantly changing, with the monopoly-oligopoly sector growing in relative prominence. In such a dual economy, the explanation for the short-fall of investment is different in the two sectors. In the concentrated sector, firms maintain prices and profit margins by restructing output; at the same time, their existing profits suffice to provide internally the bulk of whatever investment the companies desire to carry on. The level of investment, of course, will be smaller the greater the restruction in output. In the com-petitive sector, on the other hand, the risks are too great (either from direct competition with the giants, or from dependence on one or more of the giants for markets or supplies). Outsiders are unwilling to supply invest-ment funds to firms in this sector on terms attractive to entrepreneurs. The sum of investment in the two sectors, therefore, normally comes to some-thing less than full-employment saving. Internal saving by large companies is invested, but the market for external saving is increasingly reduced, and the equilibrium level of income falls increasingly short of full employment.

The dual structure, however, does not date from 1929, but from a much earlier period. (In the U.S., the first great era of combinations and trusts was the 1870s and 1880s.) Why, then, if Steindl is correct about the im-portance of economic dualism, was the Great Depression postponed until the 1930s? Why did not the panics of 1890 and 1893 develop into stagna-tion like the market crash of 1929 and the secondary decline of 1937?

Steindl's answer runs in terms of the "gearing ratio" of total capital to owned capital in the monopoly-oligopoly sector. When successful competi-tors move into the monopoly-oligopoly sector—or when oligopolistic firms extend their relative power to new geographical areas or new branches of industry—they must usually expand their physical facilities. This expansion means a burst of new investment, which in turn requires more capital than the successful competitors yet have available internally. The expanding firms must borrow from the public in the security markets.[8] This process of

---

[8] The buying of rivals' facilities, whether with one's own funds or with borrowed money, is also an important element in firm growth, but it is not pertinent to the argu-

borrowing outside capital is reflected in higher gearing ratios in the expanding firms' accounting balance sheets. The process of increasing gearing ratios Steindl finds characteristic of U.S. capitalism through the middle 1920s, but he believes that it ended in the late 1920s. He estimates the overall gearing ratio to have reached its maximum before 1929 (just as the population should reach its maximum after 1975 in the Hansen scheme), because the corporate giants are "geared up." Steindl ascribes the depression and stagnation of the 1930s to this failure of gearing ratios to continue rising. This writer is not aware of follow-up studies applying Steindl's techniques to the period since World War II. (A successful effort in this direction would have to exclude defense production if the stagnation thesis is to be tested meaningfully; such separation is difficult in practice.)

CONSERVATIVE STAGNATIONISM: SCHUMPETER

The predominant political orientation of stagnationist writers and their followers has been liberal in the twentieth-century interventionist sense, or socialist in the tradition of Karl Marx. Hansen and perhaps Keynes are exemplars of the first tradition; Baran, Sweezy, and Steindl represent the second. Conservative stagnationism has also flourished, however. It blames depressions and recessions upon unwise regulation or private business. Among professional economists, a leading spokesman has been Joseph Schumpeter, whose views are presented most fully in *Capitalism, Socialism, and Democracy.*[9]

Schumpeter was no conventional "back to Grandpa" reactionary, nor was he an Andrew Mellon (Secretary of the Treasury, 1921–30) calling for "liquidation" of farmers and trade unions. He was as convinced as any Marxist that capitalism was not the end of institutional evolution, and that it would expire in the relatively near future in favor of some form of socialism. But in opposition to the Marxists, he regarded the prospective change with more apprehension than anticipation. Socialism was to him inevitable, in the same sense as the proverbial death and taxes.

Like many other economists, Schumpeter had wondered why neither the classical stationary state nor the Marxian liquidity crisis had come about as capital accumulated in the capitalist world. His answer was "the process of creative destruction" known as innovation. (Any change in operational

---

ment here. When firm A buys the facilities of firm B, the investment by stockholders of A is balanced by disinvestment by stockholders of B, and no net investment takes place.

[9] Joseph A. Schumpeter, *Capitalism, Socialism, and Democracy* (1942; 2nd ed., 1947), Part II, ch. 5–14. An earlier version forms the closing section of Schumpeter, *Business Cycles* (1939), vol. II, ch. 15-G, pp. 1011–1050, under the heading "The Disappointing Juglar."

production functions represents to Schumpeter an innovation; the term is at once broader and narrower than technical invention.) A bare stress on innovation is conventional enough, but Schumpeter carried his analysis further than his predecessors had done. Were it not for innovation, he tells us, not only would the rate of profit and of interest fall to or near zero, but business cycles would be eliminated and capitalism would stagnate in both our uses of the term. From these propositions Schumpeter draws an important corollary: whatever encourages or accelerates innovation, regardless of its costs in "future shock," is good for capitalism; whatever discourages or retards innovation (by making it less profitable) is bad for capitalism. Innovations are made by entrepreneurs; indeed, only the innovator is the true entrepreneur; the routine "organization man" is a mere drone, whatever his title and however high he may climb the organizational pyramid. To Schumpeter, therefore, the capitalist entrepreneur is the tragic hero of capitalist decline.

The entrepreneur is a tragic hero because he digs his own grave. As capitalist enterprises grow, so do corporate bureaucracies, to the extent that they can take over part or all of the processes leading to innovation. On the engineering side particularly, they become the principal sources of innovation; the General Electric "House of Magic" is an example. (Had Schumpeter lived ten or fifteen years after 1950, he might have found in the uses of computerized operations research and management science nonengineering illustrations of the corporate bureaucrat displacing the capitalist entrepreneur.) If innovation can be institutionalized in a bureaucracy, the bureaucracy might equally well be a public as a private one. (Operating examples are the National Aeronautics and Space Agency, the Atomic Energy Commission, the Tennessee Valley Authority, the Japanese National Railways, even the Post Office.) What the entrepreneur has done, however unconsciously, has been to develop bigger and better substitutes for himself. Entrepreneurs comprise the collective Frankenstein of economic history; Schumpeter himself speaks of "the obsolescence of the entrepreneurial function."

Schumpeter, like Marx, was a Renaissance man—a ranking sociologist and intellectual historian as well as an economist. As we can see from the last paragraph, his stagnationism calls his sociology into play along with his economics. Laissez-faire capitalism, he argues, was oversold—as the California or Florida climate was oversold later on—and the overselling produced a natural reaction. Adam Smith's "obvious and simple system of natural liberty" was presented not only as obvious and simple (and natural), but as a practicable Utopia, the City Hall of "the heavenly city of the eighteenth-century philosophers." But Utopia it was not, at least not for everyone, and so it has come to be reviled in consequence later on. Capitalism had increased economic freedom, but at some cost in many

people's sense of "belonging" to society and resulting feelings of anxiety, rootlessness, "identity crises," anomie, and (non-Marxian) alienation. Perhaps more important, capitalism had also raised the social position, prestige, and power of the innovator and entrepreneur; however, one can only raise one group's social position, prestige, and power at the expense of someone else's. The capitalist's position rose at the expense of the landed aristocrat, the lay or clerical intellectual, and the military man—three groups who had ruled the roost in precapitalist times. For all of these, capitalism was decidedly sub-Utopian and sometimes positively dystopian. When capitalist institutions failed to put one hundred percent of all workers into the top ten percent of the income or wealth distribution, labor likewise became alienated and the emerging labor organizations turned against entrepreneurship, if not consciously against capitalism as a whole. All this at a time when entrepreneurship was in process of rendering itself obsolete.

There also arose anti-entrepreneurial, sometimes also anti-innovational, alliances between labor and intellectuals, such as the British Labor Party and the American New Deal Democracy. The leaders were usually intellectuals, the villains of the Schumpeterian epic. Sometimes these grand alliances included elements of "the landed interest"—aristocrats, landlords, peasants, and/or family farmers.[10] These alliances have enacted, strengthened, and enforced anti-entrepreneurial and anti-innovational legislation, which reduced the incentives to innovate by forcing entrepreneurs to share the perishable and short-run gains from innovation with other segments of society for allegedly ethical reasons. The legislative enactments have included (1) progressive taxation of income and wealth; (2) compulsory collective bargaining, with lists of "unfair labor practices" banned to entrepreneurs; (3) public-utility regulation, farm parities, and other forms of maximum and minimum price regulation; and (4) antimonopoly legislation. It was equity-oriented New Deal legislation which prolonged to stagnation what would otherwise have been ordinary depression in the 1930s. (Similar legislation had crippled British recovery from the post–World War I depression a decade earlier.) Instead of investment, such legislation encourages capitalists to consume rather than save, and to attempt hoarding of their savings. It is the anti-investment and prohoarding atmosphere that leads to the stagnation which the liberal State counteracts by "oxygen tents" of public spending. (It may also lead to capital shortages and the "alternative" stagnation depicted on left side of figure 9-1. This writer does not believe any such result was foreseen by Schumpeter himself.)

---

[10] The landed interest was generally procapitalist or at least anti-anticapitalist, but Schumpeter views the power of this ally as weakened by the progress of entrepreneurial innovation.

SUMMARY

Economic stagnation may mean (1) a declining growth rate of Y of (Y/N) at a constant level of employment (Y_e/Y_t) and/or (2) a rising unemployment rate, or a negative value of $[d(Y_e/Y_t)/dt]$. (The second of these interpretations is used here.) Also, the term refers to a primarily private economy, in which the ratio (G/Y) is small and does not rise over time. Economic evolution has in most if not all advanced countries involved expansion of the public sector relative to the private one, as well as the general avoidance of stagnation. The "mature economy" issue, therefore, remains a live one, although doctrinaires on both sides believe history has settled it "their way."

There are at least four forms of the stagnation thesis. One, orthodox Marxism, we have considered in the "Laws of Motion of Capitalism" section of chapter 5, and add nothing here. The second, or Keynes-Hansen, form, is the standard type. As presented by Hansen, it was based on the declining importance of geographic, natural-resource and demographic "frontiers," with the last-named frontier crucial for the 1930s. Hansen proposed creation of a new frontier in the civilian public service sector, anticipating the later proposals of Galbraith and others. The third, or neo-Marxian, form of stagnationism expects the Hansen new frontier to be overwhelmingly military in practice, as per the "warfare state" and "military-industrial complex." On the positive side, one neo-Marxist writer (Steindl) traces stagnation to the dual structure of mature capitalist industry as between a generally restrictionist monopoly-oligopoly sector and a highly risky competitive one. Between the two, capitalism cannot provide sufficient outlets for full-employment saving. Our fourth and last form of stagnationism, the Schumpeterian, is conservative in its political implication, although Schumpeter was himself a pessimist rather than a right-wing activist. Schumpeter's argument is that innovational entrepreneurship has been required to keep a capitalist regime running smoothly, but that capitalism had itself bureaucratized the innovational process in large firms, to the extent that the individual entrepreneur stands in danger of obsolescence. In addition, capitalism's inability to meet Utopian expectations has encouraged a labor-intellectual antientrepreneurship political combination, led by intellectuals and sometimes joined by elements of the landed interest. This has sponsored and enacted anti-entrepreneurial legislation in a number of areas—taxation, labor relations, price regulation, monopoly control. This legislation has discouraged investment, led (through hoarding) to stagnation, and reduced capitalism to dependence upon the "oxygen tent" of public expenditure.

Chapter 10

Aggregate Demand: Enter the Price Level

THE POST-KEYNESIAN COUNTERREVOLUTION

Since the late 1940s there has developed a post-Keynesian counterrevolution against the Keynesian macroeconomics of chapters 6 and 7, and a partial revival of the classical and neo-classical macroeconomics we studied in chapter 4. The counterrevolution focuses upon elements of macroeconomics either ignored or obscured by the Keynesian approach. These refinements include (1) on the demand side, a fuller exploration of the active influence of the price level directly upon real wealth and indirectly upon the Keynesian aggregates, and the implications of this analysis for the notion of underemployment equilibrium; and (2) on the supply side, the rehabilitation of classical macroeconomics in a form liberated from Say's Identity between aggregate supply and demand (regardless of the price level).[1] The first of these aspects is the subject matter of this chapter. The second aspect, and also certain policy implications of the counterrevolution, are the subject matter of Chapter 11.

Digression: What we call the post-Keynesian counterrevolution is also called the "Chicago" counterrevolution—its intellectual foundations having been laid largely by teachers and students at the University of Chicago—the neo-classical counterrevolution—by reason of its revival of the neo-classical macroeconomics—and the "anemic counterrevolution"—because it need not involve the fundamental scrapping of the Keynesian structure. Another possible term is the "neo-classical synthesis"—an expression appropriated by Samuelson's *Economics* for a different concept.[2]

The motivation for the counterrevolution is brought out in the following selection from 1958 congressional testimony by Milton Friedman, one of its founders and principal spokesmen. He is discussing the development of macroeconomics and monetary theory since 1929—his "past three decades":[3]

---

[1] We omitted from chapters 6–7 Keynes's attenuated treatment of aggregate supply as a function primarily of employment. See John M. Keynes, *General Theory of Employment Interest and Money* (1936), p. 44 f.; Alvin Hansen, *A Guide to Keynes* (1953), pp. 30–33; Sidney Weintraub, *Classical Keynesianism, Monetary Theory, and the Price Level* (1961), pp. 22–24, 35–38; Sidney Weintraub, *Some Aspects of Wage Theory and Policy* (1963), pp. 41–54. Appendix 10A to this chapter is a brief introduction to this literature.

In connection with Say's Identity (and Say's Law), the reader should review chapter 4, including the expressions (4.1), (4.3), and (4.4).

[2] Samuelson's "neo-classical synthesis" combines essentially Keynesian macroeconomics with essentially Marshallian microeconomics.

[3] Milton Friedman, "Statement on Monetary Theory and Policy," *Employment, Growth, and Price Levels* (Hearings before Joint Economic Committee, 86th Congress,

The past three decades have seen first a sweeping revolution against previously accepted economic thought about the role of monetary factors in economic change and then a counter-revolution that is still incomplete but promises to be no less sweeping. As with any successful counter-revolution, the result has not been simply to restore the status quo ante. In the process, views initially held rather uncritically have been reexamined and improved, and some elements of the revolutionary interlude absorbed. . . .

Two forces combined to produce a counter-revolution in ideas. One was strictly academic. Scholarly criticism and analysis of Keynes's ideas demonstrated a logical fallacy in one of his central propositions: namely, the proposition that, for a given stock of money, there might, even in principle, exist no price and wage level consistent with full employment; or, to put the proposition differently, than even if all prices and wages were perfectly flexible, a free market system might have no inherent tendency to full employment.

It has turned out on analysis that Keynes's proposition involved an error of omission. He neglected to take account of the effect of different levels of prices on the real value attached by the community to its wealth relative to its income, and of the effect of changes in this ratio, in its turn, on consumption expenditures. When this effect is taken into account, there is always in principle a price and wage level consistent with full employment, though of course frictions or other disturbances may prevent the economy from attaining such a position at any point of time. . . .

The second, and more obvious, though perhaps not more important, factor that produced a counter-revolution was the brute force of events. Many countries in the postwar period, including the U.S., pursued cheap-money policies, partly under the influence of ideas derived from Keynes. . . . Every such country experienced either open inflation or a network of partly effective, partly ineffective, controls designed to suppress the inflationary pressure. In every case, the stock of money rose as a result of the cheap-money policies and so did prices, either openly or in whatever disguise was most effective in circumventing the controls. No country succeeded in stemming inflation without adopting measures that made it possible to restrain the growth in the stock of money. And every country that did hold down the growth in the stock of money succeeded in checking the price rise.

THE PIGOU EFFECT ON IS

Consumption, it is agreed generally, depends upon the wealth as well as the (disposable) income of the consuming public. Hence the importance

1st Sess., May 1958), reprinted in Warren L. Smith and Ronald L. Teigen, *Readings in Money, National Income, and Stabilization Policy* (1970), pp. 112–114. (Italics added).

of markets in existing assets, particularly common stock and real estate, in triggering income fluctuations. Let us now go a step further, and subdivide real wealth W into liquid assets W' and ordinary assets W". The conventional working definition of an individual's W' is the deflated value of his money, his savings deposits in all banks, his savings and loan shares, and his holdings of public securities. All these physical assets, and returns on them are fixed in money terms.[4] All the individual's other physical assets are included in his W".

Let us now examine the effects on W of an autonomous fall in the price level, such as might result from unusually bountiful harvests or the acceleration of productivity, with nominal money stock and the nominal volume of other liquid assets constant. The nominal value $(W'')^*$ of W" will presumably fall with the level of prices generally, leaving the real value W" unchanged. The nominal value $(W')^*$ of W' remains unchanged by hypothesis, so that the real value W' will rise. With W' rising and W" approximately constant, their sum W will rise.

We have now established the wealth effects of a fall in the price level. We next proceed to investigate the influence of these effects on interest, income, and employment. As W rises, consumption will rise for any given income Y, so that the consumption function as a whole will rise and the saving function will fall. Presumably the C_o term will rise, and possibly also the marginal propensity c. If both terms rise, both the multiplicand and the multiplier increase in expressions like:

$$Y = \frac{A}{1 - c} \tag{6.5}$$

and

$$Y = \frac{A - cT_o}{1 - c + ct} \tag{6.15}$$

---

[4] In the statistician's Utopia, with unlimited information available at no cost, we could expand W' to include additional assets denominated in money terms, such as high-grade private debt securities and the present value of life insurance policies and annuities. (The volume of the individual's money debts should of course be deducted from his W'.)

Under the conventional definition, securities denominated in purchasing power rather than in nominal money are not included in liquid assets. Yet, in an inflationary environment, they are thought of by the public as superior in liquidity to any form of liquid assets.

The marginal propensity to tax—which we symbolize by t—also falls with the price level in tax systems featuring progressive taxes expressed in nominal terms. This fall strengthens the wealth effect. It also raises the Keynesian multipliers by lowering the t term in their denominators. (People are now in lower money income brackets.) By standard multiplier analysis—and also by the Islamic diagrams of chapter 7, which we shall soon review—the IS function shifts to the right. This raises both the equilibrium real income Y_e and the real interest rate r_e, neglecting any changes in the LM function. From the rise in Y_e follows a rise in the employment level N_e. This rise will extend to full employment N_f when Y_e rises to Y_f. Conversely, a higher price level is associated with lower values of income Y, interest r, and employment N, with LM constant.[5] These results are quite consistent with *microeconomic* common sense, but for the whole economy, do we not associate inflation with prosperity and deflation with depression? (This paradox will worry us throughout this chapter and the next.)

The impact of price level changes on consumption and income is called the Pigou effect, on which Friedman's conclusion (italicized above) was largely based.[6] But may not a rise in income from Y_e to Y_f require an unrealistically large fall of the price level and/or the rate of interest, from positive to negative values? To avoid this possibility, we assume [in addition to constancy of M* and (W)*] that the society's "needs" are sufficient for aggregate expenditures to exceed Y_f at some positive price level. We must also assume that, if the interest rate approaches zero, the resulting rise in W (to approach infinity) will so increase the propensity to consume and reduce the propensity to save that aggregate expenditures will equal or exceed Y_f. Neither of these assumptions seems unreasonably strong, even in a Galbraithian "affluent society."

---

[5] **Digression:**   An exogenous fall in r (such as follows reduced capital exports) raises both W' and W", and therefore also their sum W, setting off the same effect on Y and N as an exogenous fall in the price level p. Conversely, an exogenous rise in r acts like an exogenous rise in p. This results from the capitalization phenomenon. Wealth and income are related by $W = (Y/r)$. For a constant Y, a fall (rise) in r raises (lowers) W.

[6] **Terminological Digression:**   "Pigou effect" priority should probably go not to Pigou but to Gottfried von Haberler, *Prosperity and Depression* (1939), pp. 242, 389, 403. Pigou's treatments are in A. C. Pigou, *Employment and Equilibrium* (1941); "The Classical Stationary State," *Economic Journal* (December 1943); and "Economic Progress in a Stable Environment," *Economica* (August 1947). The *Economica* essay is reproduced in Friedrich A. Lutz and Lloyd W. Mints, eds., *Readings in Monetary Theory* (1951), pp. 241–251. See also Don Patinkin, "Price Flexibility and Full Employment," *American Economic Review* (September 1948) revised in Lutz and Mints, *op. cit.*, pp. 252–283.

Patinkin, *Money, Interest, and Prices* (1956, 2nd ed. 1965) uses the term "real-balance effect" in connection both with the Pigou effect and the parallel interest-induced effect mentioned in footnote 5.

OFFSETS TO THE PIGOU EFFECT

The words "Pigou effect" are in some quarters unclean. The reason is the effect's deflationary policy implications, particularly as they affect wage rates. Let us examine six principal offsets that impede its smooth and simple operation:

1. Nominal money and other liquid assets—M* and (W')*—do not, unless controlled, stay constant as the price level changes. In conformity with "needs of trade" ideology, they tend to vary in the same direction as the price level. This variation is called by its critics "perverse elasticity." It is blamed (notably by Friedman and Schwartz) for having exacerbated the Great Depression of 1929–33;[7] it is blamed more recently for "validating" inflationary wage and price movements, and accommodating petroleum and other import price rises by increasing both the money supply and its growth rate. At the same time it is defended, both on political (or "vote-fare") grounds and as an economic necessity for growth and employment.[8] Opponents agree, however, that nominal money and other liquid assets have in fact responded to price-level changes, in the "wrong" way from the viewpoint of the Pigou effect.

2. Whatever may be the comparative effects of *high* and *low* price levels, *rising* price and wage levels may be expansionary if people buy and hire (to beat the next price and wage increases, or accumulate inventories for future sales), while *falling* prices and wages may be contractionary if buyers and employers wait for further decreases (and live off their inventories.) Both consumption and investment functions are affected by these expectations. Similar expectational factors also reduce microeconomic elasticities of demand and supply for particular commodities, but only seldom do they either produce instability—defined as "functions sloping the wrong way"— or dominate particular markets for long periods. It is difficult to see why expectational factors should be more important macroeconomically— without the monetary reactions noted above.

3. Aggregate real nonliquid assets W" may indeed be invariant with respect to the price level. At the same time, they include a highly visible

---

[7] Milton Friedman and Anna J. Schwartz, *Monetary History of the U.S., 1860–1960* (1963), ch. 9, reprinted as *The Great Contraction, 1929–1933* (1965).

[8] The argument is that raising N and Y also raises M* and p, with the former moving first and appearing to be a causal factor. But if M* were prevented from increasing with N and Y, the principal result would be to check the rise in N and Y. In particular, once p has risen—in an economy with a strong labor movement, an effective system of unemployment insurance, and an income floor supported by direct relief— stagnation rather than deflation is the alleged result of tight money. Compare Sidney Weintraub, *Some Aspects of Wage Theory and Policy, op. cit.,* ch. 2, 6.

or strategic subset of assets whose prices fluctuate with, but more widely than, the general price level. For these assets, real as well as nominal values move *with* prices, and also dominate their holders' outlook upon their wealth and welfare. This tends to dampen the Pigou effect. Real estate is the most familiar strategic asset. Other "inflation hedges"—subject to losses in real value when an inflation decelerates, stops, or reverses itself— include the precious metals, art works, jewelry, old coins, postage stamps, Oriental rugs, and "collectors' items" generally. The higher the ratio of strategic assets to all ordinary assets the more the society is insulated from the Pigou effect, the weaker is the Pigou effect, and the more likely is the Pigou effect to operate in the "wrong" direction.

4. Estimates of liquid assets are often erroneously estimated gross rather than net of liquid debts. Insofar as any individual owes money, the real value of his debts rises *pari passu* with the real value of his liquid assets when the price level falls. If he is a net monetary debtor, accordingly, his consumption function will normally shift in the same direction as the price level, rather than the reverse. Should consumers as a whole be net monetary debtors to business as a whole (or to the government)—outstanding installment and mortgage debt plus accrued taxes outweighing bond and allied security holdings—the net indebtedness will militate against the Pigou effect.

5. A fall in the price level entails some redistribution of real income and wealth from debtors to creditors, and from "active" to "passive" participants in economic life. If money wages also fall, there may also be a shift from workers to capitalists, although this is less certain if the short-run elasticity of labor demand is high. Keynes concludes in the "wage-cut" chapter 19 of *The General Theory* that the net effect of these changes will be to lower both the m.p.c. and the standard multiplier. In a Pigou-effect context, such a change also operates to lower its effectiveness.

6. The Pigou effect acts more slowly, in changing real income and the level of employment, than active monetary or fiscal policy. It should, however, be noted that the Pigou effect can operate to raise employment in a progressive economy without "waiting for Godot" in the shape of falling wage rates or similar flexibilities. All that is required is a period in which money wages rise more slowly than man-hour productivity. (Keynes himself favored stable money wage rates.) The Pigou effect is therefore faster than a forthright assault upon wage rigidity, although slower than "make-work" expenditures, tax cuts, or the printing press.

Considering these several offsets, we should not be surprised that most writers (including Pigou) have downgraded the Pigou effect to a theoretical curiosum. Contrary to this conventional disregard, however, is the historical

Table 10-1
Estimates of Price-Level Elasticity of Consumption, U.S.

Investigators		
L. R. Klein (1950)	1921–41; annual, per capita	0[a]
C. Christ (1951)	1921–47; annual, aggregate	−0.19; −0.27[b]
L. R. Klein and A. S. Goldberger (1955)	1929–50; annual, aggregate	0[a]
Same	1929–52; annual, aggregate	−0.06
K. A. Fox (1956)	1929–52; annual, aggregate	−0.05
A. Zellner (1957)	1947–55; quarterly, aggregate	−0.21; −0.36[b]
Z. Griliches et al. (1962)	1947–55; quarterly, aggregate	−0.27
Same	1952–60; quarterly, aggregate	−0.30
Same	1947–60; quarterly, aggregate	−0.21
M. Morishima and M. Saito (1964)	1902–52; annual, per capita	−0.215

Notes: Except for the Klein (1950) estimate, years (or quarters) of wartime direct controls have been omitted.

[a] Not significantly different from zero.

[b] These two estimates differ mainly in their selection of "other variables."

record. Prior to 1945 at any rate, the price level *did* fall in depressions; prior to 1929 at any rate, the price decline *did* stimulate the subsequent revival, although the mechanism of stimulation is not clear. Several consumption-function studies have also sought, by introducing one or another (W')* and price level variable, to estimate the liquid-asset elasticity of consumption. Patinkin has assembled the results of a number of such studies, using U.S. data;[9] table 10-1 below, is a condensation of Patinkin's summary. The computed elasticities cluster, in the late studies dominated by post-1945 data, in the range $(−)$ .20–.30, meaning that a ten percent price fall should induce a two (or three) percent rise in real consumption expenditures, and vice versa.

A review of Keynesian Model III (chapter 7, figure 7-4) is presented as figure 10-1. For a decline in the price level from p_2 to p_1 (or for a rise from p_1 to p_2) the several panels of the figure permit the reader to translate into IS-LM diagram-language the literary argument of Haberler and Pigou, by

[9] Don Patinkin, *Money, Interest, and Prices* (2nd ed., 1965), p. 656f. Patinkin's note M (pp. 651–664) reviews other studies, including some from other countries, as well as citing more completely the studies listed, and commenting upon the inconsistencies between them.

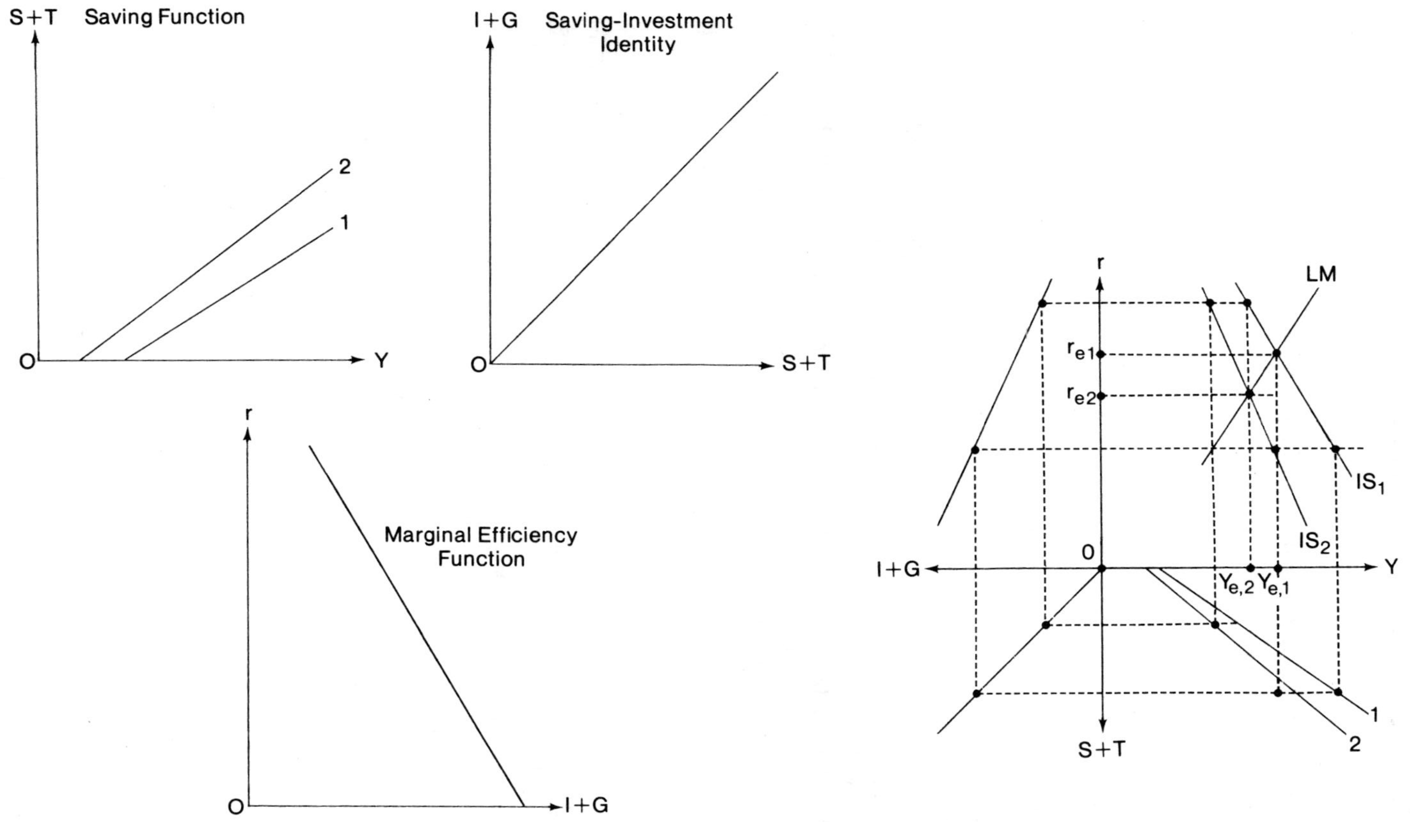

Figure 10-1 The Pigou Effect on IS

seeing how a fall (rise) in the price level moves the IS function to the right (left), raising (lowering) the income for any real interest rate.

THE KEYNES EFFECT ON LM

Lord Keynes—in chapter 19 of *The General Theory*—recognizes that a lower price level raises the real value of a constant nominal money supply. He goes on to argue that the increase in the real value of the money supply resulting from a fall in the price level lowers the interest rate and thereby raises the level of investment (but not the m.e.i. function); he also cites as offsets the considerations we have numbered (2), (5), and (6) above, which apply here as well as to the Pigou effect. The relation recognized by Keynes between the price level, the real money supply, interest, and investment is known as the Keynes effect and distinguished from the Pigou effect, but Keynes attached little policy importance to it. He considered an increase in the nominal money supply—assuming minimal inflation—to be a preferable way to achieve the same result. (It acts more quickly and avoids expectational offsets.) In the IS-LM framework, a lower price level lowers the interest rate and thereby shifts LM downward for any income level; vice versa, of course, for a higher price level. We illustrate this effect for a lower price level 1 and a higher price level 2 in figure 10-2. This figure is based on Keynesian Model IV and expands figure 7-5; it provides another opportunity to review materials from chapter 7. With an unchanged IS function, the Keynes effect of a lower (higher) price level is a higher (lower) Y_e and a lower (higher) r_e. The income consequences of the Keynes and Pigou effects upon Y_e are mutually reinforcing, while those upon r_e are offsetting.

THE REAL BALANCE EFFECT ON
INCOME AND EMPLOYMENT

Since Pigou and Keynes effects operate simultaneously, they can be combined for purposes of analysis, as on the upper panel of figure 10-3. Their income consequences are mutually reinforcing, as we have seen. Their interest-rate consequences are drawn completely offsetting, so that r_e is independent of the price level on figure 10-3. This result accords with conventional nonmonetary theories of interest, but appears here as a special case. If the Pigou effect dominates the Keynes effect, r_e and p_e will move in opposite directions. If, on the other hand, the Keynes effect dominates the Pigou effect, r_e and p_e will move in the same direction. The last case provides another hypothesis to explain the "Gibson paradox" of interest rates varying with the price level as well as with its rate of change.

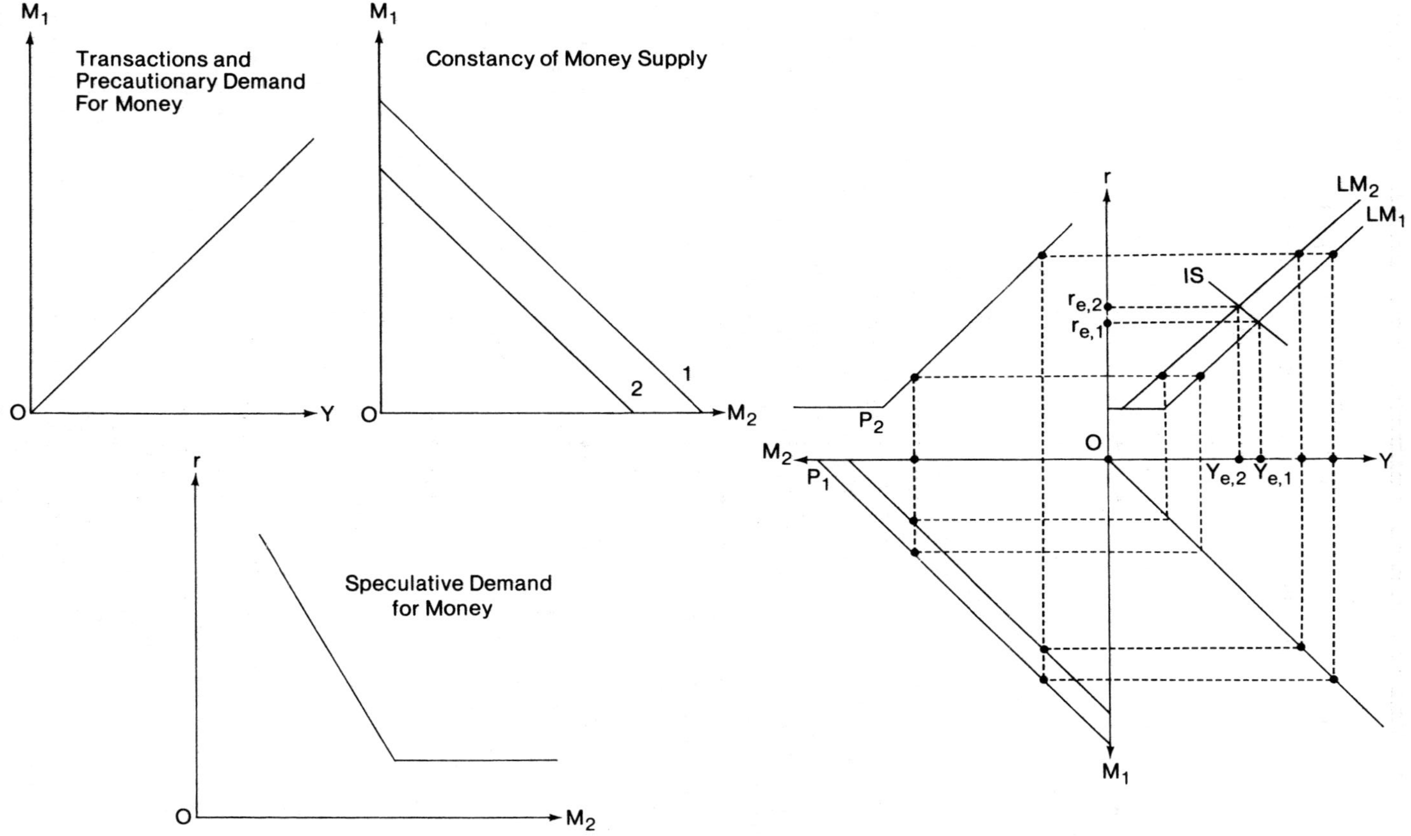

Figure 10-2 Keynes Effect on LM

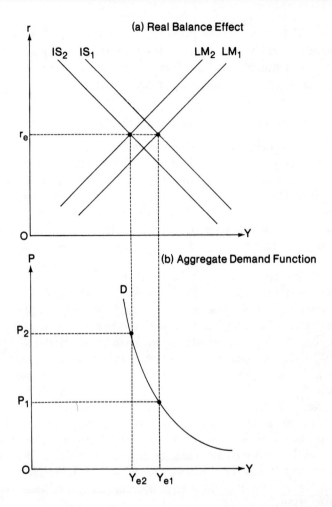

Figure 10-3 Real Balance Effect and Aggregate Demand Function

Our diagram (figure 10-3, upper panel) takes no account of any secondary interaction between Pigou and Keynes effects, in case the interest rate should vary. If the Pigou effect dominates, for example, and the real interest rate rises when the price level falls, the value of wealth is recapitalized downward and the Pigou effect is attenuated as per the argument of footnote 5. Domination by the Keynes effect, on the other hand, implies that the real interest rate and the price level move in the same direction. A price level fall, specifically, lowers the interest rate and recapitalizes value of wealth upward. The additional upward recapitalization of wealth strengthens and buttresses the Pigou effect.

Digression: The combination (summation) of Pigou and Keynes effects we call here the *real-balance effect* of the revaluation of liquid assets. This terminology is a minor departure from the ordinary usage, which follows Patinkin. (Compare the second paragraph of footnote 6.)

THE AGGREGATE DEMAND FUNCTION

Except for the definitional statement that p_2 exceeds p_1, we have not indicated explicitly the values of the price levels we are discussing. This step can, however, be taken readily. It is accomplished on the lower panel of figure 10-3. The result is an aggregate demand function in Y and p.[10] This function looks, as it should, like the demand function for a single commodity in microeconomics. It should not be confused with the aggregate expenditure function C + I + G as drawn on Keynesian cross diagrams like our figure 6-1.

The elasticity of the aggregate demand function is a measure of the importance of the real-balance effect. The higher the elasticity, the greater the importance. To call the counterrevolution "anemic" implies that the aggregate demand function is near-vertical and that its elasticity is near-zero (or even that its slope and elasticity are "wrong" from the viewpoint of stability.) In the near-vertical case, with near-zero elasticity, equilibrium real income remains independent of the price level, as in chapters 6–9.

In discussing expansion and contraction gaps in chapter 6, we raised the question, can price inflation "close" an expansion gap that is measured in real terms, or can price deflation close a contraction gap measured in real terms? Are price-level movements "functional" in gap analysis? This question can now be answered by reference to the real-balance effect—always assuming at least one of the Pigou and Keynes effects to be effective within finite time. It appears that price-level movements can indeed serve equilibrating functions.

An easy way to translate the foregoing results into algebraic form is to modify the linear equation systems of chapter 7 to include the influence of the price level p but not its rate of change (dp/dt). The Pigou effect adds terms in p to the consumption (and tax) functions used to derive IS; the Keynes effect adds terms in p to the demand (and supply) functions for money used to derive LM. The combination of neo-IS and neo-LM yields our aggregate demand function, rather than a pair of equilibrium values Y_e and r_e as in chapter 7.

---

[10] An aggregate demand function can, of course, be derived from either the Pigou or the Keynes effect by itself. For example, William Branson, *Macroeconomic Theory and Policy* (1972), pp. 69–71, derives it without reference to the Pigou effect.

For neo-IS we have, in the notation of chapter 7:

$$Y = C + I + G \tag{10.1}$$

$$C = C_o + c_1(Y - T) - c_2 p \qquad (c_1, c_2 > 0) \tag{10.2}$$

$$T = T_o + t_1 Y + t_2 p \qquad (t_1, t_2 > 0) \tag{10.3}$$

$$I + G = (I_o + G_o) - ir \qquad (i > 0) \tag{10.4}$$

$$A = C_o + I_o + G_o \tag{10.5}$$

The solution for Y or for r gives our desired result. These solutions are:

$$Y = \frac{(A - c_1 T_o) - ir - (c_2 + c_1 t_2)p}{1 - c_1 + c_1 t_1} \tag{10.6a}$$

$$r = \frac{1}{i}[(A - c_1 T_o) - (1 - c_1 + c_1 t_1)Y - (c_2 + c_1 t_2)p] \tag{10.6b}$$

(The reader can verify these results as an exercise.)

For neo-LM we use Keynesian Model V. This includes the influence of the government budget upon the real money supply, along with the income level and the interest rate. (We treat G and T as constants to simplify the algebra, and assume that high prices reduce liquidity preference.)

$$M^s = M_0^s + n_1 Y + n_2 r - n_3 p + g(G - T) \qquad (n_1, n_2, n_3 > 0) \tag{10.7}$$

$$M^d = M_0^d + m_1 Y - m_2 r - m_3 p \qquad (m_1, m_2, m_3 > 0) \tag{10.8}$$

The desired solutions for (Y, r) can be found with more tedium than difficulty as:

$$Y = \frac{(m_2 + n_2)r + g(G - T) + (m_3 - n_3)p + M_o}{m_1 - n_1} \tag{10.9a}$$

$$r = \frac{(m_1 - n_1)Y - (m_3 - n_3)p - g(G - T) - M_o}{m_2 + n_2} \tag{10.9b}$$

and a linear approximation to the aggregate demand function results from equating r-values from (10.6b) and (10.9b). Being only a function of

(Y,p), aggregate demand by itself will not yield equilibrium values for any of our unknowns. Also, being only a linear approximation, it may give meaningless (negative) values of p and/or of r for $Y = Y_f$.

A simplified form of this aggregate demand function is:

$$Y = \frac{Y_o - y_1 p + gi(G - T)}{y_2} \qquad (10.10)$$

whose slope can be viewed as a price-level multiplier:

$$\mu_p = \frac{\partial Y}{\partial p} = -\frac{y_1}{y_2} \qquad (10.11)$$

but of course the coefficients of (10.10–11) are themselves long and involved, as the reader may again verify.[11]

SUMMARY

There has arisen since World War II a counterrevolution against Keynesian systems of the sort outlined in chapters 6–7. The counterrevolution was set off largely by postwar inflationary experience. It has involved both the aggregate-demand and the aggregate-supply aspects of macroeconomic theory. In this chapter we consider only aggregate demand. Here the counterrevolution has involved a more active role for the general price level. We have derived a downward-sloping demand function for income in terms of absolute prices, such that equilibrium income Y_e may equal full-

---

[11] After we let $t_1 = t_2 = 0$ in (10.3) and $G = G_o$ in (10.4), equation (10.6b) reduces to a form consistent with (10.9b), namely:

$$r = \frac{1}{i} [(A - c_1 T) - (1 - c_1)Y - c_2 p]$$

so that, in (10.10):

$$Y_o = A - c_1 T + \frac{i}{m_2 + n_2} M_o$$

$$y_1 = c_2 + \frac{i}{m_2 + n_2} (n_3 - m_3)$$

$$y_2 = (1 - c_1) + \frac{i}{m_2 - n_2} (m_1 - n_1)$$

employment income Y_f at some positive price level. This result implies that full employment can be reached (in principle) by deflationary means, so that persistent unemployment permits the inference that wages and/or prices are above their equilibrium levels.

In developing the aggregate demand function (in words, in diagrams, and in equations), we proceed from the Keynesian IS-LM formulation by considering two effects, named for Pigou and Keynes respectively, and combining them into a real-balance effect. Assume that deflation or disinflation is being used to remedy a contraction gap. The Pigou effect then operates by the upward revaluation of liquid assets to increase wealth; the increased wealth leads to increased consumption for any income level. The Keynes effect operates in the same case by increasing the real quantity of money— assuming the nominal quantity unaffected. The rise in the real quantity of money lowers the real interest rate and therefore raises investment, even though the marginal efficiency schedule may not change. A number of offsets to both Pigou and Keynes effects are also considered, since many writers do not consider either effect important in the short run. We suggest that the real-balance effect may explain how price-level changes could close the expansion and contraction gaps discussed in chapter 6. Closing the macro-system (Price level included), requires an aggregate supply function as well, to which we turn in chapter 11.

Appendix 10a

AGGREGATE SUPPLY AND DEMAND
IN THE KEYNESIAN SYSTEM

For varying amounts of employment N, Keynes envisaged nominal demand in a form like D (in figure 10A.1). The positive slope requires no explanation. The downward concavity reflects primarily a fractional marginal propensity to spend and a stable level of investment. The aggregate supply function S on the same figure indicates the aggregate nominal sales proceeds (which Keynes calls Z) required to induce employers to provide each amount of employment. At low employment levels, D lies above S, providing incentive for further expansion. At higher levels, the reverse is true. (The pattern shown is necessary for stability.) The D and S functions intersect at point P with employment N_e and aggregate nominal income Y^*. We naturally assume $N_e < N_f$ and $Y_e^* < Y_f^*$ in the diagram as drawn.

The price level affects this picture by moving the D and S functions vertically. If wages and prices do not move together and the income distribution is changed, there may be (but need not be) additional effects. In the diagram, we suppose a rise in wages, partially at the expense of profits.

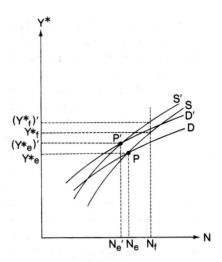

Figure 10A.1   (Keynesian) Aggregate Supply and Demand

This, we suppose further, raises D by more than would a simple all-round turn of the wage-price spiral. At the same time, it raises S by even more, by requiring higher sales proceeds as incentives for providing employment. The new equilibrium nominal income rises to $(Y_e^*)'$ but the equilibrium employment level falls to N_e'.

Chapter

11

Aggregate Supply

RELATION TO CLASSICAL MACROECONOMICS

In chapter 4 we sought to distill classical macroeconomics into the summary depicted on figure 4-1. This system included the following features:

1. An *aggregate production function*, relating real income Y to employment N, with constant stocks of land and machinery, and an unchanging spectrum of productive techniques. We have adopted a convention of placing this function in the southeast (SE) quadrant of four-quadrant diagrams.

2. A *labor market*, with separate labor-demand and labor-supply functions. These relate N to the real wage W; their intersection defines full employment. The aggregate labor-demand function maps, to a first approximation, the marginal productivity of labor (dY/dN) as determined by the slope of the production function. The aggregate labor-supply function is assumed determined by workers' labor-leisure choices. These two functions we place together in the southwest (SW) quadrant of four-quadrant diagrams.

3. The *quantity theory of money* in a rigid form that makes pY a constant, and plots as a rectangular hyperbola in p and Y in the northeast (NE) quadrant of four-quadrant diagrams. It plays in the classical system the role one might have anticipated for an aggregate demand function, in the absence of Say's Identity.

4. A *money wage function*, which is purely passive. It combines the real wage—already determined in the labor market—with the price level—determined, at full employment, by the production function and the given quantity of money. Its place is in the northwest (NW) quadrant of four-quadrant diagrams.

We shall now change this system in four fundamental ways. It will still lead to full employment under flexible prices, but with Say's Law substituted for Say's Identity. That is, we substitute

$$(M^*) \; \exists \; (P_e, W_e) : (N_e = N_f) \text{ and } (N \neq N_f) \rightarrow (W \neq W_e \text{ and-or } P \neq P_e)$$

for the

$$V(M^*) \exists (W_e) : (N_e = N_f) \text{ and } (N \neq N_f) \Rightarrow (W \neq W_e)$$

of chapter 4. The changes are:

1. The money wage rate W^* becomes an active participant in the system. It remains a rectangular hyperbola up to full employment—at which point it becomes perfectly inelastic. This construction portrays W^* as rigid

downward at less than full employment but free to increase once full employment is reached.

2. The quantity theory of money disappears; monetary influences are considered as aspects of aggregate demand. (See chapter 10.)

3. From the other three quadrants we derive an *aggregate supply function S*, in the place of the quantity theory of money on the northeast quadrant.

4. We graft the *aggregate demand* function D (developed in chapter 10) onto the northeast quadrant. The intersection of the aggregate supply function with the aggregate demand function now determines an equilibrium income and price level (Y_e,p_e). These may but need not coincide with the full employment income and price level (Y_f,p_f) on the aggregate supply function itself. If they do not, so that $Y_e < Y_f$, we are alerted to disequilibrium in the labor market. (It is possible for $p_e > p_f$ at full-employment income if aggregate demand is sufficiently high.) Geometrically, the full employment point in the labor-market quadrant determines the maximum output point on the aggregate supply function.

The diagrammatics of the preceding paragraph are illustrated in figure 11-1, with three alternative aggregate demand functions D_f, D_c, and D_x. Each of these combinations closes our macro-system.

1. The first aggregate demand function D_f gives a full-employment solution. Its parameters, with a money wage rate W^*, are employment at N_f, a real wage W_f, a real income Y_f, and a price level p_f. N_f is the maximum employment available without compulsion, and, therefore, Y_f is the maximum income attainable without compulsion.

2. The second aggregate demand function D_c illustrates a contraction (deflationary) gap with a lower employment, income, and price level; a higher real wage for those employed; and involuntary unemployment of UV. To obtain these results compare N_c with N_f, Y_c with Y_f, and so on.

3. The third aggregate demand function D_x illustrates an expansion gap. At this level of aggregate demand all real quantities (W_f, N_f, Y_f) remain at their full-employment values, but prices and money wages are above their full-employment equilibrium values (N_f, W_f, p_f). This represents the classical critique of Keynesian multiplier analysis at full employment: a shift in aggregate demand from D_f to D_x affects *no* real variables (multipliers fall to zero), but only precipitates inflation.

The reader may have noted an implicit assumption that the aggregate demand function D is independent of the aggregate supply function S. Our assumption is that a change in S (however brought about) does not

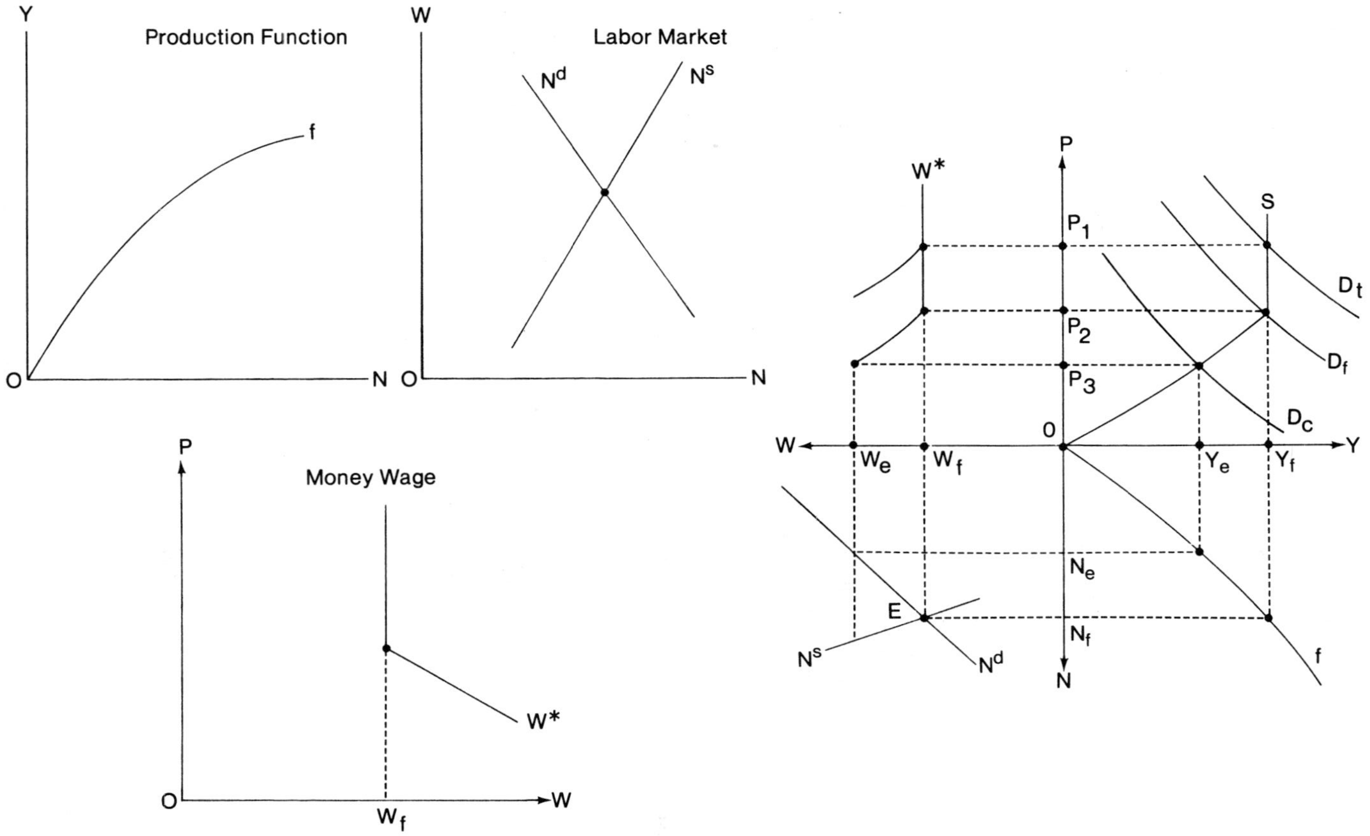

Figure 11-1 The Aggregate Supply Function

change aggregate demand D to any significant extent, and that its distributional repercussions affect almost exclusively its *composition*. This implies, in the case of a falling labor share, that decreases in the personal marginal propensities to spend (for consumption plus investment) are overcome by increases in the proportions of income received and spent by the nonpersonal (corporate and governmental) sectors.

ALTERNATIVE ROUTES TO FULL EMPLOYMENT

Nothing in the counterrevolution denies the possibility of increasing employment or decreasing unemployment by monetary or fiscal expansion, albeit at the cost of some inflation as a means of reducing real wages to their equilibrium level. Neither does it have much to say about the monetarist-fiscalist controversy, although the counterrevolutionists tend to the monetarist side. Its major implications are (1) that unemployment is a phenomenon of disequilibrium, which may be long-lasting (unemployment equilibrium is linked to certain "Keynesian special cases" relevant mainly in the short run);[1] and (2) that the classical deflationary method of dealing with disequilibrium employment is an alternative, perhaps even a preferable alternative, to inflationary expansion. (This deflationary method involves a passive rather than a direct assault upon price and wage levels. It prescribes little beyond waiting for wages or prices to fall and/or for labor productivity to rise. The authorities should refrain from making matters worse by tightening fiscal or monetary policy a la 1929–33, and compassion to the unemployed should be manifested by income supplements to the poor, including even the voluntarily unemployed.[2])

A critical point is to examine how lower money wages and/or money profits will affect income, employment, and the price level starting from an initial position of less than full employment. This mechanism involves aggregate supply to the 99-44/100 percent exclusion of aggregate demand. While leaving important intermediate stages of a full four-quadrant analysis to the reader, we can show its first and last steps in figure 11-2, under three sets of circumstances.

1. *A fall in money wages.* The initial effect is a shift from W^* to $(W^*)'$ in panel (a-1) of the figure. The ultimate effect includes a shift from S to S' in panel (a-2), with income rising from Y_e to Y_f and the price level falling from p_e to p_f. By constructing a four-quadrant diagram, the reader can show that employment rises and that the real wage must fall. Distribu-

---

[1] See Appendix 11A to this chapter, entitled "How Special Is the Keynesian Case?"
[2] Compare Milton Friedman, *Capitalism and Freedom* (1962), ch. 12.

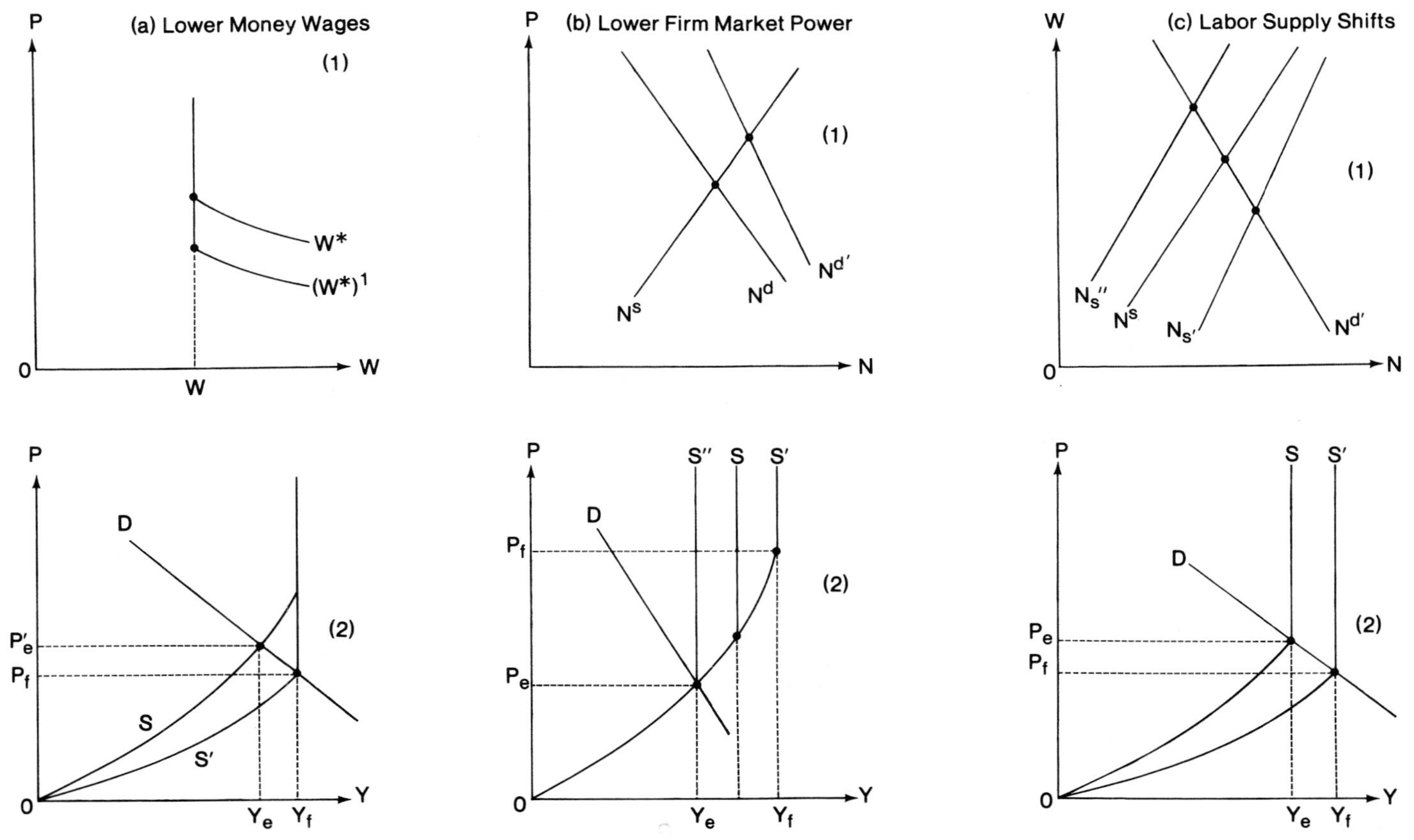

Figure 11-2 Alternative Routes to Full Employment

tionally speaking, the income share of the *previously-employed* workers falls. (We should not jump to the same conclusion about the share of labor as a *whole*, which may move in either direction but usually changes only slightly.[3])

2. *A fall in the monopoly power of business firms, in their rates of exploitation of labor, or in their power to administer market prices.* The initial effect, shown on panel (b-1) of the diagram, is an increase in the amount of labor demanded at any real wage.[4] The argument is difficult, unless the reader has had considerable microeconomic training.[5] It runs as follows: (a) A firm with substantial power, which is a price-maker rather than a price-taker as a seller of its output, a buyer of its labor and raw materials, or both at once, is called imperfectly competitive. (b) An imperfectly-competitive firm, in maximizing its profits, usually takes account of the lower selling prices (or higher selling costs) required to dispose of the additional output produced by additional employees, and also of the higher real wage rate (or lower labor quality) it must accept by expanding its labor force. Such a firm expands its employment only to the point where the worker's *marginal revenue product* (less than the value of his marginal product) equals his *marginal labor cost* to the firm (more than his wages plus fringe benefits). (c) If for any reason the firm decides to act more like a pure competitor, or is forced to do so, it will equate the value of the worker's marginal product more closely to the wage (plus fringe benefits). This will normally increase the firm's offer of employment at any wage. The ultimate effect involves a shift from S to S' on panel (b-2), with Y_e rising to Y_f and p_e falling to p_f as before. (The reader can work out intermediate details by constructing his own four-quadrant diagram.) The solution differs from case (1), however, since the shift from S to S' now involves a rise in full-employment output Y_f. (This rise results from the shift in the demand function for labor N^d.) But since a change in market power is not a "natural" equilibrating force, one cannot be sure that the existing aggregate demand D will permit the attainment of full employment without more ado. In the general case, if D crosses S' above (below)

---

[3] The near-constancy of the labor share of national income in the private sector is known as Bowley's Law.

[4] An increase in the demand for labor due to an increase in the physical efficiency of labor (or to technical progress) involves not only the sort of changes shown on panel (b-1) but also a simultaneous shift in the aggregate production function. We consider these cases in Appendix 11B to this chapter on "The Automation Problem."

[5] The standard exposition leading to our result is Joan Robinson, *Economics of Imperfect Competition* (1933), books 7–9. (Book 10 attempts a macroeconomic extension.) Compare also Martin Bronfenbrenner, *Income Distribution Theory* (1971), ch. 8.

(p_t, Y_t) the "fine-tuning" adjustment for full employment must also include a fall (rise) in D and/or a rise (fall) in the money wage level W^*.[6] Another difference from case (1) is that the real wage W will rise rather than fall, if monopoly pricing is the only reason for the initial underemployment situation.

3. A shift in the labor supply, with unchanged labor productivity. This might result from immigration, from a fall in the disutility of labor, or from reduced alternative opportunities for education and for transfer payments (relief). The shift involves the offer of more labor at any given wage rate, and is called a rise in labor supply. The impact effect [shown on panel (c-1) of figure 11-2] is to lower the full-employment real wage rate to W_e but the ultimate effect is quite different. The increase in N^s to $N^{s'}$ (with no change in D or W^*) extends the aggregate supply function S to S', increases full-employment income from Y_t to Y_t', and raises the measured unemployment percentage at Y_e [panel (c-2)]. To attain full employment, D must rise further, or W^* fall further, than before the shift. A similar analysis applies to a rise in labor productivity. This discussion runs counter to a common view in antilabor circles which blames unemployment on workers' laziness and on the availability of relief.

3a. By a similar argument, a sufficient labor supply shift in the opposite direction [to $N^{s''}$ on panel (c-2)] can solve the unemployment problem in a purely statistical sense without changing either equilibrium prices or money wages. This is a reduction in the supply of labor available at any given wage rate and a rise in the real wage required to attract any given labor supply; we call this a fall in labor supply. It leads to a shift in aggregate supply from S to S". Reductions in N^s have been achieved by encouraging emigration, expelling foreign workers, confining married women to *Kirche, Kuche, Kinder*, raising the school-leaving age, lowering the retirement age, increasing transfer payments, etc. Here the long-term effect is, as in panel (c-2) a reduction of Y_t to Y_e.

COST-PUSH INFLATION

Many texts devote separate chapters to inflation.[7] We have chosen to scatter our references to inflation and inflation theory in separate chapters.

---

[6] If this secondary adjustment is confined to a rise in D, the eventual full-employment price level p_t may exceed p_e when the new demand function D' is added to panel (2-b).

[7] Four U.S. examples are Thomas F. Dernburg and Duncan M. McDougall, *Macroeconomics* (3rd ed., 1968), ch. 17; Joseph P. McKenna, *Aggregate Economic Analysis* (rev. ed., 1965), ch. 16; Warren L. Smith, *Macroeconomics* (1970), ch. 16; William H. Branson, *Macroeconomic Theory and Policy* (1972), ch. 16. A volume of readings

We touched upon the classical theory, stressing the quantity of money, in chapter 4. We considered a standard Keynesian theory, leaning heavily upon the Keynesian Cross gap analysis in chapter 6. This has become known as "demand-pull" inflation. With the apparatus of aggregate demand and supply functions, we can now consider the so-called "new inflation"— called variously "sellers' inflation," "cost inflation," "cost-push," "wage-push," "profit-stretch," "market-power," and "administered" inflation.

A formal definition of cost-push inflation—selecting arbitrarily among the synonyms above—should cover all administrative or bargaining devices (as distinguished from impersonal and automatic developments) that push the aggregate supply function upward and to the left. These devices include both increases of market power and increases of ruthlessness in its use: price fixing, cartelization, licensure, protectionism, suppression of "economy" models, wage bargaining both collective and collusive—the list is a long one.

Expansionary policy, both monetary and fiscal, tends to validate or accommodate cost-push inflation after the fact by *relieving its consequences* of reduced output and employment. The role of public policy in this instance is painfully paradoxical. In the absence of expansionary policy or in the presence of buyers' strikes it is doubtful if any form of cost-push could be an *independent* cause of inflation. Some price increases in cost-pushful sectors would be only temporary. Others might be neutralized, as concerns the general price level, by declines in the more competitive sectors from which consumers' purchasing power had been drained. Finally, we must never forget, on the demand-pull side, the monetization of fiscal deficits (high g value in our analysis of Chapter 7) as a direct cause and accelerator of inflation, even while concentrating on its indirect accommodation of cost-pushes.

To analyze cost-push inflation diagrammatically, consider first panel (a) of figure 11-3. This is the aggregate supply and demand diagram that we have seen several times already. To apply it to long-period processes we may reinterpret Y as a percentage of a Y_f value that rises over time, so that $Y_f = 100$. Without loss of generality, we may start with an intersection α of D_1 and S_1 at the full-employment level. Full employment implies

---

on inflation theory is R. J. Ball and Peter Doyle, *Inflation* (1969). Three survey articles on inflation theory are Martin Bronfenbrenner and F. D. Holzman, "Survey of Inflation Theory," *American Economic Review* (September 1963), reprinted in American Economic Association and Royal Economic Society, *Surveys of Economic Theory* (1965), no. 2; Harry G. Johnson, "A Survey of Theories of Inflation," *Indian Economic Review* (August 1963), reprinted in Johnson, *Essays in Monetary Economics* (1967), ch. 3; David Laidler and Michael Parkin, "Inflation—A Survey," *Economic Journal* (December 1975).

tightness in both labor and product markets. Organized trade unions, oligopolies, and trade associations take advantage of this tightness to impose or bargain increases in wages and prices, which shift aggregate supply to S_2. The new intersection β of D_1 and S_2 is marked by some unemployment in consequence of the price increase. In reaction to this unemployment, the authorities require or permit monetary and fiscal measures that increase aggregate demand to D_2. Full employment is restored at γ, the intersection of D_2 and S_2, with an additional price increase. Again there are tight markets, and aggregate supply shifts in the next round to S_3. Again there is unemployment at δ, the intersection of D_2 and S_3; (for diagrammatic simplicity, we have drawn δ directly above β). Again the public authorities increase aggregate demand to D_3, and we are involved in a wage-price spiral. Note that price inflation coexists with increasing unemployment over the ranges $\alpha\beta$ and $\gamma\delta$. *The frequent assertion that macroeconomics cannot explain such "stagflation" is quite false.* The pattern indicated on this panel, with the public authorities concerned only with employment and ignoring inflation, is more typical of liberal Democratic than of conservative Republican administrations in the U.S.

Yet more controversial is a variant of the same analysis, illustrated in the right-hand panel of the same diagram (figure 11-3b). The initial situation at point α, and the initial inflationary cost push to point β, are the same as those discussed above. But now we suppose the authorities to refuse any expansion of aggregate demand. What happens next? The diagram illustrates the fears of the opponents of such a hard-line policy. Money wages and prices will continue to rise, due to the market power of firms and

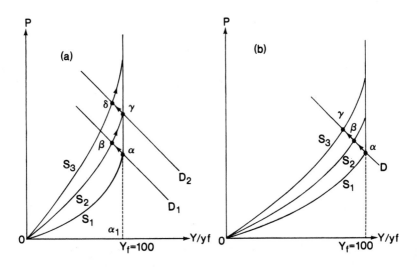

Figure 11-3　Cost-Push Inflation

unions, as combined by the processes of collective and collusive bargaining. Aggregate supply will shift to S_3, with its equilibrium point at γ, and with both inflation and unemployment more severe than before. Government, meanwhile, is under increasing pressure (especially in election years) to increase aggregate demand and put people back to work. Supporters of the hard line, however, insist that the movements of aggregate supply will stop, or even reverse themselves, if the government holds its ground, accepts some short-term unemployment and lowered growth rates, and convinces the public that it knows what it is about. Traces of such a hard line can be found in the U.S. Republican party during the Eisenhower administrations (1953–1961), and the first years of the next succeeding Republican administration (Nixon, 1969–1971).

Price and wage controls—usually under such names as guidelines, guideposts, guiding lights, or incomes policies—may be attempted in search of a short-term solution to the coexistence dilemma of rising price levels and rising unemployment, illustrated on both panels of figure 11-3. Their effects—assuming optimal enforceability—are put into an aggregate-supply context on figure 11-4. Here our initial position α is at less than full employment. Even with no change in the aggregate supply function S, increase in aggregate demand from D to D′ will produce situation β, which is inflationary but does not involve full employment. Controls plus propaganda, however, are supposed to truncate S at α, and transform its upper reaches to the horizontal segment S′, ending at the full-employment income Y_f. Under these conditions, an increase in demand to D′ will restore full employment at β', without inflation. Enthusiasts for controls think that they can go even further. By cancelling out market power, controls also take the profit out of output restriction and reduce monopoly and oligopoly to "potential" (unexercised) forms. In such a case, the "new" full employment income will exceed Y_f on the diagram, since Y_f reflects existing market power. If full-employment income exceeds Y_f, aggregate demand can be raised above D′ without inflationary consequences and without resort to rationing. This result, of course, implies optimal conditions not likely to prevail except for short periods.[8]

---

[8] For a theoretical treatment of certain problems of such controls, see Martin Bronfenbrenner, *Income Distribution Theory* (1971), ch. 17, and references cited.

The writer was subsequently accorded the opportunity to visit the USSR and discuss with Soviet economists the Soviet system of law, under which direct controls are more readily enforceable in the long term. This system includes a number of features that appear harsh in Western countries, and may include some features of over-kill.

1. Capital punishment for major "economic crimes."
2. No presumption of innocence for defendants in criminal cases.
3. No "Fifth Amendment" rights; defendant's refusal to testify may be used against him.

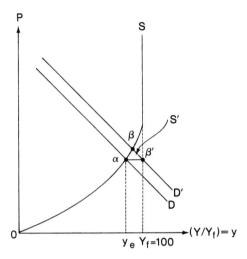

Figure 11-4   Wage-Price Controls

AN UNEASY QUADRANGLE:
AN ECONOMIC GENERATION GAP

Given the coexistence of inflation and unemployment with at least a short-run trade-off between the two, and also the difficulties of long-term direct controls over prices and money wages, what should be the primary goal of macroeconomic policy? The "humanitarian" or "compassionate" view concentrates on remedying unemployment primarily by increasing aggregate demand.[9] This may require "learning to live with inflation, or even "après nous, le déluge"—the deluge being, in this case, accelerating

---

4. "Double jeopardy" permissible; prosecution and defense have equal rights of appeal in criminal cases.
5. Defense attorneys are civil servants assigned by the court.
6. Judges serve on juries; judges and jurymen may question witnesses.
7. Twenty-five year statute of limitations.
8. Right to strike qualified by duty to work; picketing punishable as disturbance of the peace.
9. Picketing punishable as disturbance of the peace.

[9] James Tobin concludes in "Inflation and Unemployment," *American Economic Review* (March 1972) that the zero-inflation unemployment rate is not optimal, and that there is much to be said for inflation. "No one has devised a way of controlling average wage rates without intervening in the struggle over relative wages. Inflation lets this struggle proceed and blindly, impartially, and nonpolitically scales down all its outcomes. There are worse methods of resolving group rivalries and social conflict," (p. 13) whereas antiinflation policy has "persuade[d] this country to give up billions of dollars of annual output and to impose sweeping legal controls on prices and wages. Seldom has a society made such large immediate and tangible sacrifices to avert an ill-defined, uncertain, eventual evil." (p. 15).

inflation or even hyperinflation. A "traditionalist" view would safeguard the currency by letting the expansion of aggregate demand wait upon the subsidence of inflation. A "trust-busting" view would concentrate on weakening economic pressure groups. A "control" view would concentrate on enacting and enforcing direct controls. We can agree, perhaps, that an "uneasy" quadrangle exists, meaning that we can enjoy no more than three (and quite possibly less than three) of: guaranteed full employment, stable price levels, strong economic pressure groups, and freedom from direct controls.

No position is so absolute or extreme as the last paragraph implies. Few if any humanitarians, for example, would plump for expanding demand with an unemployment rate of 4 percent and a monthly inflation rate of 10 percent. Also, traditionalists would not sit on their hands very long with 25 percent unemployment and 1/100 of 1 percent annual inflation. Trust busters would not blindly dismantle concentrated industries or labor unions without investigating the ramifications on the economy as a whole. And controllers would probably "decontrol" parts of the economy if their policies created major resource misallocations. Underlying the argument between our four rival schools is some concept of the likely short-run and long-run terms of trade-off between unemployment and inflation.

There is as yet no agreement about either (1) the positive (factual) question of what the expected trade-off actually is, or about (2) the normative question of the policy appropriate to any given trade-off situation. For many people, the decision on the normative issue depends upon one's position in society. It reflects, for example, one's reaction to the fact that any given unemployment rate in the United States, with a relatively high minimum wage, implies a *higher* rate for inexperienced workers (teenagers), workers with less than a high-school education, black and Spanish-speaking workers, females, and workers near retirement age. (By the same token, it implies a lower rate for "prime-age males" with technical skills and/or superior educational backgrounds.) Turning to inflation, for "another example," the burden of the "inflation tax" (see chapter 6) is concentrated on people whose wealth is mainly in liquid assets and whose incomes are largely fixed in money terms on long-term contracts from annuities, pensions, rent, and interest. In practice, this group includes the "widows and orphans," "senior citizens," and rentiers.

In middle-class communities the disagreement has the earmarks of an

Many labor economists would assign first priority to relieving unemployment, but believe inflation could be largely avoided by retraining and "restructuring" the labor force to keep pace with the changing structure of industrial demand for labor. (This is primarily a microeconomic policy prescription.) We do not discuss "structuralism" here; a useful reference is Charles C. Killingsworth, *Jobs and Income for Negroes* (1968), pp. 49–82.

economic generation gap. High school and college students want to graduate into booming markets for their services and into a wide choice of "meaningful" jobs; the inflation rate means little to them, except as they are dependent on "senior citizens"—or face the prospect of senior citizens as dependents in the future. Parents (and teachers), however, tend to be more concerned about the inflation rate. They worry about the future purchasing power of their savings, pensions, annuities, and insurance policies. Their concern with unemployment is minimal, unless they have job-seeker dependents or have themselves lost jobs recently. Hence the generation gap.

THE PHILLIPS CURVE

Studies of the actual inflation-unemployment trade-off (and its stability over time) have focussed since 1958 upon the Phillips curve (figure 11-5). This function, in its formal presentation, relates unemployment in year $(t - 1)$ to the rate of money wage increase or decrease in year t.[10] In the diagram, the unemployment rate U is measured on the horizontal axis, and the money wage increase rate $(d \log W^*/dt)$ on the vertical axis.

It is assumed that rising productivity of labor can, on the average, permit absorption of money wage increases up to AA—perhaps 3.5 percent in the U.S., perhaps as high as 15 percent in Japan (1952–1972)—without inflationary consequences. It is also assumed that the electorate will tolerate measured unemployment rates as high as BB—perhaps 5 percent in the U.S., smaller in most other countries—without disastrous consequences to the party in power. These lines intersect at point P. A Phillips curve like F_1, passing to the southwest of P, is "good." That is to say, it implies no

---

[10] Alban W. Phillips, "The Relation between Unemployment and the Rate of Change of Money Wage Rates in the United Kingdom, 1861–1957," *Economica* (November 1958) reprinted in M. Gerald Mueller, *Readings in Macroeconomics* (1966), no. 17, and excerpted in Ball and Doyle, *op. cit.*, no. 15. The pioneer U.S. study is Paul A. Samuelson and Robert M. Solow, "Analytical Aspects of Anti-Inflation Policy," *American Economic Review* (May 1960), also reprinted in Mueller, *op. cit.*, no. 27.

Figure 11-5, as drawn, involves only these two variables. Later and more advanced Phillips-curve studies improve the empirical fit of the functions by adding additional variables. Three examples are by Richard G. Lipsey, "The Relation between Unemployment and the Rate of Change of Money Wages in the United Kingdom, 1862–1957," *Economica* (February 1960), reprinted in R. A. Gordon and L. R. Klein, eds., *Readings in Business Cycles* (1965), no. 24; L. A. Dicks-Mireaux, "The Interrelationship Between Cost and Price Changes, 1946–1959," *Oxford Economic Papers* (October 1961), in Ball and Doyle, *op. cit.*, no. 16; Saul H. Hymans, The Trade-Off between Unemployment and Inflation: Theory and Measurement," in Warren L. Smith and Ronald L. Teigen, *Readings in Money, National Income, and Stabilization Policy* (1970), pp. 152–162.

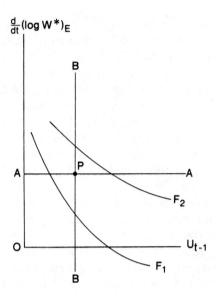

Figure 11-5 Phillips Curves

deep-seated conflict between the two goals of low unemployment and price stability.[11] Good Phillips curves appear to have been typical of industrial societies before World War II. A Phillips curve like F_2, passing northeast of P, is "bad," meaning that it implies acute conflict. Bad Phillips curves appear to have become the rule in present-day societies, possibly as a result of increased concern with maintaining full employment. Hence the call to "learn to live with inflation." For the U.S., Samuelson and Solow estimate (in the article cited in footnote 10) that the contemporary American economy must endure five to six percent unemployment as the cost of price stability.

The long-term validity of Phillips's analysis is widely disputed. Friedman,

---

[11] A more microeconomic variant of inflation theory would deny this conclusion to some extent. This is the "demand-shift" theory of Charles L. Schultze, "Recent Inflation in the United States," in Joint Economic Committee, 86th Cong., *Study of Employment, Growth, and Price Levels*, Study Paper No. 1 (1959), summarized in Smith and Teigen, *op. cit.* pp. 163–169 and in Ball and Doyle, *op. cit.*, no. 12.

Schultze argues, first, that demand shifts from good A to good B have inflationary biases in themselves, because B-prices tend to rise more quickly than A-prices fall. He argues, second, that such shifts also have inflationary biases of an indirect sort, primarily through wage rates. Wages and other costs in B not only tend to rise, but those in A tend to rise as well, by quasi-ethical "compulsive comparisons" between the workers and unions in the two industries.

for example, believes the long-run Phillips curve to be a near-vertical line.[12] That is to say, he believes an equilibrium unemployment rate to exist and to vary only randomly over time. The observed Phillips curves, he claims, represent the effects of money illusion and little more. When there is an inflationary movement, for example—including increased money wage rates—workers misinterpret such increases as increases in real wages, so that their labor supply function N^s increases in terms of true real wages. At the same time, employers misinterpret the increases in the money prices of their own outputs as including increases relative to the prices of other goods. Such a change in anticipated output prices raises the real value to them of each worker's marginal product, and so increases the labor demand function N^d. When both N^d and N^s rise, there is a rise in employment N, as well as equilibrium employment N_e. This can only be maintained, however, for as long as the money illusion persists. When the money illusion evaporates, N^d, N^s, N, and N_e return to their previous levels, unless the rate of inflation is increased and the money illusion reimposed. Friedman's analysis implies that (1) Phillips curves tend to rise vertically over time in inflationary situations, and also that (2) the inflation rate required for *maintenance* of high employment is not constant but must increase steadily and without bound.

Another line of Phillips-curve skepticism might be called institutional. In this view, Phillips curves approach the near-vertical if public policy seems incurably hard-boiled on the traditional side, and near-horizontal when policy is incurably soft-boiled on the compassionate side.[13] Statistically, this suggests that Phillips curves are volatile over time; logically, it suggests that they should not themselves be used to guide public policy in the first place.

---

[12] Milton Friedman, "The Role of Monetary Policy," *American Economic Review* (March 1968), reprinted in Friedman, *The Optimum Quantity of Money* (1969), ch. 5, esp. pp. 101–105.

During the 1970s a "rational expectations" hypothesis came into use for monetarist analysis of wage-employment problems. According to this frequently confirmed hypothesis, the market as a whole estimates the future consequences of *anticipated* policy changes quite accurately, even when individual market participants' forecasts are quite wrong. (Statisticians will recall that the sampling variance of an average is less than that of each component observation.) In the Phillips-curve case, the rational expectations hypothesis implies that any money illusion is dissipated rapidly, so that the long-term Phillips curve approaches the vertical. More generally, the hypothesis implies that monetary changes have important consequences for real variables only when they result from *unanticipated* policy decisions or when people act *irrationally*—both of which forces, interestingly enough, make for economic instability.

[13] Martin Bronfenbrenner and Franklyn D. Holzman, "Survey of Inflation Theory," *American Economic Review* (September 1963), reprinted in American Economic Association and Royal Economic Society, *Surveys of Economic Theory*, vol. i (1965), p. 80f, 84.

Empirical studies of an issue raised by Friedman—the alleged tendency of inflation to escalate when used to maintain employment—have generally led to what might be called a pro–Phillips-curve conclusion. For example, Solow concludes in *Price Expectations and the Price Level*[14] that "whatever may be true of Latin American-size inflations or even smaller perfectly steady inflations, under the conditions that really matter—irregular price increases with an order of magnitude of a few percent a year—there is a trade-off between the speed of price increase and the real state of the economy. . . . It may not be 'permanent,' but it lasts long enough for me." One such study was developed for an introductory text by two Solow students.[15] If we denote by G the gap $(Y_t - Y)$ between potential and actual income in any year, and by $(dP/dt)_{-1}$ the rise in the price index in the year immediately preceding, these writers estimate for the U.S. two relations not involving wage rates explicitly:

$$U = 2.5 + 0.06G \tag{11.1}$$

$$\frac{dP}{dt} = 1.9 - 0.028G + 0.658 \left(\frac{dP}{dt}\right)_{-1} \tag{11.2}$$

so that a gap of any given size implies both a specific unemployment rate and a specific inflation rate, if we also know the inflation rate in the previous year.

First we solve equation (11.1) for G, and substitute this value in equation (11.2):

$$G = \frac{U}{0.06} - \frac{2.5}{0.06}$$

$$\frac{dP}{dt} = 3.07 - 0.467\,U + 0.658 \left(\frac{dP}{dt}\right)_{-1} \tag{11.3}$$

If there is a "steady-state" solution, with $[dP/dt) = (dP/dt)_{-1}]$ and with "reasonable" values of both U and (dP/dt), this is evidence against the Friedman position. We have, for a steady-state solution of (11.3):

$$\frac{dP}{dt} = 8.977 - 1.365\,U \tag{11.4}$$

---

[14] Robert M. Solow, *op. cit.* (1969), p. 17.
[15] James A. Chalmers and Fred H. Leonard, *Economic Principles* (1971), pp. 194–197.

from which we can see that price stability, with $(dP/dt = 0)$, can be reached with $U = 6.577$ percent, a result not inconsistent with that of Samuelson and Solow. Other steady-state solutions, for more palatable unemployment rates, involve higher rates of inflation:

Table 11-1

U (percent)	dP/dt (percent)
3.0	4.88
4.0	3.52
5.0	2.15

Equations (11.1–2) were based on annual U.S. data for the period 1954–1967. They do not allow for any institutional reactions to "compassionate" policies designed to keep unemployment low regardless of inflationary consequences. Neither do they take account of the objections to Phillips-curve analysis. Possibly as a result, the writer believes that the dP/dt (inflation rate) figures tabulated were already too low when they were first published (1971).

INFLUENCES OF UNCERTAINTY

We have carried out nearly all our Keynesian analysis in terms of the "Keynesian economics" that has been most influential for macroeconomic policy. But at this point the rival interpretation, called by Clower and Leijonhufvud "the economics of Keynes,"[16] becomes more significant.

As Clower and Leijonhufvud interpret Keynes's message, the main theme is the importance of *uncertainty* and the resultant *volatility* of the principal Keynesian functions. These ideas can be applied to the picture we have just presented of the "deflationary" adjustment to unemployment and the consequent restoration of full employment.

In figure 11-6, D and S are again aggregate demand and supply functions that intersect at (p_e, Y_e); p_e is higher than the full-employment price level

---

[16] For an elementary introduction to this line of argument, see Axel Leijonhufvud's pamphlet, *Keynes and the Classics* (1969). The basic presentations are Robert W. Clower, "The Keynesian Counter-Revolution: A Theoretical Appraisal," in Frank H. Hahn and Frank P. R. Brechling, eds., *Theory of Interest Rates* (1965), reprinted in Clower, ed., *Monetary Theory* (1969), no. 19; and Leijonhufvud, *On Keynesian Economics and the Economics of Keynes* (1968).

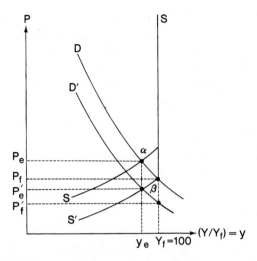

Figure 11-6   Notional and Effective Aggregate Demand

p_f, while Y_e is lower than the full-employment income level Y_f. The deflationary approach to full employment would then propose refraining from further expansion of aggregate demand beyond D, and waiting for unemployment to lower wages and profit margins (or at least to hold them below the growth rate of productivity). Holding wages and profit margins down would raise the aggregate supply function to S'. With aggregate demand remaining at D, our problem would eventually be solved.

Keynes's objection to any such policy—as Clower and Leijonhufvud read the *General Theory*—is that it increases uncertainty in a pessimistic direction. Because of widespread fear of losses and unemployment, and uncertainty as to how much wages and profit margins must fall short of previous expectations before full employment is restored, both consumption and investment demand are restrained below the previous "notional" demand function D to the lower "effective" level D'. At the same time and by the same process, suppliers hesitate to offer goods and services at what may prove to be unnecessarily low prices. Therefore "effective" supply rises to S' more slowly than "notional" supply would have done under certainty. This lag increases the fall in effective demand.

In figure 11-6, we have drawn (D', S') such that Y_e is unchanged, while prices fall to a point below p_f. This means that the deflation has done no good, even though it has been greater than one might anticipate in advance. These results represent a special case, but it is a case quite in line with the *General Theory*. (See again Appendix 11A to this chapter.)

The historical record on which Keynes's generalizations were based is primarily the record of Great Britain between 1919 and 1935, including the

Great Depression. After 1929 macroeconomic policy operated in most Western countries to *depress* aggregate demand, not to *maintain* or expand it. We cannot be sure what results might have been achieved with a less dismal record, which has given "deflation" a bad name for so long.

Four sets of consequences can be drawn from these paragraphs, three for economic policy and one for the history of economic thought:

1. Macroeconometric fine-tuning is less reliable in a world of variable uncertainties and risk aversion than in a world of certainty or risk preference. There is accordingly a need to "slant" policy recommendations in an expansionary direction to counteract any other policies that increase uncertainty.

2. It is nearly impossible to stop or even decelerate an inflation, without some social cost in unemployment created and production foregone. The cost may be sharp and concentrated in a short period. It is more likely to be long and protracted. If it is not accepted, the result is "living with inflation," under circumstances where every chance acceleration of inflation threatens to build itself into the system.

3. It is conceivable that uncertainty may some day be less of a problem than it is, and macroeconomic functions less volatile than they are, if policymakers are able and willing to explain to the public fully and honestly what they are doing and why they are doing it—and if the public is less allergic to economic reasoning.

4. Lord Keynes himself comes off better as an economic policy-strategist under the "economics of Keynes" or "volatility of functions" interpretation of his meaning than under the standard "Keynesian" interpretation in terms of special shapes of the functions we have been working with since chapter 6. (Once more, see the Appendix 11A to this chapter.)

SUMMARY

This chapter has sought to combine under one roof the derivation of the aggregate supply function and a number of its applications. (Appendix 11B develops an additional application, to automation problems.) In the earlier paragraphs the aggregate supply function is derived from the "classical model" of chapter 4, for a money wage rigid at less than full employment. In conjunction with the aggregate demand function of chapter 10, their intersection is shown to determine both the real national income and the equilibrium level of prices. The equilibrium solution, however, need not be one of full employment.

If the equilibrium solution does not involve full employment—that is, if

the equilibrium of aggregate demand and supply of output is out of phase with the equilibrium of demand and supply of labor—alternative paths to full employment are discussed. One of these is expansionary (inflationary, in the absence of direct controls). The other is deflationary, stressing decline in money wage rates, or at least lagging of these rates behind increases in productivity. The first route increases aggregate demand, and the second increases aggregate supply. The first, or Keynesian, method, usually works more quickly, particularly in the presence of downward rigidity in the labor supply function N^s. The serious consideration given the *second* route, and the acceptance of Say's Law (as distinguished from Say's Identity) are important components of the counterrevolution. The conflict between partisans of the two methods may take the form of an economic generation gap, with the young favoring aggregate-demand remedies for unemployment, and the old favoring restraint on wages and prices.

The discussion now turns to cost-push inflation, which depends (if it exists) primarily upon movements of aggregate supply that are then "ratified" or "validated" on the demand side. The aggregate supply-aggregate demand apparatus shows how inflation and underemployment can coexist, even when aggregate demand is not manipulated to validate wage and price increases. At the same time, theoretical analysis does not tell us how long such "stagflation" might persist in the absence of an active public full-employment policy. Neither does it allow explicitly for the unfavorable effects on certainty and confidence of tolerating unemployment in an inflationary situation.

The notion of an inflation-unemployment trade-off, exemplified by the Phillips curve, comes up in the same connection, and "good" Phillips curves are distinguished from "bad" ones. The claim is made that Phillips curves may be too volatile to serve as bases for policy. At the same time, in a regime of slow inflation at variable rates, the empirical evidence does not seem to support the concept of a unique long-run equilibrium unemployment rate that reestablishes itself as money illusion dies away. Neither does it support the conclusion that the inflation rate necessary to provide full employment must increase without bound.

Chapters 10 and 11 taken together graft a version of the anti-Keynesian counterrevolution to the Keynesian structure of chapters 6–9. Such treatment of controversial issues marks the "apologetic statesman of a compromising kind," and satisfies stalwarts of no school. Orthodox Keynesians would make no theoretical concessions whatever, and meet the policy challenges of inflation by a permanent network of direct microeconomic controls or "incomes policies," sometimes slanted toward prolabor redistributions of income sufficient to avoid strikes against the controls themselves. Orthodox anti-Keynesians (and some dissidents returning to "the economics

of Keynes") would scrap the Keynesian and Hicksian crosses altogether. (The nature of the proposed replacement varies from one writer to another.)

Starting as we have done from an Islamic base, this pair of chapters has three principal morals.

1. The price level makes a difference for the levels of real income and of employment.

2. In particular, underemployment can be, and often is, a sign that price levels and/or wage levels are above their equilibrium levels, as well as (or rather than) a sign of inadequacy of aggregate demand.

3. In the presence of forces pushing up prices and wages, and then calling upon government to validate the increases and overcome consumers' (buyers') strikes, there is no reason for surprise at the coexistence of unemployment, even increasing unemployment, and inflation. There is also no reason to regard the structure of macroeconomic theory as being disconfirmed by this coexistence.

TRANSITION

As we bring the macrostatic portion of this book to a close we might consider what method there has been to our madness. We have developed a series of models in chapters 4–7 and 10–11, sampling from pre-Keynesian, Keynesian, and post-Keynesian thinking. These models have not been intended as mere exercises. We have attempted to squeeze a good deal of content out of each one, and expose its implications before proceeding to another perspective or complication. There is something to be learned from each of these models. In particular, the evolution of Keynesian and post-Keynesian models should be interpreted retrospectively as a logical sequence, each step of which enriches our analytical perspective. A tabular review of what we have set out to accomplish is offered below.

MACROSTATIC THEORY: A TABULAR SUMMARY

Pre-Keynesian

Classical and Neo-Classical
    Equilibrium involves full employment.
    Output-market stress entirely on supply side; justified by Say's Identity.
    Leads to "stationary state" macrodynamics.

MARXIAN

Equilibrium normally involves unemployment.

Unemployment functional under capitalism, and not remediable under capitalist conditions.

Dynamic implications: "contradictions of capitalism" will eventually overthrow the system.

KEYNESIAN

Underemployment equilibrium much as in Marx,[17] but remediable by fiscal and monetary policies.

Exposition by a series of models, from simple to complex.

Model I. State of nature; consumption and autonomous investment only; multipliers and "Keynesian cross" diagrams.

Model II. Enter fiscal policy; public spending, taxation, and transfer payments.

Model III. Investment becomes endogenous; enter the rate of interest.

Model IV. Enter the monetary aspect; variable money demand, fixed money supply; liquidity preference and Hicksian IS-LM diagrams.

Model V. Enter variable money supply.

POST-KEYNESIAN

Equilibrium involves full employment; justified by Say's Law.

Aggregate demand; enter the price level.

Aggregate supply; reenter the classical theory.

Underemployment-inflation trade-offs? Problems of Phillips curves, stagflation, etc.

---

[17] Alternative interpretation: Labor markets adjust more slowly to disequilibrium than do other markets. Unemployment is not strictly an equilibrium condition, but results from the lag in labor-market adjustment. Labor-market disequilibria can remain obvious and severe when disequilibria in other markets are smaller and less obvious.

Appendix 11a

HOW SPECIAL IS THE KEYNESIAN CASE?

We have shown in this chapter that the macroeconomy tends generally to a position of full-employment equilibrium. But there remain a number of cases in which it does not. These are known collectively as "the Keynesian special case," as distinguished from a post-Keynesian general case. It is not completely clear which aspects of this "Keynesian" case Keynes himself may have had in mind. Indeed, if the adjustment process for a disequilibrium (money) wage rate takes the form posited by Samuelson:

$$\frac{dW^*}{dt} = \beta(W^*_e - W^*) \qquad (0 \leq \beta \leq 1)$$

one may interpret the General Theory to mean not that the adjustment coefficient β is strictly zero, but rather that it has become so small (when $W^* > W^*_e$) that a contemporary economy runs serious risks of social upheaval before the adjustment process is completed and full employment restored by the market mechanism operating on money wage rates.

The most obvious Keynesian case is precisely that of rigid disequilibrium money or real wage rates.[1] Such rigidity need not be due entirely to trade-union pressure; unorganized workers have also held out against wage cuts. Employers may likewise have a long-term interest in keeping up wages for the sake of maintaining worker morale, skill, efficiency, etc. This involves maintaining the human capital of their workers in somewhat the same way that they maintain the physical capital embodied in buildings, machinery, equipment, etc.[2]

More interesting to economists are those aspects of the Keynesian special case that would hold even with flexible money and real wages, flexible prices, and pure competition throughout the economy.

At the IS-LM level of chapter 7, without explicit consideration of price-level changes, the interest rate r is at center stage:

---

[1] Keynes himself spoke in terms of money wages only (in 1936). Subsequent inflation has dissipated workers' money illusion. Discussion in real-wage terms has therefore become more realistic.

[2] This argument I owe to Thomas Morton. See also Walter Y. Oi, "Labor as a Quasi-Fixed Factor," Journal of Political Economy (December 1962).

1. It may be "too high" because of a liquidity trap (absolute liquidity preference). In elasticity terms, the interest-elasticity of LM may be too high to permit r_e to fall to the r_f level.

2. In stagnation cases (chapter 9), the IS function may be so nearly vertical, with so low an interest-elasticity, that no positive value of r_f may exist in the system.

We pass to the aggregate-demand analysis of chapter 10, with the price level taken into explicit account. Here the aggregate demand function D may be so nearly vertical, with so low a price-level elasticity—or it may even slope "the wrong way"—that no positive p_f may exist. Or alternatively, combining the analyses of the last two paragraphs, a positive p_f may be reached only by so heavy reliance on the Keynes effect as to require a negative interest rate.

All these conditions seemed highly unrealistic to many post-Keynesian writers. A "Keynesian revival" has, however, taken place, following the work of Clower and Leijonhufvud. This newer work interprets Keynes as viewing the macroeconomic system as tending not to equilibrium at less than full employment but to no equilibrium at all, or rather to a quasi-equilibrium. It is only this quasi-equilibrium that is marked by $Y < Y_f$, but the economy can move away from quasi-equilibrium only with great difficulty.

Let us explain further. In discussing equilibrium, and the economy's adjustment to disequilibrium, we have argued as though accurate economic information were available immediately and without cost. We have also argued as though "disequilibrium" transactions, carried on under disequilibrium terms, either do not exist, are only tentative, or have no effects on the market as a whole.

Clower and Leijonhufvud view "the economics of Keynes" as founded on *departure* from such assumptions. They see the Keynesian system as directed at situations where uncertainty prevails, where information is costly in time and money, and in which the terms of disequilibrium transactions are accepted widely as indicators of equilibrium positions.

Suppose a full-employment economy suddenly disturbed by a thrift campaign, a common starting point in Keynes's earlier (1930) *Treatise on Money*. On our own curves, this is basically a fall in D, a corresponding vertical fall (horizontal rise) in S would leave equilibrium income at Y_f; but let us attempt a step-by-step account. Firms find demand for their outputs falling off by reason of the thrift campaign, but no manager knows how much of the decline in his own sales is specific to his own firm, or how long it will continue. Instead of cutting prices to new equilibrium levels, firms continue to make what sales they can at the previous prices while waiting for demand to rise again. The previous prices continue to look like

equilibrium prices to the general public, which in fact they are not. The falling sales have led rather to unplanned accumulation of inventories of finished products by firms, and later to contraction in their scales of operation.

The fall in scales of operation leads in turn to a decline in firms' demand for labor, and hence in employment. The unemployed workers do not know how much of the unemployment they perceive is specific to their own crafts or industries, or how long it may be expected to last. They also see most workers continuing in employment at previous wage rates. They consider these wage rates the equilibrium ones, which they no longer are, and see no reason (even in the absence of union organization) to accept work on less favorable terms. At what are now quasi-equilibrium prices and wage rates, then, production and employment both fall. Furthermore, the decline in production and employment leads to a further fall in demand over and above the original thrift campaign (which we suppose to be continuing) and a recession cumulates.

We return to the business firms, which we left holding unsold goods in inventories larger than had been planned. Holding excess inventories is itself costly. Firms must eventually sell other assets, or borrow from banks, or issue securities, if they are to continue holding these inventories. Both the sales of assets (including securities) and the increased loan demand increase nominal interest rates, or at least check any falls that might otherwise have resulted from the increased saving as a source for increased lending and asset demand.[3] If the incipient recession has made lenders cautious and pessimistic and the supply of money and loanable funds dries up, the rise of interest rates becomes more probable. The appearance of a liquidity trap is created, and monetary tightness is added to the recession problem.[4]

The above paragraphs suggest that downward rigidities of prices, wages, and interest rates are more than products of monopoly or imperfect competition. They are also interrelated aspects of a quasi-equilibrium competitive adjustment process in the presence of uncertainty, and under the influence of transactions at disequilibrium prices. These paragraphs also show how a disturbance of equilibrium—here, the thrift campaign—can cumulate to a

---

[3] This statement is a concession to a loanable-funds theory of interest.

[4] We can restate the argument in terms of Walras's Law, the expanded form of Say's Identity. Walras's Law states that an excess supply (demand) for goods (including labor and other inputs) must be matched by an excess demand (supply) for "bonds" (including other assets) and/or for money (including short-term financial assets complimentary with money against long-term investments).

In conditions of recession, $Y^d < Y^s$ usually implies $B^d < B^s$ and also $M^d > M^s$. The price of bonds is "too high," i.e., the interest rate is "too low" (!) for the given money supply. Or alternatively, the money supply is "too low" for the existing (disequilibrium) interest rates and asset prices.

recession under these same conditions, rather than to a full "notional" equilibrium adjustment at lower prices, wages, and interest rates than prevailed originally.

The full-equilibrium adjustment to the thrift campaign and the accompanying fall in aggregate demand remains a fall in prices, wages, and interest rates, output and employment remaining the same. What we have called a downward quasi-equilibrium adjustment under uncertainty is in "the economics of Keynes" a series of output rather than price reductions, leading to recessions with price rigidities, liquidity traps, and so on.

But which set of reactions can be expected to occur most rapidly in the real world, and therefore to dominate real economies? Granted that both sets of reactions will occur at the same time and mutually neutralize each other, which set should be called the general and which the special case? The Keynesians maintain that quasi-equilibrium adjustments necessarily are more rapid and lead to malignant recessions before full-equilibrium adjustments take hold, unless public authorities intervene with fiscal, monetary, or other assistance. The anti-Keynesians maintain, on the other hand, that full-equilibrium adjustments would lead quickly to benign deflations unless the government yields to pressures for offsetting expansions—"full employment at whatever cost"—or inadvertently contracts the economy further as the Hoover administration did in the early 1930s. The correct answer depends, we suppose, on what the private economy has historical, institutional, or political reason to anticipate. This means a Keynesian answer in an economy wedded to Keynesian policies, even when specific Keynesian policies increase uncertainty. It also means an anti-Keynesian answer in an economy wedded to "sound finance," or to monetary rules, or to nonintervention.

Appendix 11b

THE IMPACT OF TECHNICAL CHANGE:
AUTOMATION OPTIMISM AND PESSIMISM

Any technical advance, whether or not it conforms to any strict definition of "automation," raises the production function throughout its length. On a diagram like figure 11-1 a higher Y now corresponds to any N, and a lower N corresponds to any Y. Let us define the change as *automation* only if, in the neighborhood of the former equilibrium position, it also *decreases* the production function's radius of curvature. This means that, if we denote the production function by F, the marginal product of labor by F′ or (dY/dN), and the rate of change of the marginal product by F″ or

(d^2Y/dN^2), the quotient (F''/F') is smaller after the technical change than it was before.

The proposition about the radius of curvature has two economic implications:

1. To justify the title of automation, the technical improvement must increase the marginal product of the first few workers hired by more than it increases the marginal product of the Nth worker hired, if N is the preexistent volume of employment.

2. There may, for sufficiently large N, be an actual fall in the slope of the production function, i.e., in the marginal productivity of, and thus the demand for, labor. This may be true even though the total and average productivity of a given labor force increase throughout.

We can use the apparatus of this chapter to examine a highly controversial issue, the effect of automation upon employment and real wages. *Automation optimists* expect the demand for labor to increase as a result of automation, so that both employment and real wages will rise. *Automation pessimists*, on the other hand, see automated machinery as a net substitute for human labor, so that automation will lower the demand for labor, income, and employment. There is even talk of human-labor power sharing the fate of horse power. (The U.S. had nearly 27 million draft horses and mules according to 1910 census data; 50 years later, the draft horse population had suffered a decline of 95 percent or more. (Statistics were no longer collected.) Such declines are obviously easier to manage peaceably in the case of horses than in the case of human beings.

Automation optimism, of the sort eventually justified in the case of the Industrial Revolution, is illustrated in figure 11B-1 for a given labor supply. In this four-quadrant diagram the subscript 1 refers to a preautomation situation, and the subscript 2 to a postautomation one. We assume full employment in both situations. Income, employment, and real wages are all higher in the second situation, while the price level is lower; hence the optimism. This optimism is however tempered by the conclusion that, if money wages are not to fall, aggregate demand must normally be increased from D_1 to D_2 for full employment to be maintained.[1]

But things need not work out so well in the twentieth century as hind-

---

[1] Some abnormal cases can be imagined from the northeast quadrant of the diagram. If aggregate demand D passes through E_2 as well as E_1, the demand side can be neglected. If D passes to the northeast of E_2, the appropriate "fine tuning" is a decrease rather than an increase in D.

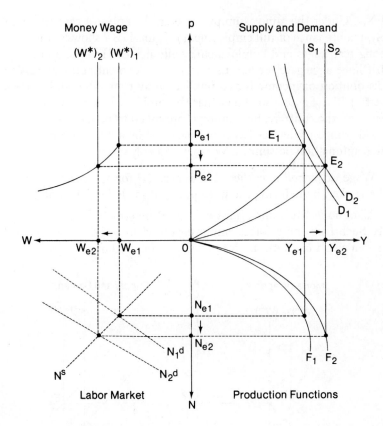

Figure 11B-1   Automation Optimism

sight suggests that they did in the nineteenth. (Contemporary opinion during the nineteenth century was by no means unanimous in complacency; read Charles Dickens's *Hard Times,* or Friedrich Engels's *Condition of the Working Class in England in 1844,* or the descriptive chapters of *Das Kapital.*) It is the conclusion of the automation pessimists that technological breakthroughs no longer have the employment-creating effects associated with the Industrial Revolution and that the unfavorable consequences of automation have been masked by military and educational expansion during the period 1950–1970.

Figure 11B-2 illustrates the pessimists' view. Geometrically, the production function F_2 has become obviously more bow-shaped than F_1. Consequently, the tilt in the marginal product function underlying the demand for labor D_n has become more extreme. Specifically, N_2^d not only crosses N_1^d, but does so at an employment level less than the original equilibrium

level N_{e1}. Under the same assumptions as in the optimist case (given labor supply, maintenance of full employment), figure 11B-2 shows automation as lowering real wages and employment, while it raises income and the price level. (Since aggregate income rises while employment and real wages fall, a redistribution of income is also implied, away from labor and in favor of property.) The figure also shows that the problem is not one of aggregate demand; on the contrary, fine-tuning is presumed to be successful.

A wide range of devices has been suggested by automation pessimists to cushion automation pessimism. We mention only seven:

1. Wage or payroll subsidies. These raise N^d for any wage rate received by the worker, by reducing the wage payment made by the employer.

2. All-or-none bargaining. This will have the same effect, within certain limits. Such bargaining forces employers off what would ordinarily be their labor demand functions, as distinguished from ordinary wage bargaining,

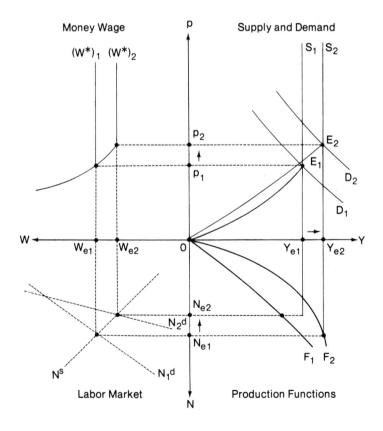

Figure 11B-2 Automation Pessimism

which leaves employers free to adjust their job offers to the bargained wage rates. The ordinary mechanism of all-or-none bargaining is indirect. It takes the form of working rules whose combined effect is to force the employer to hire more men than he wants at any given wage, on pain of obtaining no workers at all.

3. Job training and retraining. These are designed to shift the labor force from sectors where it is competitive with the new machinery to other sectors where it will be complementary with it. Hopefully, this procedure produces both some net upgrading of labor skills and some increase in D_n as in cases (1–2) above. (As one can see from the plight of unemployed and underemployed intellectuals and technicians in many countries, upgrading and increased employability do not always coexist.)

4. Withdrawing certain age, sex, and race classes from the labor market. Immigrants, married women, student-age youth, older workers eligible for pensions, are most commonly mentioned. Reasons for their withdrawal can sometimes be presented as humanitarian. These devices reduce N^s, and therefore lower aggregate income and employment. They also raise the (postautomation) price level. Their attraction, however, is that they lessen or reverse the decline in real wages brought on by automation.

5. Reducing or eliminating overtime work and multiple job-holding. This also reduces N^s, as in the previous case. To a greater extent than in (4), it also reduces N^d still further, by lessening potential employers' choice among potential employees. Its main effect is what might be considered greater "equity" in the distribution of labor income. (The same may be said of (4), if one regards as inequitable the simultaneous employment of several members of one family in a period of unemployment.)

6. Providing public employment, even of the make-work variety. We have seen (in chapter 3) that the GNP statistics evaluate the "product" of government employment (although not of "government enterprises") at the value of its payroll. It follows that, as a definitional matter or statistical artifact, the marginal product of a public employee is whatever he is paid. The effects of adding NN' public jobs at wage w to the aggregate production function F and the labor demand function N^d are as indicated by the "splints" in figure 11B-3. The published statistics will show higher N,Y,W, than before—and also lower P. What these differences actually mean depends upon the nature of the work done.

7. Breaking the nexus between income and employment are grants or social dividends that involve no obligation to seek or perform work. Such a "grants economy," as Kenneth Boulding calls it, lowers N^s by providing an alternative to labor as an income source. As in cases (4–5) above, this measure supports the real wage rate at the expense of "everything else."

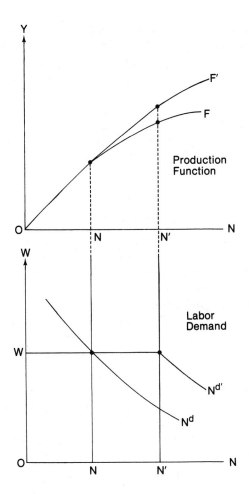

Figure 11B-3   The Public Employment "Splint"

Its main importance as an issue in social economics and social philosophy is, of course, the sharpness of its proposed break with the traditional "work ethic" of capitalist (and socialist) societies.

This discussion has been over-aggregated. The optimistic analysis tends to hold for certain major segments of the labor force who are both highly skilled and adaptable to changes in the skills required (I.Q. in excess of 120, perhaps); and the pessimistic one for other major segments (I.Q. less than 85, perhaps) who are unskilled and/or unadaptable. This combination involves troubles of its own. When high-I.Q. people can rely on social dividends as an alternative income source, one result may be a flowering of the impractical arts and sciences. When low-I.Q. people are in the same

position, the result may be brutalization and retrogression of society, with booze, dope, and raw sex playing the role of "bread and circuses" in Imperial Rome. (My high-I.Q. Duke University colleague, Thomas Havrilesky, objects to these guesses as intellectual elitism. He feels that high- and low-I.Q. people react to social dividends in much the same way. Perhaps we may soon learn which guess is correct.)

Our analysis also neglects the growth of capital. But accepting a pessimistic short-run analysis, we may suppose that "gross profits" (the income of nonworkers) will rise, permitting more saving, both personal and corporate. The same rise in profits attracts investment from entrepreneurs wishing to start new firms and expand old ones. With more saving and more investment, the capital stock rises. With more capital available, the production function is stretched out, the force of diminishing returns reduced, and the radius of curvature increased. The marginal productivity and demand for labor increases in consequence. The population, meanwhile, remains approximately constant; at least, its rate of increase is not significantly affected by changes in employment or in real wages.

The increase in gross profits, the capital stock, employment, and real wages, may continue for however long automation continues to increase real income and gross profits above what they would have been without it. Eventually, therefore, employment and real wages must rise above their preautomation values, however unfavorable may be the impact effects of automation.

This is a classical (Ricardian) model in reverse. Labor, the relatively constant productive input, occupies the position of land in the Ricardian system. Capital, sensitive to increases in income and profits, occupies the position of labor in the Ricardian system. (Gains in its total income lead to a rise in its quantity.) Finally, we are supposing policies that will secure full employment of capital at a high gross profit, quite as Ricardo expected Say's Law to provide full employment for labor at a subsistence wage.

The previous paragraphs sketch an argument, due primarily to Herbert Simon, justifying automation optimism for the long term. We can agree that (with full employment of capital) automation will raise gross profits. These may, however, be concentrated in particular enclaves of the economy where expansion possibilities and investment opportunities are limited. One such enclave is urban and suburban land, with its natural inelasticity of supply. Another is industrial monopoly and oligopoly, where (as per the Steindl argument of chapter 9) there is artificial inelasticity of investment demand if oligopolists are cautious about expanding their own capacity, and at the same time are capable of barring new competition from outsiders.

What of the parable of the horse? May not the computer make the human being obsolete (at anything approaching current real wages) in the same way that the internal-combustion engine has depreciated the horse below the value of his feed?

The obsolescence of the horse can be analyzed with three productive inputs involved: men, horses, machines. Men may be employed in processes involving horses, or in other processes involving machines. If we are pardoned "commodity fetishism," there was competition between horses and machines for the services of men. The machines won; the horses died out; the men's living standards rose. In the present instance, with two inputs (men and machines) the analogy is imperfect.

But suppose that "men" are subdivided further, into largely immutable classes. One such division may be between skilled and unskilled workers, with an elitist boundary drawn arbitrarily at an I.Q. between 80 and 90. Once again we have three services or inputs; this time they are unskilled workers, skilled workers, and machines. This time it is skilled men who may be used in processes where they work with unskilled men, or in other processes where they tend automated machines. This time, if machines win out as the pessimists fear, the national income will rise, and with it the living standards of both machine owners and skilled workers. The unskilled worker (manual or clerical) will have no economic reason for living, whatever the humanitarian objections to his extermination and the humanitarian provision of relief. Unless men are either homogeneous, or highly mobile between skill categories, we should not forget the parable of the horse.

SUMMARY

This appendix uses the apparatus of aggregate supply and demand to illustrate a controversy regarding the effects of automation upon real wages and employment. Automation optimism asserts that the effects are necessarily beneficial; automation pessimism asserts the exact opposite. Abstract theory is unable to solve this recurrent question, despite a conventional opinion that "technological unemployment" (either voluntary or involuntary) is impossible.[2] The issue is presented as depending upon the effects of automation upon the production function's radius of curvature. The more the radius is lowered by automation or by other technical change, the greater the likelihood of an unfavorable outcome. It does not seem easy to translate this technical conclusion into terms that are meaningful in the forum of public controversy. Finally, we discuss the parable of the horse as it might apply to the obsolescence of unskilled workers.

---

[2] This opinion (not discussed specifically in the text) appears to assume that the same amount of labor will be offered at any real wage above zero—N^s, in other words, is completely inelastic. It also appears to assume that the growth of aggregate demand cannot lag behind that of aggregate supply—Say's Identity, in other words, is accepted. Finally, the question of the influence of automation on wage rates is usually ignored.

Part

II

Macrodynamics: Growth, Fluctuations, Forecasting

Chapter
12

A Little
Growth Theory

TRAVERSE TO MACRODYNAMICS

Our exposition of macroeconomics in its various guises (chapters 4–11) has found neither necessary nor expedient any antiseptic separation of static from dynamic propositions and implications. The essence of the presentation has obviously been static—constant tastes, resources, institutions, and technology—and has facilitated investigating changes one-at-a-time and once-and-for-all. We have seldom needed to "date" our variables or distinguish with care between Y_t and Y_{t-1}. At the same time, the exposition has included dynamic aspects now and then, as in our "classical" chapter 4, our "Marxian" chapter 5, our "econometric" chapter 8, and our "stagnationist" chapter 9. The chapters which follow, by contrast, will deal with dynamic aspects more centrally. The present one deals with economic growth, viewed as a smooth ongoing process. The next three will deal with economic fluctuations, viewed as systematic deviations around a theoretical growth path or a statistical trend line.

Growth theory has developed, consciously or otherwise, in two directions at once. We begin with Adam Smith: "Little else is requisite to carry a state to the highest degree of opulence from the lowest barbarism, but peace, easy taxes, and a tolerable administration of justice; all the rest being brought about by the natural course of things."[1] One direction of development from Adam Smith will concern us here. It leads to study of the moving equilibrium position (stable or otherwise) of an abstract "economy," which bears some resemblance to an advanced industrialized country in the nineteenth or twentieth century. [A second direction of development from Adam Smith leads to studies that practitioners usually call Economic Development. It has also been called—by Sir John Hicks—underdevelopment economics, and described as "a practical subject which must expect to call upon any branch of theory (including non-economic, for instance sociological theory) which has any relevance to it."][2]

THE LANGE MODEL

The modern upsurge of growth theory may be dated from a 1938 essay by Oskar Lange (later Vice President of Poland), entitled "The Rate of

---

[1] This passage is not from the *Wealth of Nations* itself, but from a preliminary manuscript dated 1755 and subsequently lost. Dugald Stewart mentions this manuscript in his "Account of the Life and Writings of Adam Smith"; the passage quoted is reproduced in Edwin Cannan's "Editor's Introduction" (p. xliii) to his edition (1904) of the *Wealth of Nations* (1776).

[2] John Hicks, *Capital and Growth* (1965), p. 3.

Interest and the Optimum Propensity to Consume."[3] The title does not mention growth, but Lange uses "optimal" to mean "investment-maximizing." Investment means capital accumulation, whose main significance is as a key to growth.

Lange tried to determine what constraint most severely limited investment. Was it, as the classical writers supposed, the inadequate supply of saving? Or was it, as underconsumptionists, socialists, (and most Keynesians) supposed, inadequate demand for the investment's potential output?

Lange's solution is summarized in figure 12-1 in the familiar variables (Y, C, r), with $I = Y - C$. Lange derives an LM function (independently of Hicks) in Y and r; it is shown without reference to Lange's derivation process. Lange also uses a special (and thus far unverified) investment function $I = F(r, C)$ with $(\partial F / \partial r)$ negative and $(\partial F / \partial C)$ positive; from this he obtains a set of iso-investment curves (figure 12-1, with $I_3 > I_2 > I_1$). By differentiating totally and setting $dI = 0$, he derives the expression:

$$\frac{\partial F}{\partial r} \, dr + \frac{\partial F}{\partial C} \, dC = 0 \qquad (12.1)$$

whose slope (dr/dC) is $-(\partial F/\partial C)/(\partial F/\partial r)$. From LM, written as $M = L(Y, r)$, Lange also has, for a constant real money stock M and $dM = 0$:

$$\frac{\partial L}{\partial r} \, dr + \frac{\partial L}{\partial Y} \, dY = 0 \qquad (12.2)$$

whose slope (dr/dY) is $-(\partial L/\partial Y)/(\partial L/\partial r)$. Now, if I is a maximum and $dI = 0$, our income source equation $Y = C + I$ differentiates to $dY = dC$. Algebraically this means that we may substitute dY for dC in equation (12.1) and obtain a common solution of (12.1–2) for the slope dr/dY of figure 12-1:

---

[3] Oskar Lange, *op. cit.* reprinted in Gottfried von Haberler, ed., *Readings in Business Cycle Theory* (1944), no. 8.
Growth theory did not stand still between Smith and Lange. We have touched on the positions of Ricardo, Marx, and Schumpeter in chapters 4, 5, and 9, respectively. For fuller expositions, see Irma Adelman, *Theories of Economic Growth and Development* (1961); Hicks, *Capital and Growth, op. cit.,* ch. 4–6; Bert F. Hoselitz, ed., *Theories of Economic Growth* (1960), ch. 1–5.

$$\frac{\partial F/\partial C}{\partial F/\partial r} = \frac{\partial L/\partial C}{\partial L/\partial r} \tag{12.3}$$

Equation (12.3) has a geometric meaning. As a maximum condition for investment I, the slopes of the liquidity and investment functions are equal at their point of tangency P (where $I_2 = I_e$). There is tangency between the LM function and the investment-function map at this point on the diagram.

On the other hand, if our equilibrium point is at P' or at P" with $I_1 = I_e$, the tangency condition (12.3) does *not* hold; investment and growth are *not* maximized.

1. The first case (P') is of the sort conceived by the classical economists—too much consumption, suboptimal saving. It probably holds in many developing countries. Geometrically speaking, the slope of LM is steeper than that of the iso-investment curve I_1 at their intersection—P'.

2. The second case (P") is of the sort conceived by the underconsumptionists, including Keynesians and Marxists. It is characterized by too little consumption, suboptimal aggregate demand. It probably held in the 1930s for most developed countries. Geometrically speaking, the slope of I is steeper than that of LM at their intersection P".

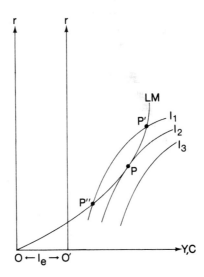

Figure 12-1   Lange Diagram

THE HARROD-DOMAR MODELS

However helpful conceptually, the Lange model has not lent itself to empirical investigation. Econometricians have not been able to use it to determine whether country A at time t is at an optimal position as Lange defines it, or if not, whether its propensity to consume is too high or too low. The model, accordingly, has not been used widely.

More influential than Lange's effort has been a series of growth models devised independently by Sir Roy Harrod in Britain and Evsey Domar in the U.S. Since they lead to identical growth paths from quite different directions, they are known collectively as Harrod-Domar models. (Harrod's work has a five-year temporal priority.) [4]

Let us denote by G the growth rate of income (dY/Y), where Y is the net national product after appropriate deduction for depreciation. Since $I = S$ and also $I = dK$ (where K is the capital stock, and I is net of depreciation), G equals:

$$\frac{dY}{I}\frac{S}{Y} \quad \text{or} \quad \frac{dY}{dK}\frac{S}{Y}$$

Harrod denotes the *saving ratio* S/Y as s. The marginal *capital-output ratio* (dK/dY), which we shall denote by v, is the amount of investment required *ex post* to increase Y by one unit.[5] It has also been called the capital coefficient and icor (incremental capital-output ratio). Its value has been estimated at between 2.5 and 3.5, a degree of constancy sufficient to justify its listing among the "great ratios of econometrics." Using these symbols, we have:

$$G = \frac{1}{v}s \quad \text{or} \quad Gv = s \tag{12.4}$$

as *Harrod's identity* regarding the determinants of the *actual* or measured growth rate G.

---

[4] Roy F. Harrod, "An Essay in Dynamic Theory," *Economic Journal* (March 1939), reprinted in Joseph Stiglitz and Hirofumi Uzawa, eds., *Readings in the Modern Theory of Economic Growth* (1969), no. 1, and in A. K. Sen, ed., *Readings in Growth Economics* (1970), no. 1. See also Roy Harrod, *Towards a Dynamic Economics* (1952), Lecture 3.

[5] Harrod sometimes uses the subscript p to denote that it is an *ex post* quantity. He eliminates the subscript for the corresponding *ex ante* quantity, which we meet in equation (12.6). See, however, Sen, *op. cit.*, p. 43n.

Besides the actual or measured rate G there are in Harrod's system two other income growth rates, the *natural* and the *warranted* rates, denoted respectively by G_n and G_w. Let G_n be a rate corresponding, in what Mrs. Robinson later called "golden-age" fashion, to the growth rate of the labor force and to the state of technology. Let v_r be the particular capital-output ratio ostensibly required by technical conditions and the composition of output, while s remains the exogenously-determined saving ratio. We no longer have an equation like (12.4); in general:

$$G_n \gtreqless \frac{1}{v_r} s \quad \text{or} \quad G_n v_r \gtreqless s \qquad (12.5)$$

The *warranted* or equilibrium growth rate G_w is one that justifies businessmen's past anticipations in the aggregate—averaging out the overly optimistic anticipations leading some to invest too much and the overly pessimistic ones leading others to invest too little. The warranted rate also leaves savers satisfied with their previous decisions to save or to consume, as denoted by a saving ratio s_r. Like the natural rate G_n, it assumes the required capital-output ratio v_r to have been planned *ex ante* as well as realized *ex post*. We therefore have:

$$G_w = \frac{1}{v_r} s_r \quad \text{or} \quad G_w v_r = s_r \qquad (12.6)$$

The equilibrium growth rate G_w is unstable. This result supposedly has important policy consequences. It leaves a greater scope for social planning than would a condition of stable growth along a given path. Let us, therefore, see how this instability, known as "knife-edge" instability along an equilibrium path, can be shown.

Suppose first that G_w, the warranted or equilibrium growth rate, exceeds both the natural rate G_n and the observed rate G. This means that G and G_n, which are by hypothesis below the equilibrium rate G_w, cannot be high enough to justify whatever investment plans may have formed the basis for G. (A higher growth path will validate *ex post* a more ambitious set of investment projects than a lower one.) If G is too low to justify the investment plans on which it is based, this implies that investment in the next period will be reduced. The observed growth rate G will fall, taking the economy further from both equilibrium (rate G_w) and full employment (rate G_n). This fall away from the equilibrium path at G_w will continue, in the absence of public intervention, until the economy hits a floor. (One such floor or buffer might be zero gross investment.)

Conversely, if G exceeds G_w—it can exceed G_n only temporarily—investors will regret not having invested more than they did. They will increase their investment plans, causing the measured growth rate G to rise further. The further rise in G will take the system increasingly out of equilibrium, until a ceiling to the exhilaration or boom is reached at (or even temporarily above) G_n.

A simple formalization of (12.6) leads to an exponential equilibrium growth path, which is also unstable. If planned saving S_r equals sY, while planned investment I_w equals $(g)(dY/dt)$ as per the acceleration principle of chapter 8, we may equate these two expressions to frame a condition of equilibrium growth:

$$g\frac{dY}{dt} - sY = 0$$

This differential equation can be solved by separating the variables and integrating.[6] The solution is:

$$\log Y = \log Y_0 + \frac{s}{g}t$$

so that, taking antilogarithms:

$$Y = Y_0\, e^{\frac{s}{g}t} \qquad\qquad (12.7a)$$

If $S = I = sY$ in general, and in particular, if $S_0 = I_0 = sY_0$, we also have:

$$I = I_0\, e^{\frac{s}{g}t} \qquad\qquad (12.7b)$$

an expression comparable, as we shall see, to Domar's independently-derived result.

---

[6] The intermediate step in the solution is:

$$\frac{dY}{Y} - \frac{s}{g}\, dt = 0$$

In integrating, it is natural to denote the constant of integration as $\log Y_0$, since it is the value of $\log Y$ at $t = 0$.

Domar's problem sprang from the stagnation controversy of the late 1930s and early 1940s.[7] Suppose that all saving is invested voluntarily, but aggregate purchasing power remains the same: Is this "full investment" enough to ward off stagnation? Not necessarily, says Domar; the investment adds to capacity, so that purchasing power must grow to maintain the employment level. Or suppose that the economy were, in fact, stagnant, as per the arguments of our chapter 9. Could the situation be saved by encouraging private investment—perhaps by tax favors, or perhaps by weakening pro-labor and antimonopoly legislation, reversing certain of the trends lamented by Schumpeter? Again Domar is pessimistic, unless aggregate demand is raised at the same time.

Investment, Domar reminds us, has two effects. The first, which he calls the *alpha effect*, is to increase income via the Keynesian multiplier. [Domar's α is the m.p.s., which we call $(1 - c)$.] The second result of investment, which Domar calls the *sigma effect*, is to increase productive capacity. [Domar's σ, or (dY/dK), is the reciprocal of the marginal capital-output ratio. In our terms, it is $1/v$.][8] To increase capacity means to increase the difficulty of utilizing it fully. "If saving is not [voluntarily] invested, we have a depression today. If it is invested, there will be an excessive accumulation of capital tomorrow, and a depression the day after."[9]

An equilibrium growth path in the Domar model is one in which the alpha and sigma effects of investment keep in step with each other. In this terminology, the alpha effect on Y can be written (dI/α), while the sigma effect (per interval of time dt) is $I\sigma dt$. Corresponding to the differential-equation development in equations (12.7), we have:

$$\frac{dI}{\alpha} - I\sigma dt = 0$$

with the solution:

---

[7] Three essays by Evsey Domar, "Capital Expansion, Rate of Growth, and Employment," "Expansion and Employment," and "The Problem of Capital Accumulation," are reprinted, respectively, from *Econometrica* (April 1946), *American Economic Review* (March 1947), and *Ibid.* (December 1948) as ch. 3–5 of Domar, *Essays in the Theory of Economic Growth* (1957). The first (and most mathematical) of the three is also reprinted in Stiglitz and Uzawa, *op. cit.*, no. 2, and in Sen, *op. cit.*, no. 2. The second essay is reprinted in M. G. Mueller, *Readings in Macroeconomics* (1966), no. 20.

[8] More complex presentations use $\Theta\sigma$ instead of σ, the Θ being the employment rate of labor (or of capital), and attaining unity under full-employment conditions. Compare Robert Eisner, *Some Factors in Growth Reconsidered* (1966), pp. 18–20, including note 1.

[9] Evsey Domar, "Problem of Capital Accumulation," in *Essays in Theory of Economic Growth, op. cit.*, p. 118.

$$I = I_0 \, e^{a\sigma t} \qquad\qquad (12.8a)$$

but since $I = S = \alpha Y$ for all values of I, including I_0, we may divide both sides of (12.8a) by α and obtain:

$$Y = Y_0 \, e^{a\sigma t} \qquad\qquad (12.8b)$$

The Domar exponential equations (12.8) are identical with the Harrod ones (12.7). The s and g of (12.7) correspond to α and $1/\sigma$ in (12.8). This is why we speak of Harrod-Domar models in hyphenated fashion. The knife-edge instability property of (12.7) also carries over to (12.8). Diagrammatically, (12.7–8) are normally upward-sloping straight lines on diagrams whose horizontal axes are time t and log Y (or log I). The slope is s/g for a Harrod model and $\alpha\sigma$ for a Domar model. When we shift to the more intuitively meaningful axes t and Y (or I), the *constant* growth *rates* of the log-linear paths become *increasing* growth *amounts*, as in figure 12-2, and the meaning of s/g or of $\alpha\sigma$ becomes less obvious. (The diagram as drawn illustrates a Harrod model.)

TWO NEO-CLASSICAL MODELS: THE SOLOW CONTRIBUTIONS

An important implication of the Harrod-Domar models is their knife-edge instability, which in turn implies a need for "planning and control" to pro-

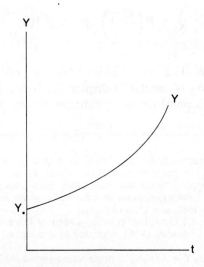

Figure 12-2   Harrod Model—Exponential Growth

vide stability. Was it this ideological threat to free enterprise that inspired a neo-classical counterrevolution in growth theory, along with the counter-revolution against Keynes? There are no obvious ideological overtones in the two models of Robert Solow, who has played in growth theory the "Friedman" role of counterrevolutionist extraordinary. The widespread acceptance of the Solow models may be another story.

Where Harrod and Domar, in the Keynesian tradition, concentrate on problems of securing adequate aggregate demand at all points on a growth path and ignoring the role of prices, the counterrevolutionists stress the supply side of the growth problem, including the role of prices. They also assume a constant high level of employment to be maintained (outside their models) by monetary and fiscal fine tuning, or by flexible prices and wages, with or without inflationary accompaniment.[10]

The first of two Solow models[11] introduces labor explicitly (along with capital) as a productive input, and allows for substitution between labor and capital in the aggregate production process. As a result, stability may be (but need not be) secured, as we shall see. We begin with a production function F:

$$Y = F(K,N)$$

linear homogeneous in K and N.[12] Its linear homogeneity property implies that:

$$\frac{Y}{N} = F\left(\frac{K}{N}, 1\right) \quad \text{or} \quad y = f(x)$$

in Solow's notation. The capital-labor ratio x is related to the Marxian "organic composition of capital" (chapter 5). It is a function of relative input prices; at each point on an equilibrium growth path, its equilibrium

---

[10] Some writers argue in favor of inflation as a spur to growth. Inflation induces people to place a higher proportion of their savings in new physical (productive) capital, and less in (unproductive) monetary assets, than does price stability or defla-tion. (They may also, however, respond to inflation by saving less, or by concentrating their savings in existing assets as inflation hedges.)

[11] Robert M. Solow, "A Contribution to the Theory of Economic Growth," *Quarterly Journal of Economics* (February 1956), reprinted in Sen, *op. cit.*, no. 7, and in Stiglitz and Uzawa, *op. cit.*, no. 4.

[12] A function such as $Y = F(K,N)$ is linear homogeneous if $\lambda Y = F(\lambda K, \lambda N)$ for any positive λ. (In the development which follows, $\lambda = 1/N$.) This condition corresponds to "constant costs" or "constant returns to scale" in microeconomics.

value is x_e, and (dx/dt) is zero as an equilibrium condition. Mathematically, this condition may be written:

$$\frac{dx}{dt} = \frac{d}{dt}\left(\frac{K}{N}\right) = \frac{1}{N}\left(\frac{dK}{dt} - x\frac{dN}{dt}\right) = 0$$

But (dK/dt) is also net investment, which equals net saving sY, with a given saving ratio s. If we recall that (Y/N) is simply y, and denote by n the employment growth rate $(dN/dt)/N$, we have

$$sy - nx = 0 \qquad\qquad (12.9)$$

as the equation of the equilibrium condition at any point in time. It is *not* an equilibrium growth *path* of aggregate y over time; in fact, it implies constant y over time. The common sense of (12.9) is that it provides for saving and investment growing just enough to retain the equilibrium capital-labor ratio as employment grows at rate n, whether n be constant or variable.

The relation of all this to stability can be clarified by a diagram (figure 12-3). The equilibrium condition (12.9) is plotted on this diagram, with axes x and (dx/dt). Income per employed worker, or y, is an increasing function of capital per employed worker, or x; diminishing returns require that its concavity be downward. Savings per employed worker sy are derived from y, with s assumed constant. On the left panel of the diagram, the employment growth rate n is also assumed constant, so that nx is a ray through the origin 0. On the right-hand panel, however, n varies with y, and therefore with x, so that (12.9) is satisfied at the three points x_1, x_2, and x_3. Also included on each panel is $(sy - nx)$ or (dx/dt), obtained by simple subtraction.

On the left-hand panel (a normal case) the variability of x suffices for a stable solution if a positive equilibrium value x_e exists. To the left (right) of x_e, sy is greater (less) than nx, so that (dx/dt) is positive (negative). As a result, the function $(sy - nx)$ cuts the horizontal axis from above. On the right-hand panel, where $n = n[f(x)]$ and so varies with x, there are three equilibrium points. The smallest of these, x_1 (the "low level equilibrium trap" of economic development theory) and also the largest, x_3 ("the affluent society") are both stable. The intermediate point x_2, like a point on a Harrod-Domar equilibrium growth path, is in unstable equilibrium, with $(sy - nx)$ cutting the horizontal axis from below. This implies for growth policy a "big push" from a situation like x_1 to get past x_2 and settle eventually at x_3, whereas a smaller "push" would simply fall back to x_1.

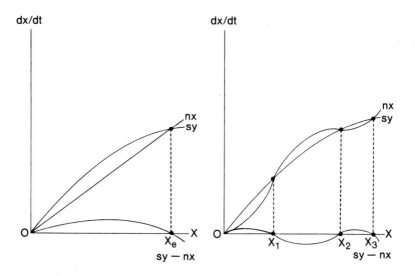

Figure 12-3   Solow Growth Model

Solow's own essay diagrams and discusses a number of other variants on the general theme of (12.9).

The second Solow essay we consider was published a year later. It is econometrically oriented.[13] This essay proposes an answer to a question that has tantalized growth theorists—namely, what proportion of growth is due to increased supplies of labor and capital inputs, and what proportion to technical progress? Attacking this problem, Solow again uses an aggregate production function, which he again assumes to be linear homogeneous in the capital stock K and employment N. Its form is:

$$Y = e^{gt} F(K,N) \qquad (12.10)$$

with the g coefficient allowing for the effects of "time" as a surrogate for technical progress. This treatment makes three implicit assumptions that later and more complex studies have sought to weaken:[14]

1. All technical progress is "disembodied" rather than "embodied" in new types of equipment and labor. It affects the productivity of "old" and "new" capital and labor in the same way and to the same extent.

---

[13] Robert M. Solow, "Technical Change and the Aggregate Production Function," *Review of Economics and Statistics* (August 1957), reprinted in Mueller, *op. cit.*, no. 23 and Sen, *op. cit.*, no. 18.

[14] These are additional to the more basic assumption of "homogenizability" or "malleability" of Y, K, and N. (The homogenizability of K, in particular, is denied by British economists of the "neo-Cambridge" school, most vigorously by Joan Robinson.)

2. All technical progress is also "neutral" and affects the productivity of labor and of capital to the same extent. In particular, it leaves unchanged the ratio of their respective marginal products.

3. The degree of substitutability of labor for capital, and vice versa, as measured by the "elasticity of substitution," is the same for new processes and for old ones already in operation.

Now let us see what can be done with equation (12.10), assumptions and all. Let G be the growth rate of Y, G_y that of product per worker (Y/N), and g the growth rate of technology—an unknown constant solved for in a statistical investigation. Let G_k and G_n be the growth rates of K and N respectively, while G_x is the growth rate of the capital-labor ratio (K/N). Finally, let s be the "property" share in Y at any given time (assumed approximately constant) and let $(1 - s)$ be the labor share. In our notation, Solow proves that:[15]

$$G = g + sG_k + (1 - s)G_n \qquad (12.11)$$

---

[15] The proofs of (12.11–12) are not difficult. Differentiating (12.10) with respect to time:

$$\frac{dY}{dt} = g e^{gt} F(K,N) + e^{gt} \left(\frac{\partial F}{\partial K} \frac{dK}{dt} + \frac{\partial F}{\partial N} \frac{dN}{dt} \right)$$

Dividing by Y (to obtain G), which equals $[e^{gt} F(K,N)]$ by (12.10):

$$G = g + \frac{1}{F(K,N)} \left(\frac{\partial F}{\partial K} \frac{dK}{dt} + \frac{\partial F}{\partial N} \frac{dN}{dt} \right)$$

Multiplying and dividing the terms in parentheses by K and N respectively, to obtain G_k and G_n:

$$G = g + \frac{K \partial F/\partial K}{F(K,N)} G_k + \frac{N \partial F/\partial N}{F(K,N)} G_n$$

Under marginal productivity assumptions, the coefficient of G_k is the property share s, while the coefficient of G_n is the labor share $(1 - s)$. Making these substitutions, we have (12.11).

We know that the growth rate of a quotient like x/y, or $[d(x/y)/dt]/(x/y) = G_x - G_y$. To apply this result, we may write (12.11) as

$$G - G_n = g + s(G_k - G_n)$$

but $G - G_n = G_y$ and $G_k - G_n = G_x$, giving (12.12).

and also:

$$G_y = g + sG_x \qquad (12.12)$$

Solow goes on to fit (12.12) to U.S. data for 1909–1949, estimating g for each year as $G - sG_x$ and comparing it with G. He concludes that output per man hour "doubled over the interval, with 87½ percent of the increase attributable to technical change and the remaining 12½ percent to the "deepening of capital."[16] The unexpectedly large "technology" component and the relatively small "capital" component shocked the economics profession, and inspired much subsequent work in the economics of technological change.

EMPIRICAL EXTENSIONS

Other writers, following up the empirical aspects of Solow's study, have carried this aspect of growth theory further in at least three principal ways:

1. Working with (12.11) rather than (12.12), to separate the contributions of capital growth from labor growth.

2. Separating the catchall g term of (12.11–12) into components g_1, g_2, . . . g_n, and estimating values for each component, that is for each of n different types of technical change.

3. Allowing for quality improvements ("embodied changes," "improvement factors," or "vintages") in capital and labor, so that we may have αK and βN instead of simply K and N, with α and β also functions of time.[17]

Exemplifying these extensions are studies by Edward F. Denison, and by Solow himself.[18] Denison, for example,[19] includes in what we have called β

---

[16] Solow, "Technical Change," *op. cit.*, p. 320. (Mueller, *op. cit.*, p. 333; Sen, *op. cit.*, p. 418.)

[17] Analytically, we may speak of G_α and G_β as improvement rates per period in K and N respectively. This permits substituting $(G_\alpha + G_k)$ and $(G_\beta + G_n)$ for G_k and G_n in expressions like (12.11–12). Also, G_x becomes the sum of $(G_\alpha - G_\beta)$ and $(G_k - G_n)$, which allows for biased growth.

[18] Edward F. Denison, *The Sources of Economic Growth in the United States* (1962); also a later study (with Jean-Pierre Poullier), *Why Growth Rates Differ* (1967); three post-1957 Solow studies are "Investment and Technical Change," in Kenneth Arrow et al., eds., *Mathematical Methods in the Social Sciences* (1959); "Technical Progress, Capital Formation, and Economic Growth," *American Economic Review* (1962); and "Capital, Labor, and Income in Manufacturing," in National Bureau of Economic Research, *The Behavior of Income Shares* (1964).

[19] Denison, *Sources of Growth, op. cit.*, table 31, p. 265.

for the U.S. over the generation 1929–1957 separate estimates of the effects of increased employment (1.31 percent per year), reduced working hours (−0.73 percent), increased quality due to a shorter working year (0.50 percent), increased education (0.93 percent), changes in the age and sex composition of the labor force (−0.01 percent), and the increased experience and better utilization of women workers in particular (0.15 percent). Of a 2.93 percent annual G, Denison ascribes 2.10 percent to the unadjusted increase in total inputs and 0.92 percent to increased overall productivity of capital and labor (our g), while −0.11 percent is lost in "adjustment factors," in which the removal of obvious statistical interactions between g, for instance, and the investment rate G_k outweigh our α and β, both of which are presumably constant.

Critics of Solow's 1957 study pointed out an anomalous implication of (12.11). Suppose the growth rate G is 3.33 percent or .0333, while the capital share s is .25. The capital-output ratio v has been 3.0 for long enough so that (K/Y) may also be 3.0. The labor-force growth rate G_n is .01, and the net saving ratio (S/Y) or (dK/Y) is .10 (all reasonably realistic assumptions under American conditions). Then G_k, which equals (dK/Y)(Y/K), is also .0333. As for g (computed as a residual), it is 0.175, slightly more than half the growth rate. Now suppose the saving ratio suddenly to double to .20, with no other changes. Then G_k would double, to 0.667, but G would rise only to 4.17 percent or 0.417 despite a real "revolution" in capital accumulation.[20] Something, the critics (and Solow himself) suspected, must be wrong somewhere.

Solow's solution has been to use investment data to construct a schedule of the *dates* or *vintages* of existing capital. He then develops a weighting system, with newer capital weighted more heavily than older. This system permits corrections for the quality of capital goods, and translation of

---

[20] The figures are:
To compute g, with G = .0333 and (S/Y) = .10:

$$g = G - [sG_k + (1 - s)G_n] = .0333 - [(.25 \times .0333) + (.75 \times .01)] = .0333 - .0158$$

To compute G, with g = .0175 and (S/Y) = .20:

$$G = g + sG_k + (1 - s)G_n = .0175 + (.25 \times .0667) + (.75 \times .01) = .0175 + .0242.$$

This g is often known as the "Abramovitz" residual, Moses Abramovitz having been among the first economists to estimate it and recognize its importance for the theory and history of economic growth.

"dollars' worth" of capital investment into "efficiency units." Solow's procedure involves the treatment of education expenditure as embodied in capital, whereas Denison's method embodies them in labor, as we have seen. Investigating U.S. data over the forty-year period 1920–1960, Solow has found an average annual G of 3.3 percent, of which 1.0 percent was due to increased employment of labor, 0.8 percent to an increased (and improved) capital stock, and 1.5 percent a residual ascribed to technical change. The total nonlabor contribution is then 2.3 percent per year, approximately ⅓ from capital and ⅔ from technological progress.

OPTIMAL GROWTH

The Lange model is a normative one, both about consumption and about growth. Lange sought to determine the optimum propensity to consume, with the aim of maximizing investment, and he aimed to maximize investment in order to promote economic growth. He assumed that growth was intrinsically a good thing, and the more of it the better. This line of thought reached its apogee in an essay by Peter Wiles entitled "Choice versus Growth."[21] Here Wiles argues that the paramountcy of growth justifies programming countries to grow faster even if the inhabitants oppose the short-run sacrifices involved, and prefer conditions closer to the classical stationary state. This brand of "growthmanship" has fallen from fashion in the MDCs (more developed countries), but survives in many LDCs (less developed countries) of the so-called Third World. It is often implicit in ranking the USSR or Japan above the U.S. and the U.K., or planned economies above free-enterprise ones, as models for LDCs to follow.

Whether taken total or per capita, gross or net, measured national or domestic product does not measure welfare. On this point there is little disagreement; we have repeated the point in chapter 3. Accordingly, GNP (for example) can possibly grow so fast as to decrease welfare. The most emphasized costs of growth have been the exhaustion of natural resources, environmental pollution in its various forms, dehumanization of working conditions, maldistribution of the gains from growth among income classes and geographical regions, and sacrifice of the miscellaneous amenities comprising the "quality of life"—from housing (neglected in favor of factories) to handicrafts (abandoned for machine-tending). From growthmanship, the pendulum of Sunday-supplement economics has swung toward zero

---

[21] Peter J. D. Wiles, "Choice versus Growth," *Economic Journal* (March 1956).

growth.[22] In a slow-growth or no-growth regime, however, more guns do indeed and immediately mean less butter, and more butter means fewer guns. More for the farmer means less for the city-dweller. More for the blacks means less for the whites. More for the poor means less for the rich. All social conflict is more abrasive, whereas growth can be a social lubricant. It is easier to sacrifice to my neighbor a substantial part of my anticipated next-year's growth dividend than an equal amount taken from my present income or wealth.

Assume the existence of a number of alternative stable-equilibrium growth paths. From among these alternatives an economy can choose, but the economy is supposed constrained to follow one such path. Which choice is optimal? A growthmanship solution is, the path giving the maximum growth rate. An environmentalist solution may restrict our choice to paths "protecting the environment," however this term is defined; no such paths may permit positive growth, either in total or per capita income. A libertarian solution may not exist, since the libertarian may deny the existence of any optimum at all. (Any growth rate resulting from the informed decisions of free men is to him the correct rate for the society in question.) A technical compromise solution is due to Edwin S. Phelps, whose criterion for an optimum is maximum consumption per capita consistent with maintaining an equilibrium capital-labor ratio as per the Solow model.[23] This solution—the so-called "Golden Rule" of Accumulation—requires that the saving ratio and the property (nonlabor) share of the national income be kept equal to each other, or conversely, that the average propensity to consume and the labor share remain equal. (Phelps does not indicate which ratio should move when the pair are in fact unequal.) Critics of consumer gadgetry, of course, object to the consumption-maximization criterion, especially when no attention is paid the value of consumers' leisure or other unmeasured aspects of consumption. Paradoxically, at least from a socialist viewpoint, most capitalist economies consume, in fact, a larger proportion of the national income (and distribute a larger share to workers) than the Phelps criterion would propose.

Phelps derives his solution algebraically; we shall use a geometric demon-

---

[22] Paul W. Barkley and David W. Seckler, *Economic Growth and Environmental Decay* (1972), ch. 1, 13; Dennis Meadows et al., *The Limits to Growth* (1972); Ezra J. Mishan, *The Costs of Economic Growth* (1967) and *The Economic Growth Debate* (1977); Erwin F. Schumacher, *Small Is Beautiful: Economics as if People Mattered* (1973).

[23] Edwin S. Phelps, "The Golden Rule of Accumulation: A Fable for Growthmen," *American Economic Review* (September 1961). A number of later developments of the Phelps rule are collected in Phelps, *Golden Rules of Economic Growth* (1966).

stration by Harry Johnson (figure 12-4).[24] The axes of this diagram are as in the Solow model (figure 12-3), and so are many of the functions drawn. In particular, x is capital per head, or K/N, while y is income per head, or Y/N. The economy is constrained to a stable Solow growth path. At x_e, the equilibrium value of x, $sy = nx$; this is shown by the intersection of the sy and nx functions at point R. Consumption per head at equilibrium is $y - sy$ or $y - nx$, the interval PR on the diagram. The slope (dy/dx) is the marginal product of capital, since (dy/dx), or $[d(Y/N)]/[d/(K/N)]$, equals (dY/dK) for any value of N. The quantity dy/dx equals (on the diagram) $(w_e y_e)/(y_e P)$.

For the situation of figure 12-4 to be optimal in Phelps's sense, PR, or consumption per head, is to be maximized. The tangent to y at P must be parallel to nx at R. This parallelism means that the triangles $0x_eR$ and $w_e y_e P$ are congruent, so that $x_e R = y_e w_e$. The meaning of $x_e R$ is clear; it is saving per head at x_e. But what is the meaning of $y_e w_e$? It is the marginal product of capital (dy/dx) multiplied by capital per head $y_e P$ to give property income per head.[25] We have, therefore, shown that saving per head equals property income per head as an optimization condition. Multiplication by

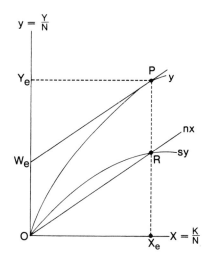

Figure 12-4   The Golden Rule of Accumulation

[24] Harry G. Johnson, *Essays in Monetary Economics* (1967), ch. 4.
[25] At the particular r_e where PR is a maximum, (dy/dx) also equals the growth rate G of the entire economy. This result follows, because the linear-homogeneous production function may be written $y = f(x)$. With x constant at x_e, both K and N must be growing at the rate n. With both inputs growing at rate n, G must also equal n, which we have shown to be the optimal value of (dy/dx).

N/Y yields the Phelps solution, equality between the property share (under socialism, the nonlabor share) and the saving ratio. This equality, incidentally, results tautologically if all labor income is consumed and all property income saved, regardless of the income distribution.

A LOOK AHEAD

This chapter has barely scratched the surface of macrodynamic growth theory.[26] Should the reader wish to pursue the subject more deeply, one important expansion would be to expand the economy into several interconnected sectors, including different types and ages of capital goods, and to consider the dynamic stability of the relations between these sectors, as well as of the economy as a whole, under different assumptions concerning the rapidity with which the price system can bring about necessary readjustments between sectors. (Under what conditions, for example, could we improve upon the simple-minded decision to let all sectors grow at the same rate? This is the subject of the so-called "turnpike theorems.") We have also mentioned, (in footnote 10) the special complications of introducing money into a growth model, as well as allowing trade and capital movements between economies that grow at different rates and with different sector proportions. When we come to optimal growth, also, more advanced treatments are concerned with population and technical change as subject to determination in the growth process, rather than as exogenous to it. Still another "problem" set of variables comprises the distributional consequences of growth in a market economy, both as between functional share (wages, rent, interest profits) and between income size classes.

As the reader was warned in advance, macrodynamic growth theory has thus far been abstract, and related only occasionally to the historical and institutional records of developing economies. Most writers hope that the gap between the two subjects can be reduced. An even more ambitious hope is to expand macrodynamics in an institutional direction, to:

> the study of the time path of a system whose structure is changing over time. In this case changes may be occurring in tastes, technology, or even in the form of economic organization. This kind of dynamic analysis poses more formidable difficulties than determining logical sequences flowing out of a given system. [It] entails all of this plus the problems of predicting when changes will occur in the system, how severe the changes will be, and what kinds of changes might occur. One has only to contemplate the problem of

---

[26] One of several textbooks on the subject is Edwin Burmeister and A. Rodney Dobell, *Mathematical Theories of Economic Growth* (1970).

predicting changes in tastes, technology, and institutions to understand what a very unsettling business this can be. [But] in order to develop rational plans for the future, an attempt at dynamic analysis of this type must be made.[27]

SUMMARY

After a methodological introduction that includes Adam Smith's laissez-faire position on economic growth policy, we pay attention initially to certain growth models based on the Keynesian system in the form of chapters 6–7. First we consider the Lange model of the optimum propensity to consume. Not overtly a growth model, it conceives the optimum as a maximization of investment and therefore of the growth rate. (Lange's optimum condition is tangency between a conventional LM function and his own idiosyncratic investment function.) We then examine in more detail the Harrod-Domar models that concern growth directly.

Harrod's analysis begins with the identity $Gv = s$, where G is the growth rate of aggregate real income, v is the marginal capital-output ratio, and s is the saving ratio or average propensity to save. This identity implies that no economy can combine a high G with both a low s and the high v characteristic of "modern industry" employing skilled and high-paid labor; something must yield. From this and related identities one can derive a warranted, or equilibrium, growth path of an exponential form, equating planned investment (as determined by a simple accelerator) with planned saving at every point in time. The Domar model derives a similar path by equating the income (multiplier) and output (productivity) consequences of investment at every point in time.

In both cases the equilibrium achieved is of a tenuous or knife-edge variety. A boom's excess of desired expenditures over actual income encourages further expansion to meet existing shortages. In Harrod's terms, it lowers the warranted rate of growth when stability would require an increase, and raises the actual rate when stability would require a decrease. Conversely, excess inventories and excess capacity in a recession lower the actual rate of growth and raise the warranted rate when the actual rate is already below the warranted rate. The unstable character of the growth path naturally implies the desirability, if not the necessity, of substantial centralized planning, at least in the aggregate.

Keynesian growth models concentrate on conditions for maintaining full employment, and concern themselves primarily with maintaining adequate

---

[27] Barkley and Seckler, *op. cit.*, p. 148. (Running quotation.)

aggregate demand. In terms of the Lange model, they assume that, in advanced countries, the threat to growth arises from the propensity to consume being below rather than above its optimum value. Neo-classical models, on the other hand, assume a high employment level as maintained by monetary and fiscal policies external to the growth model, and concentrate their attention on the supply side. The Solow model of 1956, for example, introduces a variable capital-labor ratio. Its equilibrium condition (sy = nx) does not assure stability through variation of the capital-labor ratio x, but suggests stability under what might be called normal conditions, and thereby implies less need for centralized planning and control. (In addition to the x term, the notation of this model includes the saving ratio s, income per worker y, and employment growth rate n.) Incidentally, the equilibrium value of y is (nx/s); in the absence of technological progress, this does not allow for any improvement in the average equilibrium level so long as n and s are constant.[28]

Statistical studies of growth, by Solow, Denison, and others, strive to estimate the relative importance of such causes for growth as technical changes, input augmentation, and income improvement. They have used conventional neo-classical models, but thier results appear to place greater weight on factors other than mere input augmentation than one might suspect from reading conventional static theory.

Among the infinite number of alternative equilibrium paths satisfying the Solow criterion for an equilibrium capital-labor ratio, what can we say about their relative desirabilities? Little or nothing, in any really general case. Phelps, however, has suggested the criterion of maximum consumption per worker constrained by maintenance of the equilibrium capital-labor ratio. If we accept this criterion as relevant, an optimum growth rate is derived in a high-employment market economy by equating the saving ratio to the nonlabor share of the national income. This criterion is satisfied for any income distribution, in addition, if workers consume (nearly) their entire incomes while nonworker "capitalists" save (nearly) all of their share.

---

[28] It is a useful exercise to trace through the short-run and long-run consequences of changes in n or s, using the apparatus of equation (12.9) and figure 12-3.

Chapter

13

Business Fluctuations– Traditional Theory

BUSINESS FLUCTUATIONS AND BUSINESS CYCLES

Before World War II, prospective economists did not study macro-economic analysis or aggregative economics as such. Courses and lectures that included macroeconomic materials were normally called "Business Fluctuations" or "Business Cycles." Such courses or lectures included little of the material in the first twelve chapters of this book; that little was often primarily monetary. Instead, these courses or lectures dealt in more detail with the materials we shall be discussing from now on. In addition, they included a great deal of descriptive or "institutional" material: the economic history of business fluctuations in the United States or the entire Western world, including the human consequences of depression and unemployment and suggestions for their alleviation. A long statistical section was also common, dealing with time-series analysis—methods, somewhat "cookbookish" in character, for decomposing statistical time series into trend, seasonal, cyclical, and random components and isolating the cycles.

The present chapter deals with the "cycle theory" part of an old-fashioned business cycle course. It introduces several traditional theories of fluctuations in production, income, and employment about their trend lines or growth paths. By "traditional" is meant primarily, although not exclusively, theories in greater vogue before the Great Crash of 1929, and before the appearance of Keynes's General Theory in 1936, than they are at the present time. The fullest treatment of this material is to be found in the works of Wesley C. Mitchell,[1] and of his coworkers and disciples at the National Bureau of Economic Research.

Economists use the terms "business cycles" and "business fluctuations" almost interchangeably, the former usage being somewhat more common. This usage can be misleading. To some people, use of the term "cycle" implies a regularity comparable with the physical regularities manifested by the tides or by the orbits of heavenly bodies. Such degrees of regularity seldom occur in the economy. (This writer has been asked "Do you economists still believe in business cycles?") "Business fluctuations" carries no such implication of regularity and would be the better term.

TYPES OF BUSINESS FLUCTUATIONS

Business annals, both literary and statistical, have suggested to economists three or four different patterns of business fluctuation. They differ primarily

---

[1] Particularly in Wesley C. Mitchell, Business Cycles, The Problem and Its Setting (1927), especially chapters 1 (iv) on cycle theories and 3 (iii–iv) on statistical characteristics of cycles.

in length, but all are too long to be confused with seasonal movements within a single calendar year. Fluctuations of different lengths are inter-related in that, during the upswing of a long cycle, shorter cycles usually show long periods of prosperity, short and mild periods of recession or depression; and vice versa for the downswings of long cycles. Four patterns have allegedly been isolated:

1. The *Kondratieff* cycle (30–50 years from peak to peak or trough to trough), associated with major price-level movements and perhaps also with major technological advances, such as the steam engine, the railroad, the electric motor and internal-combustion engine, etc.

2. The *Kuznets* cycle (15–25 years), associated with the economic life-time of buildings and of transport facilities such as highways and rail networks.

3. The *Juglar* cycle (7–11 years), *the* business cycle par excellence on which the bulk of academic attention has been concentrated.

4. The short or *Kitchin* cycle (18–30 months), associated with the build-ing up and drawing down of inventories of raw materials and of goods in various stages of completion.

These cycles have been named (primarily by Schumpeter) for econ-omists who have investigated them most thoroughly, following the usage of physicists who have named electrical units the volt, the ohm, the ampere, etc. Schumpeter also developed a famous and neat, but unfor-tunately not realistic schema of three Kitchins and six Juglars per Kondra-tieff.[2] (The Kuznets cycle might have been included as two Juglars per Kuznets and three Kuznetses per Kondratieff.)

Of these patterns, the most questionable is the longest (Kondratieff) cycle. Modern capitalism has not lasted long enough to provide examples sufficiently numerous to prove its existence at all conclusively. It is more plausible in price-level movements than in movements of production or em-ployment. Nikolai Kondratieff, a Soviet economist, associated upswings with wars, downswings with revolutions, and interpreted the Great Depres-sion of the 1930s as the downswing of a long cycle rather than the ultimate crisis of capitalism. (Such heresy did not fail to embroil their author, and the institute of which he was the head, with the Soviet authorities during

---

[2] The schema is illustrated in Joseph Schumpeter, *Business Cycles* (1939), vol. i, p. 213. It is made up by summing "three sine curves with periods respectively of 684, 114, and 38 months (or 57, 9½, and 3⅙ years) and with amplitudes roughly pro-portional to their periods, i.e., in the relation of 18, 3, and 1." *Ibid.*, vol. ii, p. 1051.

the Stalin period.) Schumpeter, who—as we shall soon see—associated business fluctuations with innovations, associated Kondratieff cycles with the most important ones. The whole subject of Kondratieff cycles may be more amenable to study in another century or so—if capitalism as we know it lasts so long.[3]

Following Mitchell, it has been customary for economists to divide each cycle or fluctuation into four parts: *recovery, prosperity, recession,* and *depression* in that order, with the depression period of one cycle succeeded in endless chain by the recovery period of the next one. Recovery and depression are both, in this schema, below the underlying trend or growth path, while prosperity and recession are above it. Journalists and politicians prefer to denote by recession a condition in which the growth rate of GNP, while lower than in the recent past or lower than average, remains positive, and reserve the term depression for fairly prolonged periods of absolute decline. As for the term *crisis,* Marxists use it to mean either recession or depression; conventional economists limit it to brief periods of unusually rapid and spectacular decline, approaching panic. The stock market crash of 1929, or the bank runs of 1933, deserve the name "crisis" in American business annals. The prolonged misery of the Great Depression as a whole does not, although Marxists call the entire period a "crisis of capitalism."

During the period 1945–1970, nearly all fluctuations in nearly all advanced countries have been limited to the growth rate of GNP. That is to say, growth rates fluctuated widely, but GNP itself seldom turned downward for long periods; there have been recessions but few and mild depressions. This circumstance has led some writers to speak of the prewar business cycle as being obsolete, or as being replaced by what Aaron Gordon has called the "growth cycle." Another way to look at this phenomenon is to argue that growth rates have risen while the amplitude of cyclical fluctuations has fallen, so that absolute declines in GNP are rare.[4]

---

[3] Compare Nikolai D. Kondratieff, "Long Waves in Economic Life," *Review of Economic Statistics* (November 1935), reprinted in Gottfried von Haberler, ed., *Readings in Business Cycle Theory,* 1944, no. 2; also George Garvy, "Kondratieff's Theory of Long Cycles," *Review of Economic Statistics* (November 1943), reprinted in Alvin H. Hansen and Richard V. Clemence, *Readings in Business Cycles and National Income* (1953), no. 31.

James B. Shuman and David Rosenau, *The Kondratieff Wave* (1972) is an immediately pre-oil shock popularization. As these writers interpret Kondratieff, each decade of history corresponds roughly to the decade a half-century previous. Thus they see the 1970s as a new Jazz Age boom like the 1920s and the 1980s as a depression decade like the 1930s. (They do not forecast World War III for the 1990s!)

[4] Papers presented at an international conference (London, 1967) dealing with these topics are reprinted in Martin Bronfenbrenner, ed., *Is the Business Cycle Obsolete?* (1969).

PRE-KEYNESIAN CYCLE THEORIES

Economists have known since the mid-nineteenth century that economic activity proceeded on a roughly wave-like pattern of advances and declines, rather than on a dead level interrupted by short, sharp breaks or panics. Cycle theory has, however, concentrated on explaining the upper turning points, when prosperity has given way to recession or depression, often to the accompaniment of a crisis (Black Monday, or Thursday, or Friday, as the case may be), since these crises are the most spectacular features of economic history. The lower turning point, when depression gives way to recovery, is by contrast almost neglected. Here, however, are a few explanations, common to several cycle theories but seldom stressed by theorists:

1. Fortuitous events: a good crop year (when other countries have bad ones); discovery of natural resources, particularly of precious metals; development of new innovations or technological improvements; public policy changes (protection against foreign competition, deficit financing, monetary expansion, defense or war expenditures).

2. Declines in prices, and costs, particularly wages: It is easy to read into the pre-Keynesian literature our arguments (chapters 10–11) involving movements and shifts of the aggregate demand and supply curves, although the earlier writers did not use this terminology.

3. Downward recapitalization of business property values, because of distress sales and "healthy" bankruptcies: These made it profitable (even in depressed conditions) to operate properties that had become "white elephants" by reason of high debt charges based on the higher capital values of the last prosperity period.

4. The increasing need to replace depreciating machinery and equipment, and replace depleted inventories: This is necessary if businesses are not to be discontinued (liquidated) altogether.

In table 13-1, we have assembled a number of cycle theories of the traditional type. Their discussion will comprise the remainder of this chapter. In assessing these theories, and also more "modern" ones, one should remember that (1) each episode of cycle history is different, so that theories which work well for one episode may work poorly for the next (and again vice versa); furthermore, (2) it is no trick for even a semiskilled mathematician to construct a cycle in economic variables by the use of lagged adjustments, accelerators, integrals, and similar variables.[5] The question is rather one of relating such constructs to observable phenomena.

---

[5] One simple cycle formulation is a sine curve for y, defined as the deviation of income Y from its trend line or growth path. In differential-equation terms, this sine curve is the solution of:

Table 13-1
Traditional Business Cycle Theories

I. Noneconomic Theories
    1. Astronomical Theories
    2. Psychological Theories
    3. Mathematical (Probabilistic) Theories
    4. Theological Theories
    5. Voluntarist (Great Man, Conspiratorial) Theories
II. Quasi-Economic (Technological) Theories
    1. Innovation Theories
    2. Replacement (Echo) Theories
III. Purely Economic Theories
    1. Monetary (Price Level) Theories
    2. Investment Theories
        a. Monetary Investment Theories
        b. Real Investment Theories
            (1) Cost-Price (Profit-Margin) Theories
            (2) Output (Error) Theories
            (3) Acceleration Theories
            (4) Capitalization Theories
    3. Underconsumption (Overproduction) Theories
        a. Monetary Underconsumption Theories
        b. Real Underconsumption Theories
            (1) Maldistribution Theories
            (2) Consumption Gap Theories
    4. Marxian Theories

NONECONOMIC THEORIES

Most noneconomic business cycle theories are conservative in implication. They imply some great law of rhythm in economic affairs, about which economists and social scientists can do little or nothing. Among such theories, the best known (and the most ridiculed) are the *astronomical* theories, particularly the theory relating business cycles to sunspot numbers.

The sunspot theory was devised in the 1860s and 1870s by the eminent English economist and logician W. Stanley Jevons. Jevons was one of the developers of the "utility revolution" in microeconomic price theory. He was also one of the first economic ecologists, foreseeing a decline in Britain's

---

$$y + c \frac{d^2y}{dt^2} = 0$$

where c is a constant. Despite its simplicity, this formula (and many others like it) seems to make no economic sense beyond its cyclical result. Compare Schumpeter, *Business Cycles, op. cit.*, vol. i, pp. 179–189, 205–219.

economic position as its coal supplies were exhausted.[6] He was struck by a regularity, of the sort we now call "structural," in the timing of British crises, which had been concentrated for a generation in and near years ending in 7 (1837, 1847, 1857, 1866); he traced similar movements back 150 years, and was impressed by their rough coincidence with high sunspot numbers. Not only this, but Jevons worked out an economic rationale for the influence of sunspots on the "state of trade" in Britain. The secret, he thought, lay in the effects of sunspots upon weather and in the effects of weather upon agricultural crop yields particularly in India, which was then one of Britain's major customers. High sunspot numbers meant poor crops and high food prices in India. High food prices in India meant greater food expenditures in India, evidence of what we now call an inelastic Indian demand for food. High Indian expenditures for food meant low purchasing power and low demand for textiles and other ports from Britain, and these in turn meant depressed conditions in the British textile areas.

Psychological theories of business cycles run in terms of waves of optimism and pessimism. In some theories these psychological states are themselves exogenous; in others, they are linked to the weather and other astronomical phenomena.[7] We know that marriage and conception rates (symbols of optimism) are correlated positively with business indexes. We also know that death, suicide, and morbidity rates (indexes of pessimism) are correlated negatively with business indexes. The question is, Which can most reasonably be considered the *cause* of the other? Statisticians interpret this issue in terms of leads and lags; are the correlations higher when the psychological indexes lead the business indexes, or vice versa? For many years the issue was in doubt; the indexes were roughly coincidental, and economists of the stature of A. C. Pigou (in his 1928 volume on *Industrial Fluctuations*) leaned to a psychological theory. More recently, interest has shifted away from psychological theories, less for statistical reasons than because of doubt as to the exogeneity of psychological states themselves. Are they not induced by economic factors or policies, and if they are,

---

[6] W. Stanley Jevons, "The Periodicity of Commercial Crises and Its Physical Explanation," originally published in 1878, is reprinted in Hansen and Clemence, *op. cit.*, 6. On Jevons himself, the best account is in Keynes, *Essays in Biography* (1936); section iii deals with the subject matter of this chapter. For later developments of astronomical cycle theory, see Carlos Garcia-Mata and Felix I. Shaffner, "Solar and Economic Relationships," *Quarterly Journal of Economics* (November 1934).

[7] During the Great Depression, members of American businessmen's luncheon clubs (Rotary, Kiwanis, etc.) who mentioned the word "depression" at club meetings, were sometimes required to "assume the angle" and be paddled by their fellow members. This practical application of psychological cycle theory does not seem to have played any major part in altering the course of economic life in those years.

what difference does it make whether they show themselves statistically before or after the economic consequences of these same factors or policies?[8]

Mathematical or *probabilistic* theories argue by analogy with the physical world, where the accumulation of chance events frequently produces rhythmical fluctuations about equilibrium positions or equilibrium paths. (The mathematics of such fluctuations is highly complex.) The best known application to economics is due to Ragnar Frisch.[9] The analogy Frisch uses is a freely oscillating pendulum subject both to frictions and to erratic shocks. The shocks (impulses) start the pendulum oscillating; the frictions maintain or propagate the oscillations, which might otherwise die away completely during the intervals between the shocks. Another probability theory, related less directly to physics, was developed by Eugen Slutsky, best known for his contributions to the microeconomics of consumer demand. Slutsky examined the moving sums of series of ticket numbers drawn at random. The moving sums traced patterns sometimes surprisingly similar for part of their lengths to segments selected from nineteenth-century British business cycle data.[10] The implication is clear enough; cycles are little more than chance phenomena, departures from the expected values of underlying relationships.

The two remaining categories of our noneconomic theories are taken more seriously by the general public—at least in crisis situations—than by professional economists. *Theological* theories view depressions as God's punishment for the easy living and neglect of spiritual values that characterized the preceding booms. They are popular with evangelistic preachers of the "fire and brimstone" variety, especially during recessions; Sodom, Gomorrah, and Babylon are presented as models of Main Street, Wall Street, and Washington. *Voluntarist* theories of either the "devil" or "great man" variety blame or (less frequently) praise specific individuals or groups for what they have done to the economy. For example, "the International Bankers" bring about booms by easing credit and inducing productive entrepreneurs to get into debt; then they cause depression by foreclosing their loans, and take over what the productive entrepreneurs have created. In Germany, this process has been described as a struggle between *raffendes* (exploitative) and *schaffendes* (creative) *Kapital*. This particular "devil" theory, with anti-Semitic embellishments, became part of the

---

[8] For a good summary, see Gottfried von Haberler, *Prosperity and Depression* (1937), ch. 6.

[9] Ragnar Frisch, "Propagation Problems and Impulse Problems in Dynamic Economics," in Gordon and Klein, *op. cit.*, no. 9 (Originally published 1933).

[10] Eugen Slutsky, "The Summation of Random Causes as the Source of Cyclic Processes," *Econometrica* (April 1937).

ideological stock-in-trade of Nazis and Fascists all over the world in the 1930s. A less virulent variety of the same theory ascribes to one man or one company the power to turn an economy round in a critical situation. We give two examples from Detroit: Henry Ford and the Ford Motor Company were blamed for a minor recession in 1927 because they had suspended operations for a year while converting their plants from Model T to Model A; a generation later, Harlow "Red" Curtice and General Motors were credited with American recovery from the post-Korea slump of 1953–54 by betting a billion dollars on plant expansion in 1954.

QUASI-ECONOMIC THEORIES

What we are calling quasi-economic theories invoke the effects of major shocks upon the economic system. A major shock can result from a fundamental innovation of the sort associated with the alleged Kondratieff cycle. It may also result from a major war, or from a natural catastrophe such as a major flood or earthquake in a susceptible area like Japan. Quasi-economic theories may also stress repercussions or "echoes" that such major shocks may produce in later generations.

We consider first *innovations*. Here the great name is Joseph Schumpeter, whom we have encountered more than once already. Any major innovation, for example the internal-combustion engine, induces a host of others, like the automobile self-starter, the adaptation of the storage battery to vehicular use, and improvements in gasoline as fuel for internal-combustion engines. This major innovation, with its cluster of subordinate innovations, leads at first to economic expansion as it catches on—as the automobile, for example, develops from a rich man's toy to a worker's preferred means of transport. Plants are built and employment increased to produce the new or improved goods, their parts, and their servicing facilities. Credit is expanded to finance the new operations, often with inflationary consequences. This "demand-increasing" aspect of innovations constitutes a cyclical boom. As the new or improved products come on the market, they often attain a total volume greater than any individual innovating entrepreneur had anticipated. On the other hand, competition with the "obsolete" product may be more difficult than anticipated. (The obsolescent industry may have stopped expanding or even declined, but its facilities still operate in substantial volume, like the wagon and streetcar industries in 1910–30 or the radio industry in 1950–60.) The result, an overstocking of an important market, is called the "output-increasing" aspect of innovation, and marks the recession-depression phase of the cycle. During this phase, also, credit expansion slows down or reverses itself; there may be significant price deflation. After a period of recession, it may also happen—although this is

far from certain—that businessmen will turn to further innovation (since routine measures seem ineffective), thereby starting the recovery phase once more as certain important innovations succeed.

Suppose that a wave of building is carried on at forced draft for reconstruction purposes after a war or natural catastrophe. It causes a boom, which subsequently subsides. More important for our analysis here, the structures erected during the reconstruction boom may be expected to become physically useless or economically obsolete at approximately the same time. The need to replace them gives rise to a second subsidiary wave or boom or construction activity, usually considerably less marked than the initial one. Similarly, there may be perceptible third and fourth booms when these new buildings become useless, dangerous, or outmoded. What we have said of buildings, furthermore, applies as well and often better to other facilities, such as machinery or transportation equipment.[11] This is, in rough outline, the *replacement* or *echo* theory of cyclical fluctuations. We should note that, unless the initial shock is somehow repeated, the fluctuations that it inspires will eventually be damped or die out.

PURELY ECONOMIC THEORIES

Noneconomic and quasi-economic theories of business fluctuations are to some extent conservative in their implications. If fluctuations are essentially inevitable—if their amplitude is reducible only at a high cost in delayed reconstruction or innovation—perhaps the lesser evil is to suffer in silence, or limit public efforts to palliative amelioration.[12] The economic theories, by contrast, suggest the presence of some flaw, presumably remediable, in our economic institutions themselves. Their implications are accordingly somewhat less conservative.

Our first group of economic theories is purely monetary. The so-called business cycle, Irving Fisher wrote, is merely "the dance of the dollar." By this Fisher meant the fluctuation of the price level. Excessive monetary and credit expansion, in Fisher's view, raises prices in accordance with a quantity theory of money. It simultaneously induces prosperity, because cost prices—wage rates, interest rates, rents, property taxes, utility charges—lag behind other prices, leading to rising profit margins. This state of affairs

---

[11] The standard study of periodic reinvestment cycles deals not with building construction but with shipping and shipbuilding. Johan Einarsen, *Reinvestment Cycles and Their Manifestation in the Norwegian Shipping Industry* (1938). A condensation, "Reinvestment Cycles" appeared in *Review of Economic Statistics* (February 1938); reprinted in Hansen and Clemence, *op. cit.*, no. 22.

[12] Ragnar Frisch, however, turned to detailed central planning in an effort to minimize random shocks to the economy.

cannot continue indefinitely, because the (gold) base of the monetary system will not support it. (The gold standard was part of the natural order of the economic universe when Fisher was writing.) When monetary expansion slows down or is reversed, lagging costs catch up, selling prices fall, and the real debt burden of the previous credits increases. Fisher characterizes the ensuing depression as a "debt-deflation," and his theory of depression is often called a debt-deflation theory. The flaw in the economic system seemed to Fisher the looseness of monetary controls; an obvious remedy seemed to be the stabilization of a price level.[13] Prior to the 1930s, Fisher believed price-level stabilization could best be brought about under a modified gold standard by varying the gold content of the dollar upward when prices rose and downward when they fell. This meant in practice moving the dollar value of gold bullion in the opposite direction to the price level, while withdrawing gold coin from circulation.

The most influential group of economic theories can be grouped together as *investment* theories.[14] Although the authors antedate Keynes's *General Theory* and do not use Keynesian macroeconomic analysis, we can derive from our Keynesian Model I (chapter 6) some geometry that illustrates their common features. Suppose we depict an initial normal situation (situation 1) on a Keynesian cross diagram (figure 13-1), with an aggregate expenditure function $C_1 + I_1 + G_1$ and an equilibrium income Y_1, which usually involves some unemployment. Then, for reasons that vary from one theory to the next, private investment rises to I_2, aggregate expenditure to $C_1 + I_2 + G_1$, and equilibrium income to Y_2; there is also an increase in employment. This is the prosperity phase of a business fluctuation. It is also called an *overinvestment* phase, under the assumption that much of the increased investment dI or $(I_2 - I_1)$ anticipates investment that would otherwise have been made at somewhat later dates. Eventually, after prosperity has continued for some time, the fact of overinvestment becomes increasingly clear. It is usually signaled by increases in inventory and/or in productive capacity. It therefore results in a fall of the investment level, not only to I_1 but to a lower level such as I_3, where it remains until the excess of inventory is consumed or sold, or the economy "grows into" the

---

[13] Irving Fisher, "Our Unstable Dollar and the So-Called Business Cycle," *Journal of the American Statistical Association* (June 1925). Fisher's plan for monetary reform is spelled out in *Stabilizing the Dollar* (1920). (Since the American price level was, in fact, stable in the late 1920s, Fisher was slow to appreciate the seriousness of the depression that followed.)

Ralph G. Hawtrey is the British exemplar of a monetary cycle theory, as Fisher is the American one. Hawtrey's views are outlined, with references, in Haberler, *Prosperity and Depression, op. cit.,* ch. 2.

[14] Haberler, *Prosperity and Depression, op. cit.,* ch. 2–3, treats a much broader spectrum of investment theories than we can mention here.

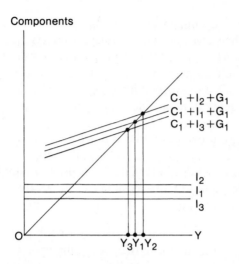

Figure 13-1   Paradigm of Investment Theories

bulk of its excess capacity while the remainder depreciates into scrap. It goes without saying that there is recession if not depression during this underinvestment phase,[15] including business failures and unemployment.

Investment theorists are by no means unanimous as to the details of the process we have just sketched. The most important division is between *monetary* and *real* investment theories. The monetary group—Knut Wicksell in Sweden, Ludwig von Mises and Friedrich von Hayek in Austria, are the best known—take the expansion of money and credit as their usual starting point, much as Fisher or Hawtrey did. But even though the measured price level does not rise—cost-saving technological progress kept it stable in the 1920s—Mises and Hayek, in particular, see expansion as leading to disguised inflation and do not share Fisher's faith in price-level stability as an ameliorative device. Monetary expansion lowers normal interest rates at least temporarily; this fall of interest is seen as the proximate cause of overinvestment based on borrowed funds. The overinvestment reverses itself when the expansion slows down and the interest rates rise again. Some monetary investment theorists—the so-called "neutral money" school—see any monetary expansion whatever as distorting relative prices in

---

[15] The terminology is imprecise and differs as between writers. Critics have enjoyed a field day at economists' expense, making fun of alleged conflicts between "overinvestment," "undersaving," "underconsumption," "overproduction," and similar terms as explanations for economic recession. My attempt to bring order out of this terminological chaos is Martin Bronfenbrenner, "Overproduction, Underconsumption, *et Hoc Genus Omne*," *Quarterly Review of Economics and Business* (February 1961).

a proinvestment and anticonsumption direction, because of its effect on interest rates. They favor avoiding unneutral effects on relative prices by holding constant M or MV, total or per capita, or tying the entire money supply more closely to a metallic base. They accept long-run price level deflation as a small price to pay for preventing short-run unmaintainable interest rate declines from setting off overinvestment booms with recessionary consequences.

Real investment theories, on the other hand, see the impetus to overinvestment in any of a large number of temporary market constellations. Among these, easier credit, lower interest rates, and profitable innovations are only examples, and not the most important examples at that. By way of further subclassification:

1. Perhaps the most influential real investment theories are *cost-price* theories. Cost-price theorists base their reasoning upon the variable sensitivity of prices to market fluctuations. In particular, selling prices received— not necessarily the prices quoted—are supposedly more sensitive than key input prices like wage rates, rents, interest rates, property taxes, and utility charges, which are governed by long-term contracts. Profit margins fluctuate as a result; simultaneous upward movements in several industries can set off an overinvestment move by either new or existing firms, as illustrated by figure 13-1.

2. Output or error theories define the basic problem as one of inadequate and costly information. When a business opportunity arises, as from a rise in selling prices relative to costs, each alert entrepreneur seizes it for his own firm, underestimating both the number of rivals who have seen it at approximately the same time and the size of these rivals' investments. The result of these errors is overproduction and excess capacity. A downturn is apt to be set off by a sharp increase in output, when the final products of everyone's new investment reach the market at the same approximate time, whatever may have happened to interest rates and other input costs in the meanwhile.

3. *Acceleration* theories regard investment as dominated in the aggregate by rates of change in aggregate income or consumption. This implies that small changes in income and consumption, whether systematic or purely random, set off larger fluctuations in investment. (We have discussed the acceleration principle itself in chapter 8, in connection with econometric investment functions. In the next chapter, we shall consider its formal interaction with the Keynesian multiplier. Here we need only point out that acceleration theories have played the role of links between older and newer theories of the cycle.)

4. During periods of prosperity or boom, business firms are often re-

organized, expanded, and combined by promoters and financiers. In the process of these manipulations, business property is often revalued on the basis of prosperity-period earnings. This process is called upward recapitalization, and upward recapitalizations often appear later on to have been inflated. In the short period, the profits of financial manipulations play a role in maintaining prosperity and encouraging the real investment with which they are intertwined. If the boom dies down and the corner is turned, "overcapitalization" leaves firms saddled with heavy debts and other fixed charges, which cannot be met under recession conditions. These inflated debt structures take time, and perhaps one or more downward recapitalizations, before they are reduced to levels the firm can support, or before the firm can grow into them. Extensive recapitalization downward, moreover, usually involves reorganization if not formal bankruptcy. This capitalization theory of business fluctuation, at least as old as Karl Marx, became the cornerstone of Thorstein Veblen's cycle theory.[16] To Veblen and his followers, financiers represent "business" distorting the productive activities and efficiencies of "industry."

The *underconsumption* or *overproduction* theories can also be presented in a diagram (figure 13-2). We start with the expenditure function and

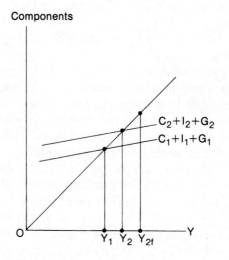

Figure 13-2   Paradigm of Underconsumption (Overproduction) Theories

[16] Thorstein Veblen, *Theory of Business Enterprise* (1904), ch. 7; also Minnie T. England, "Promoters as the Cause of Crisis," *Quarterly Journal of Economics* (August 1915).

Keynesian cross of situation 1 in figure 13-1. Let us suppose Y_1 to represent a full-employment position. As the economy grows, however, full-employment output rises to Y_{2f}. If the expenditure function rises only to $C_2 + I_2 + G_2$ and equilibrium income only to Y_2, the result is recession and a lower level of employment. Such a sequence is most commonly called underconsumption, both because personal consumption is by far the largest component of the aggregate expenditure whose rise has lagged and because the lag in consumption may have also restrained investment. But many writers object to any implication that poor consumers should have bought more out of low incomes; they prefer the term "overproduction" to describe the same sequence of events.

Underconsumption explanations for recession date back to the eighteenth century—the first edition of Bernard de Mandeville's verse "Fable of the Bees" dates from 1705, nearly three generations before Adam Smith's *Wealth of Nations* (1776). These theories have been influential among reformist and radical laymen. The British Labour Party and the American New Deal, for example, reflect strong underconsumptionist influences, perhaps focussed through the writings of John A. Hobson.[17] At the same time, professional economists have downgraded underconsumptionist writings because "with some notable exceptions, their scientific standard is lower" than many others.[18] Underconsumptionist theorists may be classified further into monetary and maldistributionist camps, depending on whether they find the economy's basic weakness in the way it distributes money and credit or the way it distributes real income and wealth.

Monetary underconsumptionists, such as the founders of the international social credit movement, were struck by the concentration of bank lending, and therefore monetary expansion, upon the *production* rather than the *consumption* of goods, particularly in recession periods. Credit is nearly always cheaper if not easier for producers than for consumers; should not the balance be at times redressed? The initial beneficiary of a loan injection into the economic circulation is normally some form of productive activity—although, of course, the injection may merely replace funds previously supplied by others. This concentration of credit upon production has led monetary underconsumptionists to the generalization that "money is used twice for production, but only once for consumption." This causes a constant tendency toward underconsumption and recession, which can be postponed but not avoided by spurts in investment activity. Writers in the monetary underconsumptionist tradition would like expan-

---

[17] On Hobson, see Keynes's appreciation in *General Theory, op. cit.*, pp. 364–371, and Alvin Hansen's in *Business Cycles and National Income* (1951), pp. 254–258.

[18] Haberler, *Prosperity and Depression, op. cit.*, ch. 5. (The quotation is from p. 119.)

sionary fiscal and monetary policy, but with the expansion in each field concentrated upon grants or loans to consumers, rather than on loans to business firms or on the financing of expenditure by the government on its own account.

Maldistributionist writers have been more influential than their monetary colleagues in the underconsumptionist camp. Some maldistributionists call themselves socialists and some do not; socialists or mere reformers, all maldistributionists find the economy's major flaw to be the underpayment or exploitation of "the poor" or "the workers"—persons with high propensities to consume. This is a matter of economics as well as of ethics. One or another pattern of redistribution could raise the economy's consumption function as its productive capacity grows, permit consumption to keep pace with production, and forestall the situation of figure 13-2. For example, underconsumptionists of the maldistributionist school blame the depression of the 1930s in the United States upon the failure of wages to rise as fast as man-hour productivity rose during the 1920s. A stronger trade union organization might have raised wages in the 1920s, and by raising them avoided 1929. A strong union movement, therefore, was encouraged and assisted by the Roosevelt administration in 1935 primarily as a recovery measure; the Wagner Act was the result.

These maldistributionist arguments are hard to support as between rich and poor, but are somewhat stronger as between labor and capital. It is true that the average propensity to consume (a.p.c.) of the poor is systematically greater than that of the rich, since the measured a.p.c. decreases as income rises. But the marginal propensity to consume (m.p.c.) is what really matters for judgments about redistribution; these are much closer as between income classes. Most if not all the differences between the m.p.c. of rich and poor seems ascribable to temporary discrepancies between measured and permanent income (chapter 8). Figures for the poor are biased upward by a preponderance of persons consuming at levels appropriate to higher incomes than they are currently receiving, and the opposite is the case for the rich. One might reasonably expect a tendency, on the other hand, for workers—with low investment opportunities in physical capital—to consume more and save less at any income, measured or permanent, than capitalists (particularly entrepreneurs) with the same income. This is borne out by many studies of measured income and consumption; it probably holds for permanent income as well. For example, the Holbrook-Stafford "generalized permanent income hypothesis"[19] in-

---

[19] Robert Holbrook and Frank Stafford, "The Propensity to Consume Separate Types of Income. A Generalized Permanent Income Hypothesis," *Econometrica* (January 1971), p. 16. Their consumption function, using the above symbols, is:

$$C = 508 + .875\,H + .862\,W + .593\,X + .463\,M + .769\,K$$

cludes separate estimates of m.p.c. for permanent labor income of a husband (H), the permanent labor income of a wife (W), permanent property income (K), permanent transfer income (X), and permanent mixed or entrepreneurial income (M). The values, in the same order, are .875, .862, .769, .593, and .463; the results are as expected, except for the surprisingly low propensity to consume transfer income.

We return to the Marxian analysis of chapter 5, to consider Marxian business-cycle theory. Marx never wrote on business fluctuation theory as such. His long-run dynamics offer us some hints and his long digressions offer others. It seems that he has elements of at least four theories, although he never combines or develops any of them fully. For example, his "liquidation crisis" (chapter 5) is an overinvestment theory, real rather than monetary. His "realization crisis" (chapter 5) is an overproduction theory of the maldistribution variety. There are also hints of a replacement or "echo" theory. Most controversial is a "disproportionality" theory based on the persistence of disequilibrium values of the capital-consumption rate between W_1 and W_2 (which we have called h in chapter 5), and also the persistence of supply-demand imbalance in the two departments. It is not clear how this disproportionality can effect the overall level of output, since excess of supply in either department implies excess of demand in the other. The answer suggested by Kosai and this writer is that when disproportionality develops, the *quickest* adjustment is by cutting production and employment in the sectors of excess supply, rather than *raising* production and employment in the sectors of excess demand.[20] Another explanation, due to Howard Sherman, is that consumption (Department 2) dominates investment (Department 1); as goes consumption, so goes the economy.[21]

SUMMARY

Business fluctuations are often called business cycles. They are not cycles in the conventional natural-science sense, but appear considerably less regular. Statisticians have, however, tentatively isolated—by methods known as "spectral analysis"—four patterns of fluctuation. In order of length, these have been called Kondratieff, Kuznets, Juglar, and Kitchin cycles. The first, longest, and most questionable (in the sense of doubt as to its

---

[20] Martin Bronfenbrenner and Yutaka Kosai, "On the Marxian Capital-Consumption Ratio," *Science and Society* (Fall 1967).

[21] Sherman also develops other Marxian relations, some of them along Keynesian lines, to obtain a mathematical theory of growth cycles, more complex than but not intrinsically different from the "modern" theory to be developed in our own next chapter. Howard Sherman, *Radical Political Economy* (1972), Appendices 3–5.

very existence) has been related to major innovations and to major price movements; wars have been noted as concentrating in their upward phases, revolutions in their downward phases. The second sort of cycle is related plausibly to the effective lifetime of buildings and transportation equipment. The third is the business cycle par excellence, with a modal length of 7–11 years; the fourth and shortest sort of cycle is associated with the build-up and run-down of investories of raw materials, of goods in process, and of finished but unsold products.

We have divided theories of business fluctuations arbitrarily into traditional and contemporary, partially on the basis of dating, but also according as they do not (or as they do) focus upon formal mathematical models. A tabulation of the traditional theories—noneconomic, quasi-economic, and primarily economic—is presented, with some subcategories, as table 13-1. In general, the first groups are more conservative in their policy implications, since they ascribe fluctuations largely to forces outside the economic system proper. Economic theories of fluctuations lead more naturally to intervention or "tinkering." While reviewing the parade of theories, the reader is given two warnings: (1) Each historical episode is to some extent unique; a theory that fits one episode may fit neither the next one, nor the previous one. (2) It is technically easy for a mathematician to superimpose cyclical oscillations upon a growth curve. The economic problem is not to construct such artificial cycles, but to relate them plausibly to observed phenomena.

In addition, the reader should also note that few of these theories are mutually exclusive. A theoretically oriented history of business fluctuations, like the historical chapters of Aaron Gordon's standard text,[22] may combine elements from several theories, from sunspots to underconsumption, in accounting for a single episode like the great Wall Street crash of October 1929.

---

[22] Robert Aaron Gordon, *Business Fluctuations* (2nd ed., 1961), ch. 14–16, traces American experience from World War I through the 1950s. Gordon extends his account in time in *Economic Instability and Growth: The American Record* (1974).

Chapter 14

Business Fluctuations– Contemporary Theory

INTRODUCTION

The contemporary theory of business fluctuations has been influenced decisively by two developments in economic thought. Each of them dates primarily from the 1930s. The first development is methodological—namely, increasing regard for and use of formal mathematical models of economic processes. (Some critics call this sterile, mechanical, and divorced from economic behavior.) The second development is substantive—namely, the Keynesian revolution, which we considered as macrostatics in chapters 6–9. An intermediate-level treatment of the resulting body of literature is found in Robin C. O. Matthews, *The Trade Cycle* (1959).

Two principal strains in this contemporary business-fluctuations literature had best be distinguished and considered separately. The first strain, more explicitly Keynesian, derives fluctuations from the interaction of the Keynesian consumption function and multiplier with the pre-Keynesian acceleration principle. Income determines consumption, while changes in autonomous expenditures (primarily investment) set off multiplier processes. At the same time, changes in consumption and income react back upon investment by way of the accelerator. Feedback theories of this sort are embodied in *multiplier-accelerator* models; the examples studied are taken from the work of Samuelson and of Hicks. The second strain of contemporary fluctuation theory uses much the same multiplier analysis, but sees investment as determined largely by fluctuations in the stock of capital—sometimes the absolute stock, more commonly the "capital-output" ratio of this stock to the national income. Theories of this sort are embodied in *capital-stock* models. The *locus classicus* of such models is the work of the Polish economist Michal Kalečki;[1] we shall refer to the more elementary models of Kaldor and Duesenberry. The reader may inquire why investment cannot be determined by both these elements simultaneously. The answer is that it can be. Models of this combined sort have indeed been developed,[2] but seem too complex for consideration here.

Neither type of model, let alone any combination of the two, has yet been developed to any easily or immediately applicable form. For the practically-minded reader, much of this chapter may seem digressive and unpromising.

---

[1] Michal Kalečki, "A Macrodynamic Theory of Economic Fluctuations," *Econometrica* (July 1935), and "A Theory of the Business Cycle," *Review of Economic Studies* (February 1937). The later essay is reprinted in Kalečki, *Essays in the Theory of Economic Fluctuations* (1939).

[2] An example is Arthur Smithies, "Economic Fluctuations and Growth," *Econometrica* (January 1957), reprinted in Gordon and Klein, *Readings in Business Cycles*, no. 4.

MULTIPLIER-ACCELERATOR MODELS: SAMUELSON

The first full-dress extension of Keynes's *General Theory* chapter 22—entitled "Notes on the Trade Cycle"—to a self-contained theory of business fluctuations was Sir Roy Harrod's *The Trade Cycle* (1936). This volume antedated its author's work on growth, which we examined in chapter 12. It featured multiplier-accelerator interaction, developed verbally and numerically. But Harrod did not, in this volume, face the problem that multiplier-accelerator interaction might not lead to any cyclical movement whatever. For example, should the accelerator be sufficiently small, we might have a simple multiplier process instead, of the type discussed in chapter 6. At the other extreme, should both multiplier and accelerator be sufficiently large, their interaction might produce simply explosive growth, with no oscillations whatever.

Two articles by Paul Samuelson, then a graduate student in his early twenties, cleared up Harrod's mathematics, formalized the multiplier-accelerator model, and established Samuelson's reputation as a *Wunderkind*.[3] The Samuelson model—our Keynesian Model I with time lags and an accelerator—requires only three equations. All variables are measured as deviations from averages or trend lines; the accelerator β is applied only to consumption rather than to total income:

$$Y_t = C_t + I_t$$
$$C_t = \alpha Y_{t-1}$$
$$I_t = \beta(C_t - C_{t-1}) = \alpha\beta(Y_{t-1} - Y_{t-2})$$

Substituting the last two equations into the first yields a single difference equation, homogeneous and of the second order:

$$Y_t - \alpha(1 + \beta)Y_{t-1} + \alpha\beta Y_{t-2} = 0 \qquad (14.1)$$

which, when solved, determines the time path of Y_t from two initial positions Y_0 and Y_1. To solve this difference equation, we begin with a change of variable. If we let $Y_t = kX^t$—the variable X has no economic meaning—(14.0) becomes:

---

[3] Paul A. Samuelson, "Interaction between the Multiplier Analysis and the Principle of Acceleration," *Review of Economic Statistics* (May 1939), and "A Synthesis of the Principle of Acceleration and the Multiplier," *Journal of Political Economy* (December 1939). The earlier essay is reprinted in Gottfried von Haberler, ed., *Readings in Business Cycle Theory*, no. 12, and in M. Gerald Mueller, *Readings in Macroeconomics*, no. 18.

$$k[X^t - \alpha(1 + \beta)X^{t-1} + \alpha\beta X^{t-2}] = 0 \quad \text{or}$$
$$X^2 - \alpha(1 + \beta)X + \alpha\beta = 0 \quad (14.2)$$

The quadratic (14.2) is called the *characteristic equation* of the difference equation (14.1). This terminology is appropriate, because the characteristics of the solution of (14.1)—a cyclical or monotonic path of Y_t, the asymptotic or damped quality of oscillations (if they exist)—depend upon the values of the roots X in (14.2). They depend more particularly upon the value of the largest X in absolute value, which dominates eventually as t increases. We leave for the Appendix to this chapter the details of the solution,[4] but can indicate already the importance of the discriminant[5] of (14.2), namely:

$$\alpha^2(1 + \beta)^2 - 4\alpha\beta$$

If $\alpha^2(1 + \beta)^2 > 4\alpha\beta$, both X-values are real numbers in (14.2), and the path of Y_t is monotonic. If $4\alpha\beta > \alpha^2(1 + \beta)^2$, the solution oscillates cyclically. Also, if $\alpha\beta > 1$, any monotonic solution is asymptotic to the multiplier value $[Y_t = Y_0/(1 - \alpha)]$, and the cycles of any oscillatory solution are damped, with their amplitude falling over time. If, on the contrary, $\alpha\beta < 1$, any monotonic solution shoots off to infinity, and the amplitude of any oscillatory solution increases in amplitude over time, meaning that the economy eventually shakes itself to pieces.

Samuelson graphs these results on a four-zone diagram; figure 14-1 reproduces the relevant portion of his diagram, with the m.p.c. $\alpha < 1$ and the multiplier $[1/(1 - \alpha)] > 1$. The boundary value between monotone and oscillatory zones is $[\alpha = 4\beta/(1 + \beta)^2]$ and the boundary value between asymptotic (damped) and explosive zones is $(\alpha = 1/\beta)$. For (α,β) values in Zone I of figure 14-1, modified multiplier processes converge asymptotically to $[Y_t = Y_0/(1 - \alpha)]$ as t increases without bound. For (α,β) values in Zone II, damped oscillations eventually converge to the same value of Y_t; additional repeated shocks are required to prevent their dying away. For (α,β) values in Zone III, oscillations not only persist but increase in amplitude with the passage of time; in the absence of ceilings, floors, or other buffers, the increases in amplitude of these oscillations is without

---

[4] See also William J. Baumol, *Economic Dynamics* (1951), ch. 9–11, or Samuel Goldberg, *Introduction to Difference Equations* (1961), pp. 5–8, 153–156.

[5] In any quadratic equation $ax^2 + bx + c = 0$, the expression $b^2 - 4ac$ is called the discriminant. If it is positive, the equation has two real roots. If it is zero, the two real roots are identical; if it is negative, there are no real roots, and the solution is a pair of complex conjugates.

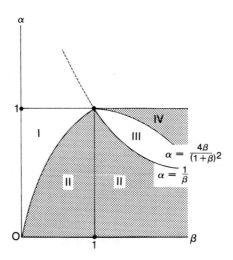

Figure 14-1   Samuelson Model and Its Characteristic Equation

bound. Finally, for (α,β) values in Zone IV, there is explosive growth without oscillations.

The "black box" aspects of the last few paragraphs can be alleviated somewhat by arithmetical sequences. Samuelson's "Interactions" article includes a number of illustrative sequences in its tables 1–2. Assume, for example, 0.5 and 1.0 as (constant) m.p.c. and accelerator values, respectively. The boundary-value equations place the pair ($\alpha = 0.5$, $\beta = 1.0$) in Zone II $[\alpha < 4\beta/(1 + \beta)^2,\ \alpha < 1/\beta]$, so that we anticipate damped oscillations. But how do the actual numbers work out? With a constant G_t of 1 unit added to (14.1) as a repeated shock, we obtain the sequence of table 14-1. Over 14 periods, it does appear to be yielding the expected damped oscillations. The first peak is 2.50; the second is lower, 2.03. The first trough is 0.0; the second is higher, 1.87. These results are consistent with eventual convergence to 2.0. (Since all numbers represent deviations from trend lines or growth paths, zero and negative values are legitimate.)

It is not entirely clear whether Samuelson considered damped oscillations with periodic shocks or explosive oscillations requiring controls as most frequently representative of actual business fluctuations. With a fluctuating accelerator, in particular, the first answer might hold in some cases and the second answer in others. The Hicks model (which follows) opts definitely for the second (explosive oscillations) answer. This writer proposes to ascribe the first (damped oscillations) answer to Samuelson, as in table 14-1, if only as an aid in distinguishing the two constructions from each other.

Table 14-1
Samuelson Multiplier-Accelerator Process
($\alpha = 0.5, \beta = 1.0$)

Period	G_t(shock)	$C_t = \alpha Y_{t-1}$	$I_t = \beta(C_t - C_{t-1})$	$Y_t = G_t + C_t + I_t$
0	0.0	0.00	0.00	0.00
1	1.0	0.00	0.00	1.00
2	1.0	0.50	0.50	2.00
3	1.0	1.00	0.50	2.50
4	1.0	1.25	0.25	2.50
5	1.0	1.25	0.00	2.25
6	1.0	1.125	−0.125	2.00
7	1.0	1.00	−0.125	1.875
8	1.0	0.9375	−0.0625	1.875
9	1.0	0.9375	0.00	1.9375
10	1.0	0.96875	0.03125	2.00
11	1.0	1.00	0.03125	2.03125
12	1.0	1.015625	0.015625	2.03125
13	1.0	1.015625	0.00	2.015625
14	1.0	1.0078125	−0.0078125	2.00

MULTIPLIER-ACCELERATOR MODELS: HICKS

Sir John Hicks's *Contribution to the Theory of the Trade Cycle* (1949) enriches the Samuelson multiplier-accelerator model with a ceiling and a floor, both of which rise over time in consequence of economic growth. It also adds a short-period "monetary" cycle to what Hicks calls the "real" cycle of the multiplier-accelerator model. At the same time, Hicks's monograph is somewhat more restrictive than Samuelson's earlier essay, in that it assumes explosive oscillation—Zone III in figure 14-1—to be the ordinary state of the world.

The ceiling to oscillations is set at any time by the output available from full employment and full-capacity operation of the economy. The floor is set by the requirement that *gross* investment may not be negative; *net* investment is, of course, negative when capital goods are not fully replaced as they wear out or become obsolete. We may speak of either the ceiling or the floor as a *buffer* to the amplitude of oscillations. As we have said, both buffers—more precisely, the income levels corresponding to both buffers—rise over time in a growing economy.

The operation of these buffers is primarily upon investment. We have

seen as part of the Samuelson model, that the investment equation embedded in (14.1) is:

$$I_t = \alpha\beta(Y_{t-1} - Y_{t-2})$$

but this quantity, when added to consumption C_t, may raise Y_t above its ceiling when $Y_{t-1} > Y_{t-2}$ and the accelerator β acts positively. The same quantity, when added to C_t, may also push Y_t below its floor when $Y_{t-2} > Y_{t-1}$ and the accelerator acts negatively. In each of these cases, the observed or ex post value of the accelerator is less than its planned or ex ante value, because of the operation of the buffer. The resulting temporary fall in the value of the accelerator suffices to reverse the course of Y_t, either at once or after a short crawl along the buffer. It also confines oscillations to the interval between the buffers, and sets limits to an unstable economy's ostensible propensity to self-destruction. (The mathematics of the buffering process is beyond the range of this study.) It leads to the implied forecast that an economy afflicted with a basic explosive-oscillation pattern will find itself frequently bumping against both of these buffers. Booms, therefore, would frequently be ended by the overstraining of capacity, and depressions by a near-zero value of gross investment. Such forecasts have not often been borne out in practice—a point not overlooked by critical reviewers of Hicks's 1949 monograph.

A merit of the Hicks model is its allowance for two cyclical processes rather than just one. The "real" cycle of the last paragraph is the main feature of Hicks's theoretical structure. It can be related plausibly to the Juglar cycle of 7–11 years (Chapter 13). But Hicks's system also includes a monetary cycle, presumably shorter, which we may associate with the Kitchin cycle of 18–30 months. The mechanism of the monetary cycle is a dynamized version of the IS-LM schema of chapter 7—which had itself been originated by Hicks twelve years before.[6]

To dynamize the IS-LM scheme, Hicks uses the Keynesian liquidity-preference theory of the rate of interest as equating primarily the supply and demand for the stock of money. His proposition is that adjustment of the rate of interest to the LM function is immediate, whereas the adjustment to the IS function involves a lag and a change of the income level.

---

[6] John R. Hicks, "Mr. Keynes and the Classics; A Suggested Interpretation," *Econometrica* (April 1937) reprinted in William Fellner and Bernard F. Haley, eds., *Readings in the Theory of Income Distribution* (1946), no. 24 and in Mueller, *op. cit.*, no. 10.

(Compare chapter 7.) If we denote the IS and LM functions as $f(Y)$ and $g(Y)$ respectively, and use time subscripts, we may write them as:

$$r_t = f(Y_{t-1}) \quad \text{and} \quad r_t = g(Y_t)$$

in figure 14-2.

It is common to suppose in microdynamics, particularly with respect to agricultural and other products with unavoidably long production periods, that demand adjusts to present prices and supply primarily to the prices of the past period in which it was decided to undertake production of the goods currently being marketed.[7] The result is a pattern of oscillations resembling a cobweb when plotted on an ordinary Marshallian-cross or supply-demand diagram. These oscillations proceed in a clockwise direction. They are damped when the supply function has a steeper slope (in absolute value) than the demand function, and vice versa. The process is the same here, except that the cobweb oscillations are now counterclockwise, and the cycles are damped when (as in figure 14-2) the slope of IS exceeds in absolute value the slope of LM. (This is a common assumption in Keynesian

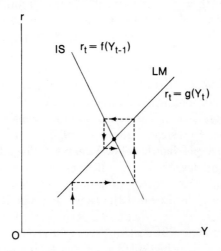

Figure 14-2   Hicks's Monetary Cycle (with Damped Oscillations)

[7] A standard reference is Mordecai J. B. Ezekiel, "The Cobweb Theorem," *Quarterly Journal of Economics* (February 1938), reprinted in Haberler, *Readings in Business Cycle Theory, op. cit.,* no. 12. Willard W. Cochrane, *Farm Prices, Myth and Reality* (1958) exemplifies a body of agricultural-economic literature that elevates the cobweb theorem to a fundamental explanation of agricultural instability.

economics, reaching extremes in doctrines of stagnation—vertical IS—and liquidity trap—horizontal LM.)

CAPITAL-STOCK MODELS: KALDOR

Primarily because of the high volatility of the acceleration coefficient β, cycle models that assume its stability have tended to fall from favor. Attention has shifted to other models based on investment functions such as:

$$I = f(Y, K, r)$$

where K is the real capital stock. The partial derivatives of I with respect to (Y,K,r) are successively positive, negative, and negative.

Of the numerous extant capital-stock models, one of the simplest was devised by Lord Kaldor.[8] Its basic apparatus is the Keynesian-cross diagram of our Keynesian Model I (chapter 6), with an investment function II replacing the autonomous quantity I_0 of that elementary model. To offset this simplicity, Kaldor makes special assumptions about the shapes of both II and the saving function SS, which wind about each other like the serpents strangling Laocöon and his sons in the classic Greek sculpture. These special assumptions have not yet been confirmed empirically.

Let the SS and II functions of Kaldor's Laocöon model be as shown in figure 14-3. Three intersections (A,B,C) correspond to income levels (Y_1, Y_2, Y_3); II is steeper than SS at the central intersection B. The intersections at A (depression, income level Y_1) and at C (boom, income level Y_3) are stable equilibrium positions, because saving exceeds investment ex ante for income levels slightly above Y_1 and Y_3, while investment exceeds saving for income levels slightly below Y_1 and Y_3. The intermediate position B, however (income level Y_2), while neither boom nor bust, is unstable by the same criterion. (Actually, these results would follow with either II or SS linear but not both, provided the slopes at point B were as shown on the diagram.)

We may also suppose with Kaldor that net investment at a starting point A is sufficiently low that the capital stock K is falling relative to anticipated long-term requirements, if not falling absolutely. Because K is falling at A, there is a capital shortage and the investment function II is rising. That is to say, it is shifting upward on the diagram. The opposite is true at point

[8] Nicholas Kaldor, "A Model of the Trade Cycle," *Economic Journal* (March 1940), reprinted in Hansen and Clemence, eds., *Readings in Business Cycles and National Income, op. cit.*, no. 23.

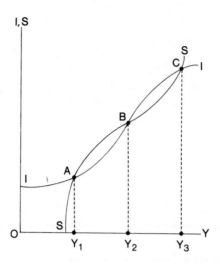

Figure 14-3   Kaldor "Laocöon" Model

C, where Kaldor supposes that II is falling, i.e., in process of shifting down-ward. There is of course some intermediate point, such as B on the diagram, where II is stable and does not shift in either direction, but such points are either not equilibrium points at all or points of unstable equilibrium. As for the saving function SS, Kaldor considers it relatively constant.

We are now ready to trace through a representative cycle, starting with a situation of depression and unemployment equilibrium at point A (in-come level Y_1). The investment function II is rising, while SS is stable. As II rises and the economy recovers somewhat from the initial depression, point B moves to the left and the two points A and B approach each other. When they coincide, their common equilibrium point—which we might call AB—is only semi-stable. That is to say, it is stable downward by our criterion, but unstable upward. As II rises still further, we have the situation of figure 14-4a. There is only one (stable) equilibrium point, at C, and the previous recovery gives way to high prosperity. But by the time equilibrium is reached in the neighborhood of C, with income in the neighborhood of Y_3, successive investments will have raised the capital stock K to an ab-normally high level relative to anticipated requirements. The specter of prospective excess capacity will have caused the investment function II to reverse its previous rises, and to begin a fall. As II falls, and with it the income level Y_3, points B and C (on figure 14-3) approach each other, eventually meeting at a semi-stable point BC. As II continues falling, recession gives way to depression, and the only stable income level is at A (on figure 14-4b). But by the time the equilibrium level A is actually reached, successive periods of low investment will have reduced the capital

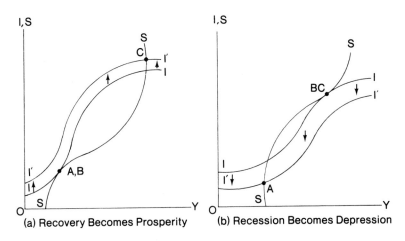

(a) Recovery Becomes Prosperity   (b) Recession Becomes Depression

Figure 14-4   Dynamics of Kaldor Model

stock once again. The investment function II will have reached bottom and begun rising once more. And so the process continues; no level at which II is constant can provide stability in the equilibrium point at which SS and II intersect. Nothing is said in this model, however, about the amplitude of the oscillations that result. Over time the amplitude may increase, decrease, and fluctuate at random. The adaptive forces summarized as "learning by experience" will tend to reduce the amplitude of fluctuations, whereas erratic shocks to the system will operate in the opposite direction.

CAPITAL-STOCK MODELS: DUESENBERRY

Limitations of space preclude tracing the full argument of James Duesenberry's *Business Cycles and Economic Growth* (1958). We accordingly take up his development *in medias res*, at a point he calls the "third simplification" of a larger model.[9] Duesenberry makes both investment I and consumption C at any period t depend upon income Y and the capital stock (wealth) K of the previous period $t - 1$. These equations are linear, as are the remaining elements of Duesenberry's four-equation model:

$$I_t = \alpha Y_{t-1} + \beta K_{t-1} \qquad (\alpha > 0, \beta < 0) \qquad (14.3)$$
$$C_t = a Y_{t-1} + b K_{t-1} \qquad (a,b > 0) \qquad (14.4)$$
$$K_t = (1 - k) K_{t-1} + I_t \qquad [0 < (1 - k) < 1] \qquad (14.5)$$
$$Y_t = I_t + C_t \qquad\qquad (14.6)$$

[9] Duesenberry, *op. cit.*, ch. 9–10. Duesenberry criticizes certain earlier writers at p. 179: "The instability of [their] models results from the use of a rigid capital coefficient and a consumption function which is independent of the return on investment."

Equation (14.3) is more flexible than alternative equations that employ the definition $I_t = K_t - K_{t-1}$ to bind β at -1 and α at K_t/Y_{t-1}. Equation (14.4) is more stable than alternatives that ignore the effects of the capital stock upon profits, on business saving, and on expenditure out of them. Equations (14.5) and (14.6) are definitional; k in (14.5) is a technically-determined depreciation rate.

From (14.3–6) Duesenberry distills a second-order difference equation comparable to the Samuelson equation (14.1) but more likely to be stable. If we substitute (14.3) into (14.5) and (14.3–4) into (14.6), the results are:

$$K_t = \alpha Y_{t-1} + (\beta + 1 - k)K_{t-1} \tag{14.7}$$

$$Y_t = (\alpha + a)Y_{t-1} + (\beta + b)K_{t-1} \tag{14.8}$$

Duesenberry seeks a difference equation in Y_t alone. His strategy is to eliminate first K_{t-1} and then K_t from (14.7–8). Elementary algebra suffices to eliminate K_{t-1} and obtain:

$$(\beta + b)K_t = (\beta + 1 - k)Y_t + [\alpha(\beta + b) - (\alpha + a)(\beta + 1 - k)]Y_{t-1}$$

This can be moved one period back and substituted directly into (14.8):

$$Y_t = [(\alpha + a) + (\beta + 1 - k)]Y_{t-1} + [\alpha(\beta + b) - (\alpha + a)(\beta + 1 - k)]Y_{t-2} \tag{14.9}$$

Equation (14.9) is of the same mathematical form as the multiplier-accelerator equation (14.1). It is at the same time more general than Samuelson's (14.1), in which Duesenberry's (not Samuelson's) β is bound at -1, while b and k are zero. Duesenberry believes the more general form less likely to explode, or yield explosive oscillations, than the special one. The argument is illustrated by figure 14-5, which is based on equations (14.7–8).

Returning to (14.7–8) we can obtain growth rates G_k and G_y of capital and income respectively. Beginning with (14.8):

$$G_y = \frac{Y_t - Y_{t-1}}{Y_{t-1}} = \frac{Y}{Y_{c-1}} - 1 = (\alpha + a - 1) + (\beta + b)\frac{K_{t-1}}{Y_{t-1}} \tag{14.10}$$

Equation (14.10) is the downward-sloping line of figure 14-5, since:

$$\frac{dG_y}{d\,(K/Y)} = (\beta + b)$$

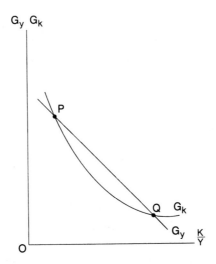

Figure 14-5   Duesenberry Capital-Stock Model

with the quantity $(\beta + b)$ assumed negative. From (14.7), in the same way:

$$G_k = \frac{K_t - K_{t-1}}{K_{t-1}} = \frac{K_t}{K_{t-1}} - 1 = \frac{\alpha}{\dfrac{K_{t-1}}{Y_{t-1}}} + (\beta - k) \qquad (14.11)$$

Equation (14.11) is the downward-sloping curve on figure 14-5, since α is positive by (14.3) and:

$$\frac{dG_K}{d\,(K/Y)} = - \frac{\alpha}{\left(\dfrac{K_{t-1}}{Y_{t-1}}\right)^2}$$

Duesenberry writes that the two growth rates (14.10–11):[10]

> are determined entirely by the ratio of capital stock to income. That being the case, the two rates of growth will remain constant if the ratio (K_t/Y_t) remains constant. The ratio of capital to income will remain constant if the rate of growth of capital equals the rate of growth of income. Consequently income can grow steadily if there is a real, positive ratio of capital to income at which the rate of growth of income equals the rate of growth of capital.

---

[10] *Ibid*, p. 204.

or, diagrammatically, if G_y and G_k intersect—under stable conditions—on figure 14-5.

The diagram shows two such points of intersection, labelled P and Q. These are equilibrium points. It remains to determine their stability and then to inquire as to their existence.

The stability properties are determined along lines that are familiar from the neo-classical growth models of chapter 12. To the right of an equilibrium point like P or Q (figure 14-5), the capital-output ratio is above its equilibrium value. If, in such a situation, G_k exceeds G_y, the capital-output ratio will rise further and the equilibrium is unstable. To the left of an equilibrium point, conversely, the stability condition is $G_k > G_y$. Applying these results to the pattern of figure 14-5, the equilibrium at P is stable but that at Q is unstable. (The reader should analyze for himself a case where G_k is tangent to G_y at a single point instead of intersecting it, i.e., a case where P and Q are identical.)

Duesenberry considers the ordinary position of the growing economy to be in the stable neighborhood to the left of point Q, although not ordinarily at point P itself. Its position is subject to shocks. These shocks may take the form of statistical deviations of G_y and G_k from equations (14.10–11); they may also involve perturbations in the parameters (a,b,α,β). These shocks may cause oscillations, which are, however, damped in the entire "stability region" to the left of Q.

Temporary instability can arise when a particular sequence of shocks drives the economy to the right of Q. Duesenberry's reading of the business annals is that such sequences may occur, but are short-lived, and that their cessation returns the economy to the stability range. A more serious source of longer-term instability might be the nonexistence of the distinct stable equilibrium point P. The G_y and G_k functions, when diagrammed as in figure 14-5, may be tangent to each other, or may never meet at all. (Duesenberry does not exclude such cases formally.) Once again, his reading of economic history reduces them to bogeyman status, at least in advanced countries. Less complacent readers of the same record, or readers of the economic history of other countries, may reach different conclusions and presumably call for a greater measure of detailed planning. One cannot from the model alone determine which view is correct.

SUMMARY

Much business-cycle theorizing since the publication of Keynes's *General Theory* has relied more heavily upon Keynesian macroeconomics—and, since World War II, upon "mechanistic" growth theory—than upon the earlier cycle theories of chapter 13. The principal models have

stressed the interaction of the multiplier and accelerator processes, or alternatively, the variability of the capital-stock and the capital-output ratio. A frequent mathematical aid has been the difference equation, particularly the second-order difference equation with constant coefficients, which we shall explore in Appendix 14A to this chapter. The practical utility of these models is not yet established; short-term forecasting models are considerably less aggregative, as we shall see in chapter 15.

As examples of multiplier-accelerator interaction models, we have chosen contributions by Samuelson and by Hicks. Samuelson points out clearly the existence of four zones determined by accelerator and m.p.c. values. In two of these zones, the model may lead to cyclical oscillations; in the other two, it does not. In two of these zones, the movements are asymptotic; in the other two, they are explosive. Examples are: a pure multiplier adjustment (asymptotic, monotonic); a damped cycle (asymptotic, cyclical); an antidamped cycle (explosive, cyclical); a pure growth process (explosive, monotonic). The Hicks model stresses explosive oscillations of increasing amplitude, restricted by moving "buffers" at the ceiling and the floor. A ceiling buffer is set by the full capacity operation of the economy, while the floor buffer is set by the requirement that gross investment be nonnegative. This is Hicks's "real cycle." In addition, Hicks introduces a shorter "monetary cycle," combining the Islamic model of our chapter 7 with the cobweb theorem of microeconomic dynamics.

As examples of capital stock models, we have chosen contributions by Kaldor and by Duesenberry. The Kaldor model uses a Keynesian cross (chapter 6) with special shapes for saving and investment functions, the latter of which is also highly volatile and sensitive to the aggregate capital stock. Cyclical oscillations arise from the mutual incompatibility of two stability conditions: (1) the saving function must be steeper than the investment function, and (2) no systematic net tendencies must be moving the investment function up or down, i.e., the capital-output ratio must also be in equilibrium. The Duesenberry model makes both consumption and investment linear functions of (lagged) income and capital. These in turn lead, in Duesenberry's view, to a generally stable solution with damped oscillations about a growth path. This result contrasts with the conclusions of Hicks and Kaldor. A policy consequence of this difference of opinion might be that confidence in the long-term stability of the economy might lead to less reliance on centralized planning than would the opposite view.

Appendix 14a

DIFFERENCE EQUATIONS AND THE SAMUELSON MODEL

MATHEMATICAL INTRODUCTION

We are given a difference equation—linear, homogeneous, second order,[1] and with constant coefficients:

$$ay_t + by_{t-1} + cy_{t-2} = 0 \qquad (14A.1)$$

We desire a solution of this equation that will take the form $y_t = f(t)$. We also know two values of y—preferably the initial values (y_0, y_1)—that will be required for the solution.[2]

The solution process makes use of a dummy variable x, such that $y_t = kx^t$. Making this substitution and dividing through by kx^{t-2}, we obtain the *characteristic equation* of (14A.1).

$$ax^2 + bx + c = 0 \qquad (14A.2)$$

The form of the solution of (14A.1) will be found to depend upon the characteristics that determine the solution of (14A.2). Hence the terminology, "characteristic equation."

To solve (14A.2) for x we use the quadratic formula of elementary algebra. In the normal or textbook case, there are two solutions, both real numbers, which we denote by (x_1, x_2).

$$x_1 = \frac{-b + \sqrt{b^2 - 4ac}}{2a} \qquad x_2 = \frac{-b - \sqrt{b^2 - 4ac}}{2a}$$

If (x_1, x_2) satisfy (14A.2), any linear combination $k_1 x_1 + k_2 x_2$ satisfies $y_t = kx^t$. We choose the particular values of k to fit the known values of y_t, namely (y_0, y_1):

---

[1] *Homogeneity* means here that multiplication by a constant λ does not affect the solution of the equation. *Order* is determined by the *highest* value of the subscript i in y_{t-i}.

[2] Two values of y are required for the solution of a second-order difference equation. More generally, n values are required for the solution of an nth order equation, but these need not all be different.

$$k_1 + k_2 = y_0 \qquad\qquad k_1x_1 + k_2x_2 = y_1$$

These equations are solved simultaneously by elementary methods. The solution of (14A.1) is, therefore:

$$y_t = (k_1x_1 + k_2x_2)^t$$

The characteristics of y_t will depend (as t increases without bound) upon the x_i with the largest absolute value. Specifically, the solution will be asymptotic if both roots x_i are less than unity, and explosive if either root exceeds unity in absolute value.[3]

ENTER COMPLEX NUMBERS

We have assumed the characteristic equation (14A.2) to have two real roots (x_1, x_2). There are, however, two other cases, depending upon the value of the *discriminant* $(b^2 - 4ac)$ of (14A.2). (Above, we assumed this discriminant to be positive.) If it is zero, there is only one real root, which we call x. In this case, we solve (14A.1) by the device of letting $x_1 = x$ and $x_2 = tx$, whereupon the solution proceeds as above, with tx the dominant root. It eventually exceeds unity in absolute value, leading to an explosive solution. If the discriminant of (14A.2) is negative, however, there are no real roots at all. We shall see in the following paragraphs that y_t oscillates cyclically in this event.

In the solution of the quadratic (14A.2) with a negative discriminant, let $(- b/2a = c)$[4] and let $[\sqrt{(b^2 - 4ac)}/2a] = di$, where $i = \sqrt{(- 1)}$. Then our solutions of (14A.2) are:

$$x_1 = c + di \quad \text{and} \quad x_2 = c - di \qquad\qquad (14A.3)$$

A number that has a real part such as c and a so-called "imaginary" part plane geometry, the length of the ray OP from the origin is $\sqrt{c^2 + d^2}$. (It and $(c - di)$, differing only in the sign of their imaginary parts, are called *complex conjugates* because their sum is real. (Here, this sum is 2c.)

Complex numbers are ordinarily represented geometrically on four-quadrant diagrams like figure 14A-1. On this diagram, the real number c is

---

[3] If the largest x_i value is negative, the successive values of y_t will alternate in sign. This oscillation will not occur unless it is also found in the observed values of y_t.

[4] This c should not be confused with the c term in (14A.1 and 2).

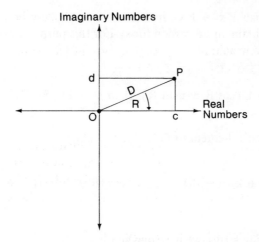

Figure 14A-1   Diagrammatic Representation of Complex Numbers

plotted on the horizontal axis, and the imaginary number d along the vertical one. (We speak of the horizontal axis as the "axis of reals" and the vertical axis as the "axis of imaginaries.") Any complex number c + di is plotted as a point P in the (c,d) plane.

Let P, then, represent a complex number. By the Pythagorean theorem of plane geometry, the length of the ray OP from the origin is $\sqrt{c^2 + d^2}$. (It is known as the *modulus;* we shall call it D.) Let R be the angle of the modulus at the origin 0. Using plane trigonometry, we can express (c,d) in terms of (D,R).

$$c = \sqrt{c^2 + d^2}\ (\cos R) = D \cos R$$

$$di = \sqrt{c^2 + d^2}\ (i \sin R) = D\, i \sin R$$

It follows that:

$$c \pm di = D(\cos R \pm i \sin R)$$

and also, using our x-values from (14A.3):

$$k_1 x_1 + k_2 x_2 = k_1 D(\cos R + i \sin R) + k_2 D(\cos R - i \sin R) \tag{14A.4}$$

The angle R can be found easily in trigonometric tables as the arc cosine of c/D or the arc sine of d/D. To solve our original difference equation for

y, which equals $k_1x_1 + k_2x_2$, however, we must show how to eliminate the i term and obtain an expression for x^t. For this purpose, we use De Moivre's Theorem, by which:

$$\text{if } x = D(\cos R \pm i \sin R); \text{ then } x^t = D^t(\cos tR \pm i \sin tR)$$

Applying this theorem to (14A.4), we obtain:

$$k_1(c + di)^t + k_2(c - di)^t = k_1D^t(\cos tR + i \sin tR) + k_2D^t(\cos tR - i \sin tR)$$

On rearranging terms, we have on the r.h.s.

$$D^t[(k_1 + k_2)\cos tR + i(k_1 - k_2)\sin tR] = D^t(e \cos tR + f \sin tR)$$

where $e = k_1 + k_2$ and $f = i(k_1 - k_2)$.

This may not seem helpful, but it is. There is a trick. This trick is that we are not limited to real numbers in our choice of (k_1,k_2). In fact, if we choose any complex conjugates $\alpha \pm \beta i$, both e and f will be real.[5] We will then have from (14A-2):

$$y_t = k_1x_1^t + k_2x_2^t = D^t(e \cos tR + f \sin tR) \qquad (14A.5)$$

All terms of (14A.5) are real, but oscillations have been introduced by the terms in the trigonometric functions.

DIGRESSION: SOLUTION DETAILS

To find (e,f) in practice, we recall that cos 0 and sin 0—which enter (14A.5) when $t = 0$ and $y = y_0$—are 1 and 0, respectively. Then, using (14A.5) and our known values (y_0,y_1):

---

[5] The proof is easy. If $(k_1 = \alpha + \beta i)$ and $(k_2 = \alpha - \beta i)$, their sum is 2α. This is our e. Furthermore, $[i(k_1 - k_2) = i(2\beta i) = -2\beta]$. This is our f.

$$y_0 = D^0(e \cos 0) = e$$

$$y_1 = D(y_0 \cos R + f \sin R) = \sqrt{c^2 + d^2}\left(y_0 \frac{c}{\sqrt{c^2 + d^2}} + f \frac{d}{\sqrt{c^2 + d^2}}\right)$$

$$= cy_0 + fd$$

$$f = \frac{y_1 - cy_0}{d}.$$

Using these values for (e,f), we can find y_t in terms of (y_0, y_1, c, d, t). This is the solution of the difference equation (14A.1) when the discriminant of the characteristic equation (14A.2) is negative. We write the solution below in terms of the modulus D and the angle R to simplify the notation.

$$y_t = D^t\left(y_0 \cos tR + \frac{y_1 - cy_0}{d} \sin tR\right) \qquad (14A.6)$$

APPLICATION TO THE SAMUELSON MODEL

The remainder of this appendix applies our mathematical results in the special case of the Samuelson multiplier-accelerator model. Samuelson's difference equation is:

$$Y_t - \alpha(1 + \beta)Y_{t-1} + \alpha\beta Y_{t-2} = 0 \qquad (14.1)$$

so that (a,b,c) of (14A.1) are, respectively $[1, -\alpha(1 + \beta),$ and $\alpha\beta]$, where α is the m.p.c. and β is the accelerator. The corresponding characteristic equation is

$$X^2 - \alpha(1 + \beta)X + \alpha\beta = 0 \qquad (14.2)$$

with the discriminant

$$\alpha^2(1 + \beta)^2 - 4\alpha\beta \quad \text{or} \quad \alpha = \frac{4\beta}{(1 + \beta)^2}$$

This last expression is precisely one of the Samuelson boundary conditions illustrated in figure 14-1. When it is negative, the solution of the Samuelson model (14.1) is oscillatory.

The other Samuelson boundary condition is more difficult to derive.[6] It is, that the value of the highest X equal unity. [If it exceeds unity, (14.1) is explosive; if it is fractional, the solution is asymptotic.] We can show, however, that either both values of X exceed unity or neither value does.[7] Under these circumstances, the condition for an explosive solution is that the product X_1X_2 exceed unity. This product reduces to $\alpha\beta$; the second Samuelson boundary condition is therefore $(\alpha = 1/\beta)$, the rectangular hyperbola in figure 14-1.

To prove the key statements in the last paragraph, we find the product of the two roots of the characteristic equation (14.2):

$$X_1X_2 = \frac{\alpha(1 + \beta) + \sqrt{\alpha^2(1 + \beta)^2 - 4\alpha\beta}}{2} \cdot$$

$$\frac{\alpha(1 + \beta) - \sqrt{\alpha^2(1 + \beta)^2 - 4\alpha\beta}}{2} = \alpha\beta$$

If one root X_i exceeds unity and the other not, the product $(x_1 - 1)(x_2 - 1)$ is negative. We then have:

$$\frac{[\alpha(1 + \beta) - 2] + \sqrt{\alpha^2(1 + \beta)^2 - 4\alpha\beta}}{2} \cdot$$

$$\frac{[\alpha(1 + \beta) - 2] - \sqrt{\alpha^2(1 + \beta)^2 - 4\alpha\beta}}{2}$$

The product of these two numerators reduces to $(4 - 4\alpha < 0)$, which in turn implies $1 < \alpha$, a value ruled out by the economics of our problem. (The m.p.c. is a proper fraction.)

It follows that, with fractional m.p.c., the two roots of the characteristic equation (14.2) must fall on the same side of unity in the Samuelson model. In this case, their product (X_1X_2) tells us on which side this is. Our boundary condition is then $[(X_1X_2) = 1]$ or $(\alpha = 1/\beta)$.

---

[6] Compare Hyman P. Minsky, "A Linear Model of Cyclical Growth," *Review of Economics and Statistics* (May 1959), reprinted in Gordon and Klein, *op. cit.*, no. 5.

[7] This statement assumes two distinct values of X. We have shown already that the result will be explosive if the two values are identical.

Chapter
15

Macroeconomic
Forecasting

EVERY MAN A FORECASTER

(Almost) everyone is an economic forecaster, whether or not he or she realizes the fact. When one goes (or does not go) to college or university, selects a career, buys a house, moves (or does not move) from one place or job to another, or plans one's family size, he or she is implicitly forecasting that certain things will happen in the economy and that certain other things will not happen. The argument applies equally well to the decisions of organizations like churches, business firms, or trade unions.

There are two exceptions to this generalization:

1. Economically isolated people completely unaffected by the state of the economy. Subsistence farmers are examples. So are hippies in communes, if the communes are sufficiently removed from the rest of society.

2. People so acrobatically flexible, at least in their own estimations, that they can adjust equally easily to any event whatever.

Most people and most organizations do not forecast overtly. This usually causes them to act as though they expected some important economic variables not to change—because they have not considered the possibility of their changing. For example, they may be acting as though they expected this year to be just like last year, or this year's change from last year's conditions to be just like last year's change from two years ago. Other "nonforecasters" simply do not put their forecasts in quantitative terms, or spend much time and effort on making them, or care to defend them. Our point, however, is that "nonforecasters" usually do forecast in fact, and show the effects of their forecasts in their actions, even though the forecasting be done in some informal and amateurish way hopefully adequate for their purposes.

THE PROOF OF THE PUDDING

Macroeconomic forecasts may be based, at one extreme, on guesses, hunches, extrasensory perception (E.S.P.), or rules of thumb. Or, at the other extreme, they may be based on sophisticated macroeconomic theories and econometric models. By and large, on the whole, and other things equal, it should in the long run become apparent, if certain macroeconomists are indeed talking sense, that macroeconomic forecasts based on the particular views of these macroeconomists (as properly understood by competent people) perform significantly better than macroeconomic forecasts based upon alternative theories and models—or upon soothsayers' readings of the entrails of birds. This is all we mean by applying to macro-

economics and to forecasting the old adage that "the proof of the pudding is in the eating." Here, of course, the macroeconomics is the pudding and the forecast is the eating.

At the same time, the old adage does *not* imply any of the following propositions:

1. Even the best of theories will provide perfect forecasts at all times.

2. Detailed factual knowledge is unnecessary for forecasting.

3. The practical man's hunches will never outperform the specialist's theories.

4. Forecasting will soon be reduced to computer science.

5. The special intelligence, ability, and flair of the particular forecaster will eventually become unimportant.

MAKE OR BUY?

Some business firms and other organizations, especially large ones directly concerned with economic activity, make their own macroeconomic forecasts. They hire economists and statisticians in research departments to make such forecasts on an "in-house" basis, often under the supervision of senior executives. Other firms and organizations buy either regularly or occasionally the specialized forecasting services of outside consultants and research organizations. Still other firms and organizations combine both methods. One recent development is the specialized branch of the knowledge industry that applies its own stock of data and computer expertise to dynamic models largely devised by its customers. (It may even dispatch its own personnel to help customers improve the models they are using.)

Before paying out large sums for outside forecasting services, potential consumers should be warned that chicanery and hokum exist in this field and be advised to develop a certain modicum of sales resistance. Sometimes the forecasts of Great Name, Inc., may in fact be products not of Mr., Dr., or Prof. Great Name's extensive skills and experience but of one or more of his office clerks, secretaries, or programmers—the customer could hire equally good ones for less money. Or the "confidential" information the service dispenses—numbers and equations included—may be copies of, or condensations from, materials in the public domain, such as the U.S. Department of Commerce *Business Conditions Digest* (formerly *Business Cycle Developments*) and *Survey of Current Business*. In which case, it may be cheaper to hire or train a research assistant to locate and extract these same materials than to pay an outside service.

ALIBIS, ALIBIS

The notorious track record of economic forecasters is no secret. It embodies little or nothing to inspire jealousy among meteorologists, horse-race handicappers, or astrologers. The lackluster performance of recognized and semi-official professionals has to some extent encouraged the do-it-yourselfers and outright frauds on the fringes of economic forecasting, and given rise to a vicious circle of disrepute.

Acknowledging all this, the critic should also recognize the special problems which economic forecasters face and which they do their feeble best to overcome. These include the following:

1. There are critical lags in basic data, which require the forecaster to begin by "forecasting the present." We now have 1929 data, but forecasters for 1930 in the fall of 1929 had data for only two or three quarters of 1929[1] and no way to estimate the effects of the stock market collapse of October.

2. To make matters worse, such data as are available for the immediate past are usually "preliminary." This means that they are "blow-ups" from samples or subsamples that are occasionally badly biased. The resulting errors are particularly marked when one attempts to deal with differences and differentials. For this reason, the use of terms like $[dC, d(dC/dY),$ or $d(C/Y)]$ as forecasting tools has not progressed in practice to the extent that one might expect from a practical-minded reading of Keynesian theory.

3. Forecasts may be either qualitative or quantitative. Other things equal, a quantitative forecast is usually more useful to its recipients. At the same time, precision should not be confused with accuracy. A quantitative forecast should, therefore, include some measure of its anticipated range of error, just as a qualitative one should include some indication of the probability of its being wrong.[2] The point at issue is primarily the *standard* error of a quantitative forecast, and secondarily the standard errors of the key parameters of its estimating equations. If standard errors (or equivalents) are omitted from published forecasts, the consumer runs the risk of being sold precision in lieu of accuracy. On the other hand, if standard errors are included, the consumer may complain that he is getting no more for his money than he knew before—as when two standard errors above the fore-

---

[1] These data did not include series on national income, national product, employment and unemployment, and their components. Such series became available on a regular basis in the subsequent decade.

[2] Meteorological forecasters have come increasingly to recognize this point, particularly as regards rainfall. Standard practice in the U.S. has accordingly shifted from including or omitting the word "rain"—depending on whether the estimated probability of rainfall was more or less than fifty percent—to including the probability itself, which may, of course, be zero or unity.

cast GNP may represent a super-boom while two standard deviations below the forecast represent a major depression.

4. The meaning of important variables may be uncertain in the data available, or may have changed over time in the data available for estimation purposes. Unemployment is perhaps our best example here, as we have seen in chapter 2. The meaning of the figures changes with the treatment of part-time employment and the search for it, the treatment of voluntary unemployment, the care taken to locate "discouraged workers," the ease of obtaining make-work jobs and outright relief, and the stringency of enforcement of regulations against the numerous variations upon the theme of "hustling." Other examples are found frequently in price and interest-rate statistics, and likewise in data for international trade and capital movements. Here the economic significance of published figures refer more closely, in certain countries at certain times, to the nature and enforcement of the direct controls than to economic conditions in the country publishing the figures.

5. Were clouds systematically "seeded" with silver iodide and other chemicals in accordance with weather forecasts, to bring rain here or to avoid it there, the work of the meteorologist would be more difficult than it already is, and his batting average lower. Yet this is precisely the position of the economic (and social) forecaster. If his projection is to be useful, it must be to some extent public. And if it is public, people may act upon it to falsify (or verify) it.[3] For a generation including the middle of the nineteenth century, years ending in seven were years of crisis and depression (1837, 1847, 1957). This periodicity inspired, as we saw in chapter 13, astronomical theories of the business cycle, notably the sunspot theory of W. Stanley Jevons. It also led to widespread forecasts, by factually minded and theoryless empiricists and practical men, of another crisis in 1867. Preparing for this crisis a year before it was due, businessmen and investors seem to have lowered their marginal efficiency of investment functions (m.e.i., in chapter 6), and increased their liquidity preferences correspondingly. The result was a significant depression in 1866.[4] (The ten-year periodicity ended seven years later, when the Panic of 1873 arrived completely out of phase.) In the 1920s the eminent "bear" forecaster Roger Babson,

---

[3] It is possible to take account of this effect in theoretical models by appending "reaction functions" that relate what the values of principal variables might have been in a predictionless society to their values in a society where correct public predictions were made and accepted. It has been more difficult to fit such reaction functions empirically.

[4] This was by no means the sole cause of the 1866 downturn. More important, especially in America, may have been the ending of the Civil War (and its accompanying inflation) in 1865.

who had been predicting a stock market crash for several years before it happened, was blamed for causing it when it finally arrived.

6. We have left to the end the forecaster's major bugaboo—important structural changes in the underlying social and economic system. Forecasts for Japan in 1923 made no allowance for the disastrous Tokyo-Yokohama earthquake of that September, which was to set back the country's economic development for the better part of a decade. Forecasts for the Western World in 1939 were made in the immediate post-Munich atmosphere of "peace in our time," and did not allow for the outbreak of World War II in August and September. Forecasts for Cuba in 1959 took account of neither the sudden collapse of the Batista government in January or the rapid anticapitalist shift in the policies of the successor (Castro) regime. Forecasts for the U.S. in 1971 could not anticipate the "Nixon shocks" and direct controls introduced in mid-August. Forecasts for Europe and America in 1974 could not allow for the rise of OPEC and the oil embargo, and so on. At its annual November "Conferences on the Economic Outlook" for the following year, the University of Michigan Research Seminar on Quantitative Economics (R.S.Q.E.) frequently offers a spectrum or menu of alternatives, each keyed to a different outcome of certain unsettled legislative and administrative problems, notably in monetary and fiscal policy. It also indicates which of these alternatives it considers most probable. This "spectral" device makes it easier for persons whose political forecasts differ from the R.S.Q.E.'s to use the quantitative results presented. At the same time, it adds to the critic's difficulty in assessing the Michigan group's predictive performances.

A CASE IN POINT: THE POSTWAR FORECASTS OF 1944-45

What alibis apply in important specific cases? Let us choose for our example the notorious "postwar forecasts" of American economists. Developed in 1944-45 by a number of specialists in both public and private employment,[5] probably influenced by each other's results as well as by the experience of the 1930s, these forecasts envisaged renewed depression after World War II, with unemployment of from five to eight million workers, instead of the labor shortage and inflation that actually ensued.[6] The under-

---

[5] Of the optimistic minority, the most outstanding and outspoken member was Wladimir L. Woytinsky of what was then the Social Security Board.

[6] During the McCarthy period of the 1950s, the forecasters as a group were accused of deliberate pessimism as a pro-Soviet and anti-American tactic. This charge has never been proved even against particular forecasters who may have had leftist sympathies, let alone against "the forecasters" as a group.

lying theory of most of these forecasts was the Keynesianism of our chapter 6; the shortcomings of the forecasts encouraged the counterrevolutions against Keynesian doctrine discussed in chapters 8, 10, and 11. The techniques used in 1944–45 included, in embryonic form, those of the econometric forecasts that came to dominate the field a generation later. The shortcomings of the postwar forecasts may have delayed the acceptance of econometrics for a decade or more.

"What went wrong" seems to have been a series of easily understandable errors, none of them particularly serious in itself, but all of them operating in the same (pessimistic) direction.[7] Their total impact on the *unemployment* estimate, in particular, was devastating.

The several forecasting models were all different. Few of them were explicitly "dynamic" in the sense of specifying particular lag structures. All were forced to depart from standard textbook formulations, however, by the special "structural" problems of rapid reconversion from a war to a peace economy. A representative "least-common-denominator" model is given below in our notation; it omits all references to international trade and uses real values, whereas many of the forecasts were largely in nominal terms.

$$Y = C + I + G \qquad (15.1)$$

$$C = C_1 + C_2 + C_3 \qquad (15.2)$$

$$C_1 = C_{10} + c_1(Y - T) \qquad (15.3)$$

$$C_2 = \hat{C}_2 \qquad (15.4)$$

$$C_3 = \hat{C}_3 \qquad (15.5)$$

$$I = \hat{I} \qquad (15.6)$$

$$G = G_o \qquad (15.7)$$

$$T = T_o + tY \qquad (15.8)$$

$$A = C_{10} + \hat{C}_2 + \hat{C}_3 + \hat{I} + G_o \qquad (15.9)$$

$$L = L_o \qquad (15.10)$$

$$N = N_o + nY \qquad (15.11)$$

$$U = L_o - N \qquad (15.12)$$

The solution of this model for Y is a modified form of equation (6.15), derived from (15.1–9):

$$Y = \frac{A - c_1 T_o}{1 - c_1 + c_1 t} \qquad (15.13)$$

In the model above and in the great majority of the postwar forecasts, consumption is subdivided or disaggregated into C_1 (nondurable goods),

---

[7] For alternative views compare Lawrence Klein, "Post-Mortem on Transition Predictions of National Product," *Journal of Political Economy* (August 1946), and Michael Sapir, "Review of Economic Forecasts for the Transition Period," *Studies in Income and Wealth*, vol. 11 (1949).

C_2 (durable goods), and C_3 (services, including rental housing). This was done because the sectoral consumption function for nondurables as computed for 1929–39 had continued to fit well for the war years 1940–45, although the conventional Keynesian consumption function as a whole had failed to function—the result, it was believed, of wartime shortages. The estimates of C_2 and C_3, and also of $I(\hat{C}_2, \hat{C}_3, \hat{I})$ in (15.4–6) represent the estimates of specialists—engineers and business administrators—of maximum output in their respective areas; they may be said to "suppress" the corresponding Keynesian estimates under special conditions of shortage. The estimate of G_0 reflected the anticipated reductions from wartime levels resulting from rapid demobilization of the armed forces.

In this instance, all the estimates (15.3–7) were uniformly low. So, therefore, was the estimate of Y in (15.13). Equation (15.3), for C_1, was the greatest disappointment of the group. It proved an underestimate even after addition of an adjustment factor for special "reconversion" expenditures by demobilized troops. This may have been because the Pigou effects of wartime liquid-asset accumulation (chapter 10) were forgotten or overlooked, or because no distinction was made between long-run and short-run consumption functions (chapter 8). The underestimates in (15.4–6), on the other hand, cannot be blamed on economists. "Practical" experts underestimated the practicable speeds of reconversion and of constructing new civilian facilities, and economists believed them. The underestimate of (15.7) was a horse of still another color. The main element in the delayed reduction rate in federal military spending was undoubtedly the deteriorating relationship with the Soviet Union, which culminated in the Cold War.[8] But in addition, fear of the anticipated postwar depression may have led, as a countermeasure, to the maintenance of public spending. To whatever extent this was the case, it exemplifies the argument presented above.

Equations (15.10–12) deal directly with the labor force, employment, and unemployment. They are not involved in the derivation of (15.13), but in the context of the postwar forecasts, they introduced serious problems of their own. The estimates of the labor force L in (15.10) were too high, because of reliance on sociologists' sample-survey results to indicate the postwar plans both of demilitarized troops and of civilian war workers. A smaller proportion of demobilized servicemen went immediately to work than had indicated it would do so. More chose additional education or the

---

[8] The predominant view in 1944 and early 1945 had been that the Soviet Union would be too weak as a result of the Nazi invasion, or too occupied with internal reconstruction, to oppose a worldwide Anglo-American hegemony exercised by men of good will.

"52-20 club"[9] under the provisions of the "G.I. Bill of Rights" than had been anticipated. At the same time, a larger proportion of the war workers left the labor market than had reported plans to do so. "Rosie the Riveter," in particular, married and became pregnant earlier than she seems to have anticipated. At the same time, the estimates of employment N in (15.11) were too low, not only because of the underestimate of Y in (15.13) but because of the underestimates of the parameters in (15.11) itself. An anticipated increase in productivity was slow in occurring when prime-age males replaced women, older men, and "4-Fs" in industry. Apparently both "the Army way" and "the Navy way" of doing things were further from "the right way" than had been assumed. And so, with income Y and employment N both underestimated and the labor force L overestimated, the differential identity (15.12) proved a catastrophic overestimate of unemployment U.

SOME ELEMENTARY METHODS

Qualitative forecasting is aimed particularly at anticipating turning points in business conditions. As Shakespeare said,

There is a tide in the affairs of men
Which, taken at the flood, leads on to fortune

and the qualitative forecaster aims at isolating that "flood" with its corresponding "ebb." Qualitative forecasting is dominated in the U.S. by a set of elaborate barometric methods developed at the National Bureau of Economic Research (N.B.E.R.) by Wesley C. Mitchell and his disciples (Arthur F. Burns, Geoffrey H. Moore). Quantitative forecasting, on the other hand, is aimed at reliable numbers without special attention to turning points. It is dominated by large-scale econometric models, with Lawrence Klein playing among the model builders the role Wesley Mitchell once played in the world of business barometers.[10]

We shall take up N.B.E.R. methods and econometric models in good time. But before doing so, we need a catchall title under which to consider the multitude of other macroeconomic forecasting methods in everyday use in the business world. We shall use the term "elementary methods," although in no sense of invidious disrepute, since one or more of these

---

[9] To ease their psychological readjustment to peacetime conditions, returning veterans were permitted up to 52 weeks of idleness at $20 per week in 1946 dollars. This arrangement was called derisively "the 52-20 club."

[10] Compare Deborah Dewitt Malley, "Lawrence Klein and His Forecasting Machine," *Fortune* (February 1975).

methods may solve more of our problems better than any of the more elaborate ones currently in fashion. These methods are elementary in the sense that most (although not all) of them involve relatively little economic or mathematical sophistication, and also because most (but not all) require less long-run expenditure of resources on a continuing basis.

We shall also subdivide our sample of so-called elementary forecasting methods into half-a-dozen subgroups, namely:

1. Esoteric methods, which involve extrasensory perceptions or secret channels of information.

2. Statistical extrapolations of single series, which usually involve spectral or harmonic analysis, or other forms of "charting."

3. Historical analogies with past developments.

4. Business barometers, other than those developed at the N.B.E.R. and the U.S. Department of Commerce.

5. Cross-cut analyses.

6. Opinion-poll methods.

1. **Esoteric Methods.** Here are two examples. The first involves the special qualities of "genius." The second involves the special techniques of astrology:

> The kind of intelligence a genius has is a different sort of intelligence. The thinking of a genius does not proceed logically. It leaps with great ellipses. It pulls knowledge from God knows where.
>
> A genius who knew absolutely nothing about economics and who rarely read a newspaper, an hour after landing in America after a long absence, stood and looked into the street from his publisher's office on Madison Avenue and said, "Within a year this country will have a terrible financial panic." In answer to the obvious question, why he thought so, he replied impatiently, "I don't think. I *know*. Can't you *see* it, *smell* it? I can *see* people jumping out of windows on this very street." Within a year the crash came—and when reminded, he could not recall his prediction at all.[11]
>
> The House of Taurus, the bull, is a domestic house, often the zodiacal sign of successful bankers and entrepreneurs. Into the Taurian House loomed giant Saturn, bringing delays and restrictions upon finance. And the Earth felt them, the economy boggled, and people of all occupations stood in fear because there was no longer the promise of security, guarantee of work, or knowing the value of the dollar. Then, in June 1971, Saturn

---

[11] Dorothy Thompson, in *Ladies Home Journal* (December 1956). The "genius" is the novelist Sinclair Lewis, to whom Miss Thompson was married in the late 1920s.

finished its 30 months in the House of Commerce and moved in with Taurus' neighbor, Gemini. The financial fog began to lift.[12]

A different esoteric method is exemplified by a stock market forecaster who believed, as many do, that the market is "rigged" by insiders. But he went further. In these days of electronic surveillance, he believed, insiders cannot trust the mails or the telephone to communicate with each other. They have, however, hit upon the device of having special "signals" inserted in newspaper comic strips! He (the forecaster), after reading the "funnies" with special care, had figured out what some of the signals were, and could sell you the benefits of his information in the form of tips on what to sell and what to buy.

It is easy for the rationalist to laugh off these and other esoteric methods, and it is hard to evaluate them seriously. Such methods cannot be proved wrong; they are used widely in Western culture; they are relied upon even more widely in certain other cultures.

2. **Statistical Extrapolations.**   Conventional statistical analysis of time series aims at breaking such series down into components for a number of purposes, including forecasting. *Long-term trend* and *seasonal variation* are ordinarily eliminated first by more or less mechanical methods. Deviations from trend-and-seasonal are then broken down further into *cyclical* and *random* components. Harmonic or spectral analysis, mathematically more advanced, seeks to isolate cycles of varying lengths in data from which trend alone has been removed. The method has proved itself particularly in astronomical and meteorological forecasting; tables of sunrise and sunset, of lunar phases, and of tidal movements depend vitally upon spectral analysis of time-series data. It has been natural to apply the same methods to economic time series. The classification of business cycles by length (chapter 13) has been a result. Short-term forecasts achieved by this method, however, have thus far fallen short of those achieved in the natural sciences. For example, the following running quotation from a (temporarily) influential "scientific" study is memorable mainly for the number and pervasiveness of its mistakes in forecasting developments following the end of World War II:

> Here, in summary, are some findings of which we may be relatively sure:
> 1. The underlying 54-year rhythm of wholesale prices is on the decline. It turned in 1925; the pattern is due to reach bottom in 1952.

---

[12] Tom Crone, "Ouija Believe There's a Profit in Prophecy?" *Northliner Magazine* (Summer 1972), p. 14.

2. The shorter 9-year pattern in wholesale prices—a rhythm that applies also to iron, steel, and stock market prices—which had its last high in 1937, reaches for another high in 1946. The pattern is due to turn down until 1951.

3. The 3½-year pattern which is almost universal in business is due for a peak in 1947. Other peaks in the 3½-year rhythms are due in 1950 and 1954. Lows are due in 1948 and 1951.

4. The 18⅓-year pattern in building activity apparently reached its peak about late 1942. In general, building and real estate patterns are due to decline to a low around 1953.

5. The 15-year pattern in the index of the purchasing power of beef cattle prices, an exceedingly interesting index for the farmer, was scheduled for a high around 1944, thereafter declining to a low due in 1951. OPA regulations and wartime black markets veiled the meaning of free market statistics. But declines after 1946 would not be surprising.

These findings are not offered as unqualified forecasts. The data do not go back far enough to permit unqualified assurance that the observed rhythms are beyond the result of chance. Still, with all these qualifications, it is worth noting that the expectancies facing us do not suggest any lengthy postwar boom. On the contrary, the number of important rhythms that come to a low together around 1952 suggest the possibility of a growing postwar crisis. The reader familiar with this method of analysis will not expect the crisis to be avoided or halted by any preventive measures which the government might decide to take. Probably the most we can hope for would be some sort of palliative action if the blows fall.[13]

In addition to spectral analysis, at least two other methods of extrapolation—deducing the future course of a series from its own past—should be cited. One is the quadrature (integration) method that Roger Babson used in forecasting the 1929 crash. The other is the Dow theory in its multifarious variations, beloved of Wall Street "chartists" for generations.

Quadrature theories are based on areas above and below trend lines. The Babson variant relied upon the notion that "what goes up must come down." This meant that any area above the trend would shortly be balanced by an approximately equal area below it. When the stock market boomed after 1925–26 (opening up an increasingly large area above a preestimated trend), Babson began predicting an offsetting large slump on the downward side. When the Great Depression actually arrived, however, it far overbalanced the preceding boom. Babson "adjusted" his trend line to fit the requirements of his theory by assuming that an upward trend of the American economy had ceased temporarily with the inauguration of

---

[13] Edward R. Dewey and Edwin F. Dakin, *Cycles, the Science of Prediction* (1947), p. 226 f.

Franklin D. Roosevelt and the commencement of New Deal policies in March 1933!

Dow theories, variations upon a single original model, are unusual in their multitude and variety, and also in their secrecy. They involve examination of patterns in the successive peaks and troughs of stock price series, which may or may not be "confirmed" by patterns in series of transaction volumes for the same period. For example, suppose a bull market in some security, naturally interrupted by short oscillations and "technical readjustments." The failure of one oscillatory peak to equal the last one is considered evidence that this particular bull market may have run its course, especially if the preceding and/or the following trough is also lower than its predecessor, and if interest in the stock appears to be decreasing as measured by the volume of transactions. In contrast to courses in such business subjects as investments and security analysis, courses in macroeconomics devote little attention to the Dow theory and its variations, primarily because their applications have been predominantly microeconomic, focusing upon particular security prices.

3. **Historical Analogies.**   Historical-analogy forecasts were particularly popular during the Great Depression of the 1930s. Measuring on the basis of one or another statistical series, one or another investigator determined how many months were required to go from peak to trough, or from trough to full recovery, in other major depressions—the 1870s, the 1890s—and forecast turning points or recoveries accordingly. This sort of procedure is now passé, except for a theory of primary and secondary postwar movements devised by Leonard P. Ayres. Ayres's theory was that each major war is followed by a primary postwar boom and depression centering in nondurable goods. But satiation of the nondurable goods market still leaves the markets for durables and for housing unfilled, so that there ensues a long secondary postwar boom, followed by an even longer and more serious postwar depression set off by a money panic (as in 1873) or a stock-market crash (as in 1929). After World War II, the first three of these phases came "on schedule," with the primary postwar depression in 1949–50. For this reason, every recession of the 1950s and early 1960s was hailed in some quarters as the long-awaited secondary postwar depression and the new 1929. Such talk was most audible during the relatively serious recession of 1957–58. But the "secondary postwar depression" never arrived. When the American economy slowed down again in 1969–71 and 1974–75, the phrase was seldom mentioned.

4. **Business Barometers.**   A business barometer is a series, or a combination of series, which can be expected to turn up (or down) before such

aggregates as income and employment do, just as barometric pressure usually turns up (or down) before the weather turns clear (or stormy). The most elaborate of the barometric systems, devised at the National Bureau of Economic Research, is discussed later in this chapter. We limit our attention here to simpler systems.

The most elementary barometric systems use single series. One such series is an industrial stock price index, seen as a measure of public confidence. Others are series for new orders of capital goods or for the value of building permits as precursors of investment activity. (We recall that private investment is the most volatile element in the Keynesian system.) Still another such series is bank debits—outside New York City, where stock-market influences are greatest—as a precursor of expenditures in general. A more obscure barometer—which illustrates a pitfall of the method—was once linseed oil sales. Linseed oil moved ahead of paint, which led building activity, which was a major factor in investment. But when linseed oil was displaced as a major component of paint, it lost its barometric function as well.

The most prestigious barometric forecasting method of the 1920s was the A-B-C system developed at Harvard University. The Harvard A series (speculation, as indicated by stock prices) led the B series (business, as represented chiefly by the Federal Reserve index of industrial production), which in turn led the C series (money, or rather money rates as represented by the rates of return on bonds). In the A-B-C theory, the important series B was apparently caught between A and C. When A was falling with C still rising, B would soon fall as well. And vice versa, if A was rising while C was still falling. This system fell out of favor when it failed to forecast either the 1929 crash or the seriousness of the succeeding depression.

Empirically minded and antitheoretical readers may ask: Why not feed into a computer a number of series that one thinks ought to make a good barometer, and leave to the computer and its programmers the job of devising weights for all these series, so that the resultant compound will come as close as possible to leading, say, GNP, by six months or a year? This too was done in the 1920s, long before the days of either electronic computers or GNP series. The Brookmire Economic Service devised a series that "back-cast" the federal index of industrial production with a six-month lead. It then failed miserably as a forecaster.

5. **Cross-Cut Analyses.**   Cross-cut and check-list analyses usually involve combinations—often simple additions—of elementary forecasts of the principal components of each of these in turn. Also, alternatively or additionally, the forecaster may choose to estimate separately the GNP contributions of each of the country's principal industries and industrial groups,

and add the results. Usually, in check-list forecasting, there is also at least a side glance at monetary developments, at labor-force and employment conditions, at foreign economies as determinants of major exports and imports, and at indicators of general optimism or pessimism.

The merit of this method is in forcing the forecaster to justify each of his totals as the sum of its parts, and so to prevent ridiculous inconsistencies. In addition, the forecaster has the opportunity to ask himself, and to determine graphically or algebraically, whether his partial forecasts are consistent with each other on the basis of past experience. (For example, do his separate forecasts of income and of employment involve unusually large or unusually small changes in output per worker?) But at the same time, there is nothing in the cross-cut or the check-list to prevent rosy glows of optimism or black palls of pessimism from biasing the entire structure of the forecaster's estimates.

6. **Opinion Polls.** There are several types of opinion polls and economic surveys. They may be based upon quantitative questions—How much do you think the consumers' price index will rise or fall this year?—or upon qualitative ones—Are you better off this year than last? They may be addressed to selected samples of well-informed or influential persons—business leaders, statisticians, economists, journalists, politicians—or to random samples of the general public. The responses may be presented with substantial precision—50 percent of a sample of Indiana business leaders believe this year's unemployment rate will be over 4.0 but less than 4.5 percent—or in general terms—35 percent of Canadian housewives don't know whether they can expect to be better off next year than this.

The more precise and formal polling of the influential and well-informed is exemplified by the periodic polls conducted by *Fortune* magazine, and also by the "business outlook" sessions that feature the conventions of the American Statistical Association. More general polling of the general public is exemplified by the work of the Survey Research Center at the University of Michigan and of the National Opinion Research Center (N.O.R.C.).

It is interesting and informative to know what the influential and the well-informed think about the shape of things to come. But one cannot be sure to what extent their supposed opinions are independent of each other, or on what evidence or analysis they may themselves have been based. The experts sometimes lead each other astray by ordinary "mob psychology." Two examples are the "new era" opinions of 1928–29 and the postwar pessimism of sixteen years later. Or they may be providing us with little more than naive forecasts, of one of three sorts: (a) things will continue as they have been; (b) the trend of past events will continue into the near future; or (c) some imprecise statistical average of (a) and (b). In any

case, opinion-poll forecasts work out quite well in calm periods, but do badly in anticipating turning points in either direction.

Much the same difficulties beset the results of opinion polling of the general public, except that we are less likely to confuse precision with accuracy, since the results are usually presented in less precise form. The special problems in survey research, on the other hand, include: (1) the greater dependence of the answers upon the precise wording of the questions and (in oral surveys) on the personalities of interviewers, (2) the greater likelihood of transitory influences from the headlines on the particular day the survey is made, and (3) the difficulty of interpreting the frequently large "don't know" percentage of the responses.

The results of opinion polls are often useful auxiliary ingredients in economic forecasts. We have mentioned the possibility of their inclusion in check-list forecasting. They may be equally useful as auxiliary independent variables in fitting any or all of the econometric functions mentioned in chapter 8. To rely exclusively or primarily upon them, however, seems suspiciously close to "the blind leading the blind."

NATIONAL BUREAU METHODS

The N.B.E.R. barometric system, based on *reference cycles* and *diffusion indexes*, is in a class by itself. Much of the data in the official U.S. Department of Commerce *Business Conditions Digest* is keyed to this system. The system has also been adapted widely to conditions other than the U.S. For detailed explanations, one must rely on technical N.B.E.R. publications, but textbook-level treatments are available.[14]

For each of 862 statistical series in the N.B.E.R. armory, the reference cycle is its average or representative pattern of movement over those fluctuations in which its behavior has been observed. The following five steps are required to work out this reference cycle:

1. Cycles are dated by reference to historical business annals, with special reference to their beginning troughs (called Stage I), their peaks (Stage V), and their ending troughs (Stage IX).

2. For each fluctuation or cycle, nine stages are determined by dividing equally the periods of rise (Stages I–V) and fall (Stages V–IX). Thus the

---

[14] Three basic N.B.E.R. publications are: Arthur F. Burns and Wesley C. Mitchell, *Measuring Business Cycles* (1946); Geoffrey H. Moore, ed., *Business Cycle Indicators* (2 vols., 1961); Geoffrey H. Moore and Julius Shiskin, *Indicators of Business Expansions and Contractions* (1967). Good textbook-level treatments are Robert A. Gordon, *Business Fluctuations* (2nd ed., 1961), pp. 515–522, and Michael K. Evans, *Macroeconomic Behavior* (1969), ch. 16.

third and fourth periods (from Stage III to Stage IV and from Stage IV to Stage V) are of equal length. So are the fifth and sixth periods (from Stage V to Stage VI and from Stage VI to Stage VII). The fourth and fifth periods, however, are of different lengths.

3. The average value of the series over each fluctuation is computed by averaging its values at each of the nine stages. If there is an upward trend, the average value at Stage IX will be higher than the average value at Stage I, and vice versa. No attempt is made to eliminate trends where they exist, but adjustments are made for seasonal variations.

4. Cycle relatives (percentages of the averages computed in point 3 above) are computed at each of the nine stages.

5. Median cycle relatives for the nine stages are computed and plotted diagrammatically, along with much supplementary information about both the cycle relatives and the series itself.[15]

To be considered for inclusion in the N.B.E.R. "short list" of published series, let alone for consideration as a *leading* series, the series in question must be of some general economic significance. To be a leading series, its reference cycle should generally have its peak *before* Stage V and its trough *before* Stage IX of the representative fluctuation. (Some series do much better in this respect at peaks than they do at troughs, or vice versa.) In addition, the pattern of cycle relatives should be regular, with relatively small variance.[16] The twelve leading series as of 1966 are listed in table 15.1, replacing an earlier list dating from 1960.[17] To rationalize the presence of any particular series on the list of twelve is not a difficult task for the serious student of macroeconomics. It is more difficult to rationalize the absence of such other series as business failures and rates of change in such aggregates as our Y and C.

---

[15] Two supplementary items are worthy of special mention. The first is the variability of the cycle relatives at each stage. The second is the *specific* cycle of the series, which is computed by repeating steps 1–5 with the beginning and ending dates of fluctuations determined by the behavior of the series itself, without reference to the economy as a whole. (Some series, particularly agricultural ones, have specific cycles quite different from and more pronounced than their reference cycles.)

[16] The N.B.E.R. uses a complex but basically subjective scoring system for inclusion in its short list. Six criteria are included: economic significance, statistical adequacy, conformity, timing, smoothness, and currency. These criteria are explained and illustrated in Moore and Shiskin, *op. cit.*, pp. 8–28.

[17] Six series on the earlier list were dropped. Some had been discontinued or replaced by improved series not available in 1960. Others seemed largely to duplicate the information supplied by other listed series. In two cases, their postwar conformity records had been disappointing. *Ibid*, table 8, p. 69.

Table 15-1
Twelve N.B.E.R. Leading Indicators

Short Title	First Cycle Turn	Timing at Peaks and Troughs				
		Num-ber	Leads	Coinci-dences[a]	Lags	Median Lead (months)
1. Average work week (production workers)	1921	19	13	4	2	5
2. Nonagricultural placements	1945	10	8	4	1	3
3. Net business formation	1945	10	8	3	0	7
4. New orders, durable goods	1920	20	16	7	0	4
5. Contracts and orders, plant and equipment	1948	8	7	2	1	6
6. New building permits, private housing	1918	22	17	5	1	6
7. Change in manufacturing and trade inventories	1945	10	9	2	0	8
8. Industrial materials prices	1919	21	13	9	2	2
9. Stock prices, 500 common stocks	1873	44	33	14	5	4
10. Corporate profits after taxes	1920	20	13	11	2	2
11. Ratio, price to unit labor cost, mfg.	1919	21	17	10	3	3
12. Change in consumer installment debt	1929	14	11	4	1	10

[a] Includes short leads and lags (3-months or less)
Source: Moore and Shiskin, op. cit., table 7, p. 68.

In addition to the leading series identified by the reference-cycle method, the N.B.E.R. has come to stress diffusion indexes as indicators of economic change. The basic idea of a diffusion index is simple. Assume that the economist is working with 100 series, each with the same importance or weight. (Few diffusion indexes include differential weighting features.) It seldom or never happens that all 100 of these series point in the same direction. When 50 or more seem to be moving in a favorable direction, the overall situation may be called prosperous. Conversely, when 50 or more

seem to be moving unfavorably, we may call the situation a recession or depression.

Suppose that the number of "favorable" series were to decline from 80 to 70, perhaps after having remained at or near 80 for some time. Although conditions are still predominantly prosperous, the decline of the diffusion index is taken as a sign of possible downturn in the fairly near future. In the opposite case, an increase in the number of "favorable" series from 20 to 30, after the number had been stable or falling, is a sign of impending recovery, although conditions remain on the whole depressed.

Diffusion indexes may be partial. That is to say, they may relate specifically to production, price, or employment series. Or they may be more general, referring to economic activity as a whole and comprising series of many different types. Elementary illustrations of diffusion-index methodology are the frequent comparisons by television commentators of the numbers of stock issues whose prices rose and fell during a particular period. This information presumably adds to the usefulness of the commentators' main stock-in-trade, the movements of the various stock price indexes. At the very least, a rise in a stock price index is more significant if the number of issues whose prices rose exceeds by a wide margin the number whose prices fell than it would have been if the number of declines had been equal to or greater than the number of increases.

The economic-theory background of the N.B.E.R. barometers and indicators is not highly developed. The reference-cycle method in particular has been assailed, in an influential review of the 1946 Burns-Mitchell *Measuring Business Cycles*, as "Measurement Without Theory" and as casual empiricism on a level not greatly superior to a cookbook or an old farmer's almanac.[18] The diffusion indexes have also been attacked as representing the rate of change of economic activity,[19] and as adding little to our knowledge of whatever underlying processes produced the pattern of

---

[18] Tjalling Koopmans, "Measurement Without Theory," (1947), reprinted in Robert Aaron Gordon and Lawrence R. Klein, eds., *Readings in Business Cycles* (1965), no. 10. A reply (by Rutledge Vining) and subsequent controversy may be found in Gordon and Klein, *op. cit.*, nos. 11–13.

[19] If "economic activity" is the sum of a number of equally weighted disparate series with equal amplitudes of fluctuation, and if it can be represented roughly by a sine curve, the larger the number of components that are moving upward, the steeper will be the upward slope of the curve, with a point of inflection where this number is a maximum. Also, the larger the number of components that are moving downward, the steeper will be the downward slope of the aggregate curve, with another point of inflection where this number is a maximum. The first derivative of the sine curve, i.e., the cosine curve, has these characteristics, and is accordingly traced out by the diffusion index. Compare Sidney Alexander, "Rate of Change Approaches to Forecasting— Diffusion Indexes and First Differences," in Gordon and Klein, *op. cit.*, no. 33.

economic activity in the first place. The N.B.E.R. has defended itself with the aid of numerous allies, and there has been much methodological controversy.

The generation since 1945 has been marked not only by a number of small recessions—and an absence of large ones—but by a number of false leads, threatened downturns that never quite came off. The N.B.E.R. methods could not in practice distinguish between the genuine and the pseudo-downturns, and gave a number of false leads in the downward direction.[20] None of these false signals were as serious in their consequences, however, as the postwar forecasts treated earlier.

THE COMPOSITE INDEX

The U.S. Department of Commerce has gone beyond the N.B.E.R. by combining and summarizing the results of its own experimentation with leading series in a single index. Its "composite index of leading indicators" receives wide newspaper and television publicity. In the United States, like the N.B.E.R. lists, the composite index is subject to revisions when (as in 1974) it fails to forecast a turning point correctly, or when it gives a false alarm.

Twelve leading indexes are combined in this widely publicized forecasting tool (1975 version). The deviations of each of these indexes from its own moving average (in standard-deviation units) are weighted unequally; their weighted average is a single number, the composite index itself. The weights (scores) are themselves composites, reflecting subjective judgments by Department of Commerce economists and statisticians as to each index's economic significance ($\frac{1}{6}$ of the total weight), its statistical adequacy ($\frac{1}{6}$), its historical conformity to business history ($\frac{1}{6}$), its smoothness and freedom from random fluctuations ($\frac{2}{15}$), its timing at peaks and troughs ($\frac{2}{15}$ each, or $\frac{4}{15}$ in total), and the recency of available data ($\frac{1}{10}$). The components and their weights are presented in table 15.2.[21] Comparing this composite with its predecessor (which failed to predict the 1974 downturn), an important change is the greater use of price deflators to avoid being misled. Another change, interesting particularly to monetarists, is the inclusion of two money and near-money variables (nos. 8–9, table 15.2), which were not used before.

---

[20] The section entitled "False Leads" in Alexander, op. cit. (pp. 636–639 of the Gordon-Klein collection) discusses eleven "false peaks" in addition to the eight "true ones" disclosed by Moore's historical diffusion index over the period 1919–1956.

[21] Details and results are presented in Victor Zarnowitz and Charlotte Boschan, "Cyclical Indexes: An Evaluation and New Leading Indexes," *Business Conditions Digest* (May 1975). Table 15.2 is based on their table 3, p. 11.

Table 15-2
Components and Weights, Department of Commerce
Composite Index of Leading Indicators (1975 version)

Number	Component	Weight
1.	Average workweek of production workers, manufacturing	73
2.	Layoff rate, manufacturing (inverted)	71
3.	Index of net business formation	70
4.	Index of stock prices, 500 common stocks	80
5.	Index of new private housing units authorized by local building permits	76
6.	Vendor performance, percent of companies reporting slow deliveries	69
7.	Contracts and orders for plant and equipment, in 1967 dollars	74
8.	Money balances [Friedman's M_1] in 1967 dollars	79
9.	Percent change in total liquid assets	69
10.	Net change in inventories on hand and on order, in 1967 dollars (excluding capital and defense goods)	65
11.	New orders for consumer goods and materials, in 1967 dollars	74
12.	Percent change in sensitive prices (wholesale price index of crude materials, excluding food and feeds)	70

ECONOMETRIC MODELS

Econometric forecasting dates from two monographs by Tinbergen, prepared for the League of Nations in the 1930s to test rival cycle theories of that day.[22] Elementary econometric forecasts failed badly, as we have seen, in the postwar forecasts of 1944–46, but the econometricians were not discouraged. Primary credit for the econometric revival goes to Lawrence Klein, his associates, and his students at American, European, and Japanese universities and research institutes.[23]

By the 1970s, Eckstein tells us:[24]

[22] Jan Tinbergen, *Statistical Testing of Business-Cycle Theories* (2 vols., 1939).

[23] Particularly influential have been the Klein-Goldberger model of the 1950s and the Brookings Institution-Social Science Research Council model of the 1960s, although both of these are now obsolete. Lawrence Klein and Arthur Goldberger, *An Econometric Model of the United States, 1929–52* (1955); James Duesenberry, Gary Fromm, Lawrence Klein, and Frederick M. Kuh, eds., *The Brookings Quarterly Economic Model of the U.S. Economy* (1969).

[24] Otto Eckstein, "Econometric Models and the Formation of Business Expectations," *Challenge* (March-April 1976), p. 13f.

Large-scale econometric model forecasting [had] swept the field. Today, virtually all serious national economic forecasting [in the U.S.] is done with large-scale econometric models. Virtually every major business subscribes to one of the major models, and some subscribe to more than one. The government agencies [including the Office of Management and Budget and the Council of Economic Advisers] and congressional committees concerned with economic policy also use the models as part of their analyses. . . . [T]he distinction between "informal" and econometric forecasting has disappeared as the model managers have learned to use information not directly built into the models, and as [other] forecasters have learned to use the models through time-shared computor systems.

Similar conditions hold in most developed market economies, although the status of econometric forecasting as "the wave of the future" seems clearer in North America than it does in Europe. An ambitious "Project LINK" aims at the interconnection of several country models into a single model for the world economy.[25] Another project proposes to enlarge the scope of country models beyond the conventional limits of economics, by adding "social indicators" to their dependent and independent variables. (Professor Klein is an active participant in both of these projects.)

Contemporary economic models have advanced beyond the "Model T" pre-1950 vintages in a number of ways. Many of these are related more intimately to econometrics than to macroeconomics:

1. They are becoming increasingly larger and less aggregated, with increasingly specialized attention paid to individual sectors and subsectors.[26]

2. The basic data have been improved, so that quarterly models have replaced the annual ones of the 1940s. Monthly models may be in the offing.

3. Equations are commonly stated and fitted in differential form, with all variables expressed in terms of deviations from the previous period. This change concentrates attention upon the most relevant problems of economic change.

4. Equations are explicitly dynamic, in the sense that dependent variables y_t are associated with previous values $x_{t-1}, \ldots, x_{t-n}$ of several independent

---

[25] Jan Walbroek, ed., *The Models of Project LINK* (1976) is a technical compendium of methods and accomplishments through 1975. Less technical reports, usually authored or coauthored by Klein, appear in the Social Science Research Council journal, *Items*.

[26] There is little point to comparing lists of equations and unknowns. Readers interested in comparing middle-sized econometric forecasting models may find samples (all now obsolete) in Evans, *op. cit.*, chapter 18, and in Gordon and Klein, *op. cit.*, pp. 302–304, 584–589, and 604–611.

variables. Each model, therefore, specifies a particular lag structure. The dynamic character of the model means that "tracking" is possible, given values of all variables at time t_1, for the future paths of the dependent variables at times $t_2, t_3, \ldots t_n$, under various assumptions as to economic policies and policy changes. The method can also be applied counterfactually. Given values for the U.S. in the late 1920s, for example, simulations can be made of the possible course of the U.S. economy under policy decisions more expansionary than those actually followed by the Hoover administration.[27]

5. The behavioral equations of forecasting models are seldom of the simple linear forms assumed in this book. More complex forms frequently fit the data better. These forms are sometimes so complex as to involve difficulties in computer programming. Months of high-level programming work were required, for instance, before the Brookings model could be "run" at all.

6. The ordinary least-squares method of curve fitting, familiar to students of elementary statistics, is often replaced or supplemented by other methods—two-stage least squares, reduced forms, limited information methods, etc. In fitting any single equation of an n-equation model, these modifications take account of the fact that the other $(n - 1)$ equations of the model hold as well, and also of the fact that errors or deviations from any equation are usually interrelated both with each other and with errors or deviations in other equations.[28]

No econometric model can be completely neutral as between rival macroeconomic theories, however objective its builders try to be. Their choice of variables and equational relationships to include and test reflects their theoretical preconceptions. Most of the earlier models were Keynesian and fiscalist,[29] at least to the extent of taking the interest rates, money supply, and other financial variables as given (exogenous). A minority, represented by the St. Louis model,[30] were monetarist. More recently, certain of the

---

[27] The best-known counter-factual "simulation of the U.S. economy in recession," however, deals with the recession of 1957–58 under alternative policy assumptions. James Duesenberry, Otto Eckstein, and Gary Fromm, "A Simulation of the United States Economy in Recession," in Gordon and Klein, *op. cit.*, no. 15.

[28] For a fuller and more intelligible explanation of the statistical issues involved in the so-called simultaneous-equations approach to curve fittings, the reader should consult a technical econometrics text, such as John Johnston, *Econometric Methods* (1963), ch. 9.

[29] These have been the orientations of Professor Klein.

[30] This model was developed at the Federal Reserve Bank of St. Louis. See Leonall C. Andersen and Keith M. Carlson, "A Monetarist Model for Economic Stabilization," Federal Reserve Bank of St. Louis *Review* (April 1970) and "St. Louis Model Re-

larger models attempt a greater degree of neutrality, with both monetary and fiscal sectors fully developed and related to each other. Examples are the F.R.B.-M.I.T. or "Mad Fit" model developed for the Federal Reserve Board of Governors with M.I.T. assistance, and the P.M.S. (or M.P.S.) development of the "Mad Fit," which combines the talents of M.I.T. and University of Pennsylvania economists under the aegis of the Social Science Research Council.[31] Crews has prepared diagrammatic "flowcharts" of two models (F.R.B.-M.I.T., St. Louis) that indicate graphically the patterns of interrelation that the models assume between their key variables.[32]

The record of the current generation of large-scale, computerized, and highly disaggregated econometric forecasting models has been mixed. Five major points can be made in favor of these models.

1. They have passed the "market test" of acceptance by hardheaded businessmen and bankers, and at high prices. Concurrently, commercial sellers of models, and of estimates based on them, have made fortunes.[33]

2. They have avoided such egregious errors as the "new era" euphoria of 1926–29, the bleak pessimism of 1944–45, or the mindless extrapolation of trend-and-cycle into the future.

3. Nor has their role been merely passive. Their early-warning signals may have assisted in avoiding any "secondary postwar depression." Also, most of them were right when the "composite index of leading indicators" was wrong with regard to the downturn of 1974.

---

visited," *International Economic Review* (June 1974). Another monetarist model is Arthur Laffer and R. David Ransom, "A Formal Model of the Economy for the Office of Management and Budget" (mimeographed, 1971). A non-monetarist and strictly classical model is Thomas J. Sargent's "Classical Macroeconomic Model of the United States," *Journal of Political Economy* (April, 1976).

[31] Frank de Leeuw and Edward Gramlich, "The Federal Reserve—M.I.T. Econometric Model," *Federal Reserve Bulletin* (January 1968) and "The Channels of Monetary Policy" (*ibid.* (June 1969). Also compare Eckstein, *op. cit.*, pp. 13–15.

[32] Joseph Crews, "Econometric Models: Monetarist and Non-Monetarist Views Compared," Federal Reserve Bank of Richmond *Monthly Review* (February 1973). (This article, plus the 1974 Andersen-Carlson and the 1969 de Leeuw-Gramlich studies, mentioned in the two preceding footnotes are condensed in Thomas M. Havrilesky and John T. Boorman, eds., *Current Issues in Monetary Theory and Policy* (1976), nos. 11–13.) An earlier diagrammatic flowchart presentation of two (older) econometric models is Kiichiro C. Kogiku, *Introduction to Macroeconomic Models* (1968), ch. 9. [Kogiku's examples are the Brookings-Social Science Research Council and the Department of Commerce (Office of Business Economics) models.]

[33] Data Resources, Inc. (D.R.I.), founded and headed by Otto Eckstein, reported 1976 gross receipts of $17 million and profits of $1.5 million. Chase Econometrics, headed by Michael K. Evans, is affiliated with the giant Chase Manhattan Bank. "To the Prophet Go the Profits." *Time* (26 September 1977). Also Lawrence Minard, "Cheerful Days in the Dismal Science," *Forbes* (8 January 1979).

4. They have become increasingly eclectic as between alternative economic theories, and broadened their scope and the range of variables they estimate endogenously. Their makers have also been willing and able to learn from and to avoid their past mistakes.

5. They have provided empirical answers to important questions of detail, where smaller models are locked into other answers that are usually wrong. Such cases involve the effects of shifts *within* the broader aggregates, or the effects of concentrating some macroeconomic change on one subsector rather than another. (Examples: A shift from defense to civilian public expenditures, with a constant G; an expansion of new investment dI in residential housing rather than plant and equipment.) Models limited to single (G,I,C,T) terms, however accurately constructed, can only answer "no effects at all" to such questions as the above, but this answer tells us the limitations of the small model rather than the facts of the real world. Similarly, a small model cannot apportion (among *types* of consumption, for instance) the consequences of one or another change in any exogenous variable (say, a change in the tax laws). These less aggregative questions on the border between micro- and macroeconomics are obviously interesting to business concerns, which have assisted generously the large-model experimentation.

At the same time, the larger econometric models have disappointed some of their supporters' more sanguine expectations:

1. Their forecasts of such basic aggregates as Y, N, and p have not yet reached the point of outperforming consistently smaller models or even naive models.[34]

2. Some econometric success may be due less to objective correctness than to subjective judgment. Judgment—frequently defended as "T.L.C."

---

[34] A naive model is a mechanical forecast of some variable (call it x) according to some such rule of thumb as: $X = x_{-1}$, $x - x_{-1} = x_{-1} - x_{-2}$, or a recursive equation fitted by least squares:

$$x = a_0 + a_1 x_{-1} + a_2 x_{-2} + \cdots + a_n x_{-n}$$

Support for the contention in the text comes from, among others, Carl Christ, "Aggregate Econometric Models," in Gordon and Klein, *op. cit.*, no. 17, Herman O. Stekler, "Forecasting with Econometric Models," *Econometrica* (July–October 1968), and especially Ronald Cooper, "Predictive Performance of Quarterly Econometric Models of the U.S." in Bert Hickman, ed., *Econometric Models of Cyclical Behavior* (1972), vol. ii. But see, in opposition, the "horse race" in Evans, *op. cit.*, pp. 516–519 and table 18.3; also (in reply to Cooper) E. Philip Howrey, Lawrence Klein, and Michael McCarthy, "Notes on Testing the Predictive Performance of Econometric Models," *International Economic Review* (June 1974).

(tender loving care) of one's model[35]—includes allowance for policy changes, strategic insertion of deviations from equations, special treatments of "difficult" periods—omission, subsuming their effects into dummy variables—and revisions of equations that worked badly last year. The result is that, when a summary table shows organization X's model to have done nobly for each of the past ten years, one would do well to inquire about the frequency and significance of the "T.L.C." adjustments made by the X staff during the decade. The version that did so well last year may be quite different from the one which did so well ten years ago, and no version has had ten years of testing.[36]

3. The back-casting performance of a model can be improved by empirical gimmicks with little justification beyond "improving the fit" over some past period. There are two dangers here: (a) The results may be peculiarly sensitive to these gimmicks; more important (b) the gimmickry that worked in the past may not continue to work in the future.[37]

4. The degree of disagreement between rival models—fiscalist, monetarist, and eclectic—remains large enough to baffle and confuse the econometric layman and inspire distrust of both economics and econometrics. This is seldom true of forecasts for next quarter or next year; it becomes embarrassingly apparent, as Christ has shown,[38] when forecasts are "tracked" over long periods.

---

[35] For a defense of T.L.C., see Howrey, Klein, and McCarthy, *op. cit.*, pp. 370–372. At the other extreme, Benjamin Ward's *What's Wrong with Economics?* (1972), takes an ultra-harsh view of price-level adjustments in particular (p. 147):

> [T]hese big models, in which as much as $1 million of research funds may be invested, have been performing so poorly in recent months that some of those with the best reputations are reputedly inserting 'fudge-factors' to get a better prediction of price changes than the models can give. That is, the economists have the laborious calculations entailed in using the model carried out on the computer, and then jack up the price data that comes out by a few points, because they have more faith in their own intuitive judgment than in these great empirically estimated models.

[36] To lessen their dependence on T.L.C., some model builders add variables representing the contemporary state of public confidence, sacrificing the "tracking" capability discussed above. Ray C. Fair's *Short-Run Forecasting Model of the U.S. Economy* (1971) includes as independent variables, "an index of consumer sentiment based on five questions about consumer attitudes" (p. 30), "the percent of manufacturing firms reporting inventory condition as high minus the percent reporting [it] as low" (table 2-1, p. 25), the planned volumes of new car purchases, plant and equipment investment, and inventory investment. See also Eckstein, *op. cit.*, p. 18 f.

[37] On sensitivity, see Martin Bronfenbrenner, "Sensitivity Analysis for Econometricians," *Nebraska Journal of Economics and Business* (Fall 1972). Evans (*op. cit.*, p. 516) observes: "With today's modern technology, good sample period fits and good ex post forecasts are limited only by the amount of available computer time, the number of research assistants, and one's own patience."

[38] Carl Christ, "Judging the Performance of Econometric Models of the U.S. Economy," *International Economic Review* (February 1975), especially the tables and diagrams of pp. 65–72.

5. Numerous important questions can be "answered" by even the most elaborate models with hesitation, diffidence, and special assumptions. Some relate to the *minutiae* of timing. One such case arose in connection with the American "stagflation" of 1969–70. What would be the timing (with special relation to the 1970 and 1972 elections) of the price-level and unemployment effects of an administration "game plan" of tight money, heavy defense expenditures, and minimal interference with market prices? In particular, would the inflation rate fall before the unemployment rate rose? (No model gave a firm answer, and the infirm answers differed from one model to the next.) And half a decade later, what would be the macroeconomic effects of a default in the municipal debt of New York City? (Data Resources Institute assumed this would be equivalent to a 50 percent reduction in local capital expenditures and went on from there. The initial assumption was arbitrary, but D.R.I. had signed a contract to provide an answer.)

Here are two rival summaries of the econometric forecasting record, between which each reader may take his choice or compute an average. On the optimistic side, we condense the concluding paragraph of the Evans text.[39]

> Thirteen years after the trough of the Great Depression, the Employment Act of 1946 was passed, assuring that no such situation would occur again. Now that we know much more about the use of monetary and fiscal policy tools, it is time to extend this Act and make it effective against less severe recessions. The theory of how monetary and fiscal tools can be applied, and the numerical calculations showing their approximate effects, suggest that if the cycle cannot be completely eliminated, it can be mitigated to such an extent that the economy will remain near full employment at all times.

But the pessimists claim that econometric forecasts are not good enough for such ambitious purposes and cannot be expected to become good enough in the near future.

> If we take account of the subject [matter] of economic forecasts it becomes likely that their accuracy can in future only be improved very slowly and to a constantly diminishing degree. The econometrician will have to reconcile himself to falling short of the precision of science.[40]

---

[39] Evans, *op. cit.*, p. 607. See also his "Predictive Record" section, *ibid*, pp. 516–530.

[40] C. A. van den Beld, "Werden Konjunkturpropheten immer irren?" *Der Volkswirt* (24 December 1969), p. 89 f. (tr. Erich Streissler). Van den Beld wrote as a director of the Nederlandsche Centraal Planbureau, a Dutch institution with Western Europe's longest experience in econometric forecasting and projection. Benjamin Ward (*op. cit.*, ch. 10) exemplifies the same view.

An Austrian econometrician explains the reasons for his own pessimism in more detail:

He is a bad statistician who gives a forecast without error margin; for all statistical phenomena are subject to variation. He is a better statistician who adds some thoughts on the likely deviation around the mean value of his estimate. But the best statistician is he who remembers that even the confidence limits of a forecast can be next to pointless: this procedure assumes that we have to reckon only with the same variation as that registered in the past. The great problem of forecasts is not that they are subject to error, but that we must remain ignorant about the size of the error we commit. The econometric garb of the forecasting problem is the lack of information on the real confidence region of our forecasts.

The ability to forecast in economics rests upon the preponderance of past habits, the continuation of chains of reaction already initiated, the continuity of institutions shaping economic life. As a first approximation, the effect of government on income and growth may then be considered constant. Needless to say, such continuity of government policy or of the political climate can change quickly as in France in 1968; the added difficulty for the forecaster being that a victorious party previously in opposition may or may not fall short of changing economic policy in a way vociferously promised.[41]

SUMMARY

Nearly everyone indulges in explicit or implicit economic forecasting as an element in even noneconomic decisions involving the future. It is therefore a mistake to look down one's nose at people who forecast professionally. Furthermore, one test of the applicability—not necessarily the abstract "truth"—of a macroeconomic theory is the comparative performance of forecasts based on that theory and forecasts based on other theories or on as pure empiricism as possible. An important issue for the businessman or public body is that of "make or buy"—whether to construct one's own forecasts, to buy the forecasts of others in the marketplace, or to combine the two in some manner.

Also, before scorning the forecaster or "economic fortune teller," one should realize the difficulties of the forecaster's position. As a case in point, consider the notorious American "postwar forecasts" of 1944–46. Here underdeveloped economics and econometrics combined with misinformation from noneconomists to produce a series of honest errors that were all in a pessimistic direction.

---

[41] Erich Streissler, *Pitfalls in Econometric Forecasting* (1970), pp. 55–57 (running quotation).

Controversy heats up when we consider rival forecasting methods, both qualitative and quantitative. We mention a great number of "informal" or "elementary" methods—i.e., relatively noneconomic and generally non-theoretical. Many of these, such as opinion polling, business barometers, "charting," and cross-cut analysis, retain their popularity in business circles and government offices. We then pass to what are in the U.S. the principal rival approaches: qualitative systems aimed particularly at forecasting cyclical turning points; econometric models aimed at quantitative forecasting year in and year out. Exemplifying the first of these rivals, we discuss the reference cycles, leading indicators, and diffusion indexes of the N.B.E.R. and the U.S. Department of Commerce. Contemporary econometric forecasting is largely the province of large-scale (multi-equation) models, largely Keynesian and tending toward fiscalism in theoretical orientation. It is impossible to select a single exemplar for this entire group, but these models are distinguished from those that performed so badly in 1944–46. The records of the big models of the 1970s are considered over a period that seems relatively uneventful at least by comparison with the seventeen years 1929–46. We contrast rival views of the prospects of further improvement and application of econometric-model forecasting, which presently has the best claim to "wave-of-the-future" status in economic forecasting generally.

Name Index

Subject Index

Structural unemployment, 16
Subemployment, 17
Suffrage and wages, 62
Sunspot cycle theory, 281, 282
Supply and demand
  aggregate of, 217, 218
  notional and effective aggregate demand, 237
  and Say's law, 59
  and Solow models, 263–268
Swedish budget, 28

Tableau economique, 33
Taxes
  and built-in flexibility, 103, 104
  and circular flow, 9
  and fiscal policy model, 98–102
  marginal propensity for taxing, 206
  valued-added taxation, 21, 22
Technology
  frontiers of, 194
  impacts of, 245–252
  optimism and pessimism, 245–252
Theological cycle theories, 283
Theory of the Consumption Function, 164
Theory of money and price levels, 4, 5
Tight money policies, 120
Time trend in Hickman's function, 176, 177
The Trade Cycle, 296
Trade unions and wages, 62
Transfer payments, 36
Treatise on Money, 243
Turnpike theorems, 273

Uncertainty, influence of, 236–238
Underconsumption theories, 289, 290
Underemployment, 17
Underinvestment phase, 287
Unemployment. See Employment
Unemployment insurance, 62
USSR, accounting system of, 27

Value-added statement, 20
Value-added taxation, 21, 22
Value theory, 4
Variable investment model, 118–125
VAT, 21, 22
Vintages of capital, 269
Voluntarist cycle theories, 283
Voluntary unemployment, 17

Wage and price controls, 229, 230
Wages
  and classical macrodynamics, 56
  fall in, 223, 225
  and the Great Depression, 57
  and Keynesian special case, 242–245
  and Pigou effect, 207
  rigidity of, 60–63
  subsidies, 248
Wagner Act, 291
Walras's Law, 149, 244
War economy and employment, 49, 50
Warranted growth rate, 260
Wealth, 205, 206
Wealth-adjustment hypothesis, 167-169
Welfare, 42, 43
World view, 8–11

Zero growth, 42